NEGIMA!

Ken Akamatsu

TRANSLATED BY
Hajime Honda

ADAPTED BY
Peter David and Kathleen O'Shea David

LETTERED BY
Studio Cutie

D O N

Published in the United Kingdom by Tanoshimi in 2006

1 3 5 7 9 10 8 6 4 2

First published in serial form by Shonen Magazine comics and subsequently published in book form by
Kodansha Ltd., Tokyo in 2003. Copyright © 2003 by Ken Akamatsu

Published by arrangement with Kodansha Ltd., Tokyo and with Del Rey,
an imprint of Random House Inc., New York

Tanoshimi
The Random House Group Limited
20 Vauxhall Bridge Road, London, SW1V 2SA

Random House Australia (Pty) Limited
20 Alfred Street, Milsons Point, Sydney
New South Wales 2061, Australia

Random House New Zealand Limited
18 Poland Road, Glenfield
Auckland 10, New Zealand

Random House (Pty) Limited
Isle of Houghton, Corner of Boundary Road & Carse O'Gowrie
Houghton 2198, South Africa

Random House Publishers India Private Limited
301 World Trade Tower, Hotel Intercontinental Grand Complex,
Barakhamba Lane, New Delhi 110 001, India

Random House Group Limited Reg. No. 954009

www.tanoshimi.tv
www.randomhouse.co.uk

A CIP catalogue record for this book is available from the British Library

Papers used by Random House
are natural, recyclable products made from wood grown in sustainable forests.
The manufacturing processes conform to the environmental regulations of the country of origin.

ISBN 9780099504153 (from Jan 2007)
ISBN 0 09 950415 4

Printed and bound in Germany by GGP Media GmbH, Pößneck

Translator – Hajime Honda
Adaptor – Peter David and Kathleen O'Shea David
Lettering and Text Design – Studio Cutie
Cover Design – David Stevenson

A Word from the Author

Hi, this is Ken Akamatsu. It's been a while.

After taking over a year off after *Love Hina*, I have returned to work with my new serial, *Magister Negi Magi*! I hope you enjoy it.

The protagonist of *Negima!*, Negi, is cute, smart and talented—the kind of protagonist you'd never find in my previous manga! Ironically enough, though, top student personalities like him don't usually stand out (ha ha)!

So, are you gonna take the plunge!?

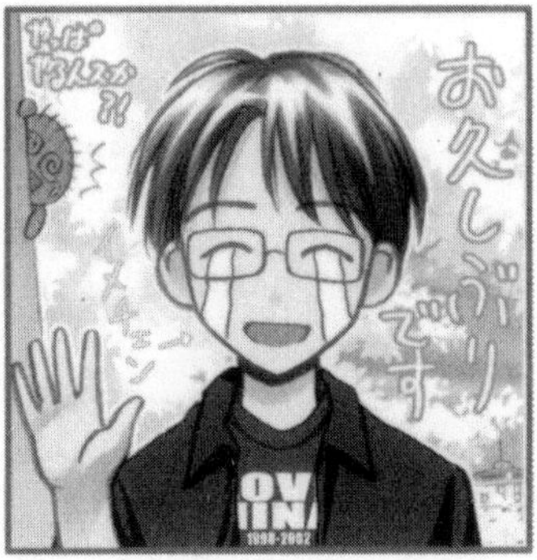
お久しぶりです

It's been so long.

The 31 beautiful girls in his class all have unique personalities, each with her share of trials and tribulations. (Actually, some of them aren't even human. . . .) Maybe they're the real protagonists of *Negima!*?

So let's take our time and watch over Negi as he grows up.

Ken Akamatsu
http://www.ailove.net

Honorifics

Throughout the Tanoshimi Manga books, you will find Japanese honorifics left intact in the translations. For those not familiar with how the Japanese use honorifics, and more important, how they differ from English honorifics, we present this brief overview.

Politeness has always been a critical facet of Japanese culture. Ever since the feudal era, when Japan was a highly stratified society, use of honorifics—which can be defined as polite speech that indicates relationship or status—has played an essential role in the Japanese language. When addressing someone in Japanese, an honorific usually takes the form of a suffix attached to one's name (example: "Asuna-san"), or as a title at the end of one's name or in place of the name itself (example: "Negi-sensei," or simply "Sensei!").

Honorifics can be expressions of respect or endearment. In the context of manga and anime, honorifics give insight into the nature of the relationship between characters. Many translations into English leave out these important honorifics, and therefore distort the "feel" of the original Japanese. Because Japanese honorifics contain nuances that English honorifics lack, it is our policy at Tanoshimi not to translate them. Here, instead, is a guide to some of the honorifics you may encounter in Tanoshimi Manga.

-*san*: This is the most common honorific, and is equivalent to Mr., Miss, Ms., Mrs., etc. It is the all-purpose honorific and can be used in any situation where politeness is required.

-*sama*: This is one level higher than *san*. It is used to confer great respect.

-*dono*: This comes from the word *tono*, which means *lord*. It is an even higher level than *sama*, and confers utmost respect.

-*kun*: This suffix is used at the end of boys' names to express familiarity or endearment. It is also sometimes used by men among friends, or when addressing someone younger or of a lower station.

-chan: This is used to express endearment, mostly toward girls. It is also used for little boys, pets, and even among lovers. It gives a sense of childish cuteness.

Sempai: This title suggests that the addressee is one's "senior" in a group or organization. It is most often used in a school setting, where underclassmen refer to their upperclassmen as "sempai." It can also be used in the workplace, such as when a newer employee addresses an employee who has seniority in the company.

Kohai: This is the opposite of *sempai*, and is used toward underclassmen in school or newcomers in the workplace. It connotes that the addressee is of lower station.

Sensei: Literally meaning "one who has come before," this title is used for teachers, doctors, or masters of any profession or art.

-[blank]: Usually forgotten in these lists, but perhaps the most significant difference between Japanese and English. The lack of honorific means that the speaker has permission to address the person in a very intimate way. Usually, only family, spouses, or very close friends have this kind of permission. Known as *yobisute*, it can be gratifying when someone who has earned the intimacy starts to call one by one's name without an honorific. But when that intimacy hasn't been earned, it can also be very insulting.

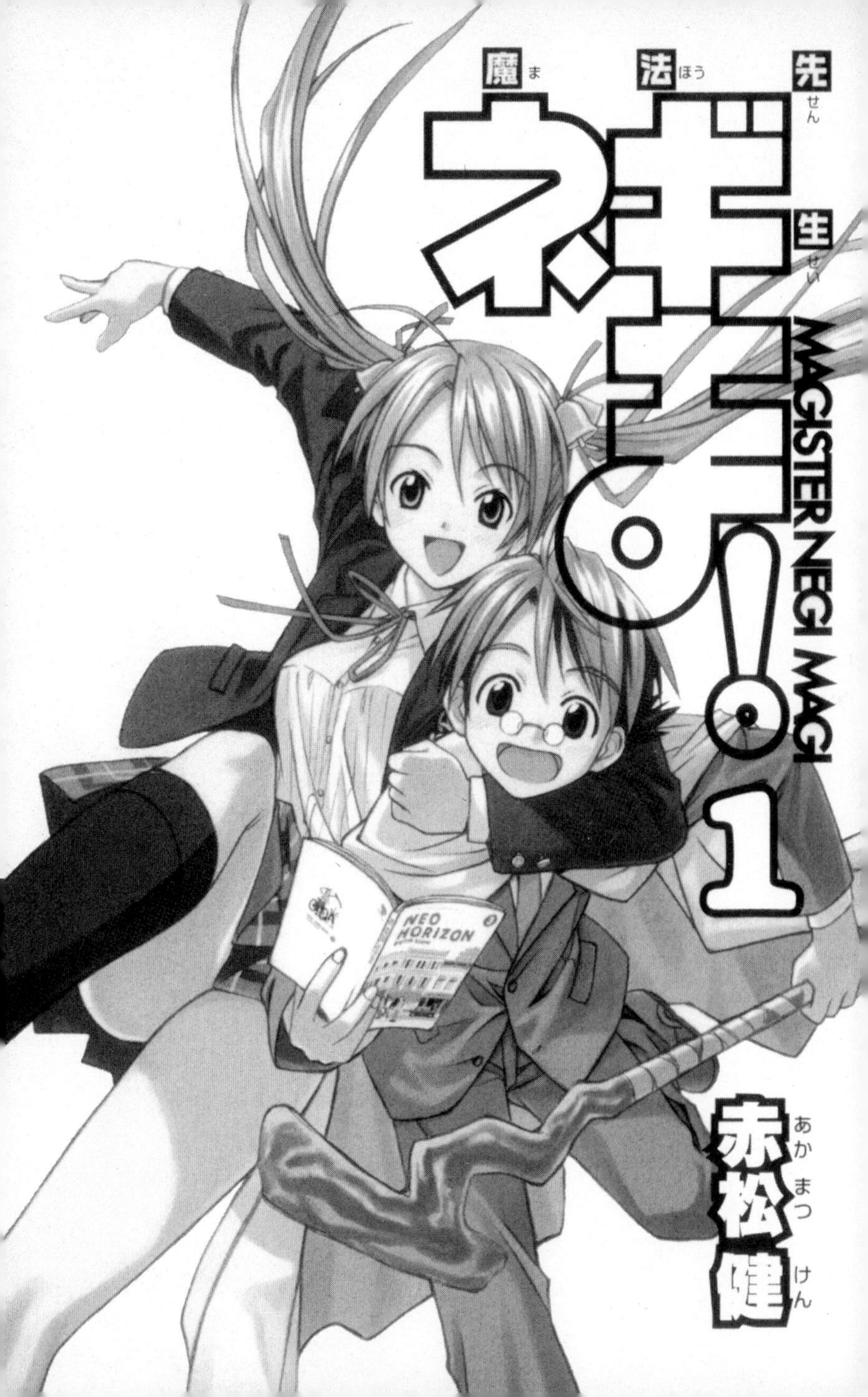

魔法先生
ネギま！
MAGISTER NEGI MAGI
1
赤松健
NEO HORIZON

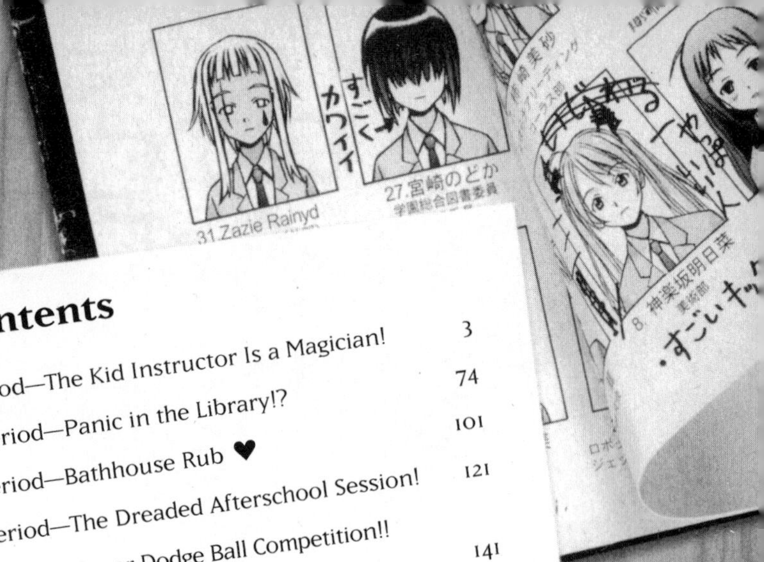
すごくカワイイ
31.Zazie Rainyd
27.宮崎のどか
学園総合図書委員
8.神楽坂明日菜
美術部

Contents

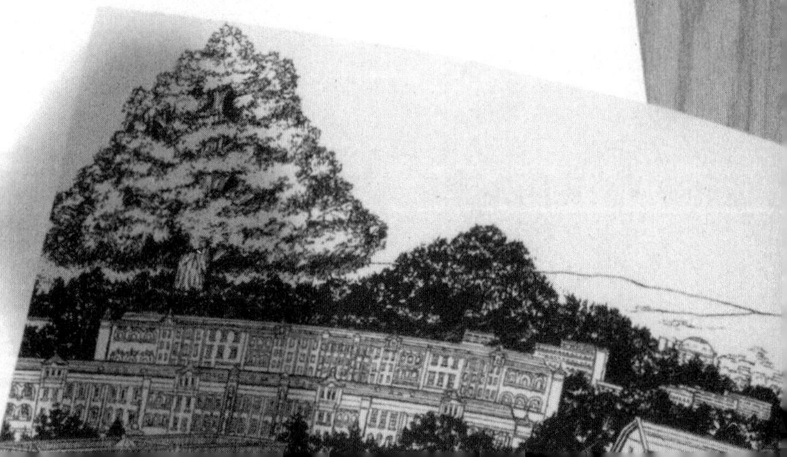

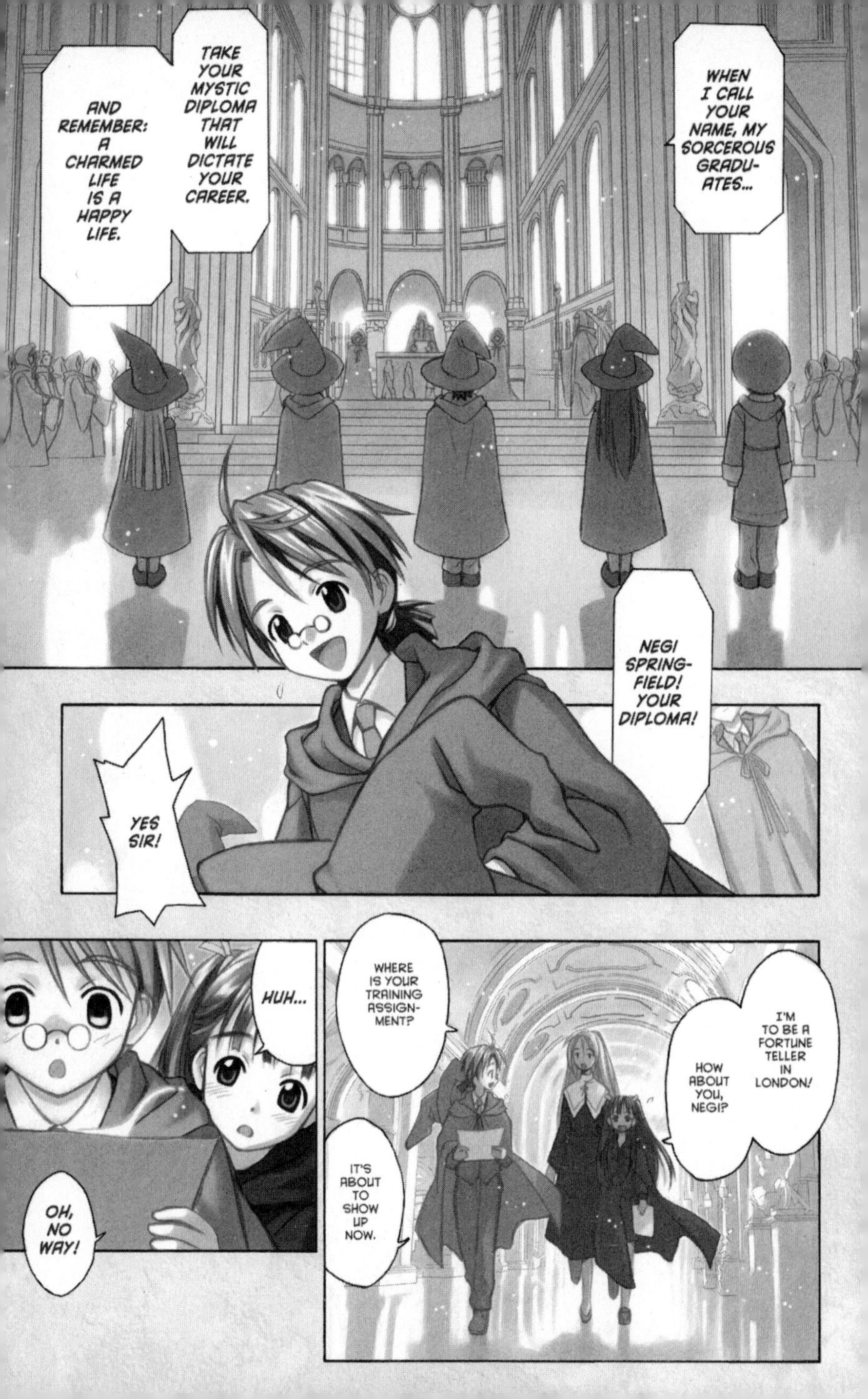
WHEN I CALL YOUR NAME, MY SORCEROUS GRADUATES...
TAKE YOUR MYSTIC DIPLOMA THAT WILL DICTATE YOUR CAREER.
AND REMEMBER: A CHARMED LIFE IS A HAPPY LIFE.
NEGI SPRING-FIELD! YOUR DIPLOMA!
YES SIR!
I'M TO BE A FORTUNE TELLER IN LONDON!
HOW ABOUT YOU, NEGI?
WHERE IS YOUR TRAINING ASSIGN-MENT?
IT'S ABOUT TO SHOW UP NOW.
HUH...
OH, NO WAY!

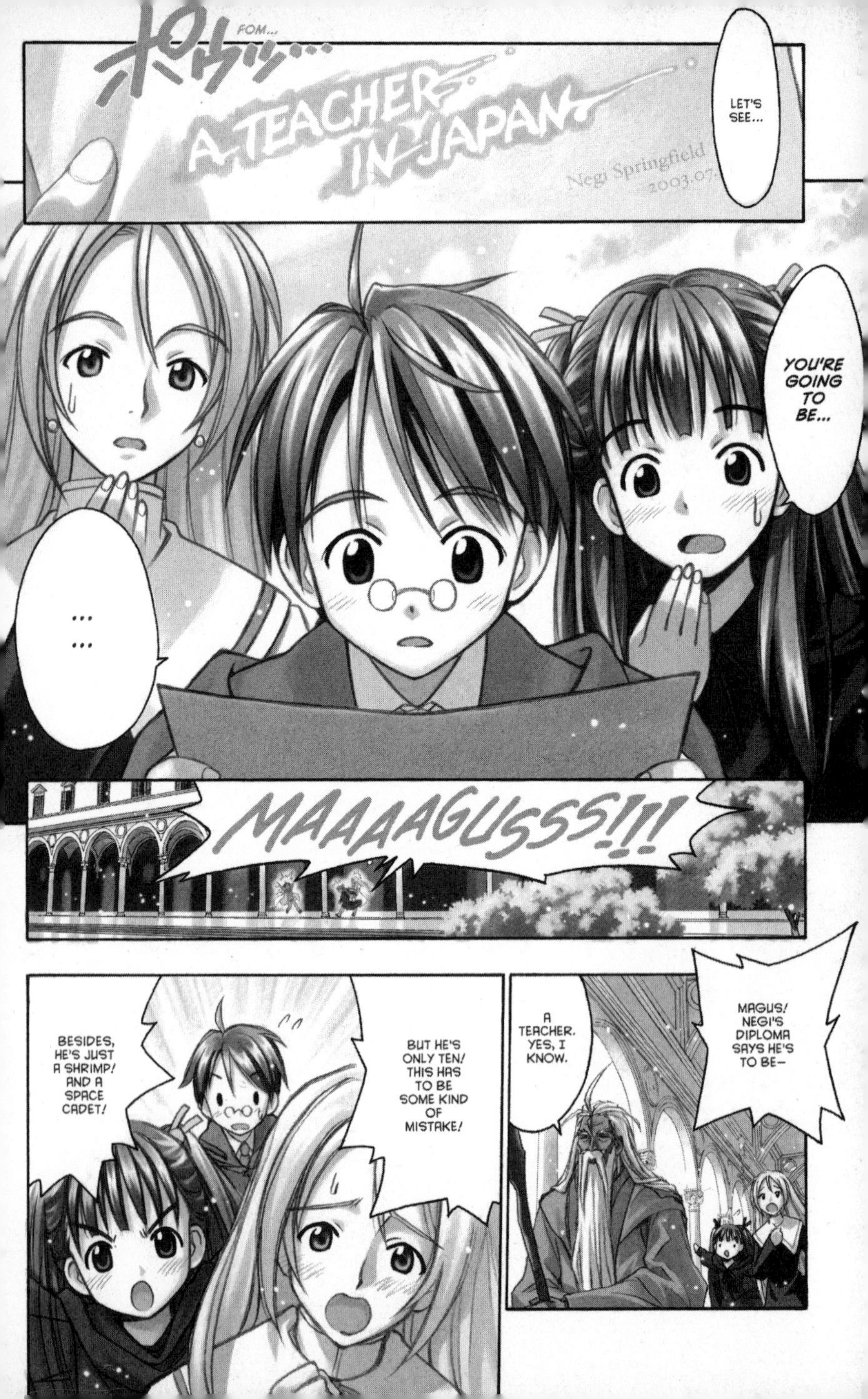
FOM...
A TEACHER IN JAPAN
Negi Springfield 2003.07
LET'S SEE...
YOU'RE GOING TO BE...
...
...
MAAAAGUSSS!!!
MAGUS! NEGI'S DIPLOMA SAYS HE'S TO BE—
A TEACHER. YES, I KNOW.
BUT HE'S ONLY TEN! THIS HAS TO BE SOME KIND OF MISTAKE!
BESIDES, HE'S JUST A SHRIMP! AND A SPACE CADET!

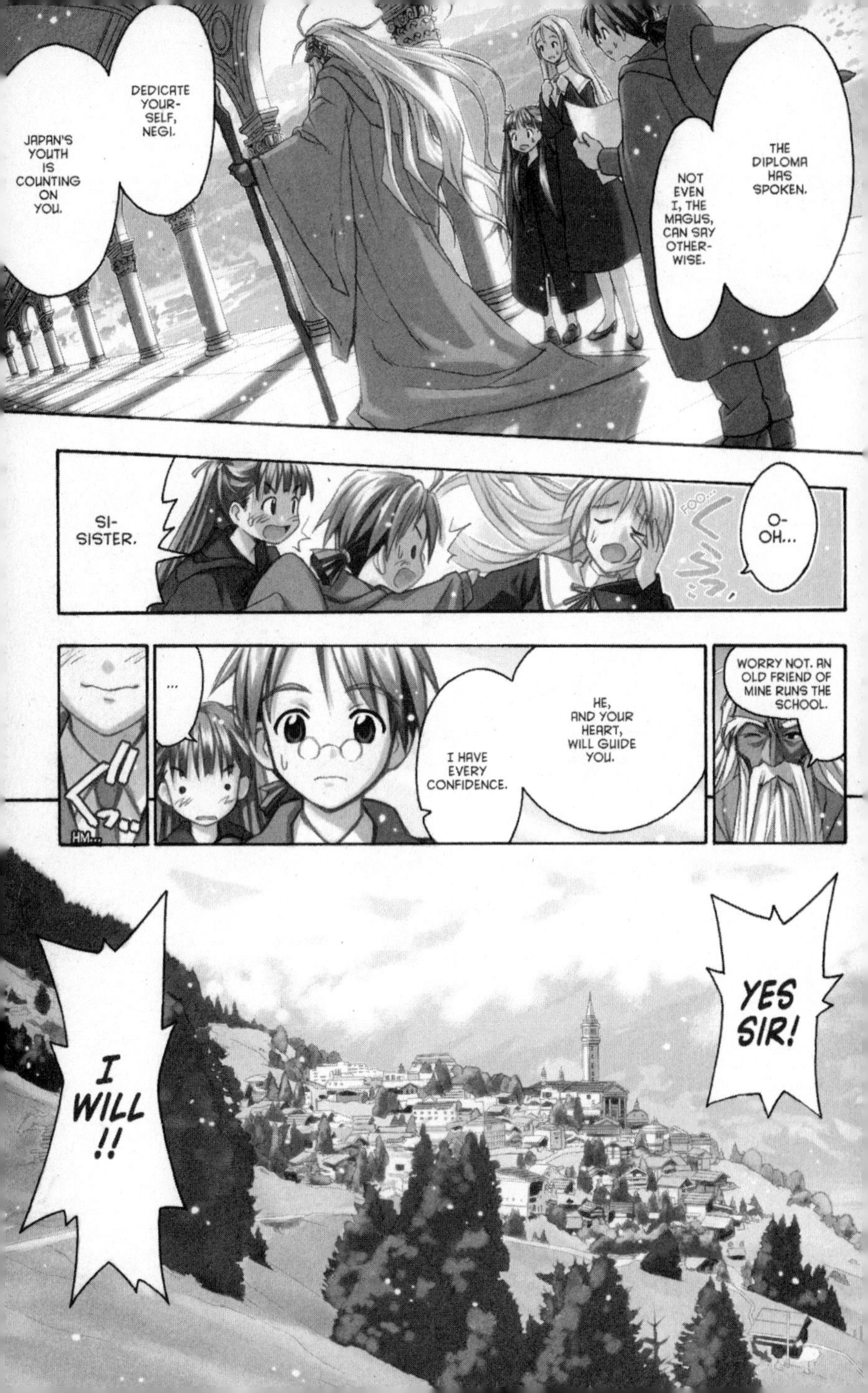
THE DIPLOMA HAS SPOKEN.
NOT EVEN I, THE MAGUS, CAN SAY OTHER-WISE.
DEDICATE YOUR-SELF, NEGI.
JAPAN'S YOUTH IS COUNTING ON YOU.
O-OH...
FOO...
SI-SISTER.
WORRY NOT. AN OLD FRIEND OF MINE RUNS THE SCHOOL.
HE, AND YOUR HEART, WILL GUIDE YOU.
I HAVE EVERY CONFIDENCE.
...
HM...
YES SIR!
I WILL!!

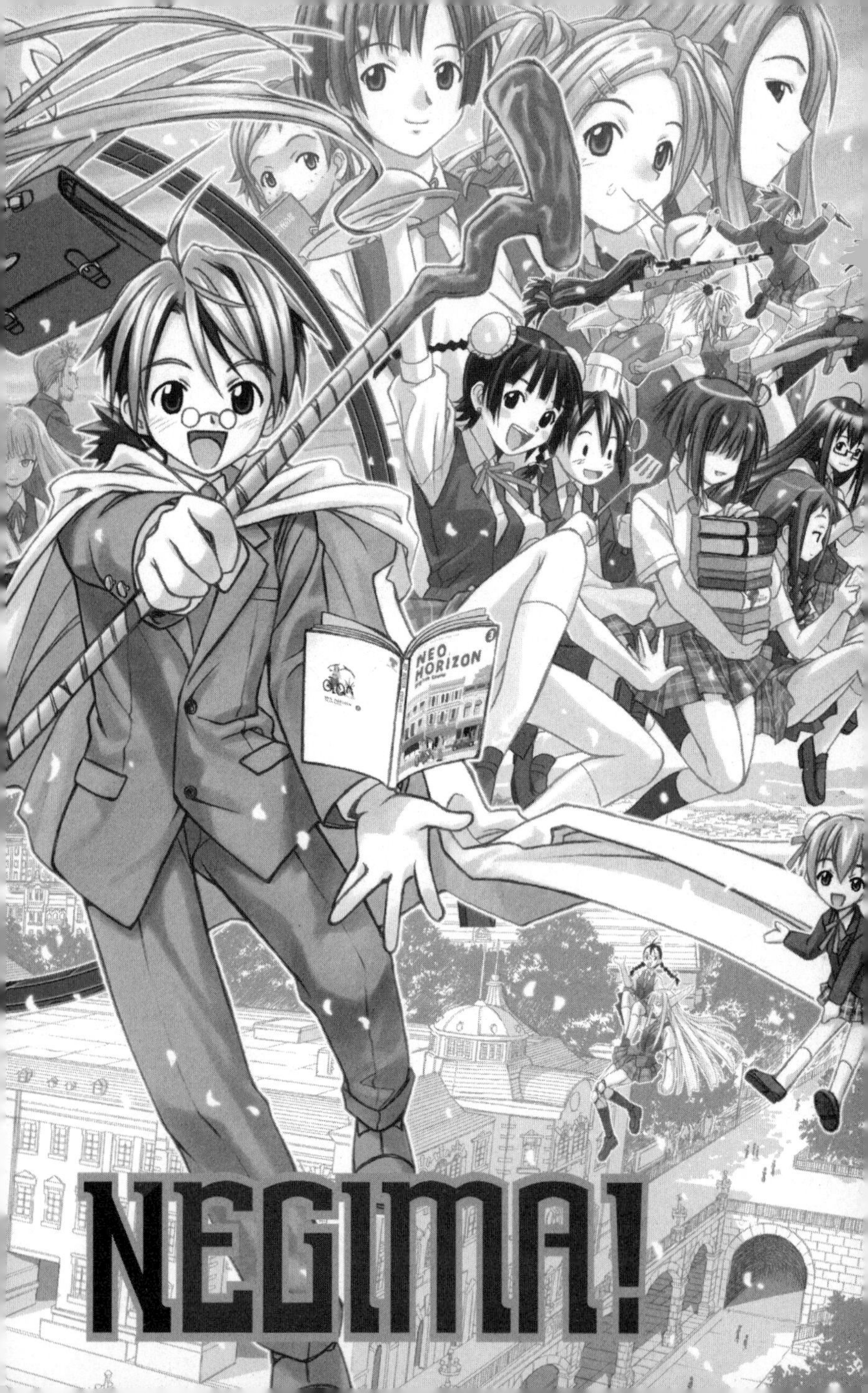
NEO HORIZON
NEGIMA!

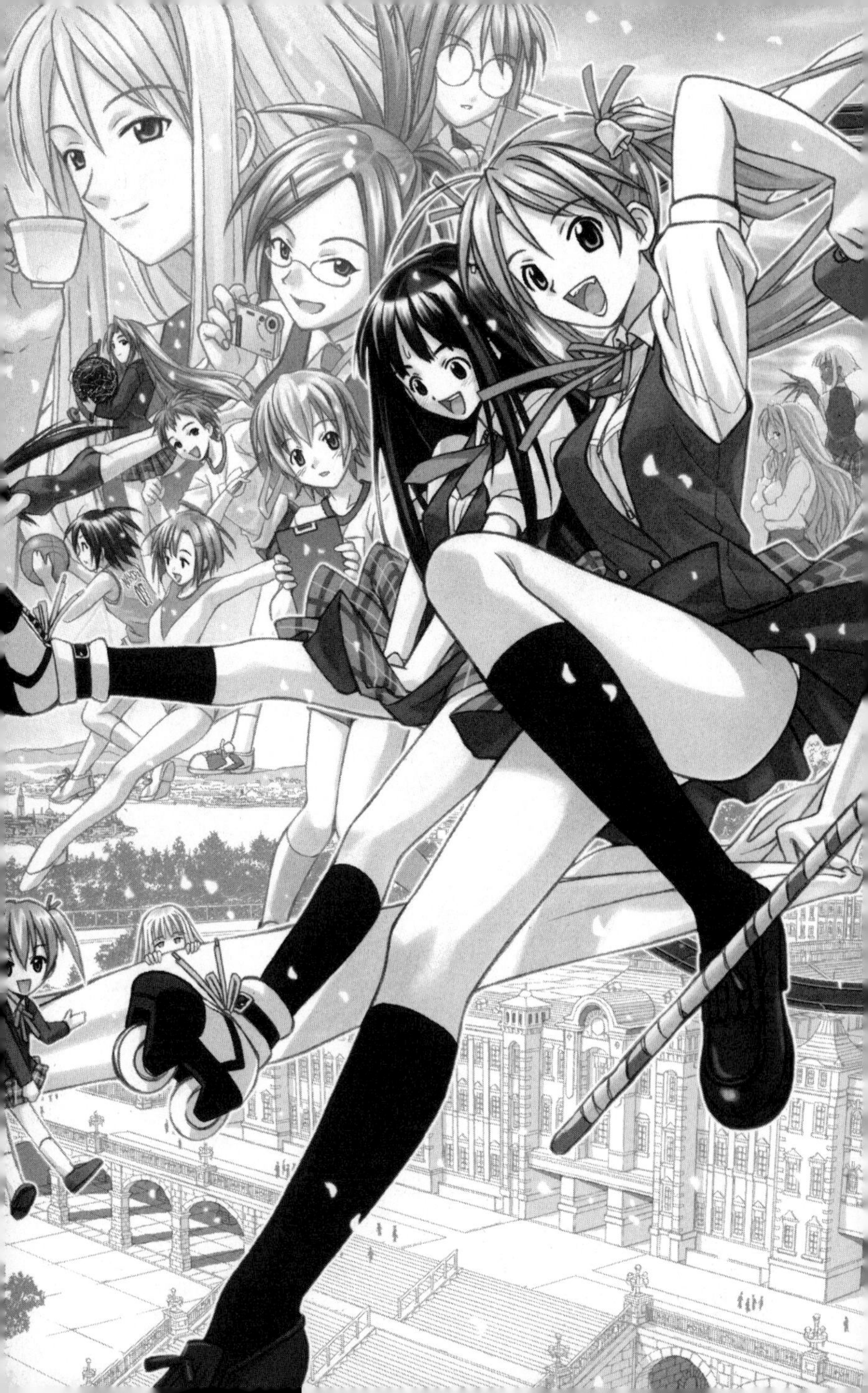

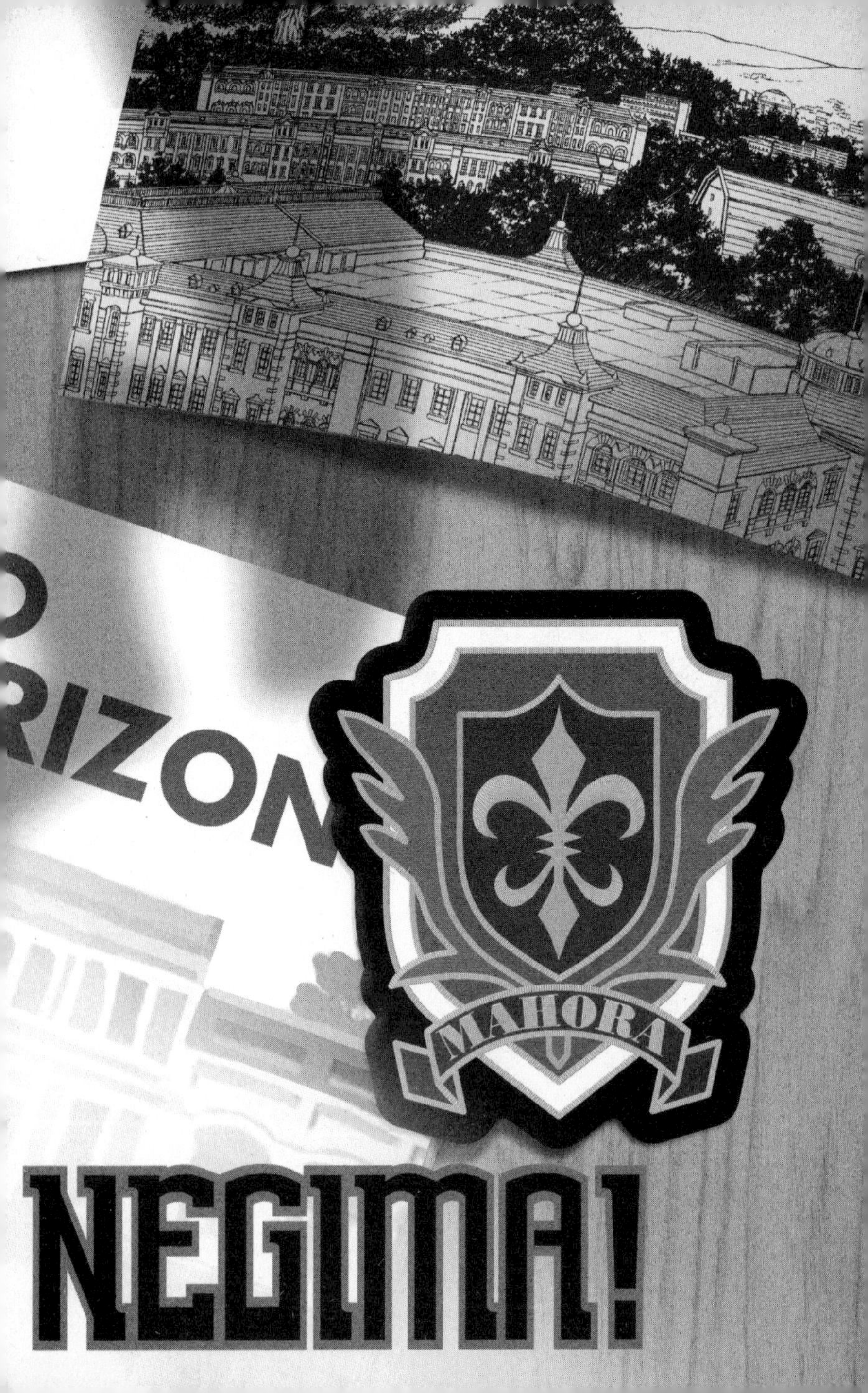
MAHORA
NEGIMA!

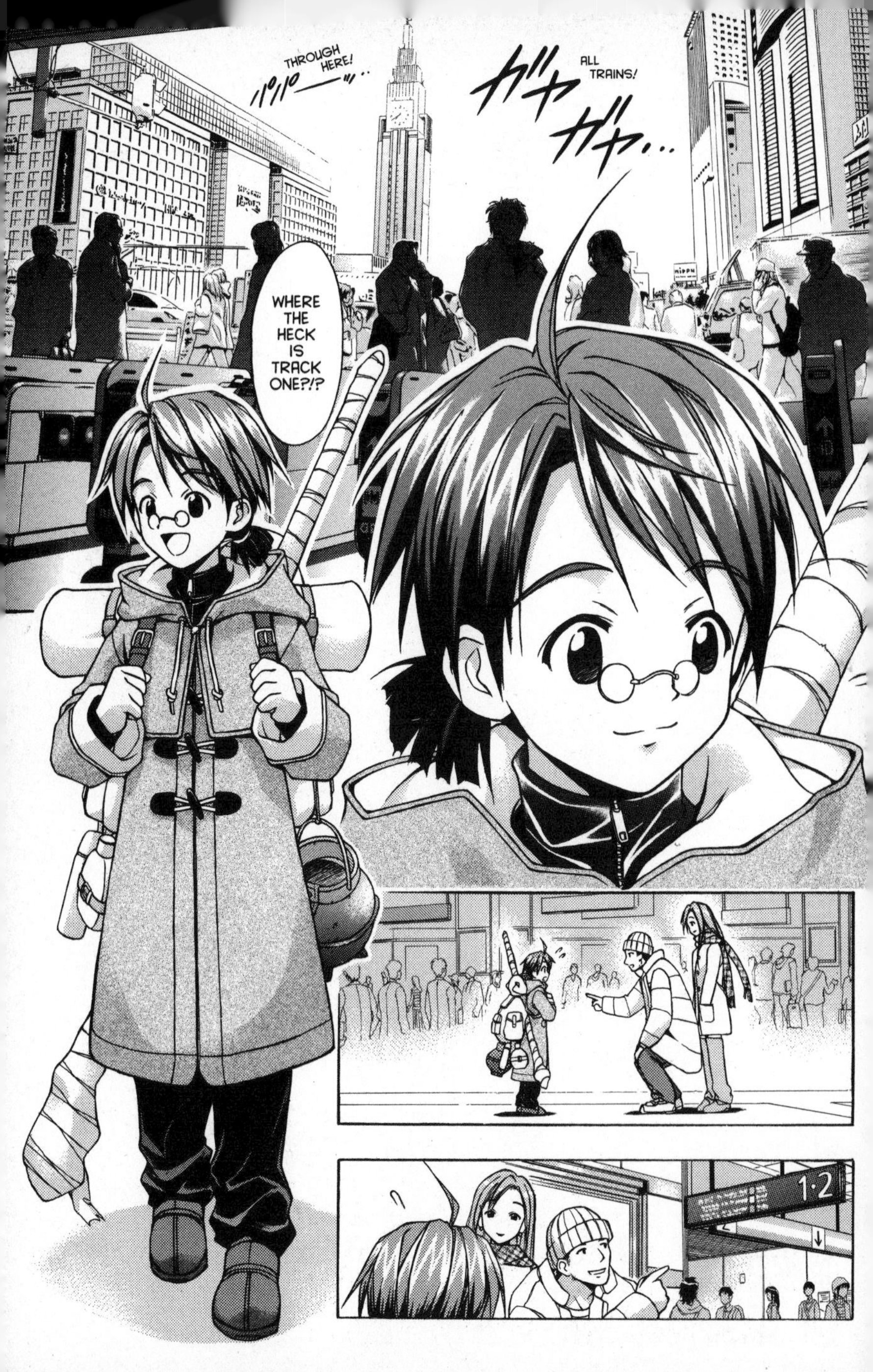
ALL TRAINS!
ガヤガヤ…
THROUGH HERE!
パパー…
WHERE THE HECK IS TRACK ONE?!?
1·2

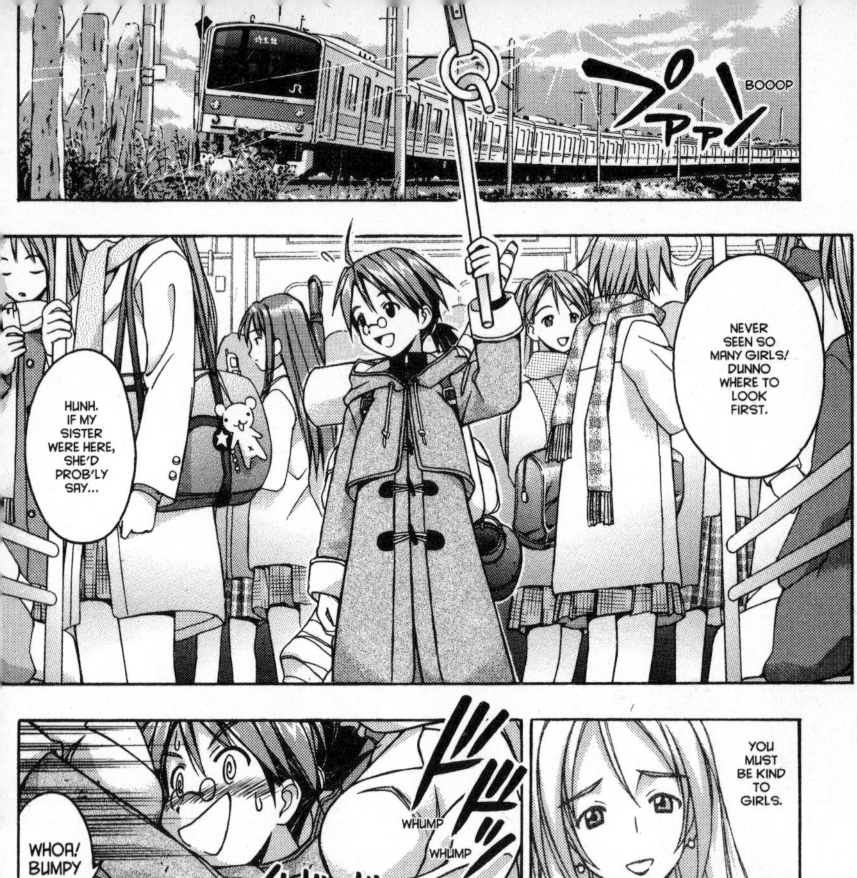
BOOOP
NEVER SEEN SO MANY GIRLS! DUNNO WHERE TO LOOK FIRST.
HUNH. IF MY SISTER WERE HERE, SHE'D PROB'LY SAY...
YOU MUST BE KIND TO GIRLS.
WHUMP
WHUMP
WHOA! BUMPY RIDE!
SQUISHH
OKAY, SISTER.
S'MATTER, SHRIMP? NOT USED TO TRAINS?
OH, BE NICE FOR ONCE!?
TEE HEE
AHA
URK

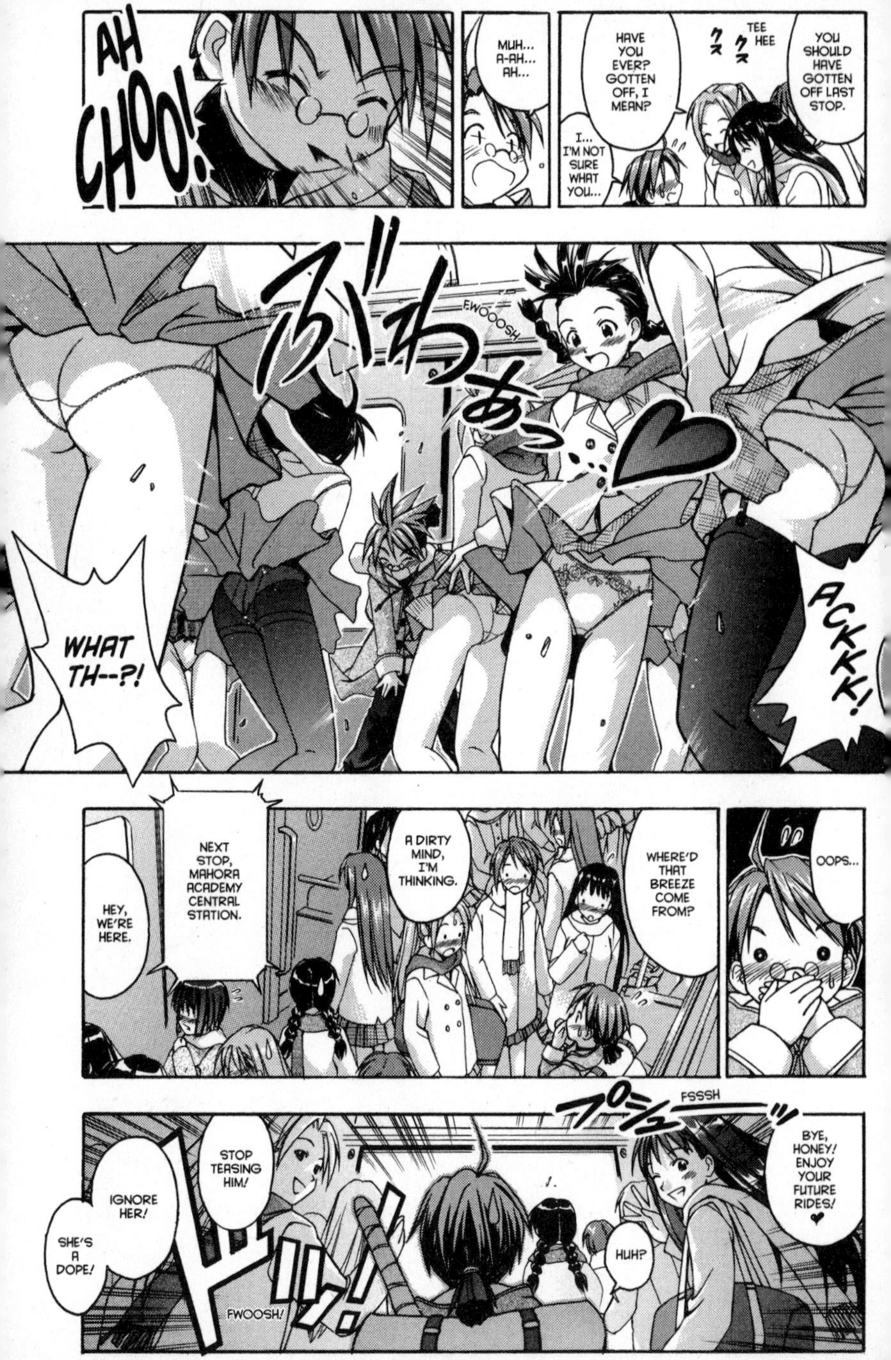
YOU SHOULD HAVE GOTTEN OFF LAST STOP.
クスクス
TEE HEE
HAVE YOU EVER? GOTTEN OFF, I MEAN?
I... I'M NOT SURE WHAT YOU...
MUH... A-AH... AH...
AH CHOO!
ぶわあっ
FWOOOOSH
ACKKK!
WHAT TH--?!
OOPS...
WHERE'D THAT BREEZE COME FROM?
A DIRTY MIND, I'M THINKING.
NEXT STOP, MAHORA ACADEMY CENTRAL STATION.
HEY, WE'RE HERE.
FSSSH
BYE, HONEY! ENJOY YOUR FUTURE RIDES! ❤
HUH?
STOP TEASING HIM!
IGNORE HER!
SHE'S A DOPE!
FWOOSH!

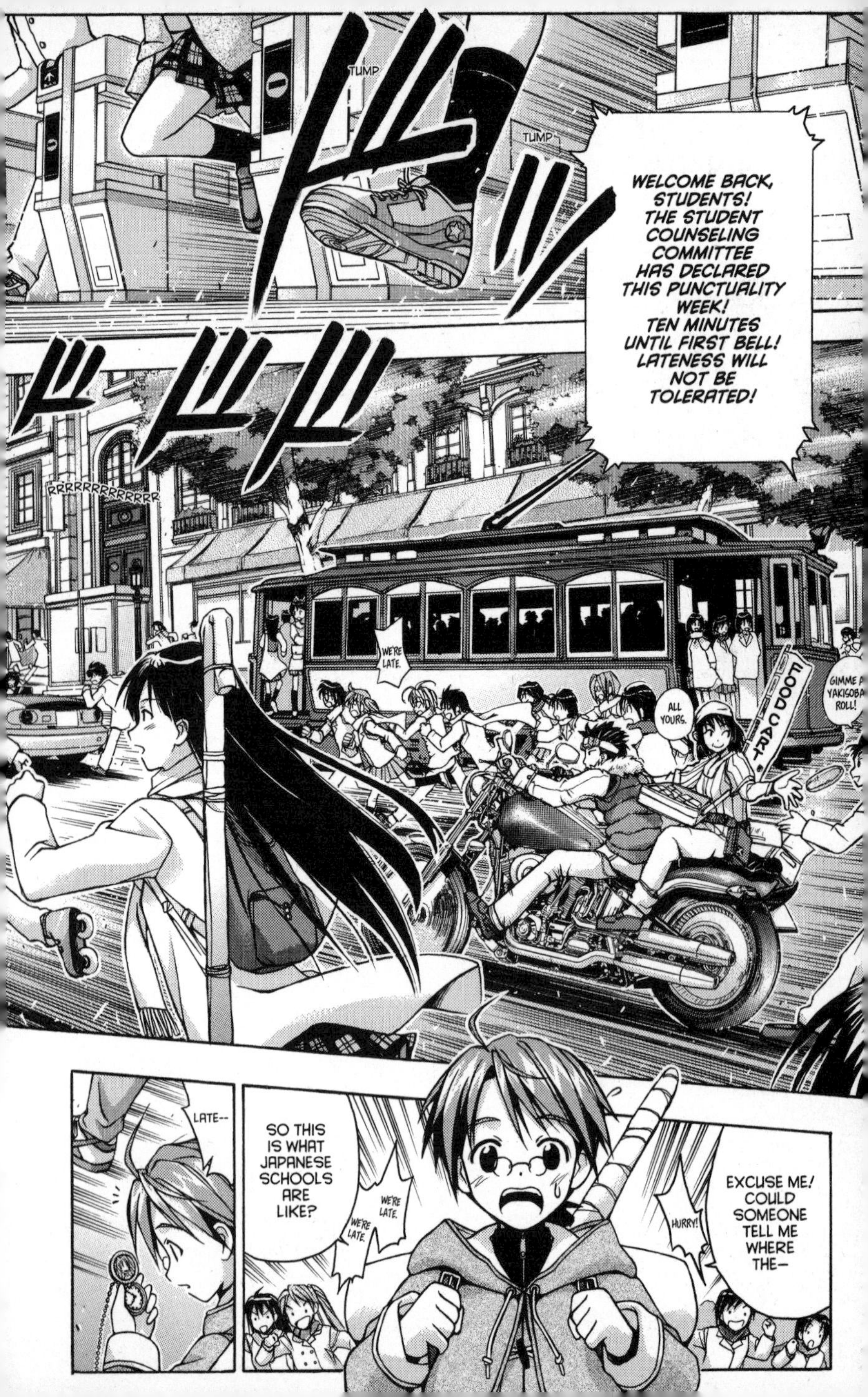
TUMP
TUMP
WELCOME BACK, STUDENTS! THE STUDENT COUNSELING COMMITTEE HAS DECLARED THIS PUNCTUALITY WEEK! TEN MINUTES UNTIL FIRST BELL! LATENESS WILL NOT BE TOLERATED!
RRRRRRRRRRRRRR
WE'RE LATE.
FOOD CART
GIMME A YAKISOBA ROLL!
ALL YOURS.
LATE--
SO THIS IS WHAT JAPANESE SCHOOLS ARE LIKE?
WE'RE LATE.
WE'RE LATE.
HURRY!
EXCUSE ME! COULD SOMEONE TELL ME WHERE THE—

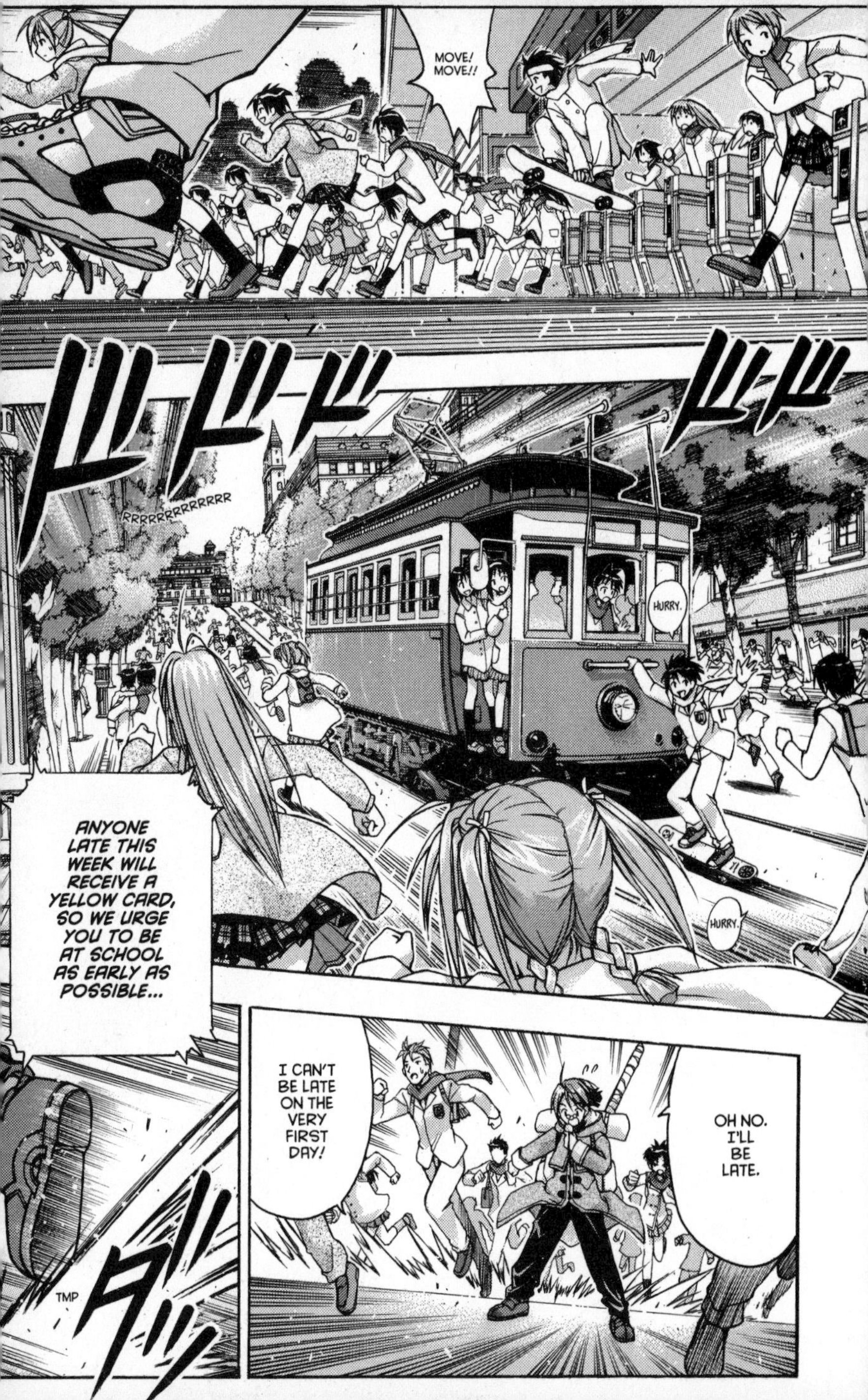
MOVE! MOVE!!
ドド
ドドドド
RRRRRRRRRRRR
HURRY.
HURRY.
ANYONE LATE THIS WEEK WILL RECEIVE A YELLOW CARD, SO WE URGE YOU TO BE AT SCHOOL AS EARLY AS POSSIBLE...
OH NO. I'LL BE LATE.
I CAN'T BE LATE ON THE VERY FIRST DAY!
ダッ
TMP

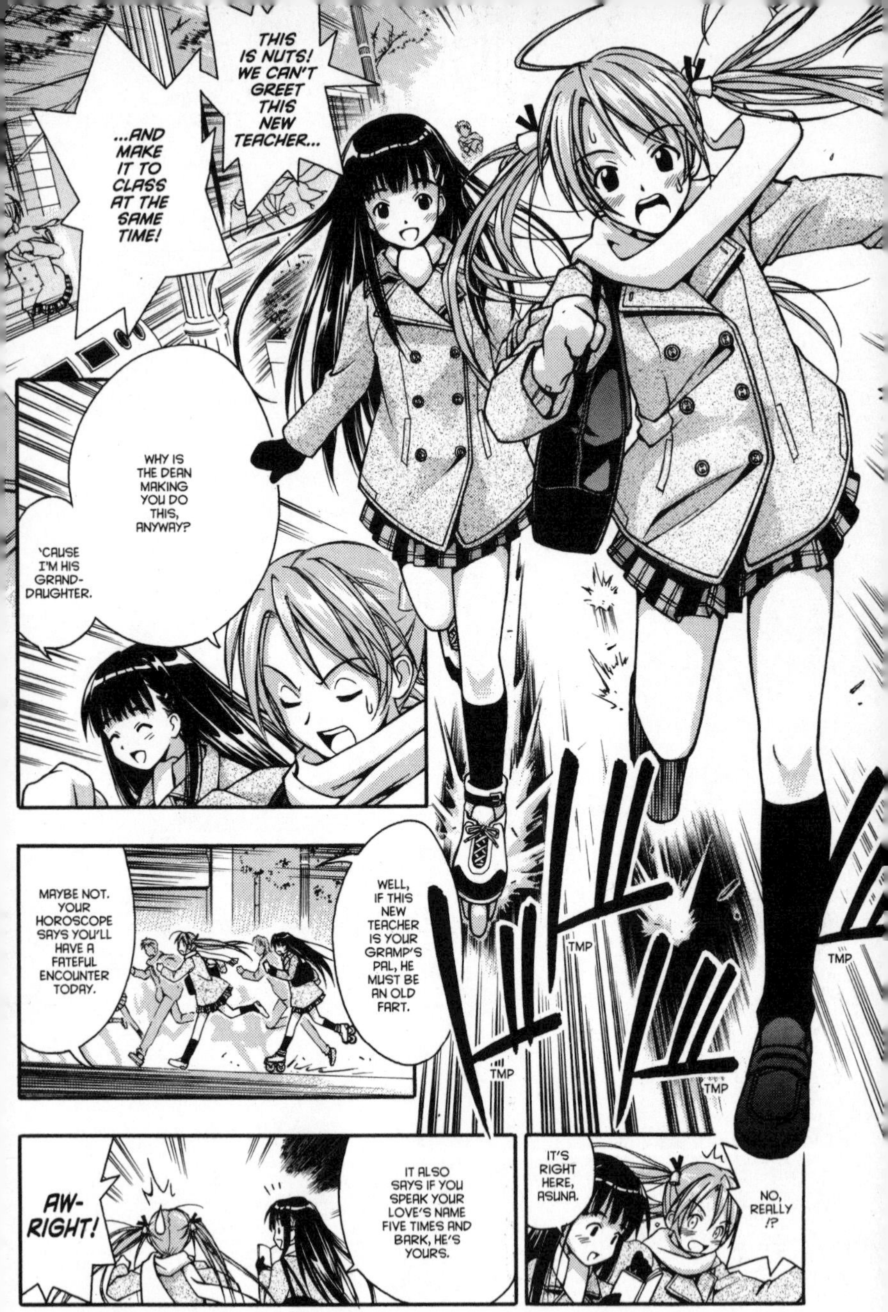
THIS IS NUTS! WE CAN'T GREET THIS NEW TEACHER...
...AND MAKE IT TO CLASS AT THE SAME TIME!
WHY IS THE DEAN MAKING YOU DO THIS, ANYWAY?
'CAUSE I'M HIS GRAND-DAUGHTER.
WELL, IF THIS NEW TEACHER IS YOUR GRAMP'S PAL, HE MUST BE AN OLD FART.
MAYBE NOT. YOUR HOROSCOPE SAYS YOU'LL HAVE A FATEFUL ENCOUNTER TODAY.
TMP
TMP
TMP
TMP
NO, REALLY !?
IT'S RIGHT HERE, ASUNA.
IT ALSO SAYS IF YOU SPEAK YOUR LOVE'S NAME FIVE TIMES AND BARK, HE'S YOURS.
AW-RIGHT!

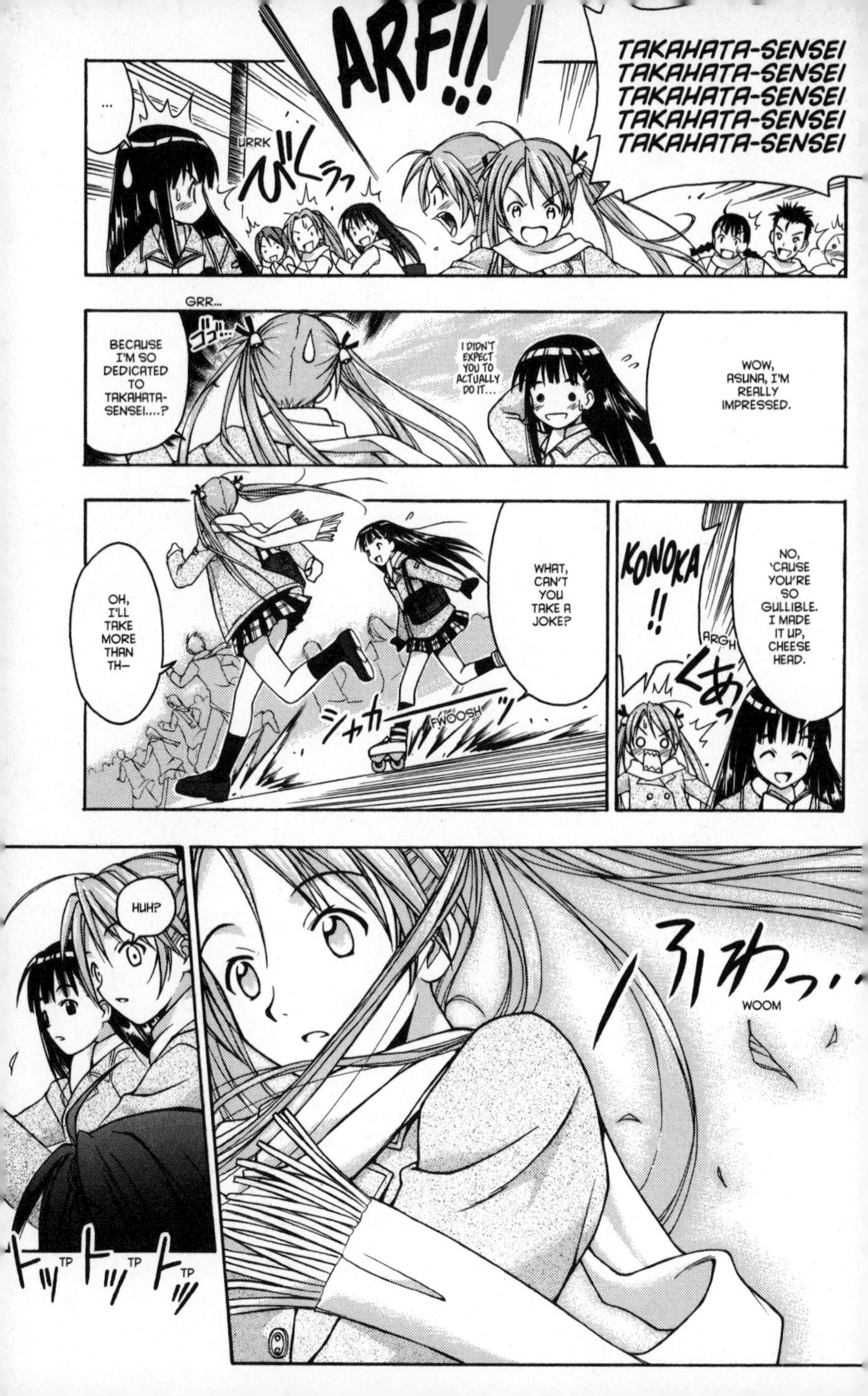
TAKAHATA-SENSEI TAKAHATA-SENSEI TAKAHATA-SENSEI TAKAHATA-SENSEI TAKAHATA-SENSEI
ARF!!
URRK
...
WOW, ASUNA, I'M REALLY IMPRESSED.
I DIDN'T EXPECT YOU TO ACTUALLY DO IT...
GRR...
BECAUSE I'M SO DEDICATED TO TAKAHATA-SENSEI....?
NO, 'CAUSE YOU'RE SO GULLIBLE. I MADE IT UP, CHEESE HEAD.
KONOKA!!
ARGH
WHAT, CAN'T YOU TAKE A JOKE?
FWOOSH
OH, I'LL TAKE MORE THAN TH–
WOOM
HUH?
TP
TP
TP

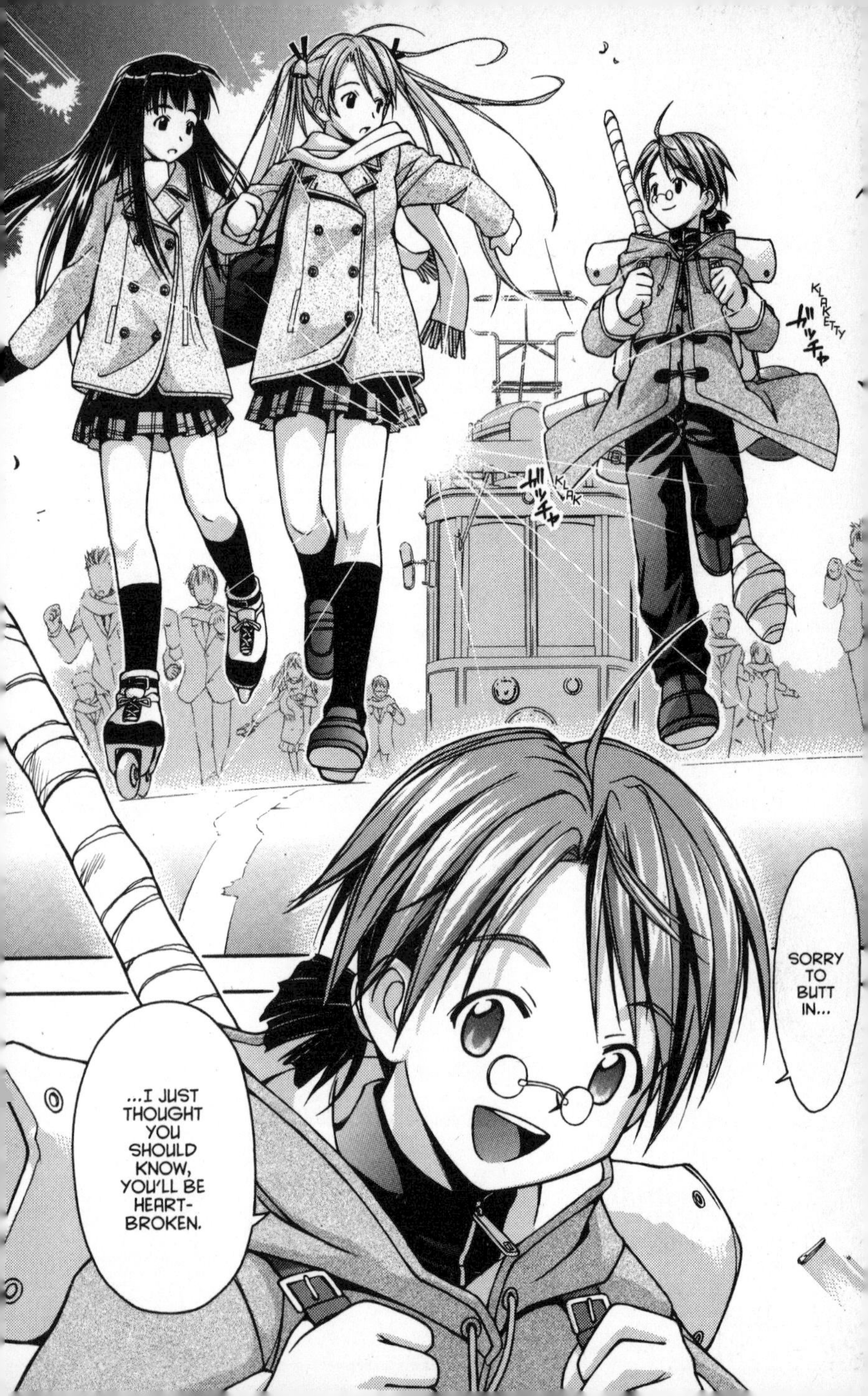

KLAKETTY
ガッチャ
ガッチャ
KLAK
SORRY TO BUTT IN...
...I JUST THOUGHT YOU SHOULD KNOW, YOU'LL BE HEART-BROKEN.

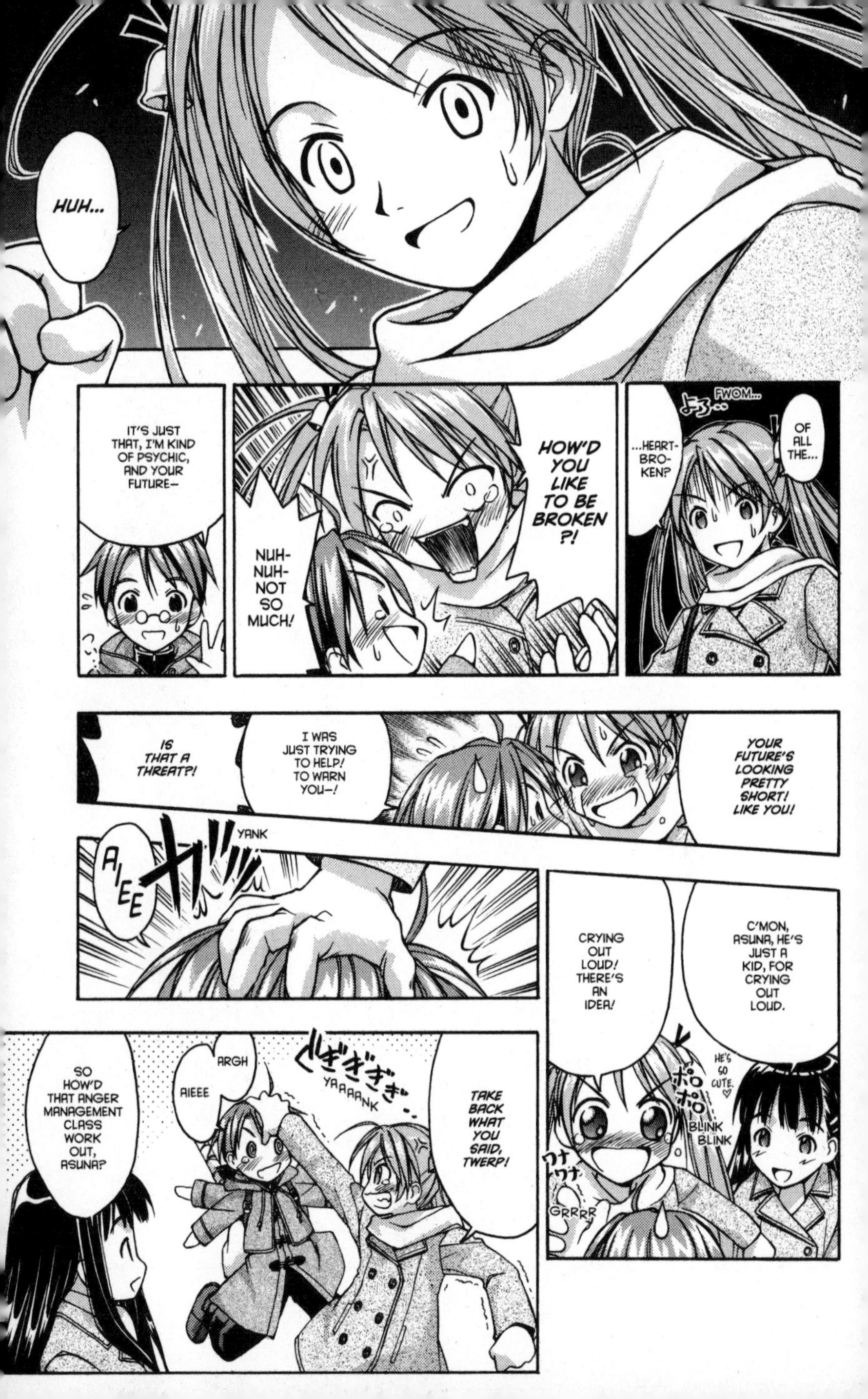
HUH...
OF ALL THE...
FWOM...
...HEART-BROKEN?
HOW'D YOU LIKE TO BE BROKEN?!
NUH-NUH-NOT SO MUCH!
IT'S JUST THAT, I'M KIND OF PSYCHIC, AND YOUR FUTURE–
YOUR FUTURE'S LOOKING PRETTY SHORT! LIKE YOU!
I WAS JUST TRYING TO HELP! TO WARN YOU–!
IS THAT A THREAT?!
C'MON, ASUNA, HE'S JUST A KID, FOR CRYING OUT LOUD.
CRYING OUT LOUD! THERE'S AN IDEA!
HE'S SO CUTE.
BLINK BLINK
GRRRR
YANK
AIEE
TAKE BACK WHAT YOU SAID, TWERP!
YAAAAANK
ARGH
AIEEE
SO HOW'D THAT ANGER MANAGEMENT CLASS WORK OUT, ASUNA?

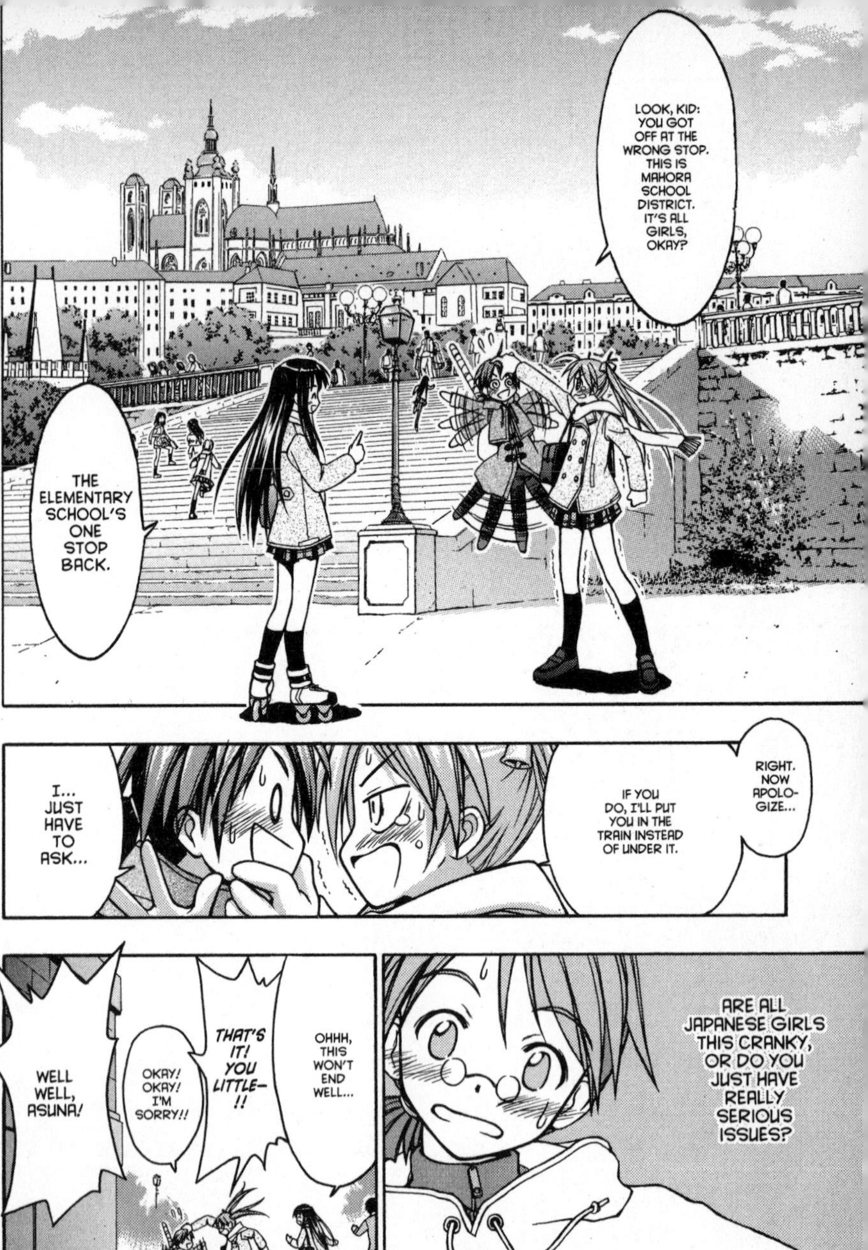
LOOK, KID: YOU GOT OFF AT THE WRONG STOP. THIS IS MAHORA SCHOOL DISTRICT. IT'S ALL GIRLS, OKAY?
THE ELEMENTARY SCHOOL'S ONE STOP BACK.
RIGHT. NOW APOLOGIZE...
IF YOU DO, I'LL PUT YOU IN THE TRAIN INSTEAD OF UNDER IT.
I... JUST HAVE TO ASK...
ARE ALL JAPANESE GIRLS THIS CRANKY, OR DO YOU JUST HAVE REALLY SERIOUS ISSUES?
OHHH, THIS WON'T END WELL...
THAT'S IT! YOU LITTLE—!!
OKAY! OKAY! I'M SORRY!!
WELL WELL, ASUNA!

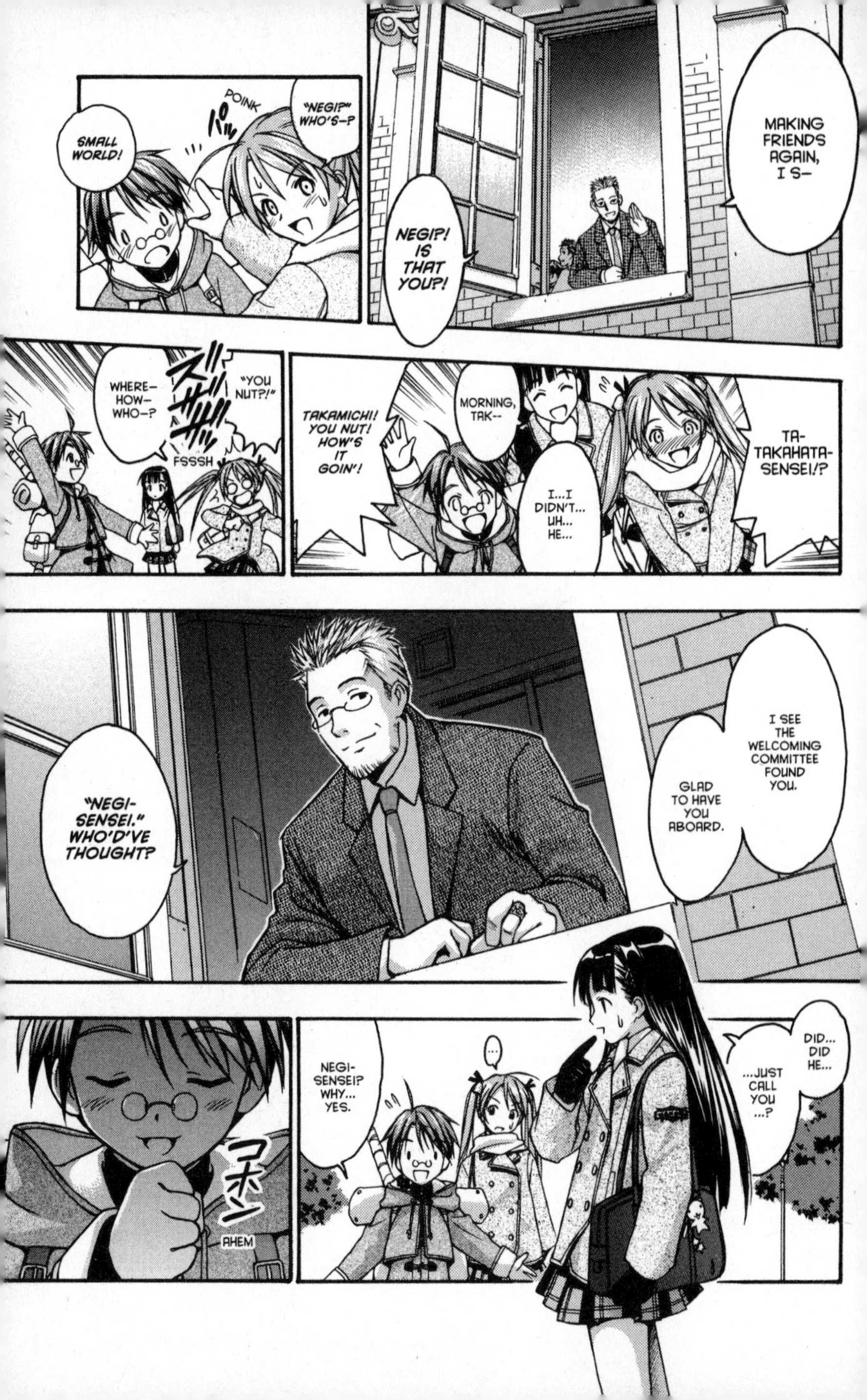

MAKING FRIENDS AGAIN, I S—
NEGI?! IS THAT YOU?!
"NEGI?" WHO'S—?
POINK
SMALL WORLD!
TA-TAKAHATA-SENSEI!?
I...I DIDN'T... UH... HE...
MORNING, TAK--
TAKAMICHI! YOU NUT! HOW'S IT GOIN'!
"YOU NUT?!"
FSSSH
WHERE-HOW-WHO-?
I SEE THE WELCOMING COMMITTEE FOUND YOU.
GLAD TO HAVE YOU ABOARD.
"NEGI-SENSEI." WHO'D'VE THOUGHT?
DID... DID HE...
...JUST CALL YOU ...?
...
NEGI-SENSEI? WHY... YES.
AHEM

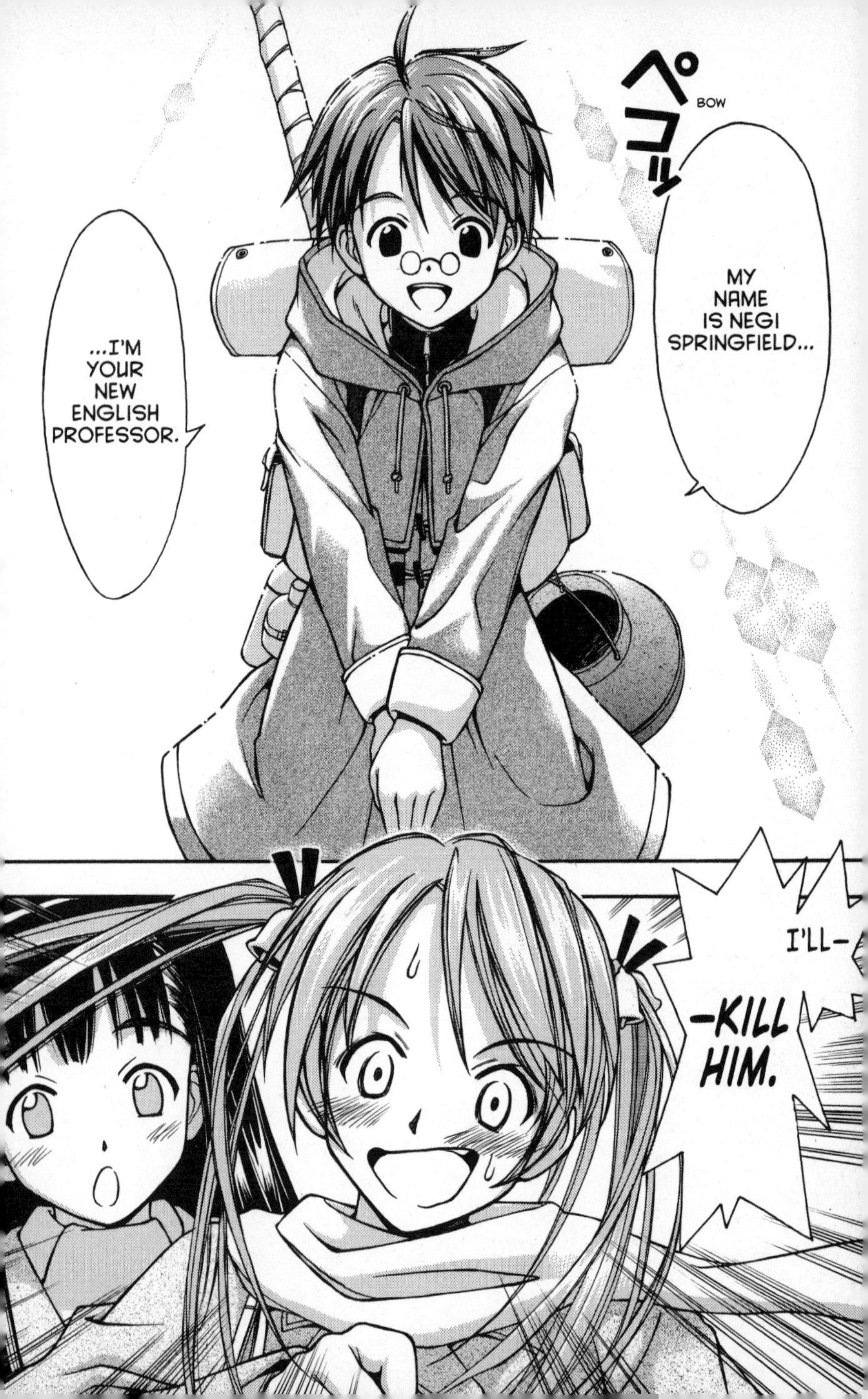
ペコッ
BOW
MY NAME IS NEGI SPRINGFIELD...
...I'M YOUR NEW ENGLISH PROFESSOR.
I'LL-
-KILL HIM.

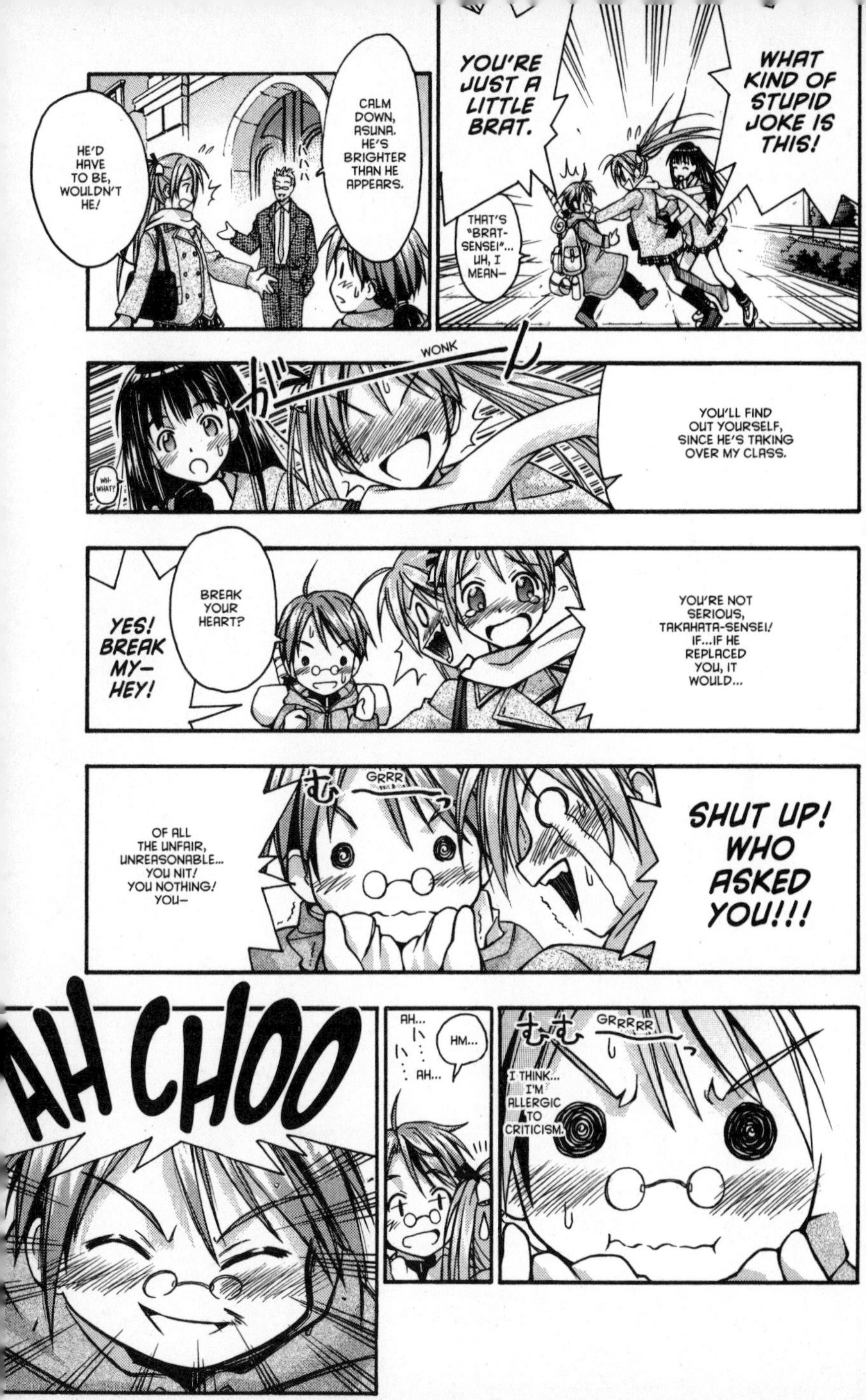
WHAT KIND OF STUPID JOKE IS THIS!
YOU'RE JUST A LITTLE BRAT.
THAT'S "BRAT-SENSEI"... UH, I MEAN—
CALM DOWN, ASUNA. HE'S BRIGHTER THAN HE APPEARS.
HE'D HAVE TO BE, WOULDN'T HE!
YOU'LL FIND OUT YOURSELF, SINCE HE'S TAKING OVER MY CLASS.
WONK
WH-WHAT?
YOU'RE NOT SERIOUS, TAKAHATA-SENSEI! IF...IF HE REPLACED YOU, IT WOULD...
BREAK YOUR HEART?
YES! BREAK MY—HEY!
SHUT UP! WHO ASKED YOU!!!
GRRR
OF ALL THE UNFAIR, UNREASONABLE... YOU NIT! YOU NOTHING! YOU—
GRRRRR
I THINK... I'M ALLERGIC TO CRITICISM.
AH... AH...
HM...
AH CHOO

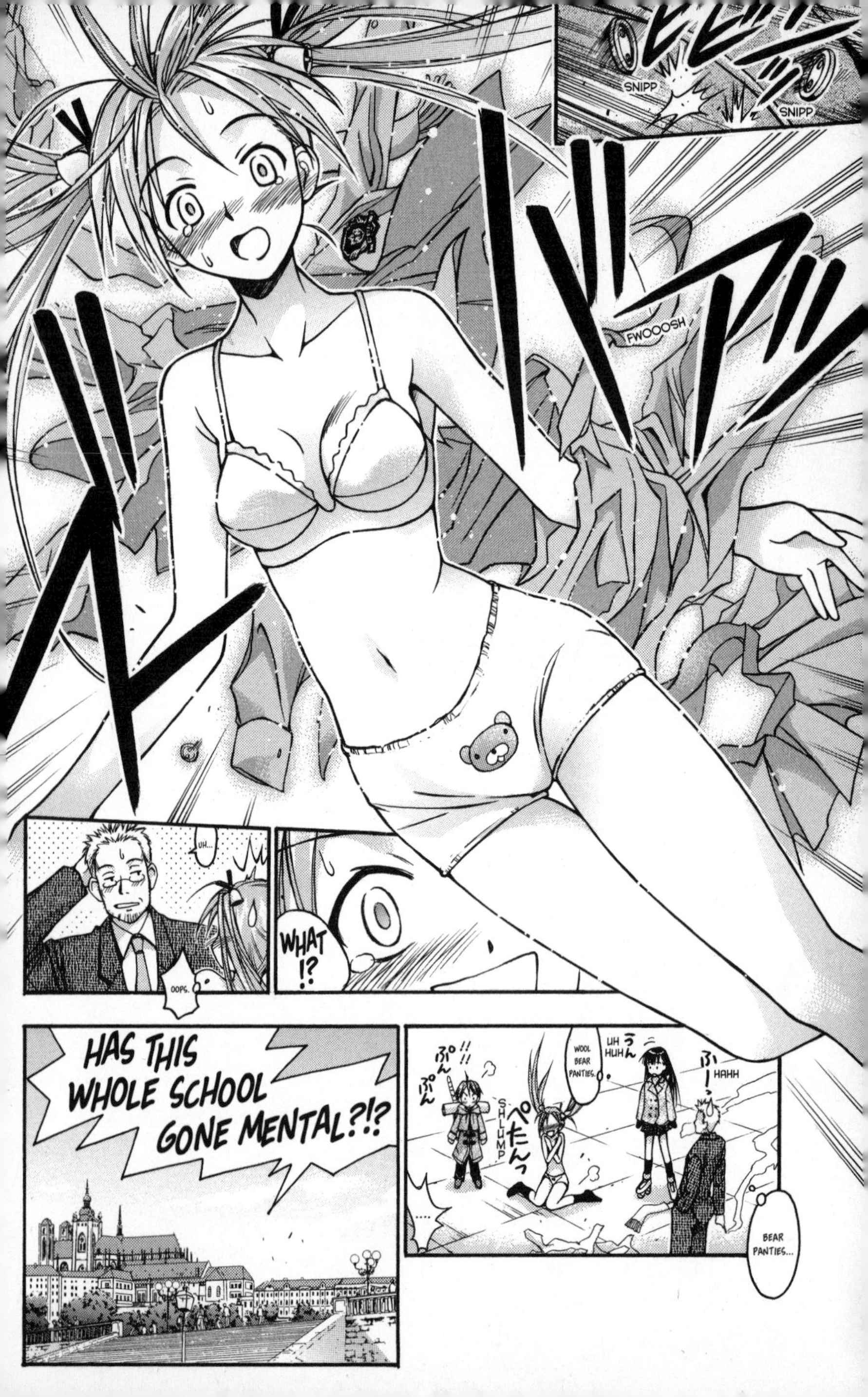
SNIPP
SNIPP
FWOOOSH
UH...
OOPS.
WHAT!?
HAS THIS WHOLE SCHOOL GONE MENTAL?!?
WOOL BEAR PANTIES.
UH HUH
HAHH
SHLUMP
....
BEAR PANTIES...

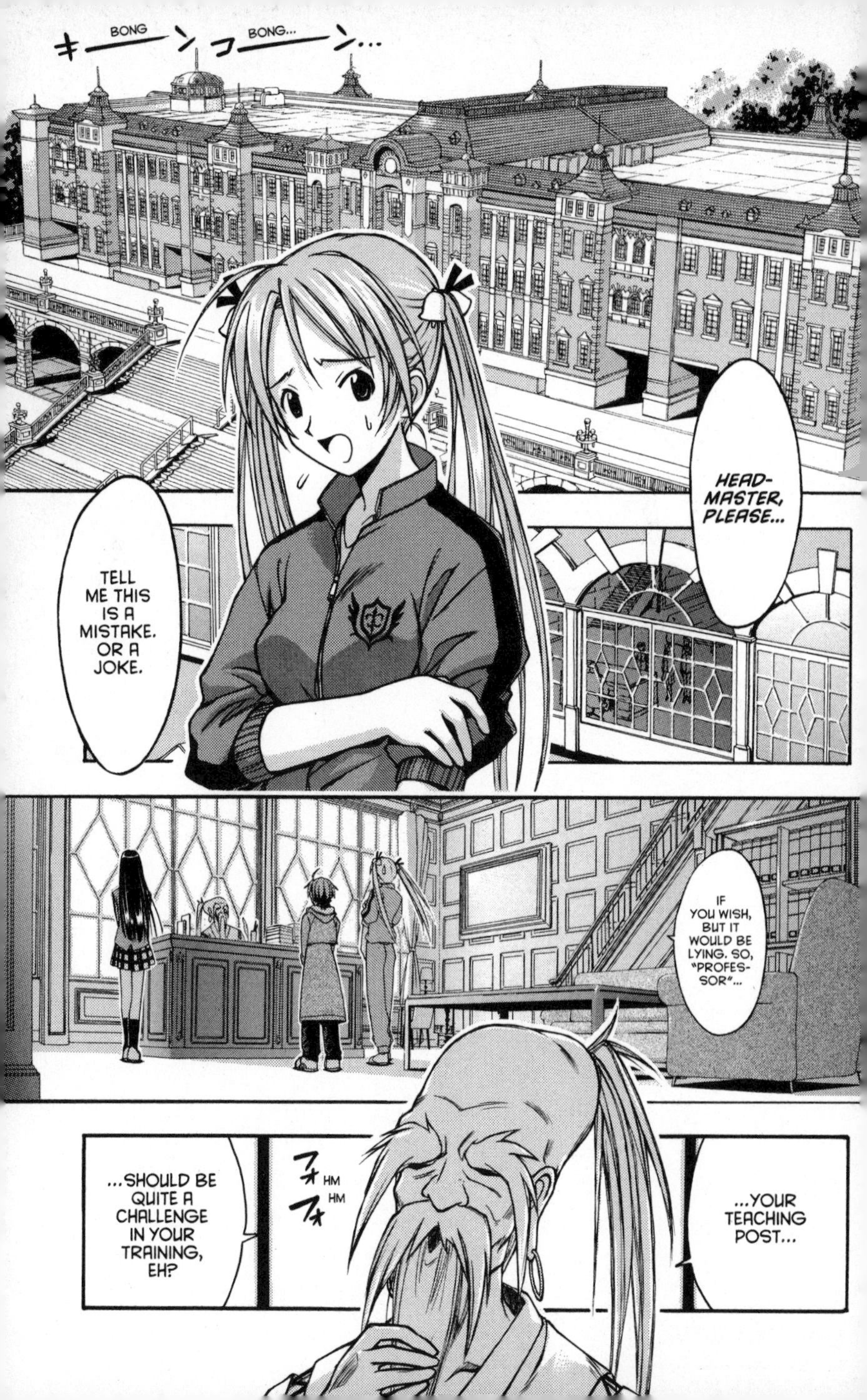

キーンコーン…
BONG BONG...
HEAD-MASTER, PLEASE...
TELL ME THIS IS A MISTAKE. OR A JOKE.
IF YOU WISH, BUT IT WOULD BE LYING. SO, "PROFES-SOR"...
...YOUR TEACHING POST...
フォ HM
フォ HM
...SHOULD BE QUITE A CHALLENGE IN YOUR TRAINING, EH?

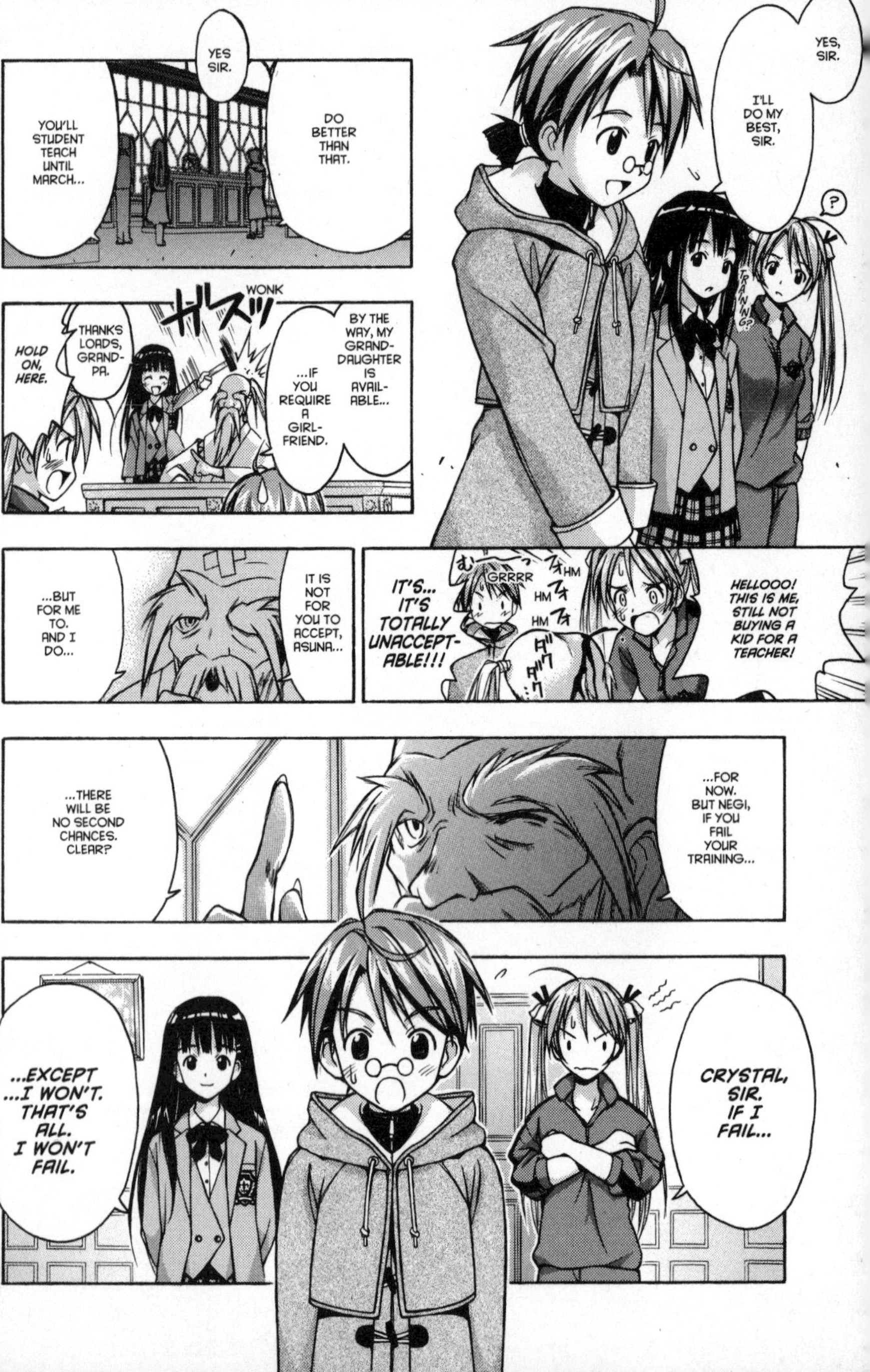
YES, SIR.
I'LL DO MY BEST, SIR.
?
TRAINING?
YES SIR.
DO BETTER THAN THAT.
YOU'LL STUDENT TEACH UNTIL MARCH...
BY THE WAY, MY GRAND-DAUGHTER IS AVAIL-ABLE...
...IF YOU REQUIRE A GIRL-FRIEND.
WONK
THANKS LOADS, GRAND-PA.
HOLD ON, HERE.
HELLOOO! THIS IS ME, STILL NOT BUYING A KID FOR A TEACHER!
HM
HM
HM
GRRRR
IT'S... IT'S TOTALLY UNACCEPT-ABLE!!!
IT IS NOT FOR YOU TO ACCEPT, ASUNA...
...BUT FOR ME TO. AND I DO...
...FOR NOW. BUT NEGI, IF YOU FAIL YOUR TRAINING...
...THERE WILL BE NO SECOND CHANCES. CLEAR?
CRYSTAL, SIR. IF I FAIL...
...EXCEPT ...I WON'T. THAT'S ALL. I WON'T FAIL.

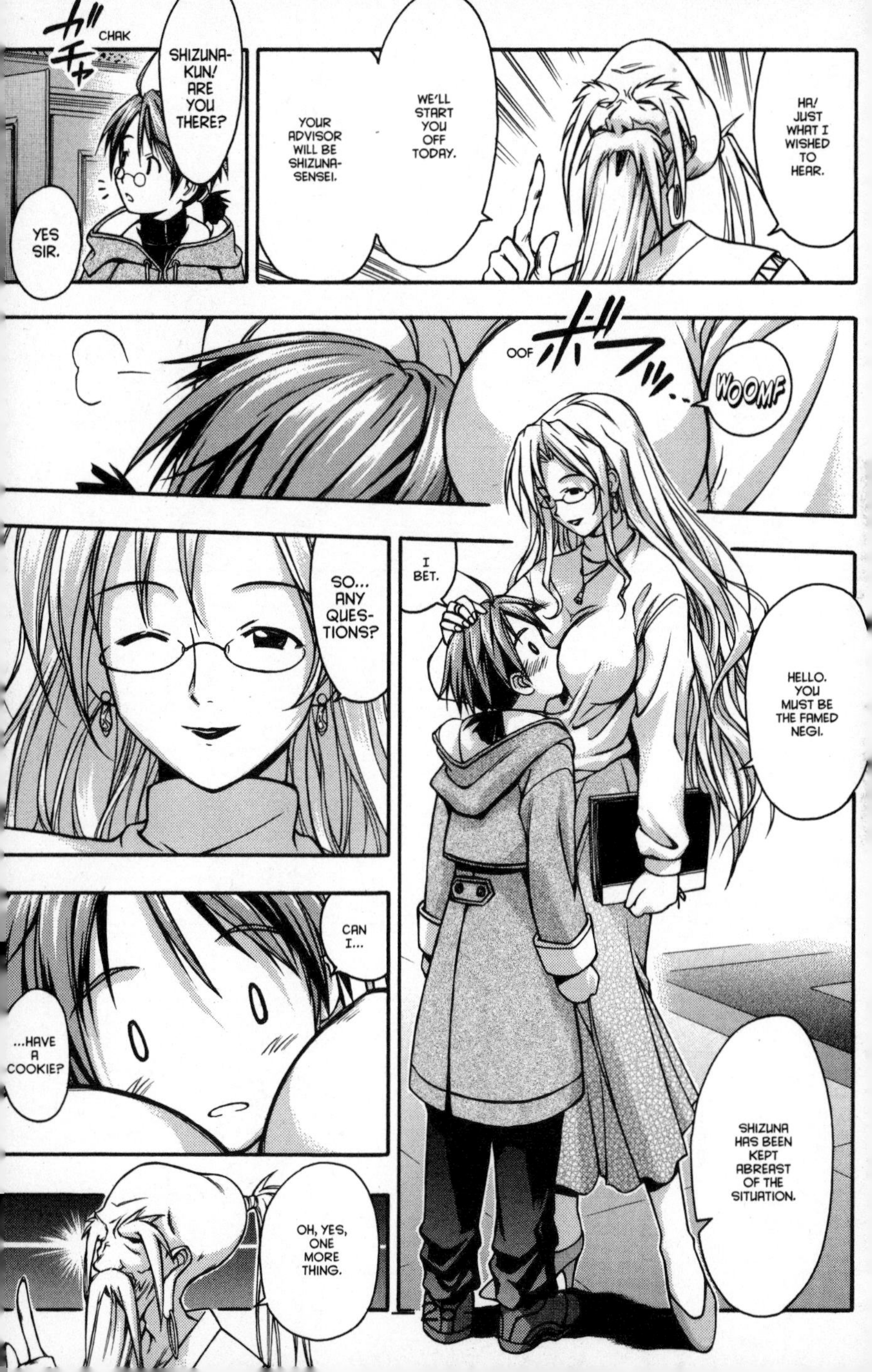
HA! JUST WHAT I WISHED TO HEAR.
WE'LL START YOU OFF TODAY.
YOUR ADVISOR WILL BE SHIZUNA-SENSEI.
CHAK
SHIZUNA-KUN! ARE YOU THERE?
YES SIR.
OOF
WOOMF
HELLO. YOU MUST BE THE FAMED NEGI.
I BET.
SHIZUNA HAS BEEN KEPT ABREAST OF THE SITUATION.
SO... ANY QUESTIONS?
CAN I...
...HAVE A COOKIE?
OH, YES, ONE MORE THING.

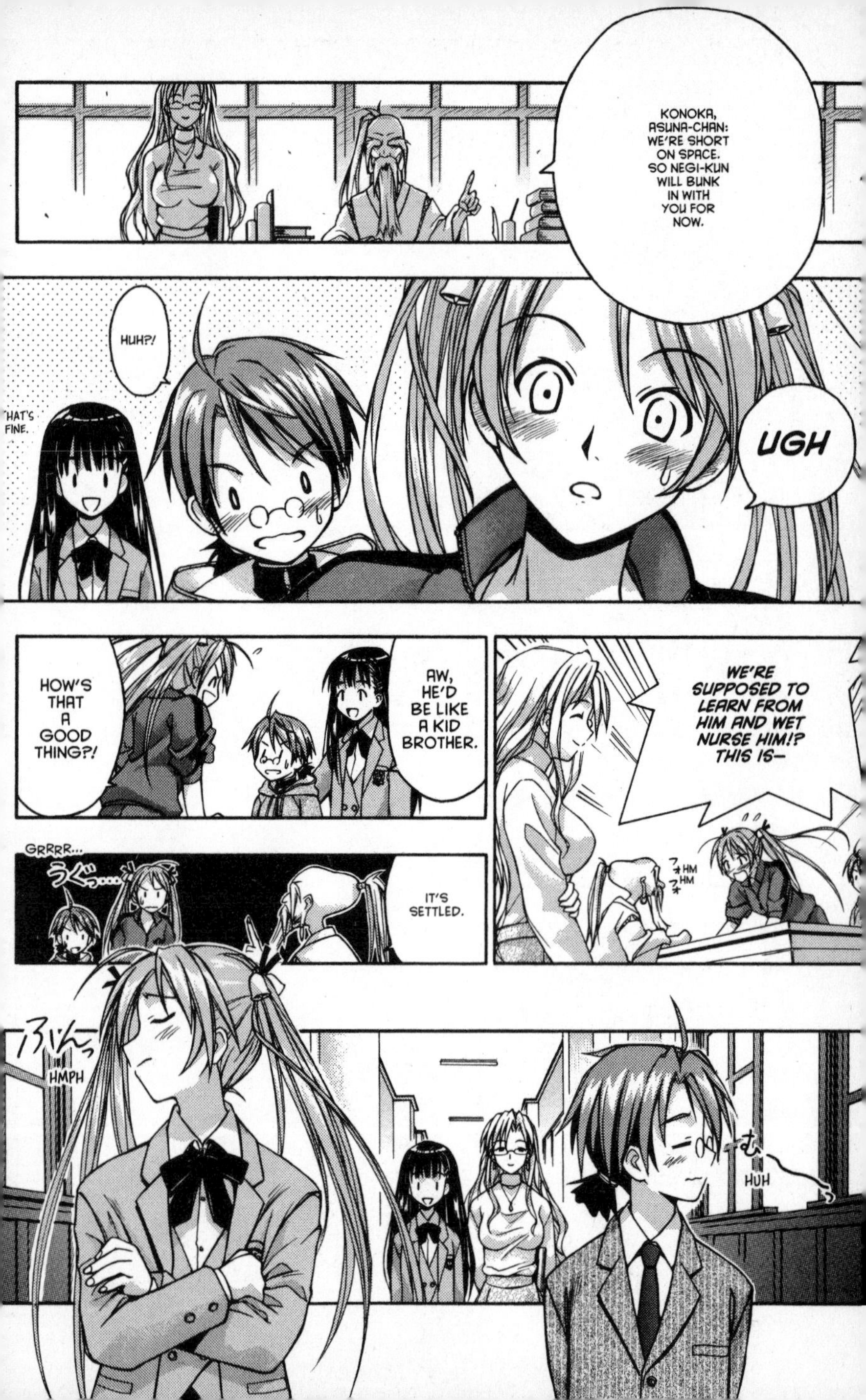
KONOKA, ASUNA-CHAN: WE'RE SHORT ON SPACE. SO NEGI-KUN WILL BUNK IN WITH YOU FOR NOW.
UGH
HUH?!
HAT'S FINE.
WE'RE SUPPOSED TO LEARN FROM HIM AND WET NURSE HIM!? THIS IS—
フォ HM フォ HM
AW, HE'D BE LIKE A KID BROTHER.
HOW'S THAT A GOOD THING?!
IT'S SETTLED.
GRRRR... うぐっ...
む HUH
ふんっ HMPH

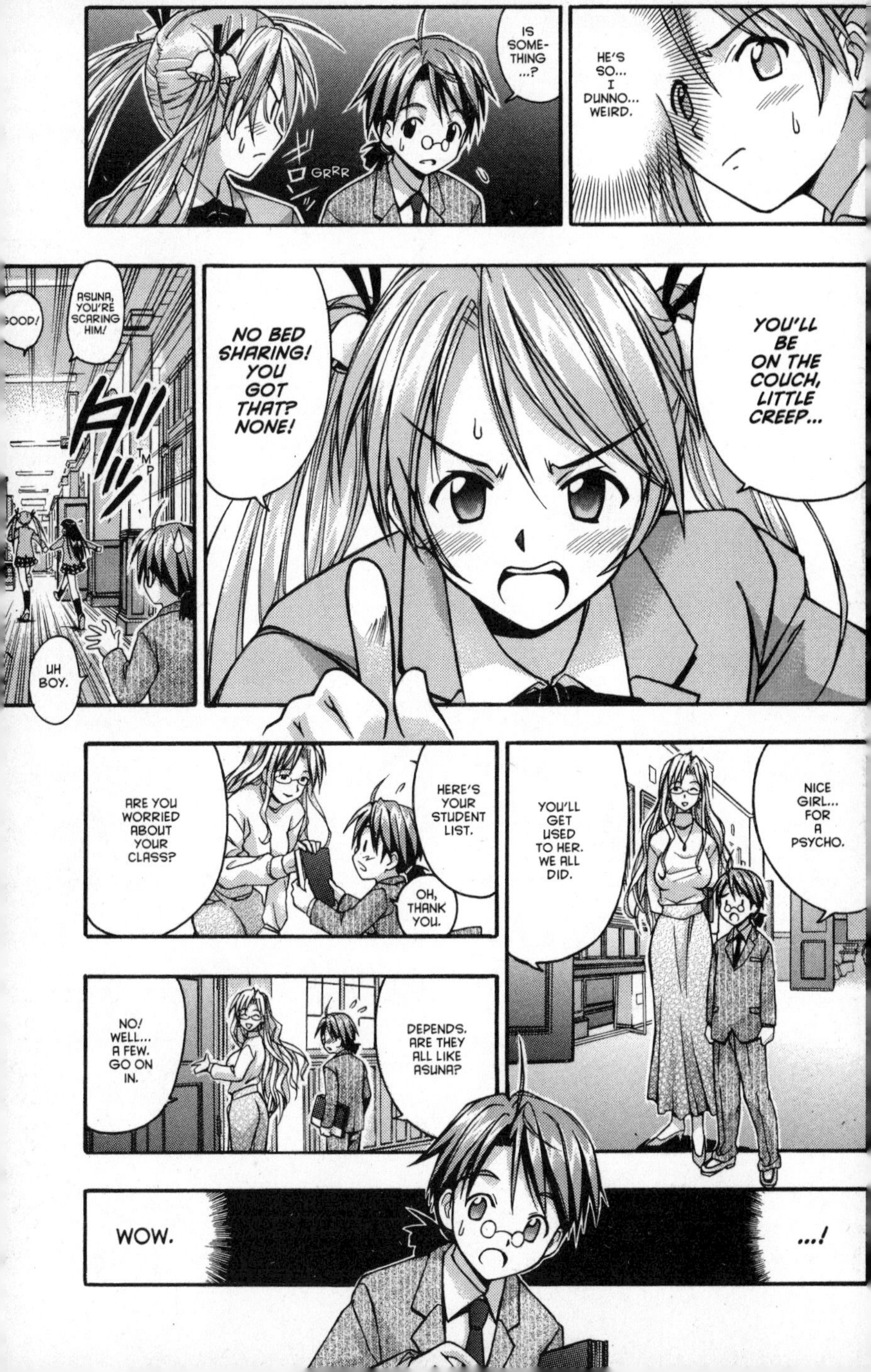
HE'S SO... I DUNNO... WEIRD.
IS SOME-THING ...?
GRRR
YOU'LL BE ON THE COUCH, LITTLE CREEP...
NO BED SHARING! YOU GOT THAT? NONE!
ASUNA, YOU'RE SCARING HIM!
GOOD!
TMP
UH BOY.
NICE GIRL... FOR A PSYCHO.
YOU'LL GET USED TO HER. WE ALL DID.
HERE'S YOUR STUDENT LIST.
OH, THANK YOU.
ARE YOU WORRIED ABOUT YOUR CLASS?
DEPENDS. ARE THEY ALL LIKE ASUNA?
NO! WELL... A FEW. GO ON IN.
...!
WOW.

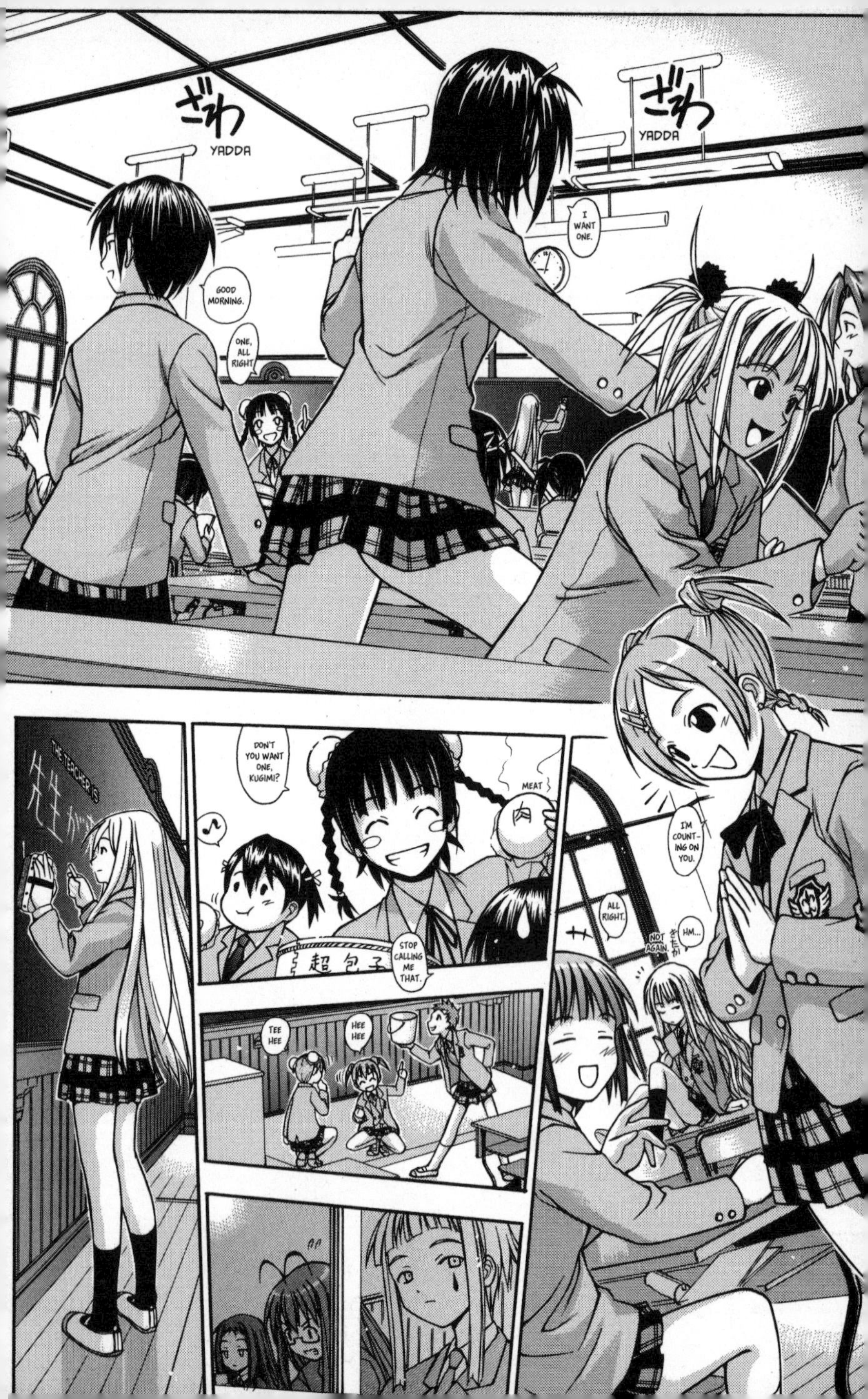
ざわ
YADDA
ざわ
YADDA
I WANT ONE.
GOOD MORNING.
ONE, ALL RIGHT
I'M COUNTING ON YOU.
ALL RIGHT.
HM...
きたか
NOT AGAIN.
MEAT
肉
DON'T YOU WANT ONE, KUGIMI?
STOP CALLING ME THAT.
超包子
THE TEACHER IS
先生が
HEE HEE
TEE HEE

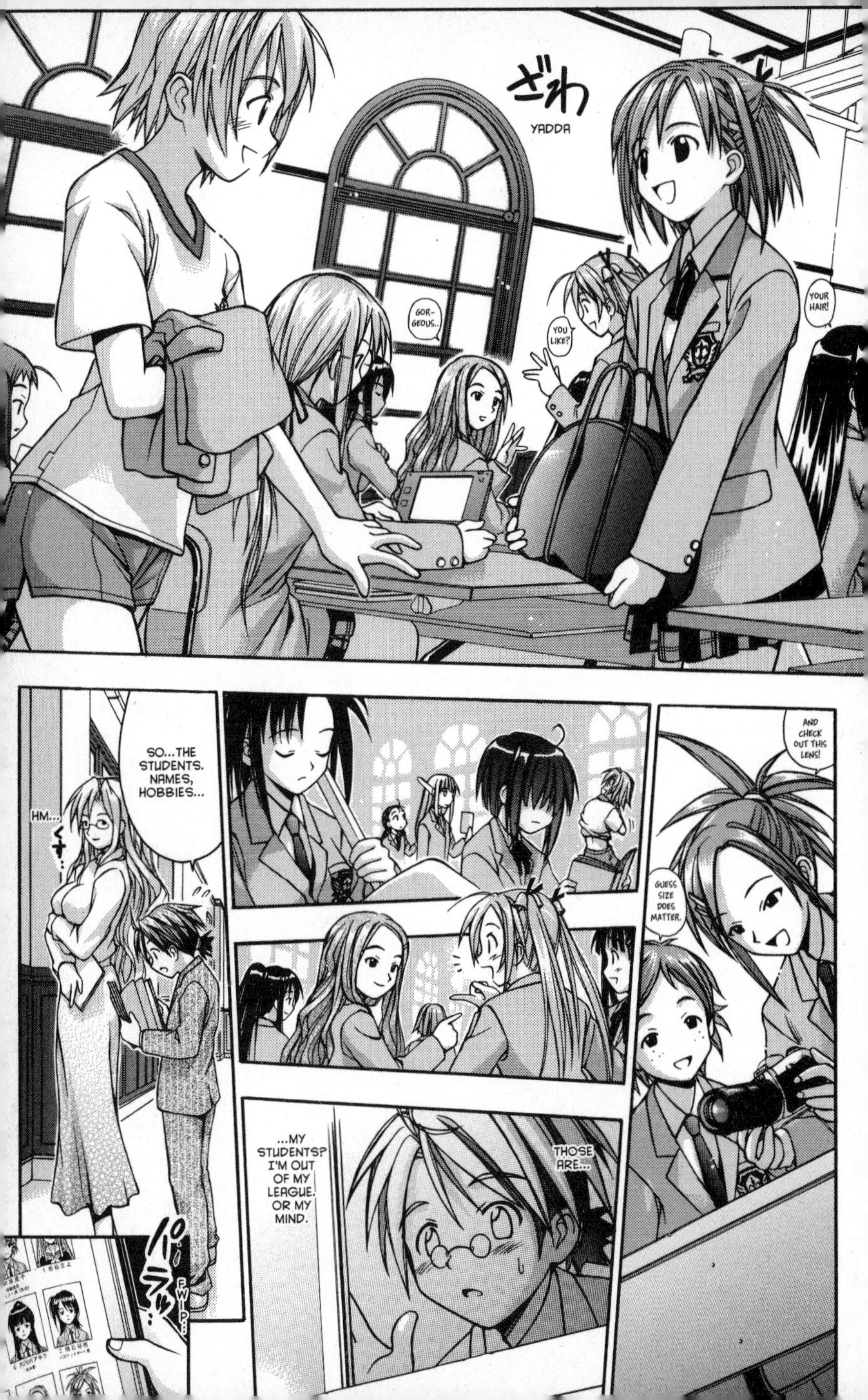
ざわ
YADDA
YOUR HAIR!
YOU LIKE?
GOR-GEOUS..
AND CHECK OUT THIS LENS!
GUESS SIZE DOES MATTER.
SO...THE STUDENTS. NAMES, HOBBIES...
HM...
くす...
THOSE ARE...
...MY STUDENTS? I'M OUT OF MY LEAGUE. OR MY MIND.
パラッ
FWIP...

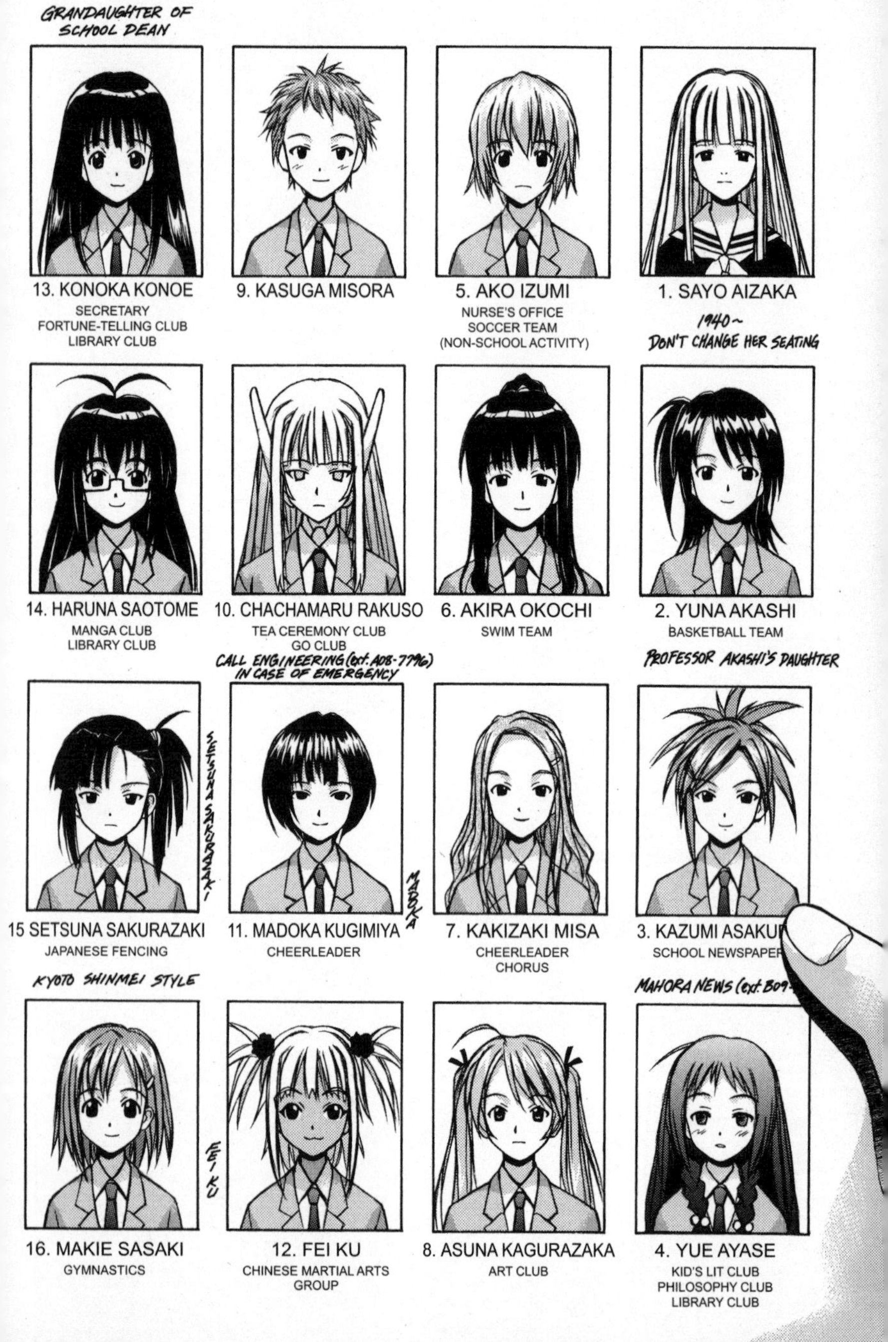

GRANDAUGHTER OF SCHOOL DEAN
13. KONOKA KONOE
SECRETARY
FORTUNE-TELLING CLUB
LIBRARY CLUB
9. KASUGA MISORA
5. AKO IZUMI
NURSE'S OFFICE
SOCCER TEAM
(NON-SCHOOL ACTIVITY)
1. SAYO AIZAKA
1940~
DON'T CHANGE HER SEATING
14. HARUNA SAOTOME
MANGA CLUB
LIBRARY CLUB
10. CHACHAMARU RAKUSO
TEA CEREMONY CLUB
GO CLUB
CALL ENGINEERING (ext. A08-7796) IN CASE OF EMERGENCY
6. AKIRA OKOCHI
SWIM TEAM
2. YUNA AKASHI
BASKETBALL TEAM
PROFESSOR AKASHI'S DAUGHTER
SETSUNA SAKURAZAKI
15 SETSUNA SAKURAZAKI
JAPANESE FENCING
KYOTO SHINMEI STYLE
MADOKA
11. MADOKA KUGIMIYA
CHEERLEADER
7. KAKIZAKI MISA
CHEERLEADER
CHORUS
3. KAZUMI ASAKU
SCHOOL NEWSPAPE
MAHORA NEWS (ext. 809-
16. MAKIE SASAKI
GYMNASTICS
FEI KU
12. FEI KU
CHINESE MARTIAL ARTS
GROUP
8. ASUNA KAGURAZAKA
ART CLUB
4. YUE AYASE
KID'S LIT CLUB
PHILOSOPHY CLUB
LIBRARY CLUB

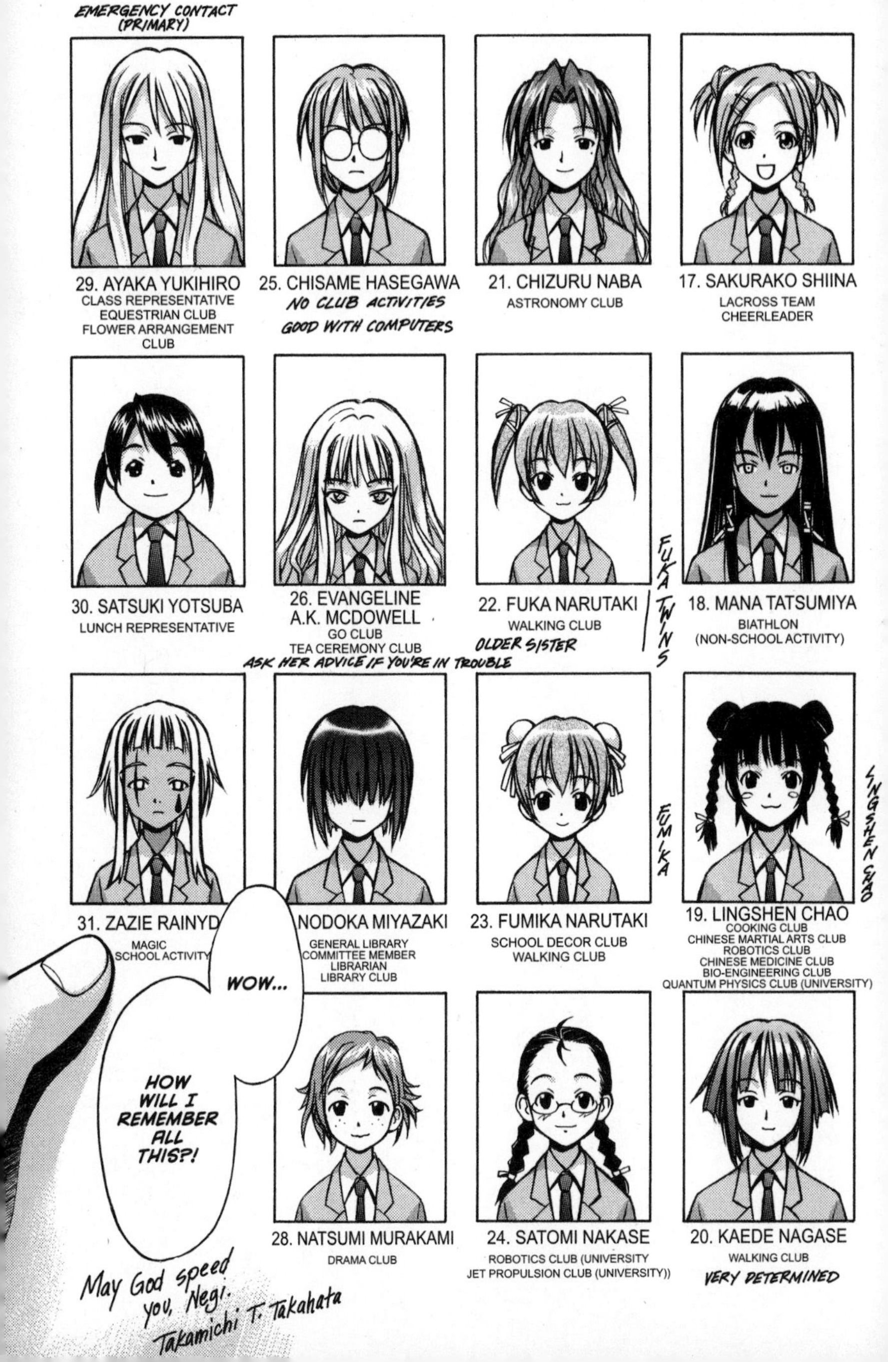

EMERGENCY CONTACT (PRIMARY)
29. AYAKA YUKIHIRO
CLASS REPRESENTATIVE
EQUESTRIAN CLUB
FLOWER ARRANGEMENT CLUB
25. CHISAME HASEGAWA
NO CLUB ACTIVITIES
GOOD WITH COMPUTERS
21. CHIZURU NABA
ASTRONOMY CLUB
17. SAKURAKO SHIINA
LACROSS TEAM
CHEERLEADER
30. SATSUKI YOTSUBA
LUNCH REPRESENTATIVE
26. EVANGELINE A.K. MCDOWELL
GO CLUB
TEA CEREMONY CLUB
ASK HER ADVICE IF YOU'RE IN TROUBLE
22. FUKA NARUTAKI
WALKING CLUB
OLDER SISTER
FUKA TWINS
18. MANA TATSUMIYA
BIATHLON
(NON-SCHOOL ACTIVITY)
31. ZAZIE RAINYD
MAGIC
SCHOOL ACTIVITY
NODOKA MIYAZAKI
GENERAL LIBRARY COMMITTEE MEMBER
LIBRARIAN
LIBRARY CLUB
23. FUMIKA NARUTAKI
SCHOOL DECOR CLUB
WALKING CLUB
FUMIKA
19. LINGSHEN CHAO
COOKING CLUB
CHINESE MARTIAL ARTS CLUB
ROBOTICS CLUB
CHINESE MEDICINE CLUB
BIO-ENGINEERING CLUB
QUANTUM PHYSICS CLUB (UNIVERSITY)
LINGSHEN CHAO
WOW...
HOW WILL I REMEMBER ALL THIS?!
28. NATSUMI MURAKAMI
DRAMA CLUB
24. SATOMI NAKASE
ROBOTICS CLUB (UNIVERSITY
JET PROPULSION CLUB (UNIVERSITY))
20. KAEDE NAGASE
WALKING CLUB
VERY DETERMINED
May God speed you, Negi.
Takamichi T. Takahata

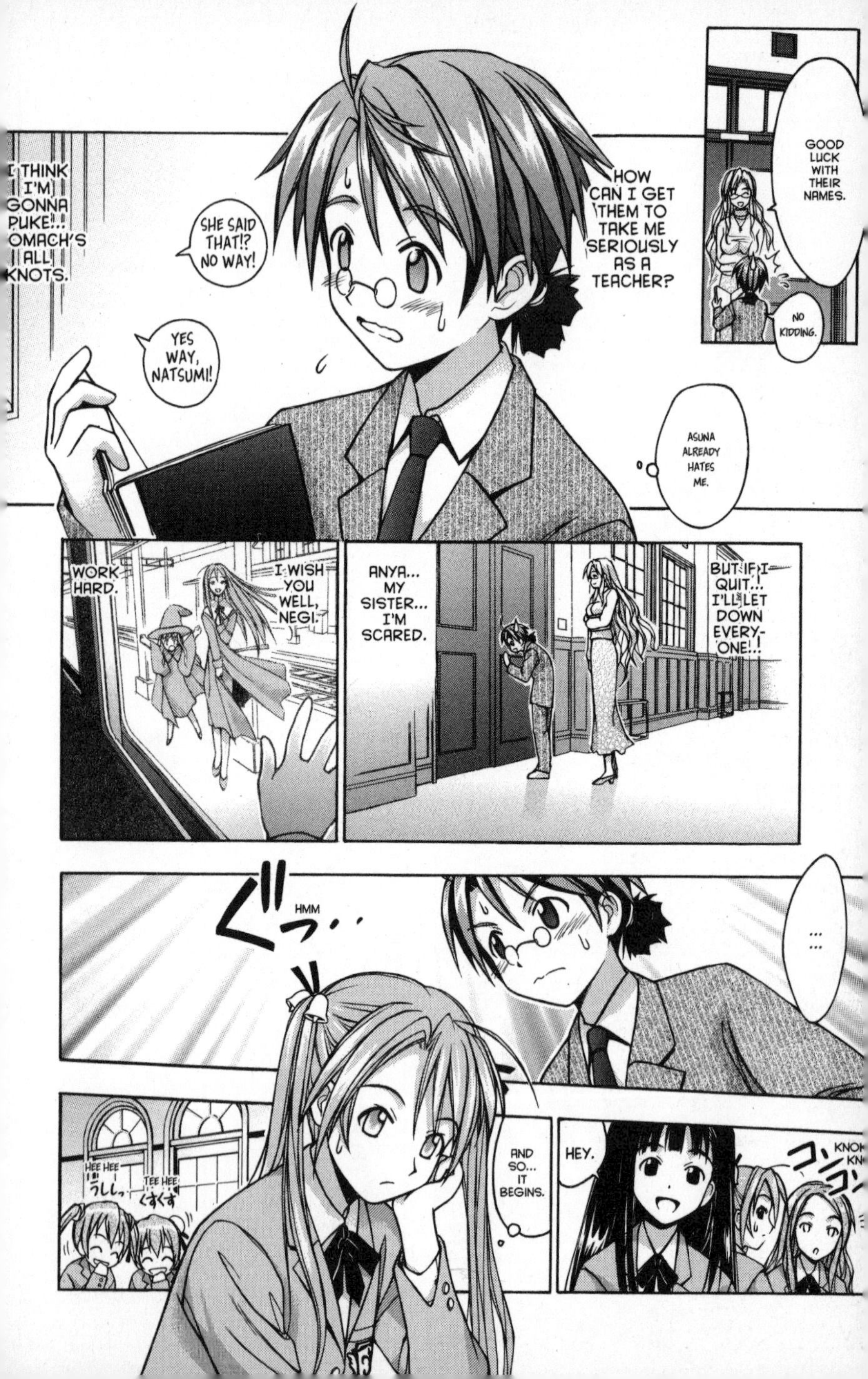
GOOD LUCK WITH THEIR NAMES.
NO KIDDING.
HOW CAN I GET THEM TO TAKE ME SERIOUSLY AS A TEACHER?
ASUNA ALREADY HATES ME.
SHE SAID THAT!? NO WAY!
YES WAY, NATSUMI!
I THINK I'M GONNA PUKE... OMACH'S ALL KNOTS.
BUT IF I QUIT... I'LL LET DOWN EVERY-ONE...!
ANYA... MY SISTER... I'M SCARED.
I WISH YOU WELL, NEGI.
WORK HARD.
......
ぐっ・・
HMM
コンコン
HEY.
AND SO... IT BEGINS.
うしし。
HEE HEE
くすくす
TEE HEE

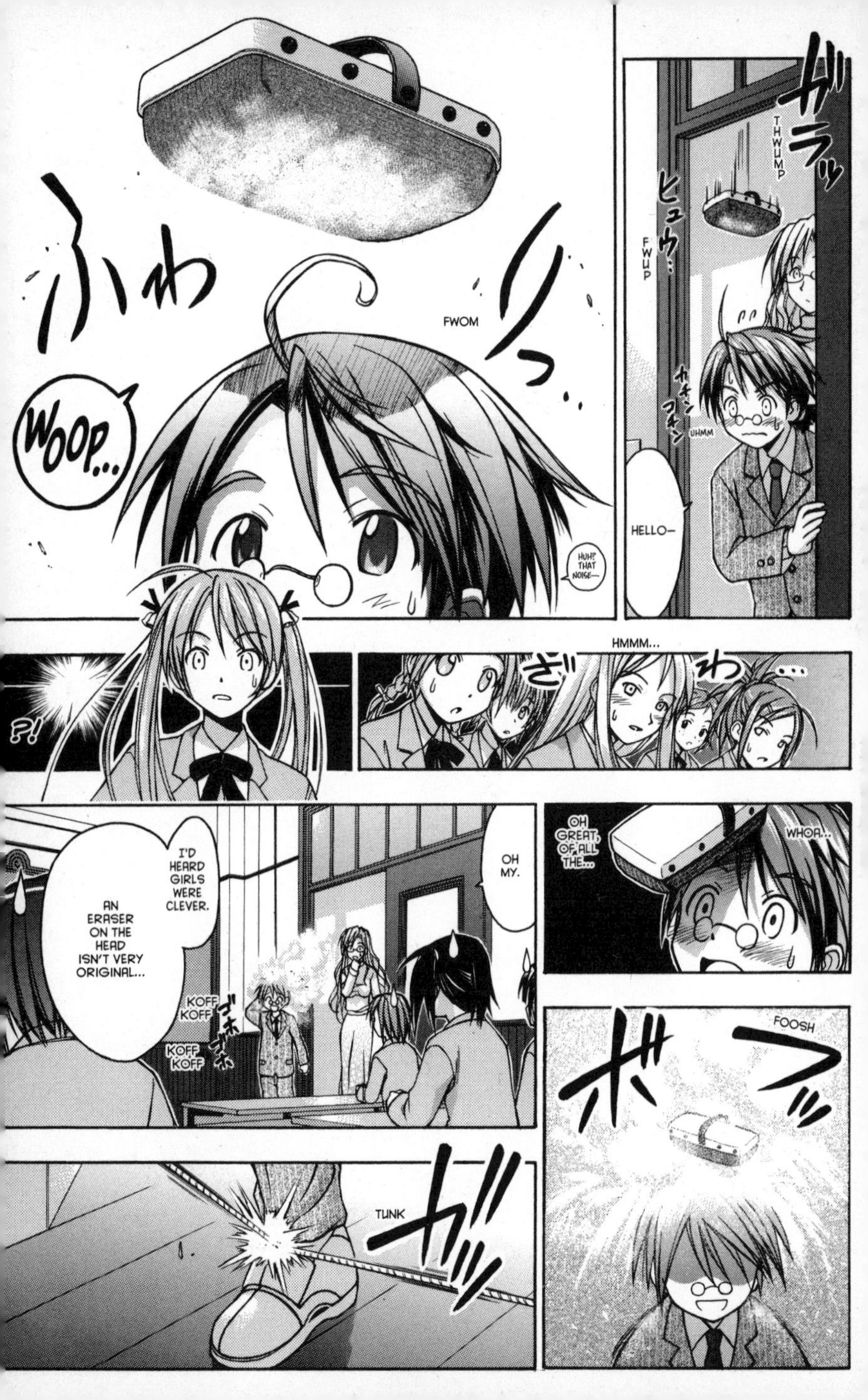
ガラッ
THWUMP
ヒュウ…
FWUP
カチン コチン
UHMM
HELLO—
ふわりっ…
FWOM
WOOP...
HUH? THAT NOISE—
ざわ…
HMMM...
?!
OH GREAT, OF ALL THE...
WHOA...
OH MY.
I'D HEARD GIRLS WERE CLEVER.
AN ERASER ON THE HEAD ISN'T VERY ORIGINAL...
KOFF KOFF
ゴホ ゴホ
KOFF KOFF
ボフッ
FOOSH
ガッ
TUNK

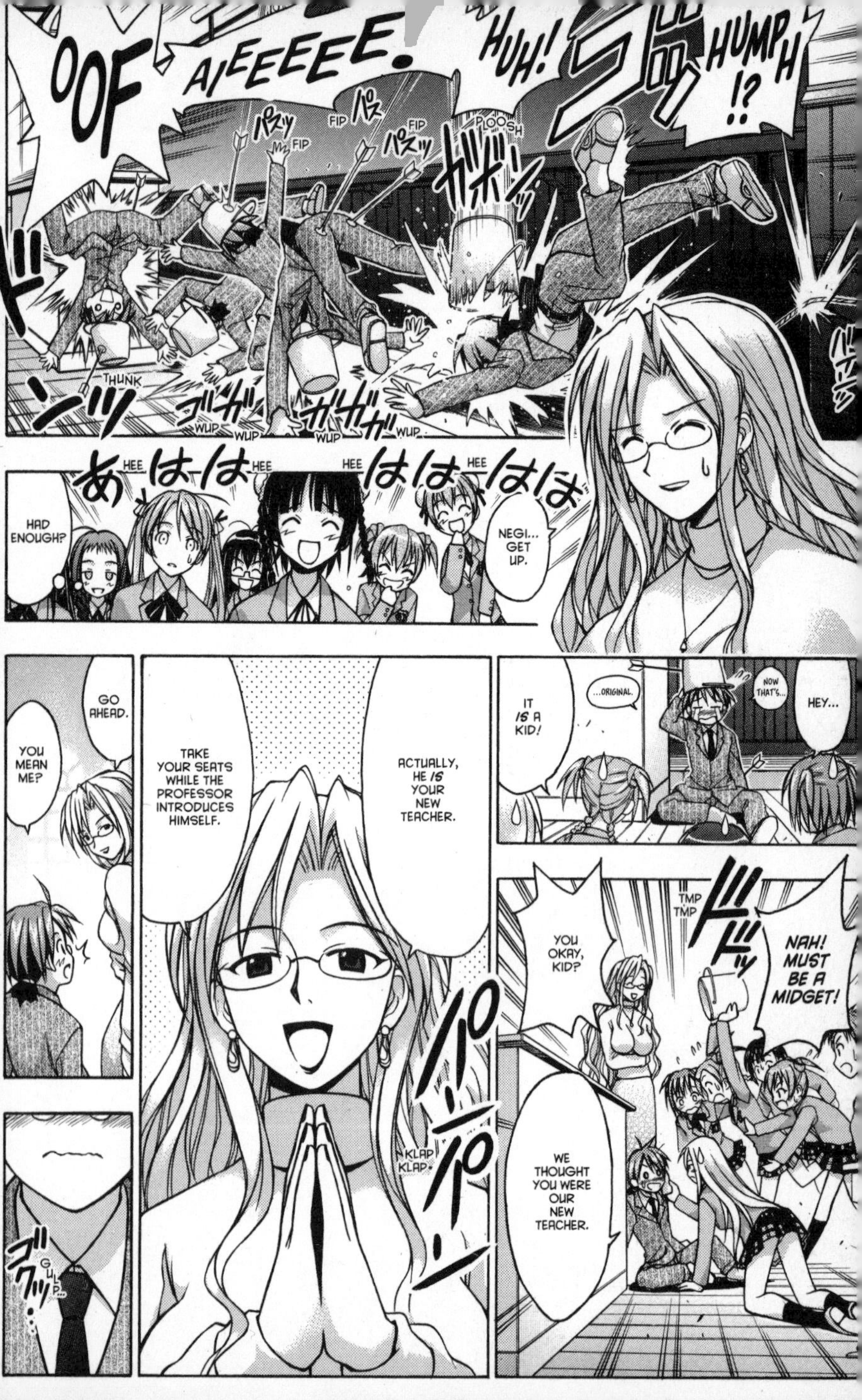
HUMPH !?
HUH!
AIEEEEEE.
OOF
FIP
FIP
FIP
PLOOSH
THUNK
WUP
WUP
WUP
WUP
HEE
HEE
HEE
HEE
NEGI... GET UP.
HAD ENOUGH?
HEY...
NOW THAT'S...
...ORIGINAL.
IT IS A KID!
ACTUALLY, HE IS YOUR NEW TEACHER.
TAKE YOUR SEATS WHILE THE PROFESSOR INTRODUCES HIMSELF.
GO AHEAD.
YOU MEAN ME?
TMP TMP
NAH! MUST BE A MIDGET!
YOU OKAY, KID?
WE THOUGHT YOU WERE OUR NEW TEACHER.
KLAP KLAP
GULP...

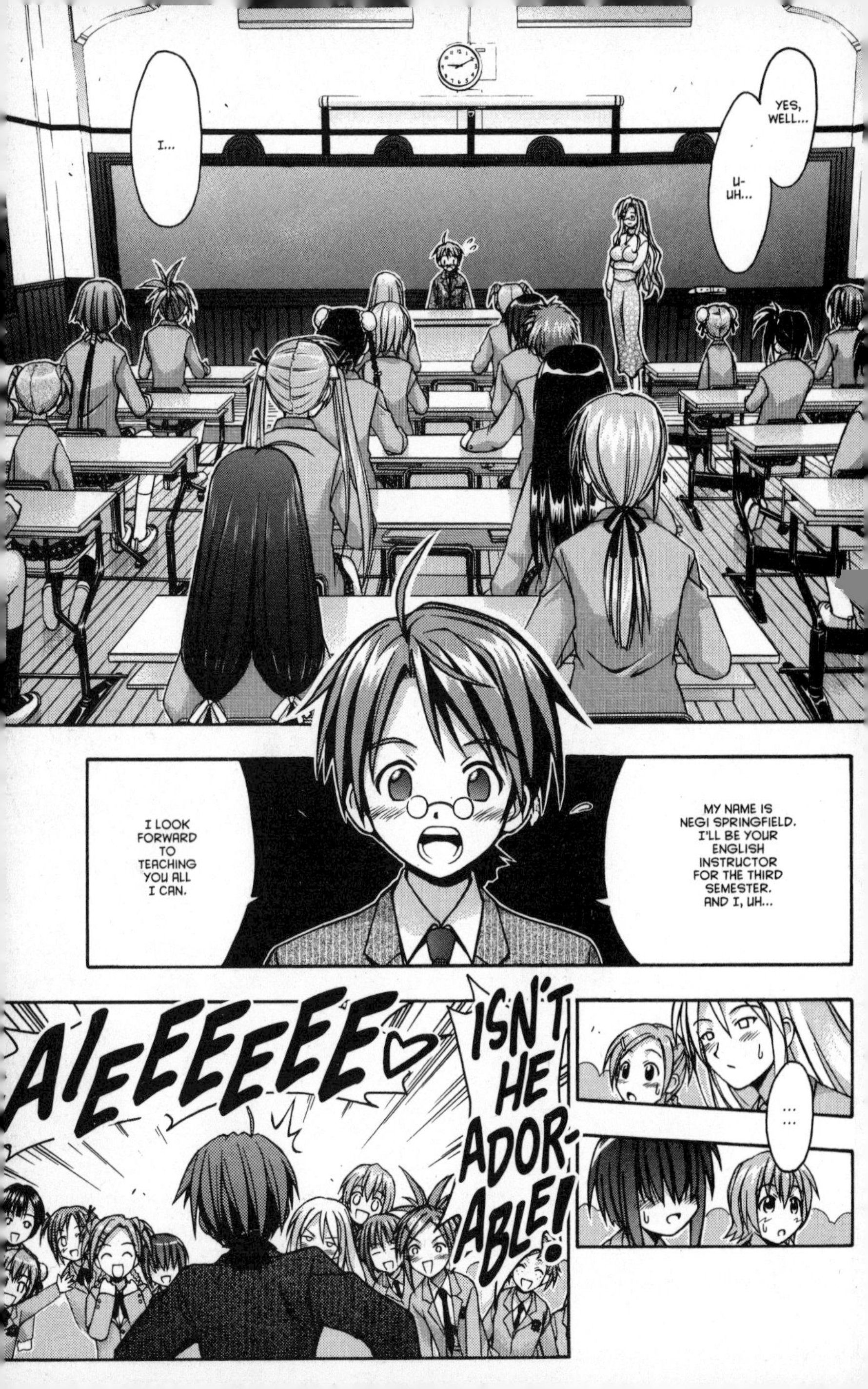
YES, WELL...
U-UH...
I...
MY NAME IS NEGI SPRINGFIELD. I'LL BE YOUR ENGLISH INSTRUCTOR FOR THE THIRD SEMESTER. AND I, UH...
I LOOK FORWARD TO TEACHING YOU ALL I CAN.
... ...
ISN'T HE ADORABLE!
AIEEEEEEE♡

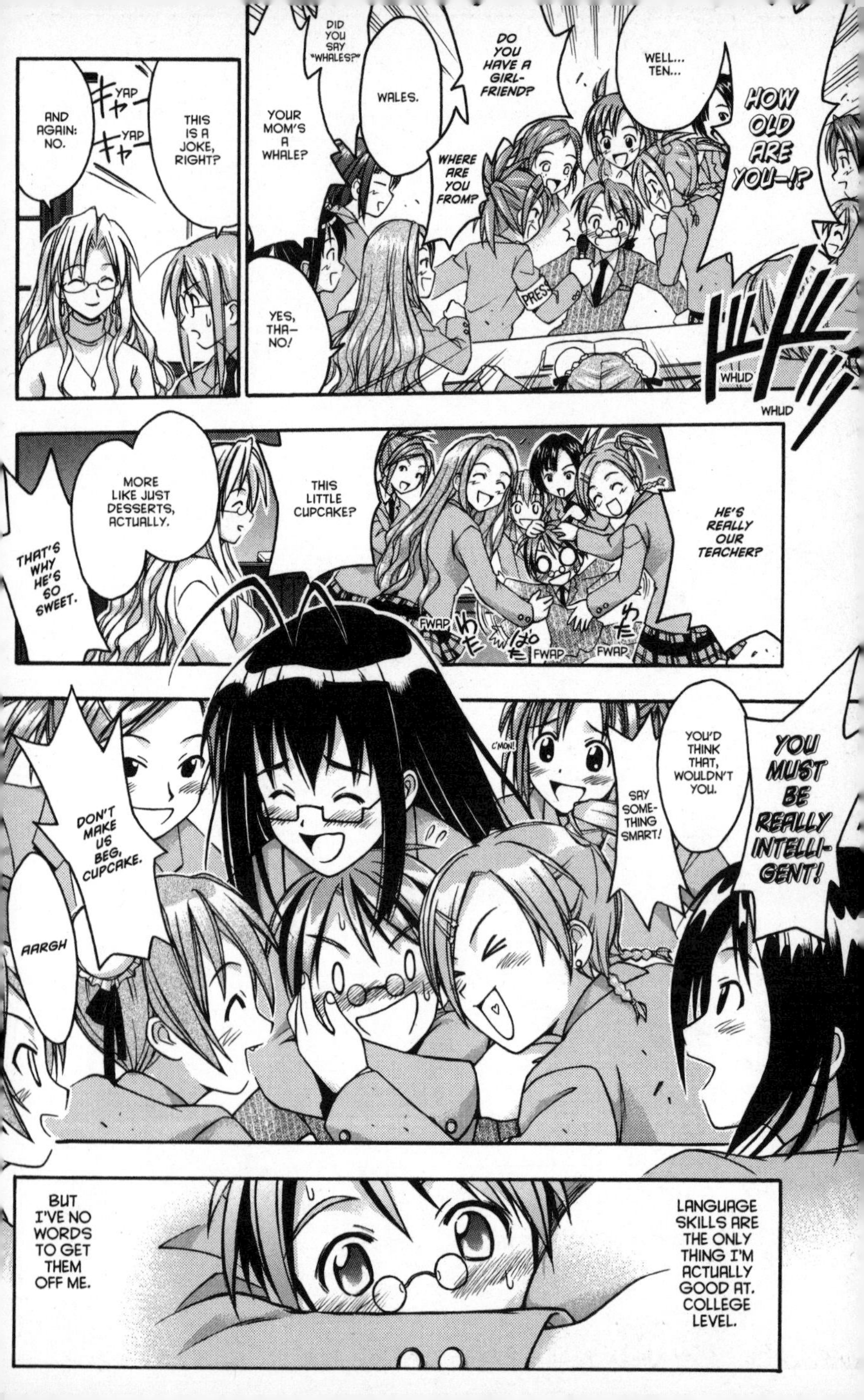
HOW OLD ARE YOU—!?
WELL... TEN...
DO YOU HAVE A GIRL-FRIEND?
WHERE ARE YOU FROM?
WALES.
DID YOU SAY "WHALES?"
YOUR MOM'S A WHALE?
YES, THA— NO!
WHUD
WHUD
THIS IS A JOKE, RIGHT?
AND AGAIN: NO.
YAP
YAP
HE'S REALLY OUR TEACHER?
THIS LITTLE CUPCAKE?
MORE LIKE JUST DESSERTS, ACTUALLY.
THAT'S WHY HE'S SO SWEET.
FWAP
FWAP
FWAP
YOU MUST BE REALLY INTELLI-GENT!
YOU'D THINK THAT, WOULDN'T YOU.
SAY SOME-THING SMART!
C'MON!
DON'T MAKE US BEG, CUPCAKE.
AARGH
LANGUAGE SKILLS ARE THE ONLY THING I'M ACTUALLY GOOD AT. COLLEGE LEVEL.
BUT I'VE NO WORDS TO GET THEM OFF ME.

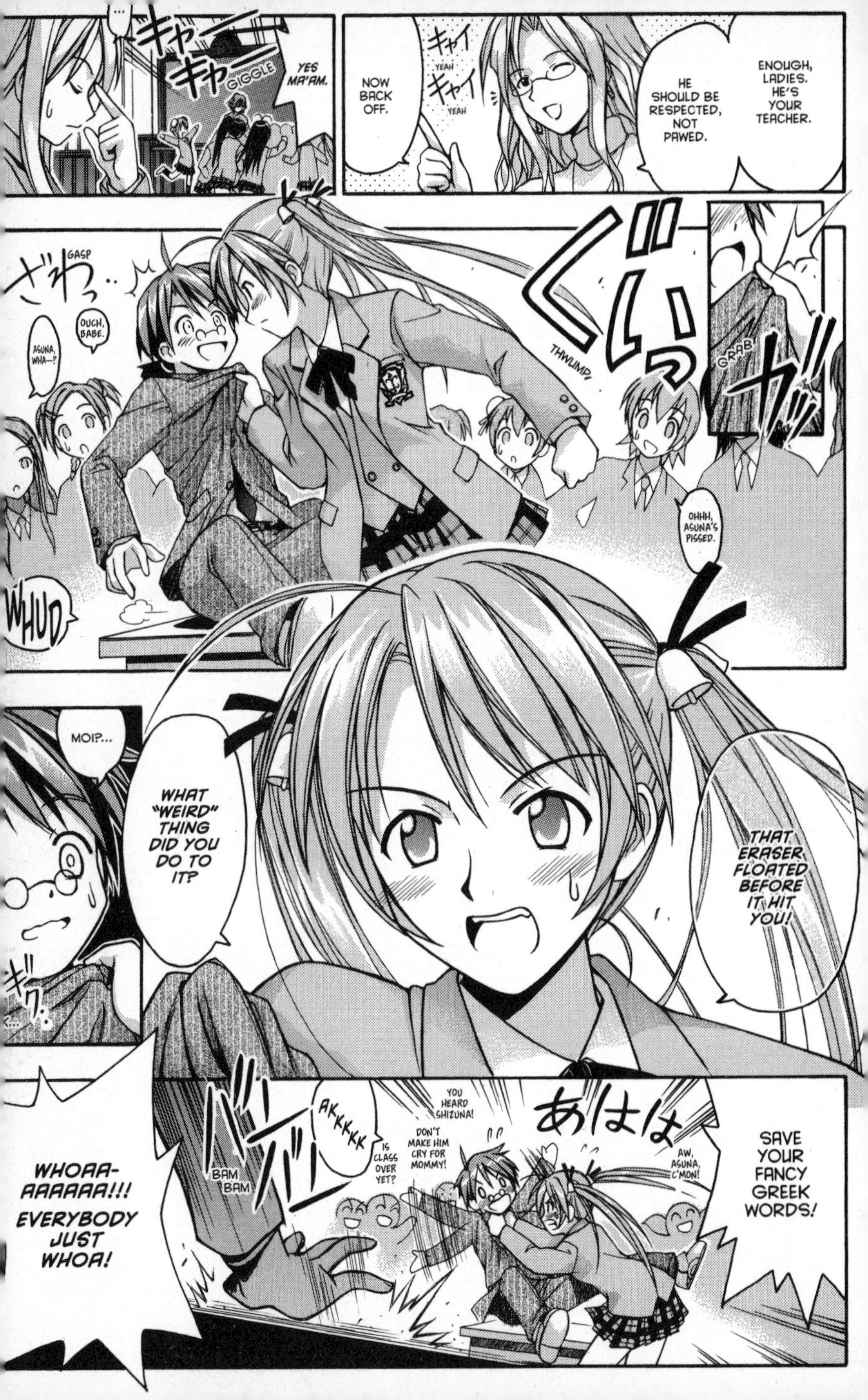
ENOUGH, LADIES. HE'S YOUR TEACHER.
HE SHOULD BE RESPECTED, NOT PAWED.
キャイ YEAH キャイ YEAH
NOW BACK OFF.
YES MA'AM.
キャー キャー GIGGLE
...
GRAB
くいっ
THWUMP
OHHH, ASUNA'S PISSED.
OUCH, BABE.
ASUNA, WHA—?
ざわっ GASP
WHUD
THAT ERASER FLOATED BEFORE IT HIT YOU!
WHAT "WEIRD" THING DID YOU DO TO IT?
MOI?...
SAVE YOUR FANCY GREEK WORDS!
AW, ASUNA, C'MON!
あはは
YOU HEARD SHIZUNA!
DON'T MAKE HIM CRY FOR MOMMY!
IS CLASS OVER YET?
AKKKKK
BAM BAM
WHOAA-AAAAAA!!! EVERYBODY JUST WHOA!

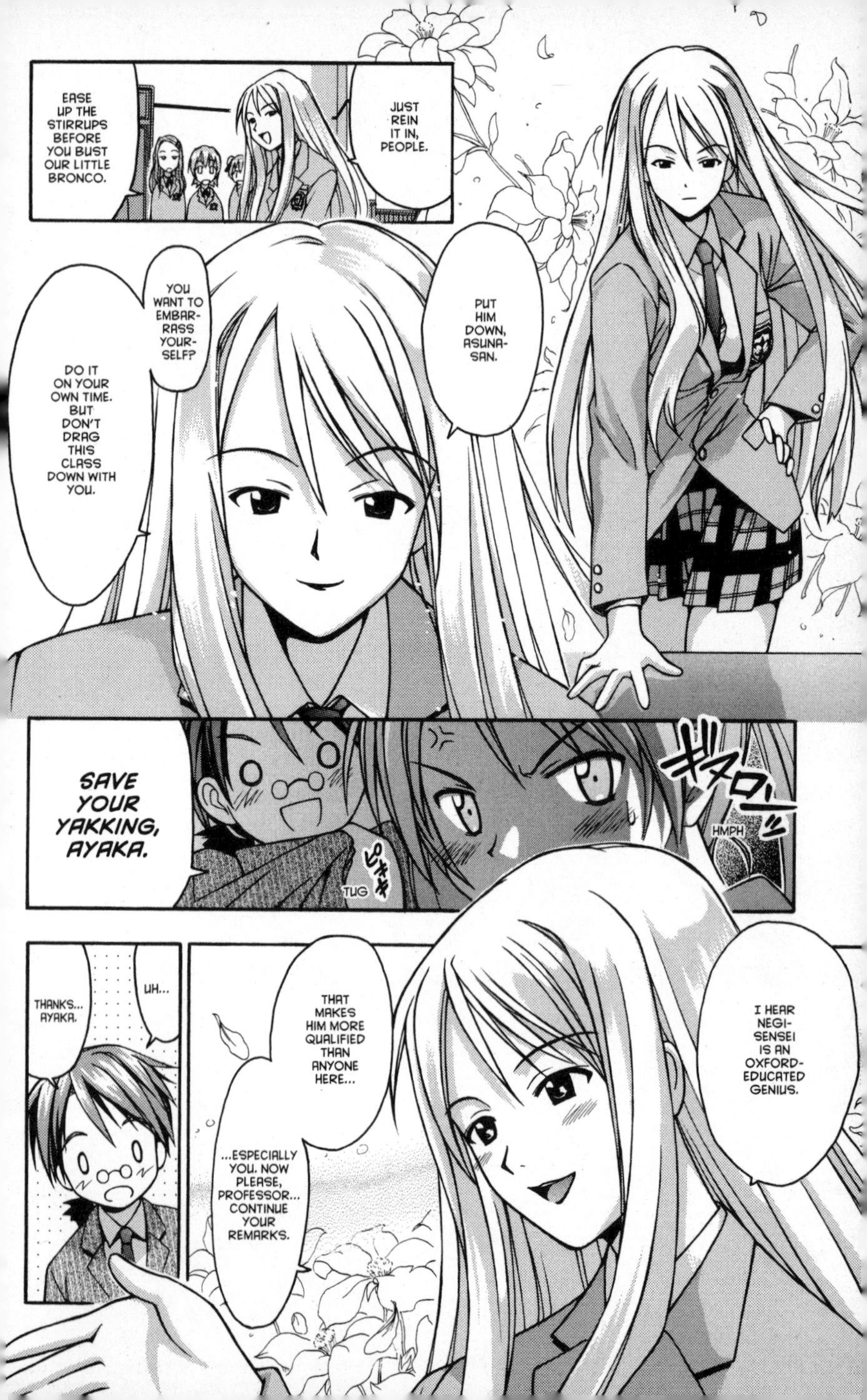

JUST REIN IT IN, PEOPLE.
EASE UP THE STIRRUPS BEFORE YOU BUST OUR LITTLE BRONCO.
PUT HIM DOWN, ASUNA-SAN.
YOU WANT TO EMBAR-RASS YOUR-SELF?
DO IT ON YOUR OWN TIME. BUT DON'T DRAG THIS CLASS DOWN WITH YOU.
HMPH
SAVE YOUR YAKKING, AYAKA.
TUG
I HEAR NEGI-SENSEI IS AN OXFORD-EDUCATED GENIUS.
THAT MAKES HIM MORE QUALIFIED THAN ANYONE HERE...
...ESPECIALLY YOU. NOW PLEASE, PROFESSOR... CONTINUE YOUR REMARKS.
UH...
THANKS... AYAKA.

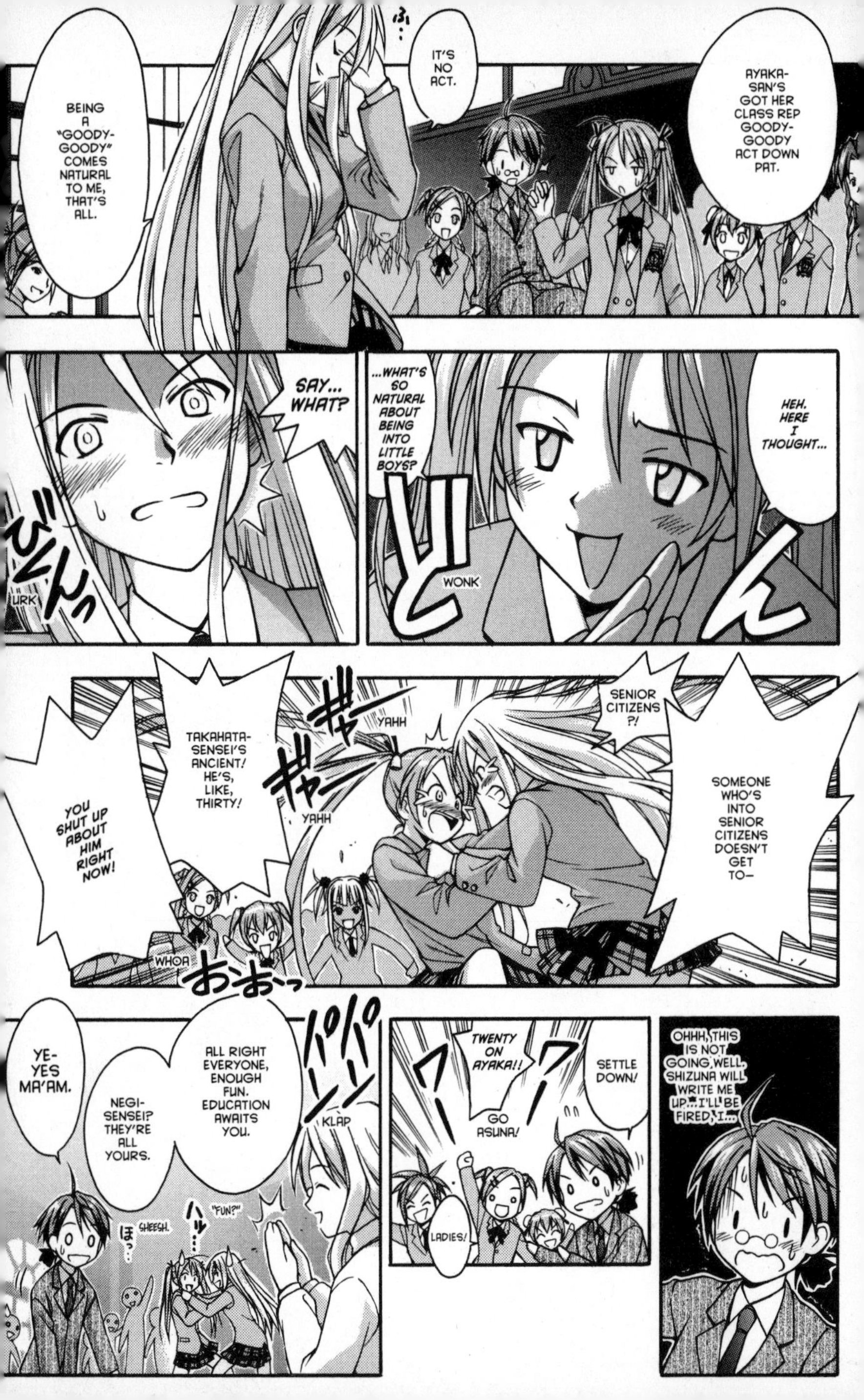
AYAKA-SAN'S GOT HER CLASS REP GOODY-GOODY ACT DOWN PAT.
IT'S NO ACT.
BEING A "GOODY-GOODY" COMES NATURAL TO ME, THAT'S ALL.
HEH. HERE I THOUGHT...
...WHAT'S SO NATURAL ABOUT BEING INTO LITTLE BOYS?
WONK
SAY... WHAT?
URK
SENIOR CITIZENS?!
SOMEONE WHO'S INTO SENIOR CITIZENS DOESN'T GET TO—
YAHH
YAHH
TAKAHATA-SENSEI'S ANCIENT! HE'S, LIKE, THIRTY!
YOU SHUT UP ABOUT HIM RIGHT NOW!
WHOA
OHHH, THIS IS NOT GOING WELL. SHIZUNA WILL WRITE ME UP... I'LL BE FIRED, I...
SETTLE DOWN!
TWENTY ON AYAKA!!
GO ASUNA!
LADIES!
KLAP
ALL RIGHT EVERYONE, ENOUGH FUN. EDUCATION AWAITS YOU.
NEGI-SENSEI? THEY'RE ALL YOURS.
YE-YES MA'AM.
"FUN?"
SHEESH.

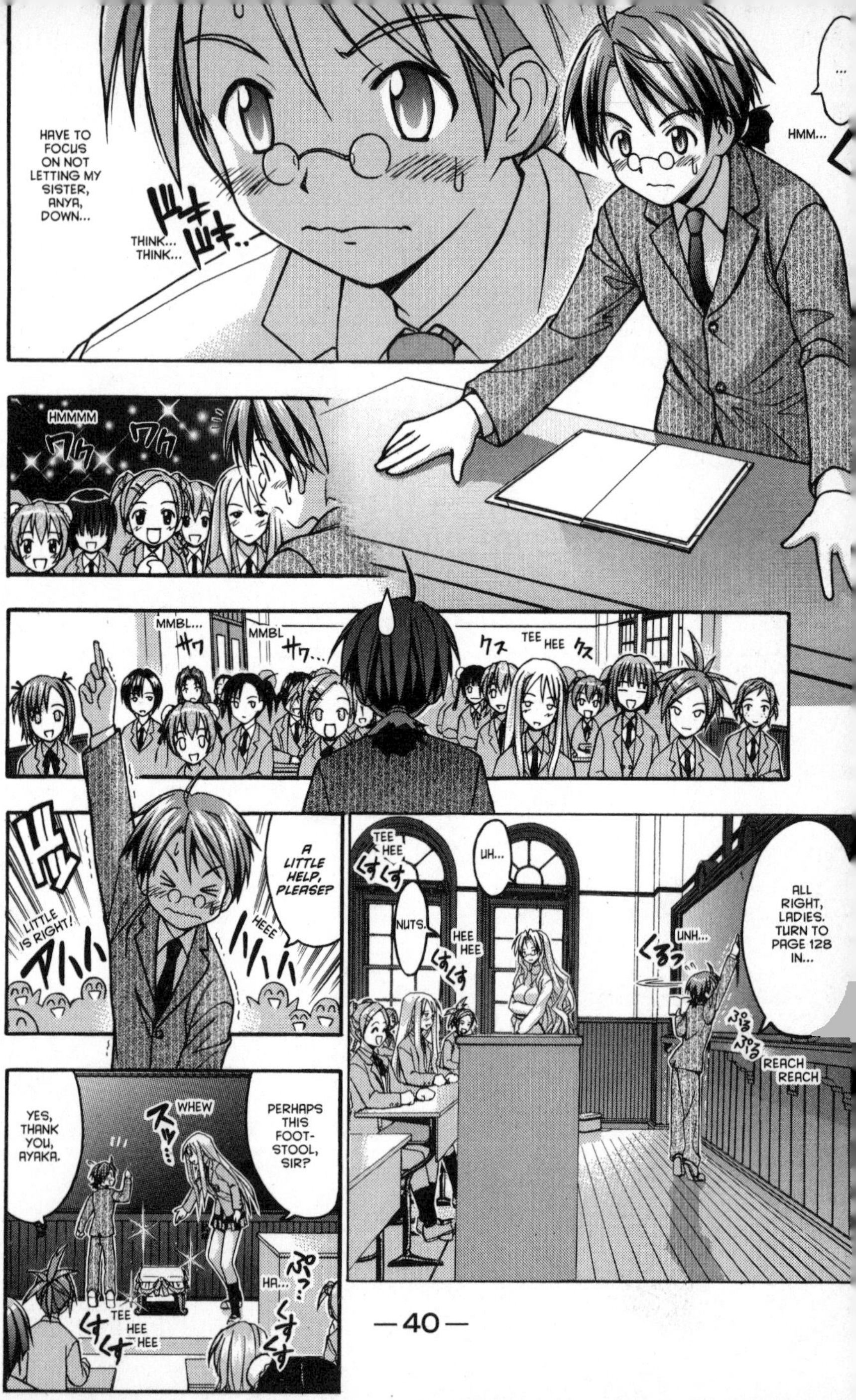
...
HMM...
HAVE TO FOCUS ON NOT LETTING MY SISTER, ANYA, DOWN...
THINK... THINK...
HMMMM
ワク ワク
MMBL...
サワ
MMBL
サワ...
クス
TEE HEE
クス
ALL RIGHT, LADIES. TURN TO PAGE 128 IN...
UNH...
くるっ
ぷるぷる
REACH REACH
UH...
TEE HEE
くすくす
NUTS.
HEE HEE
くすくす
A LITTLE HELP, PLEASE?
HEEE
ハハハ
LITTLE IS RIGHT!
アハハ
PERHAPS THIS FOOT-STOOL, SIR?
WHEW
スッ...
YES, THANK YOU, AYAKA.
HA...
ぷっ
くすくす
TEE HEE
くすくす
HEE

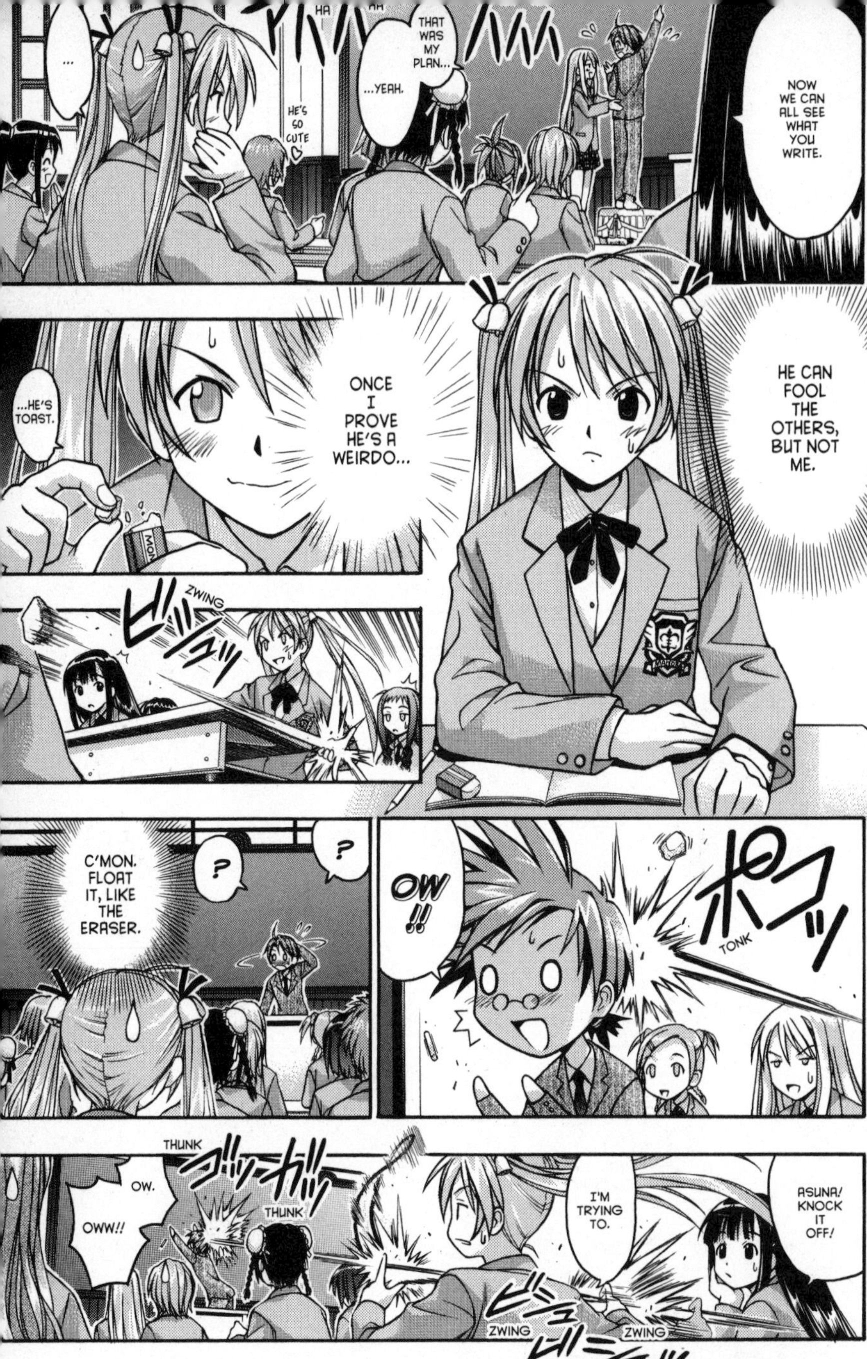
NOW WE CAN ALL SEE WHAT YOU WRITE.
HA
THAT WAS MY PLAN...
...YEAH.
HE'S SO CUTE
...
HE CAN FOOL THE OTHERS, BUT NOT ME.
ONCE I PROVE HE'S A WEIRDO...
...HE'S TOAST.
ZWING
TONK
OW!!
?
?
C'MON. FLOAT IT, LIKE THE ERASER.
ASUNA! KNOCK IT OFF!
I'M TRYING TO.
ZWING
ZWING
THUNK
THUNK
OW.
OWW!!

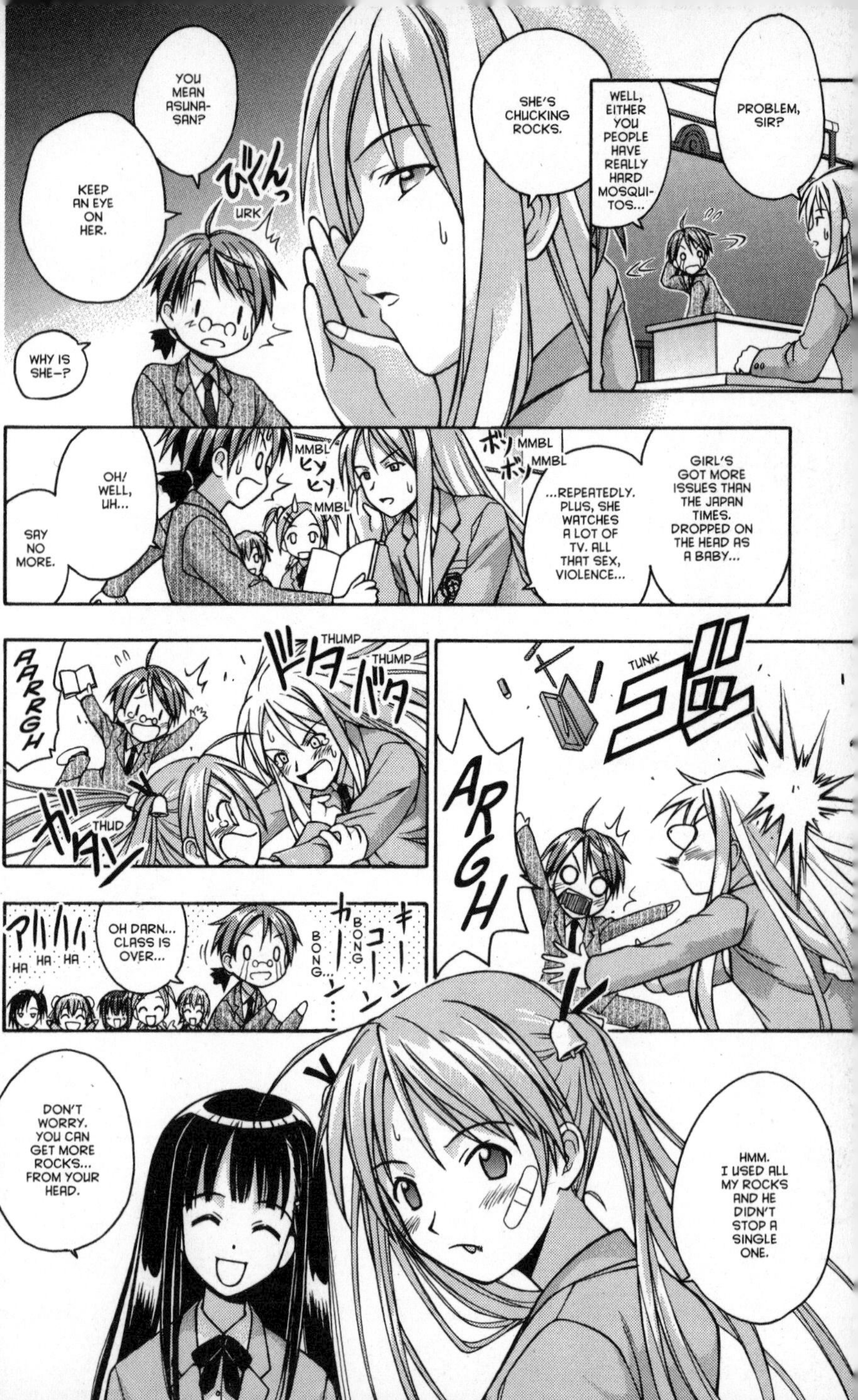
PROBLEM, SIR?
WELL, EITHER YOU PEOPLE HAVE REALLY HARD MOSQUITOS...
SHE'S CHUCKING ROCKS.
YOU MEAN ASUNA-SAN?
KEEP AN EYE ON HER.
URK
WHY IS SHE–?
GIRL'S GOT MORE ISSUES THAN THE JAPAN TIMES. DROPPED ON THE HEAD AS A BABY...
...REPEATEDLY. PLUS, SHE WATCHES A LOT OF TV. ALL THAT SEX, VIOLENCE...
MMBL
MMBL
MMBL
MMBL
OH! WELL, UH...
SAY NO MORE.
TUNK
ARGH
THUMP
THUMP
AARRGH
THUD
BONG
BONG...
OH DARN... CLASS IS OVER...
HA HA HA
HMM. I USED ALL MY ROCKS AND HE DIDN'T STOP A SINGLE ONE.
DON'T WORRY. YOU CAN GET MORE ROCKS... FROM YOUR HEAD.

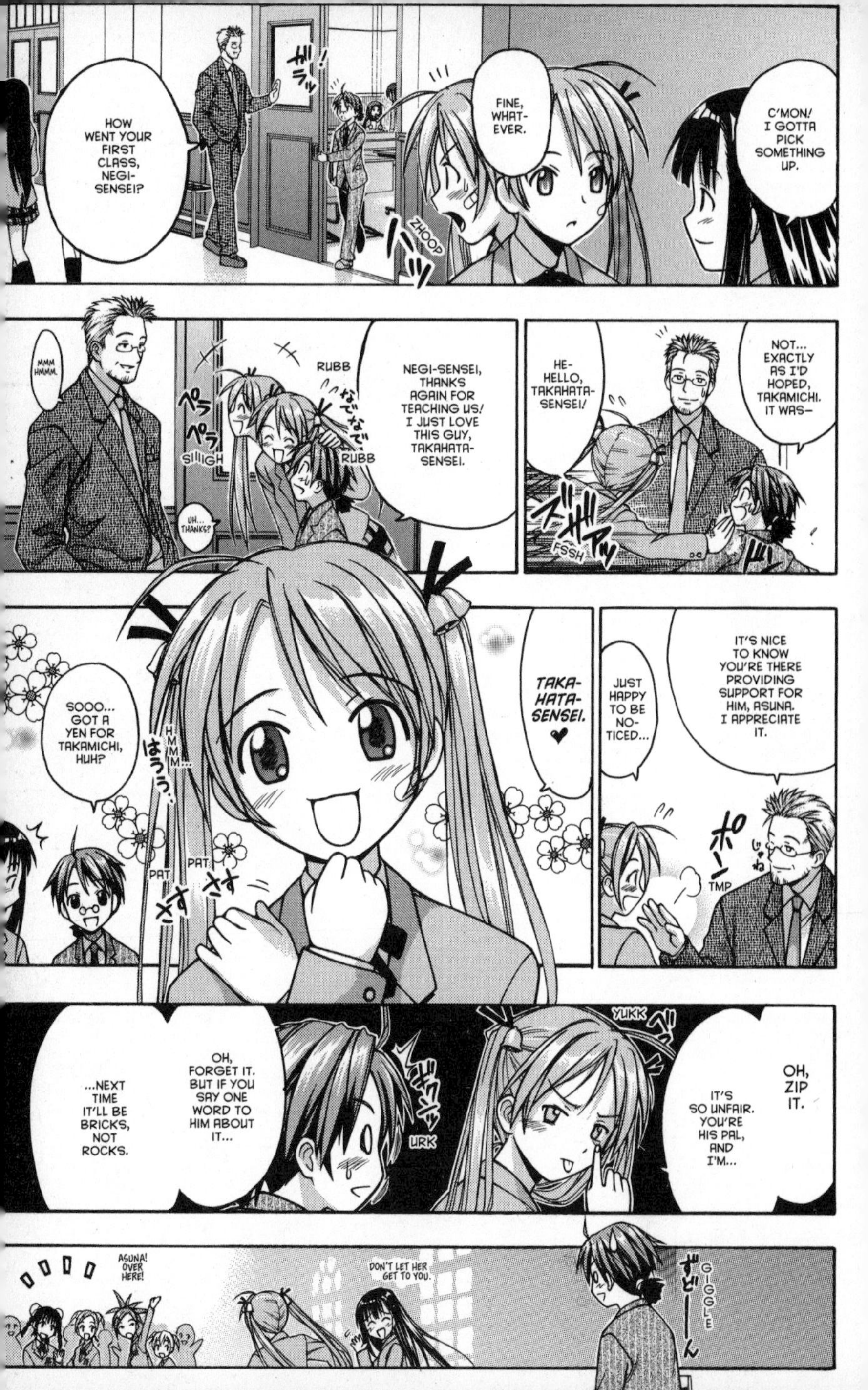
C'MON! I GOTTA PICK SOMETHING UP.
FINE, WHATEVER.
ZHOOP
HOW WENT YOUR FIRST CLASS, NEGI-SENSEI?
NOT... EXACTLY AS I'D HOPED, TAKAMICHI. IT WAS—
HE-HELLO, TAKAHATA-SENSEI!
FSSH
NEGI-SENSEI, THANKS AGAIN FOR TEACHING US! I JUST LOVE THIS GUY, TAKAHATA-SENSEI.
RUBB
RUBB
SIIIGH
MMM HMMM.
UH... THANKS?
IT'S NICE TO KNOW YOU'RE THERE PROVIDING SUPPORT FOR HIM, ASUNA. I APPRECIATE IT.
JUST HAPPY TO BE NOTICED...
TMP
TAKA-HATA-SENSEI. ❤
HMMM...
SOOO... GOT A YEN FOR TAKAMICHI, HUH?
PAT
PAT
OH, ZIP IT.
IT'S SO UNFAIR. YOU'RE HIS PAL, AND I'M...
YUKK
URK
OH, FORGET IT. BUT IF YOU SAY ONE WORD TO HIM ABOUT IT...
...NEXT TIME IT'LL BE BRICKS, NOT ROCKS.
GIGGLE
DON'T LET HER GET TO YOU.
ASUNA! OVER HERE!

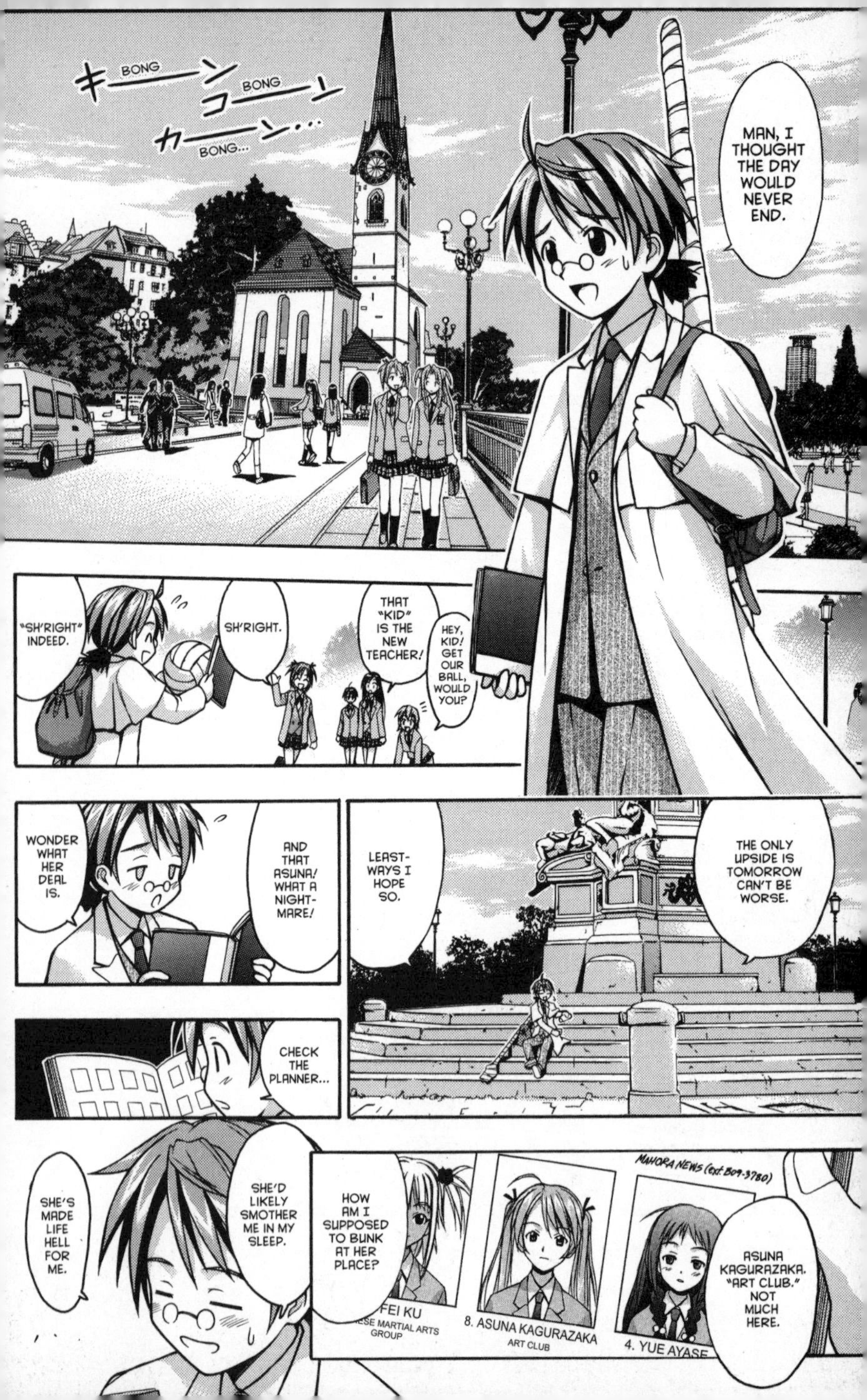
キ—ン BONG
コ—ン BONG
カ—ン… BONG...
MAN, I THOUGHT THE DAY WOULD NEVER END.
HEY, KID! GET OUR BALL, WOULD YOU?
THAT "KID" IS THE NEW TEACHER!
SH'RIGHT.
"SH'RIGHT" INDEED.
THE ONLY UPSIDE IS TOMORROW CAN'T BE WORSE.
LEAST-WAYS I HOPE SO.
AND THAT ASUNA! WHAT A NIGHT-MARE!
WONDER WHAT HER DEAL IS.
CHECK THE PLANNER...
MAHORA NEWS (ext. 809-3780)
ASUNA KAGURAZAKA. "ART CLUB." NOT MUCH HERE.
4. YUE AYASE
8. ASUNA KAGURAZAKA
ART CLUB
FEI KU
MARTIAL ARTS GROUP
HOW AM I SUPPOSED TO BUNK AT HER PLACE?
SHE'D LIKELY SMOTHER ME IN MY SLEEP.
SHE'S MADE LIFE HELL FOR ME.

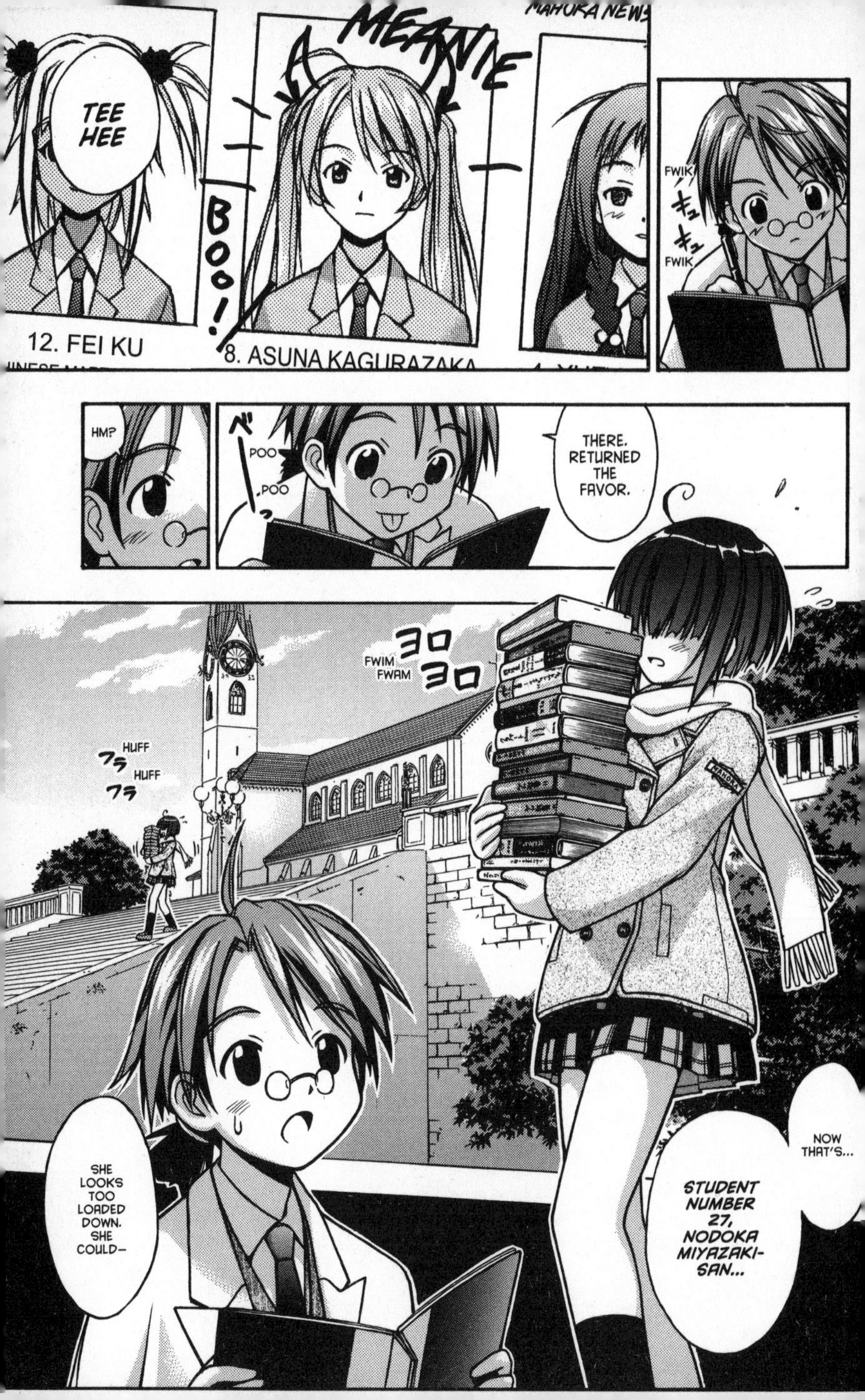
MAHORA NEWS
TEE HEE
12. FEI KU
MEANIE
BOO!
8. ASUNA KAGURAZAKA
FWIK
キュ
キュ
FWIK
HM?
ベ
POO
POO
THERE. RETURNED THE FAVOR.
ヨロ
ヨロ
FWIM
FWAM
フラ
HUFF
フラ
HUFF
NOW THAT'S...
STUDENT NUMBER 27, NODOKA MIYAZAKI-SAN...
SHE LOOKS TOO LOADED DOWN. SHE COULD—

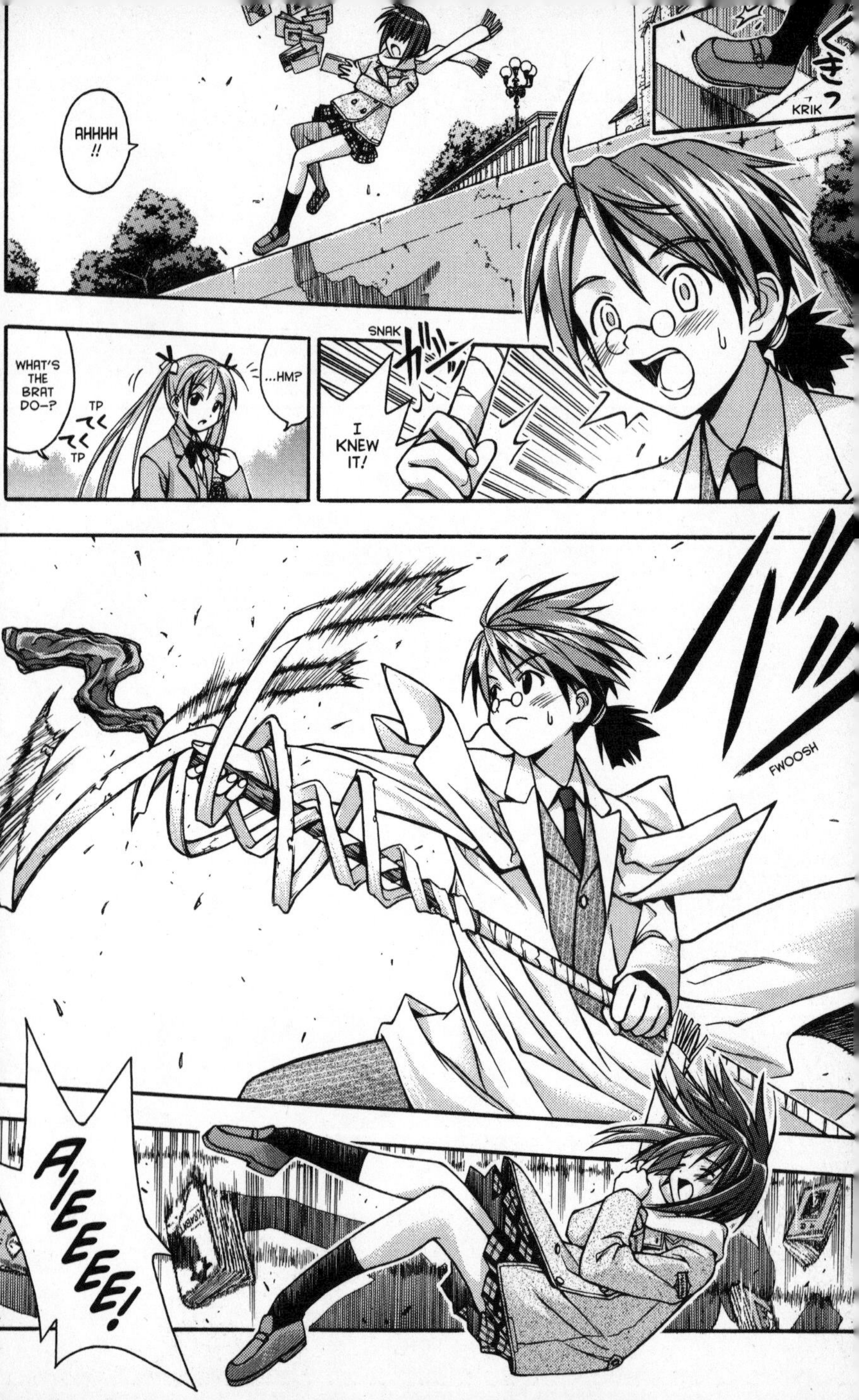
くきっ
KRIK
AHHHH!!
SNAK
I KNEW IT!
...HM?
WHAT'S THE BRAT DO—?
TP てく てく TP
FWOOSH
AIEEEE!

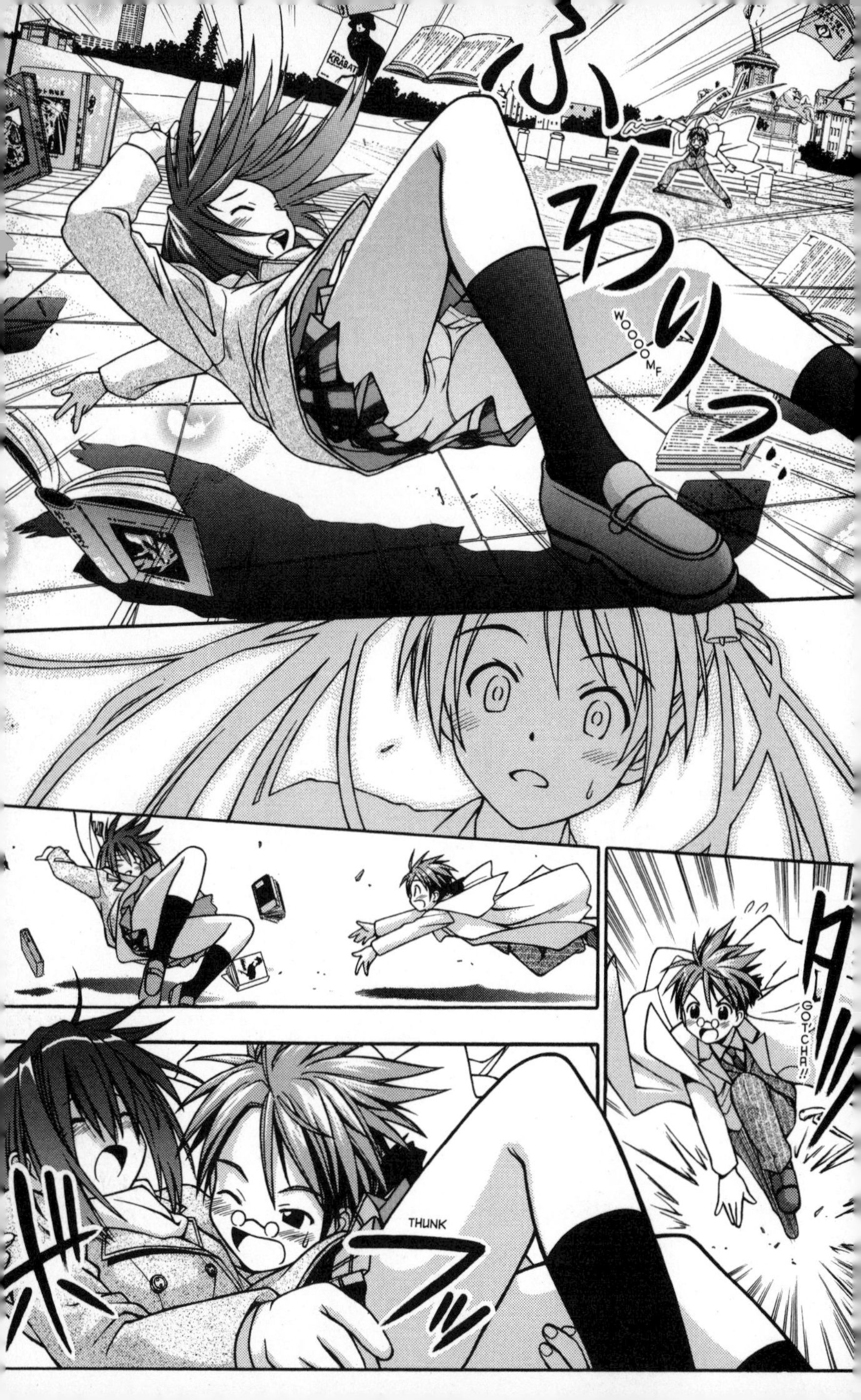
KRABAT
ふわりっ
WOOOOMF
GOTCHA!!
THUNK

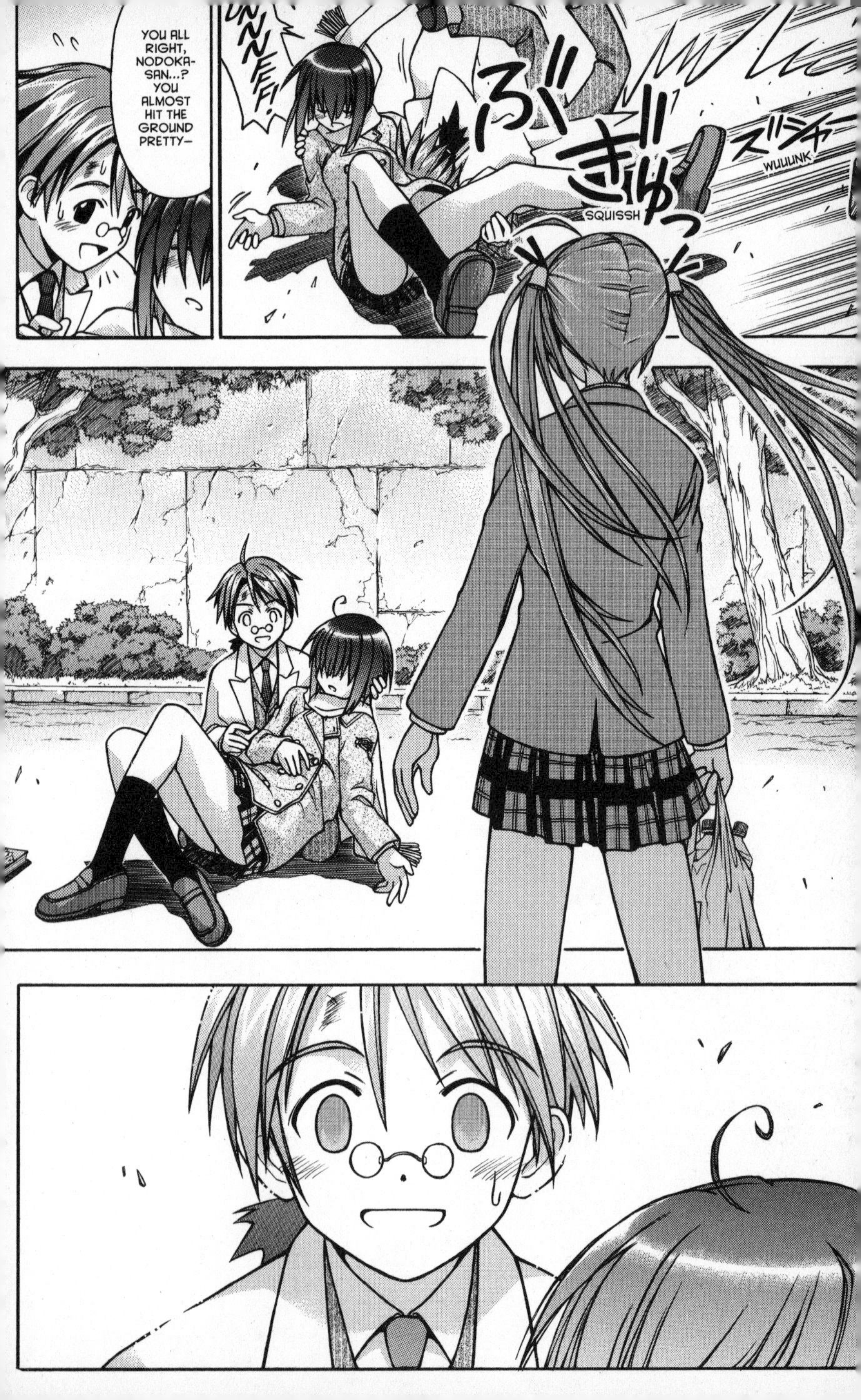
ズシャ
WUUUNK
ぎゅっ
SQUISSH
UNNEFF!
YOU ALL RIGHT, NODOKA-SAN...? YOU ALMOST HIT THE GROUND PRETTY—

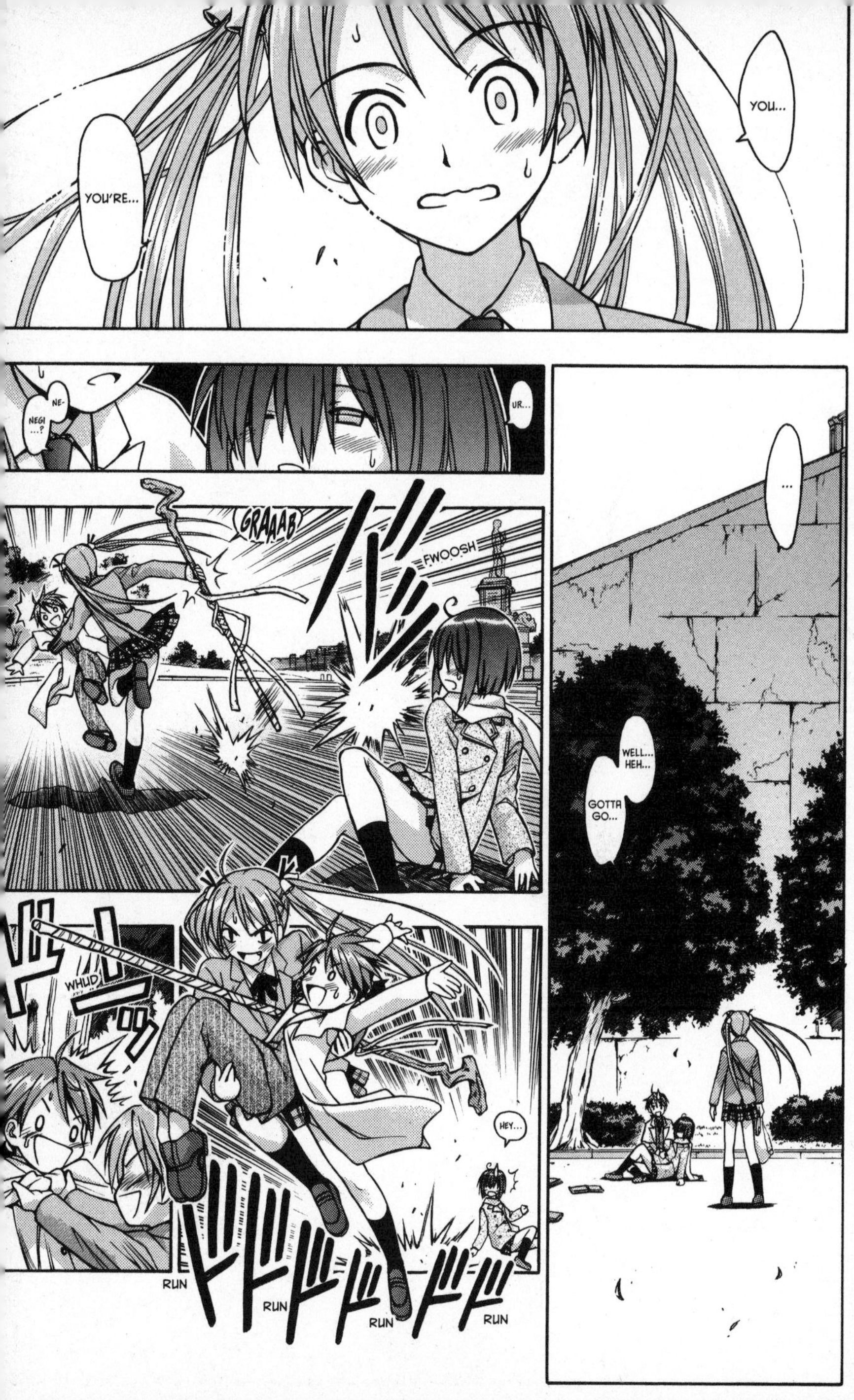
YOU...
YOU'RE...
...
WELL... HEH...
GOTTA GO...
NE- NEGI ...?
UR...
FWOOSH
GRAAAB
WHUD
HEY...
RUN
RUN
RUN
RUN

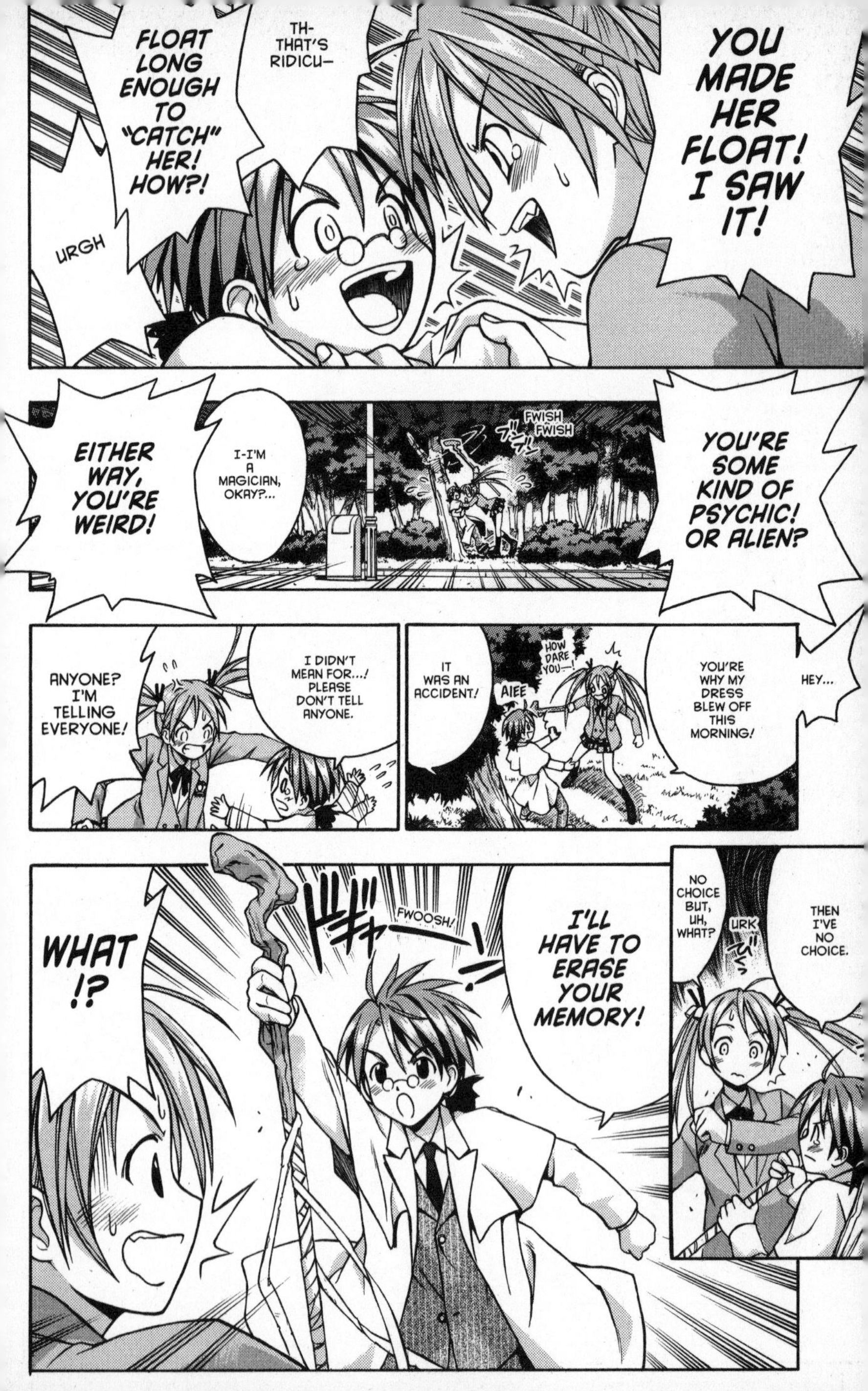

YOU MADE HER FLOAT! I SAW IT!
TH-THAT'S RIDICU—
FLOAT LONG ENOUGH TO "CATCH" HER! HOW?!
URGH
YOU'RE SOME KIND OF PSYCHIC! OR ALIEN?
FWISH FWISH
I-I'M A MAGICIAN, OKAY?...
EITHER WAY, YOU'RE WEIRD!
HEY...
YOU'RE WHY MY DRESS BLEW OFF THIS MORNING!
HOW DARE YOU—!
AIEE
IT WAS AN ACCIDENT!
I DIDN'T MEAN FOR...! PLEASE DON'T TELL ANYONE.
ANYONE? I'M TELLING EVERYONE!
THEN I'VE NO CHOICE.
URK
NO CHOICE BUT, UH, WHAT?
FWOOSH!
I'LL HAVE TO ERASE YOUR MEMORY!
WHAT!?

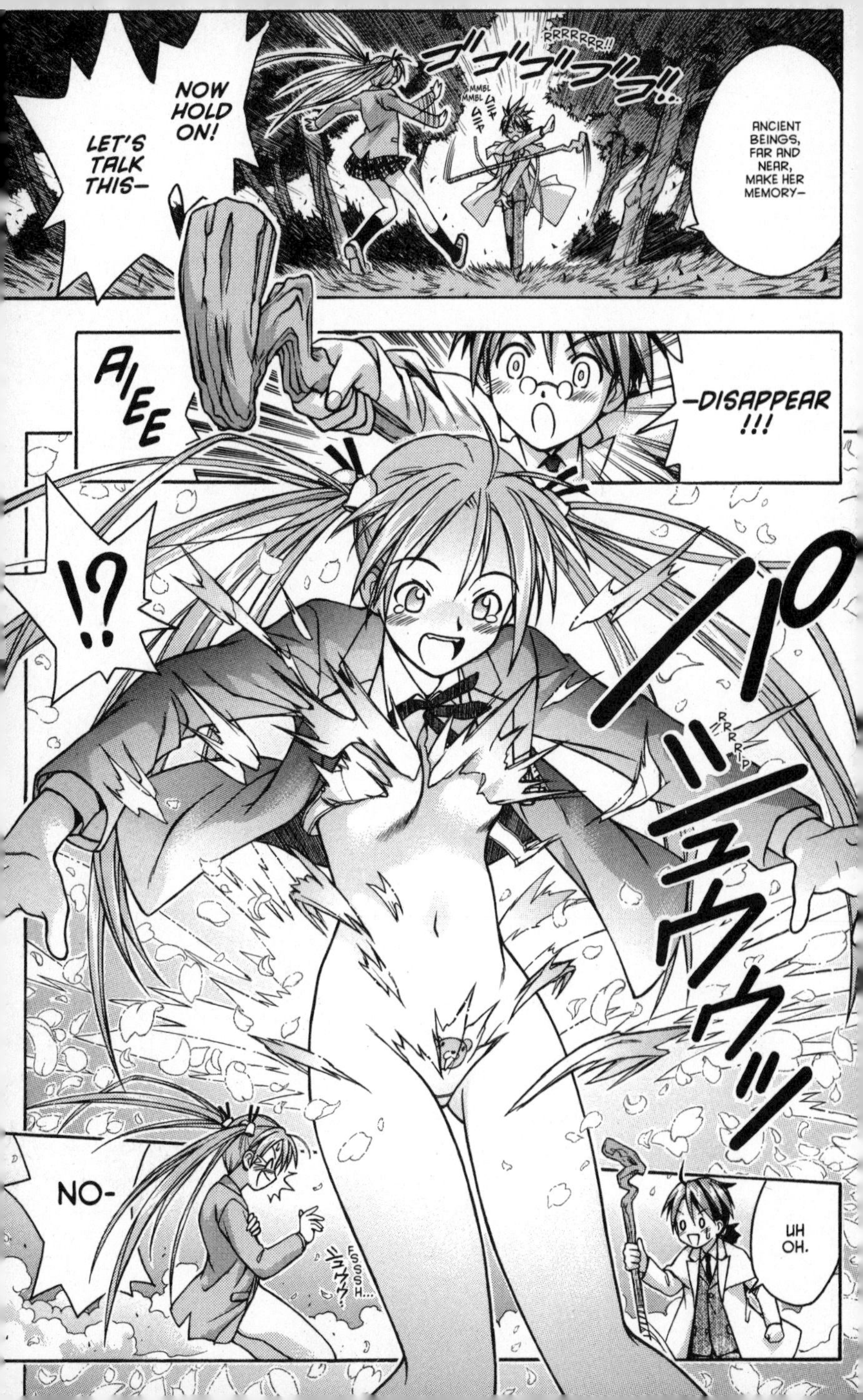
ANCIENT BEINGS, FAR AND NEAR, MAKE HER MEMORY—
RRRRRRRR!!
MMBL MMBL
NOW HOLD ON!
LET'S TALK THIS—
—DISAPPEAR !!!
AIEE
!?
RRRRRIP
UH OH.
NO-
FSSSH...

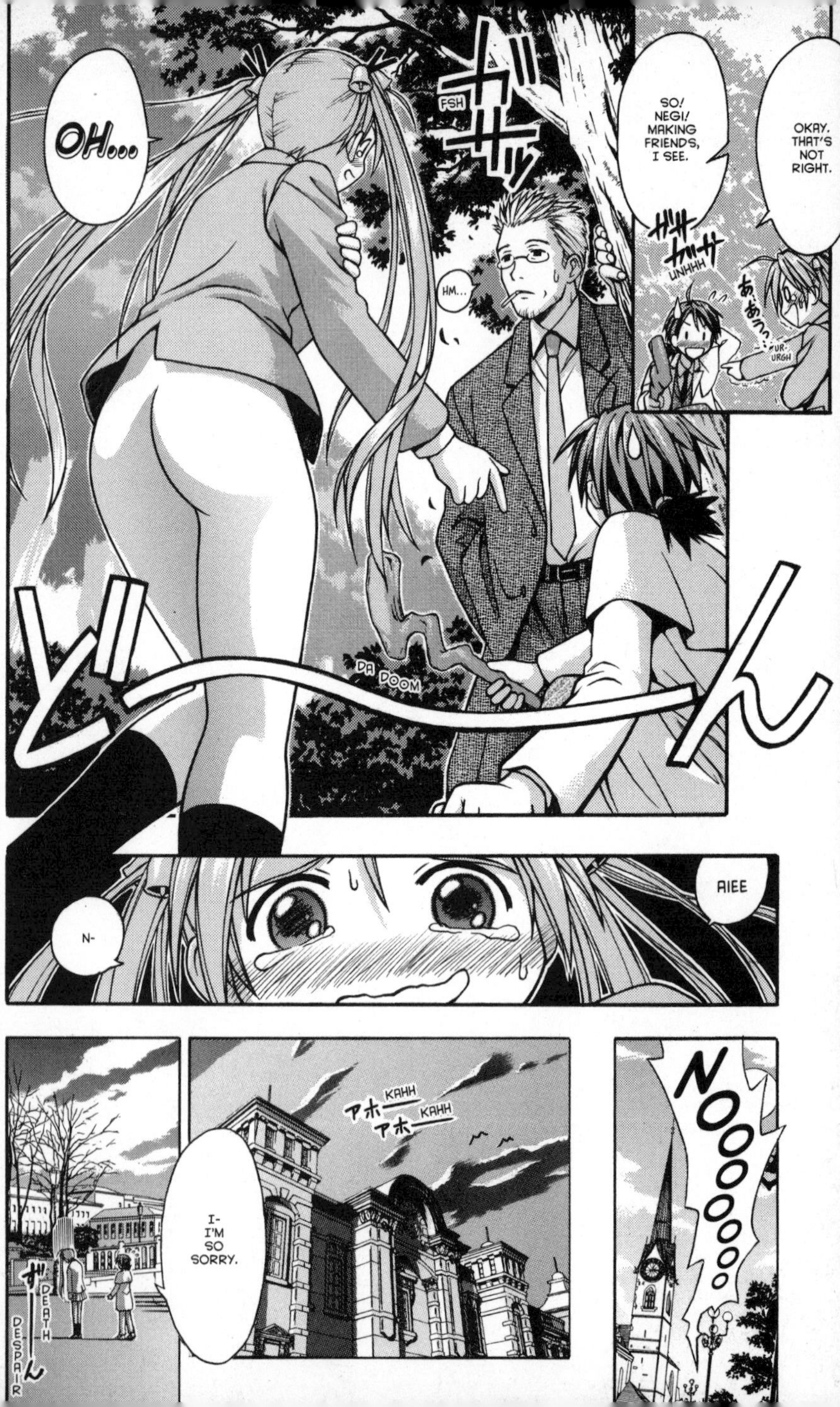

OKAY. THAT'S NOT RIGHT.
SO! NEGI! MAKING FRIENDS, I SEE.
UNHHH
UR-URGH
FSH
HM...
OH...
DA DOOM
AIEE
N-
NOOOOOOOO
KAHH
KAHH
I- I'M SO SORRY.
DEATH
DESPAIR

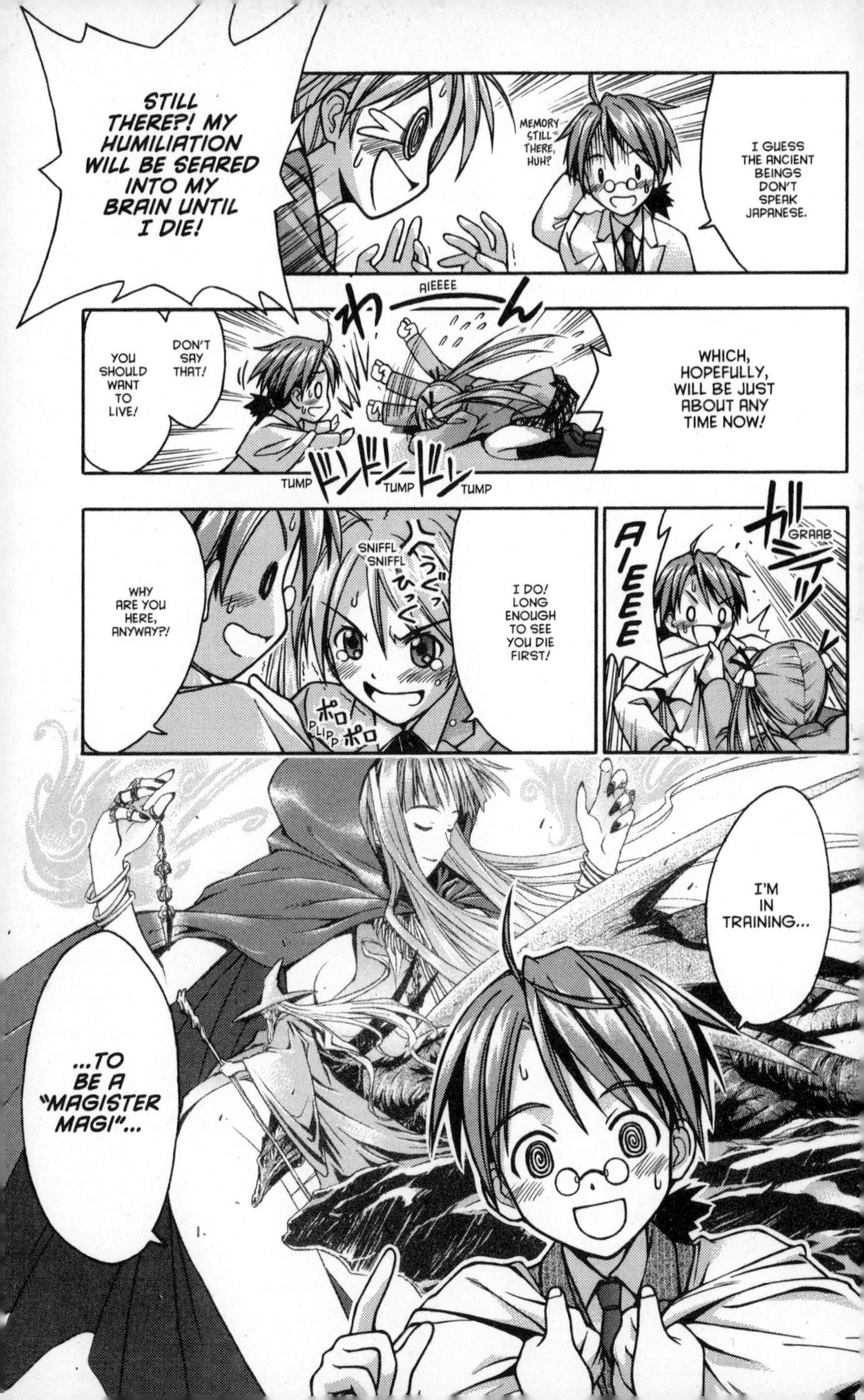
I GUESS THE ANCIENT BEINGS DON'T SPEAK JAPANESE.
MEMORY STILL THERE, HUH?
STILL THERE?! MY HUMILIATION WILL BE SEARED INTO MY BRAIN UNTIL I DIE!
WHICH, HOPEFULLY, WILL BE JUST ABOUT ANY TIME NOW!
AIEEEE
DON'T SAY THAT!
YOU SHOULD WANT TO LIVE!
TUMP
TUMP
TUMP
GRAAB
AIEEE
I DO! LONG ENOUGH TO SEE YOU DIE FIRST!
SNIFFL
SNIFFL
PLIPP
WHY ARE YOU HERE, ANYWAY?!
I'M IN TRAINING...
...TO BE A "MAGISTER MAGI"...

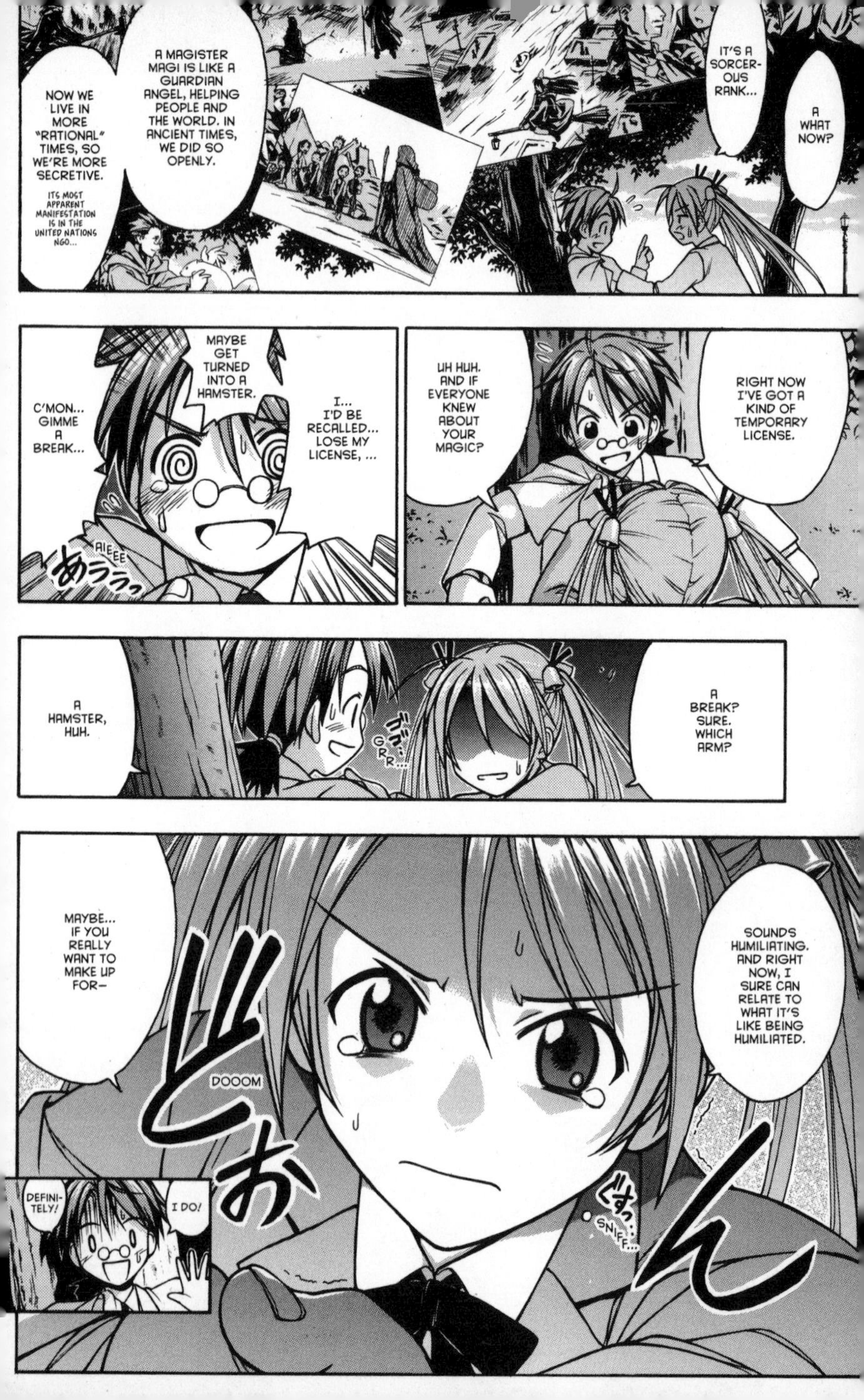

A WHAT NOW?
IT'S A SORCEROUS RANK...
A MAGISTER MAGI IS LIKE A GUARDIAN ANGEL, HELPING PEOPLE AND THE WORLD. IN ANCIENT TIMES, WE DID SO OPENLY.
NOW WE LIVE IN MORE "RATIONAL" TIMES, SO WE'RE MORE SECRETIVE.
ITS MOST APPARENT MANIFESTATION IS IN THE UNITED NATIONS NGO...
RIGHT NOW I'VE GOT A KIND OF TEMPORARY LICENSE.
UH HUH. AND IF EVERYONE KNEW ABOUT YOUR MAGIC?
I... I'D BE RECALLED... LOSE MY LICENSE, ...
MAYBE GET TURNED INTO A HAMSTER.
C'MON... GIMME A BREAK...
AIEEE
A BREAK? SURE. WHICH ARM?
GRR...
A HAMSTER, HUH.
SOUNDS HUMILIATING. AND RIGHT NOW, I SURE CAN RELATE TO WHAT IT'S LIKE BEING HUMILIATED.
SNIFF...
DOOOM
MAYBE... IF YOU REALLY WANT TO MAKE UP FOR–
I DO!
DEFINITELY!

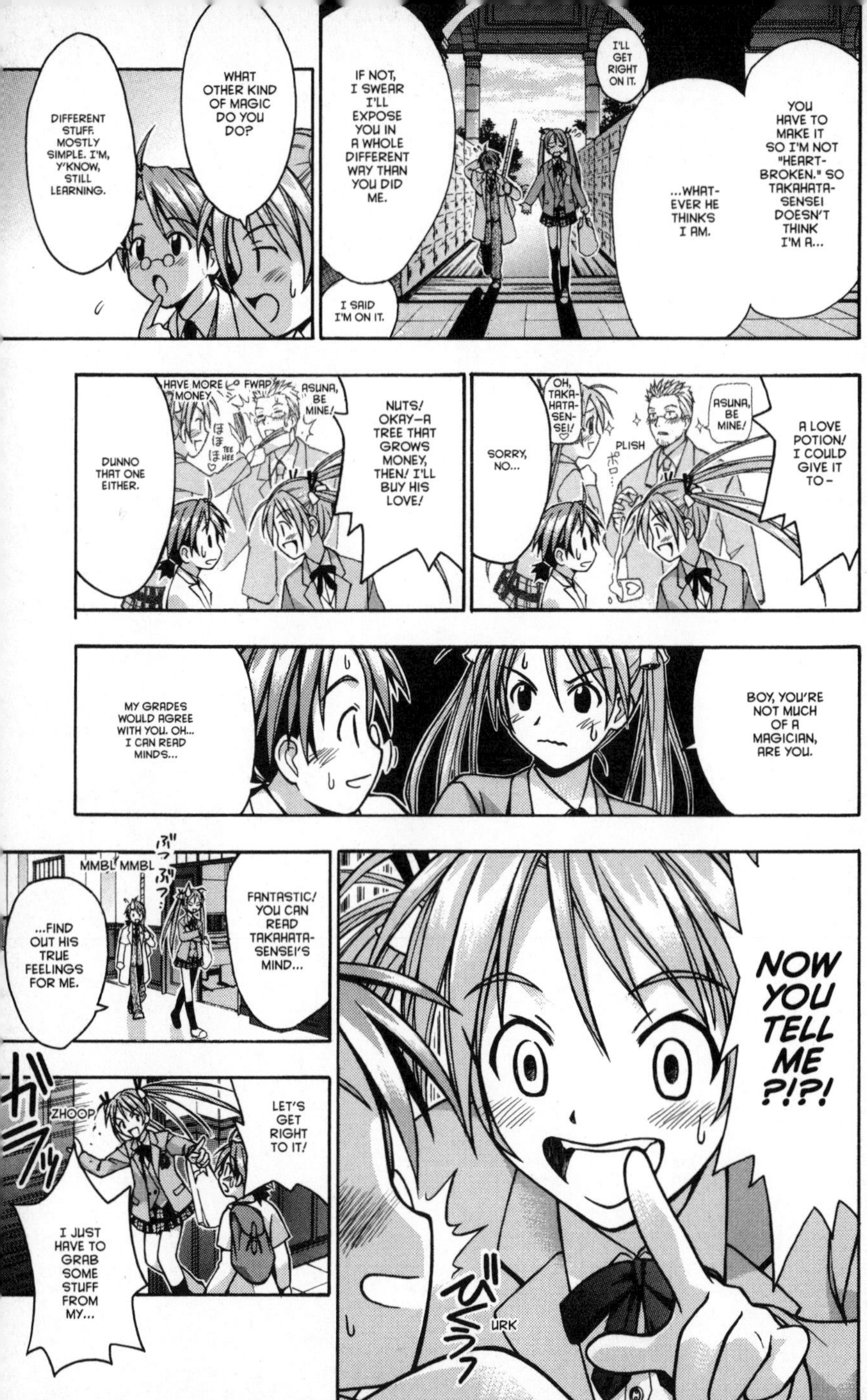
YOU HAVE TO MAKE IT SO I'M NOT "HEART-BROKEN." SO TAKAHATA-SENSEI DOESN'T THINK I'M A...
...WHATEVER HE THINKS I AM.
I'LL GET RIGHT ON IT.
IF NOT, I SWEAR I'LL EXPOSE YOU IN A WHOLE DIFFERENT WAY THAN YOU DID ME.
I SAID I'M ON IT.
WHAT OTHER KIND OF MAGIC DO YOU DO?
DIFFERENT STUFF. MOSTLY SIMPLE. I'M, Y'KNOW, STILL LEARNING.
A LOVE POTION! I COULD GIVE IT TO–
ASUNA, BE MINE!
OH, TAKAHATA-SENSEI! ♡
PLISH
SORRY, NO...
NUTS! OKAY—A TREE THAT GROWS MONEY, THEN! I'LL BUY HIS LOVE!
ASUNA, BE MINE!
FWAP
HAVE MORE MONEY
TEE HEE
DUNNO THAT ONE EITHER.
BOY, YOU'RE NOT MUCH OF A MAGICIAN, ARE YOU.
MY GRADES WOULD AGREE WITH YOU. OH... I CAN READ MINDS...
NOW YOU TELL ME?!?!
URK
FANTASTIC! YOU CAN READ TAKAHATA-SENSEI'S MIND...
MMBL MMBL
...FIND OUT HIS TRUE FEELINGS FOR ME.
LET'S GET RIGHT TO IT!
ZHOOP
I JUST HAVE TO GRAB SOME STUFF FROM MY...

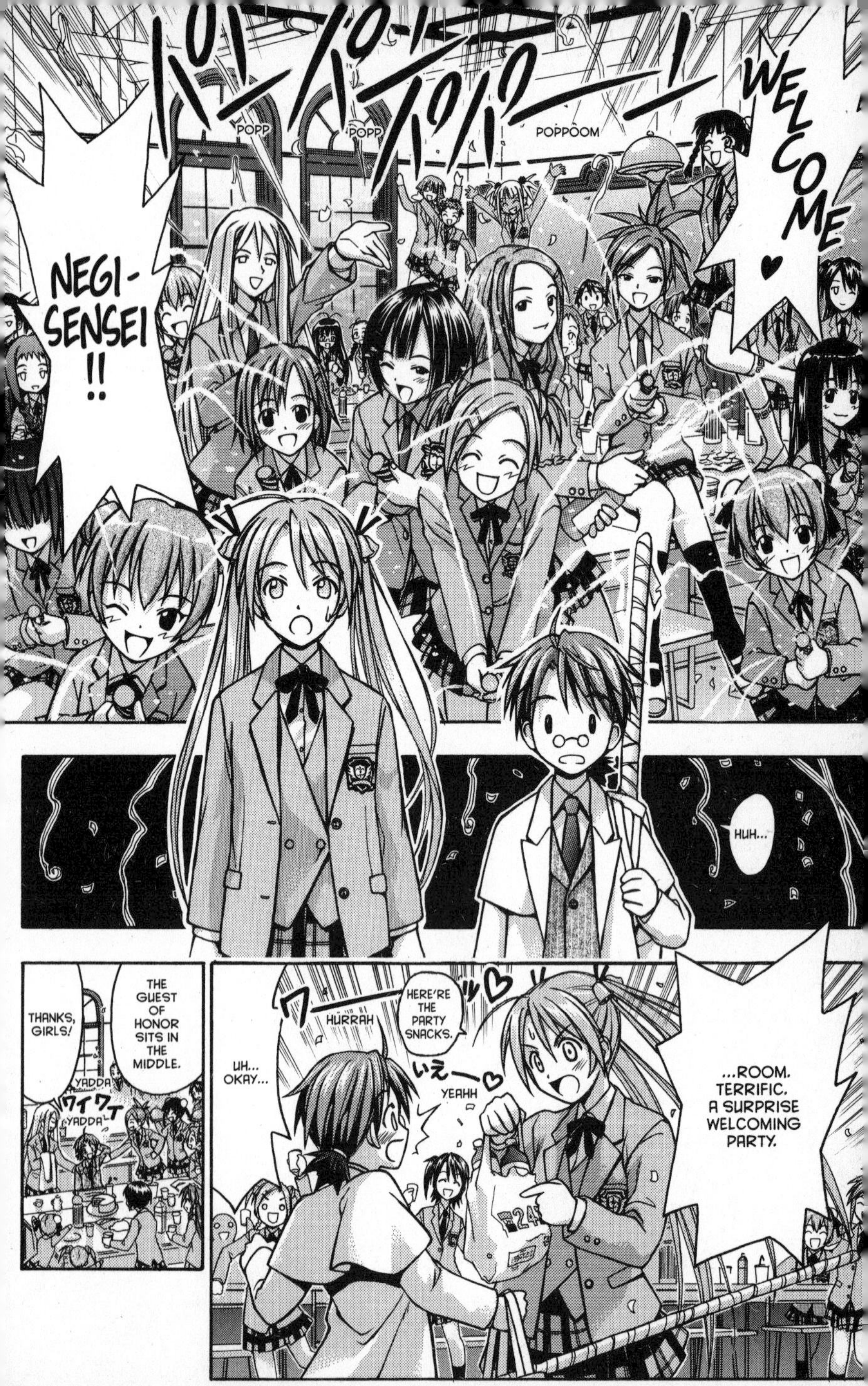

POPP
POPP
POPPOOM
WELCOME ♥
NEGI-SENSEI !!
HUH...
...ROOM. TERRIFIC. A SURPRISE WELCOMING PARTY.
HURRAH
HERE'RE THE PARTY SNACKS.
YEAHH
UH... OKAY...
THE GUEST OF HONOR SITS IN THE MIDDLE.
THANKS, GIRLS!
YADDA
YADDA

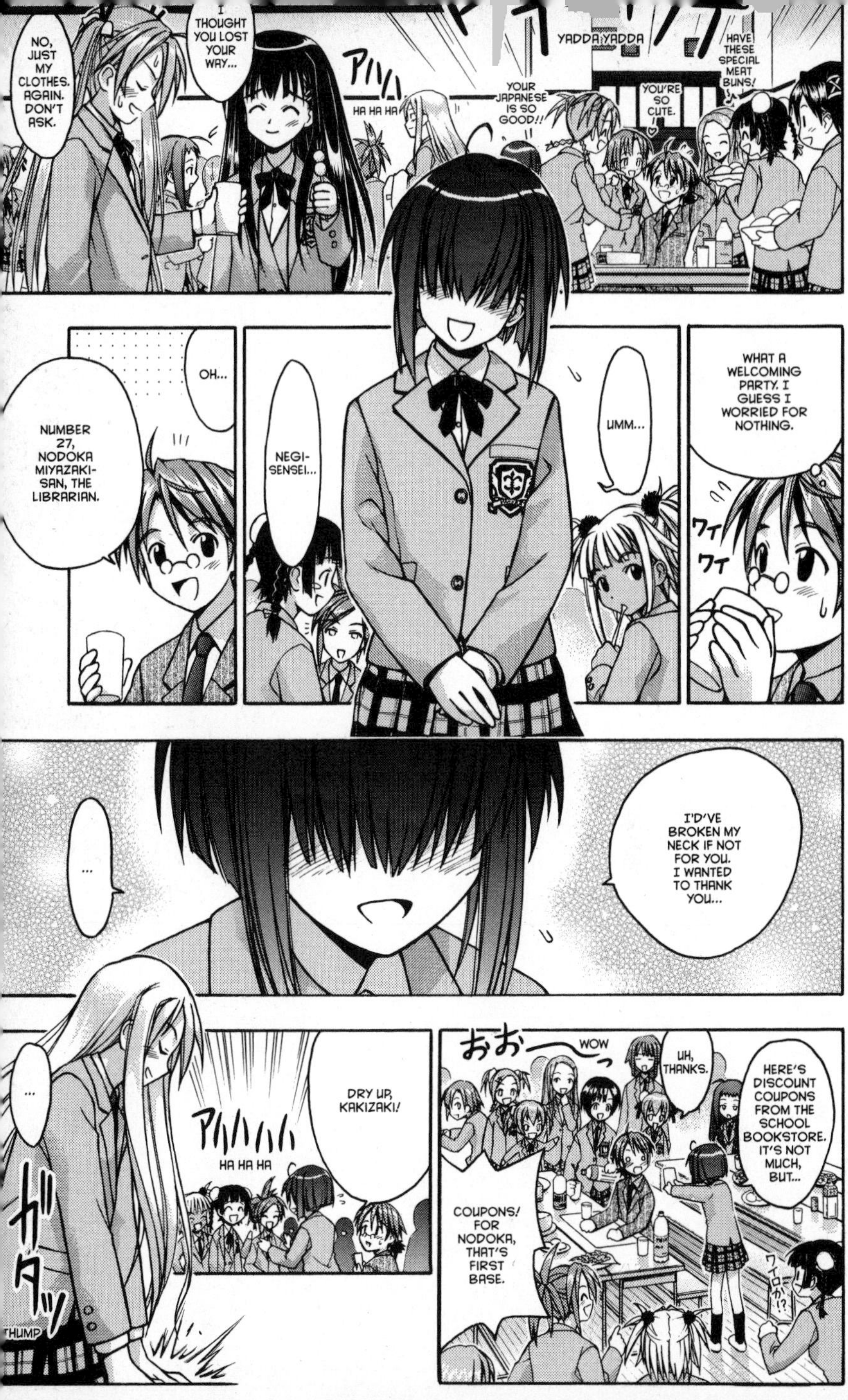
HAVE THESE SPECIAL MEAT BUNS!
YOU'RE SO CUTE.
YOUR JAPANESE IS SO GOOD!!
YADDA YADDA
HA HA HA
I THOUGHT YOU LOST YOUR WAY...
NO, JUST MY CLOTHES. AGAIN. DON'T ASK.
WHAT A WELCOMING PARTY. I GUESS I WORRIED FOR NOTHING.
UMM...
NEGI-SENSEI...
OH...
NUMBER 27, NODOKA MIYAZAKI-SAN, THE LIBRARIAN.
I'D'VE BROKEN MY NECK IF NOT FOR YOU. I WANTED TO THANK YOU...
...
HERE'S DISCOUNT COUPONS FROM THE SCHOOL BOOKSTORE. IT'S NOT MUCH, BUT...
UH, THANKS.
WOW
COUPONS! FOR NODOKA, THAT'S FIRST BASE.
DRY UP, KAKIZAKI!
HA HA HA
...
THUMP

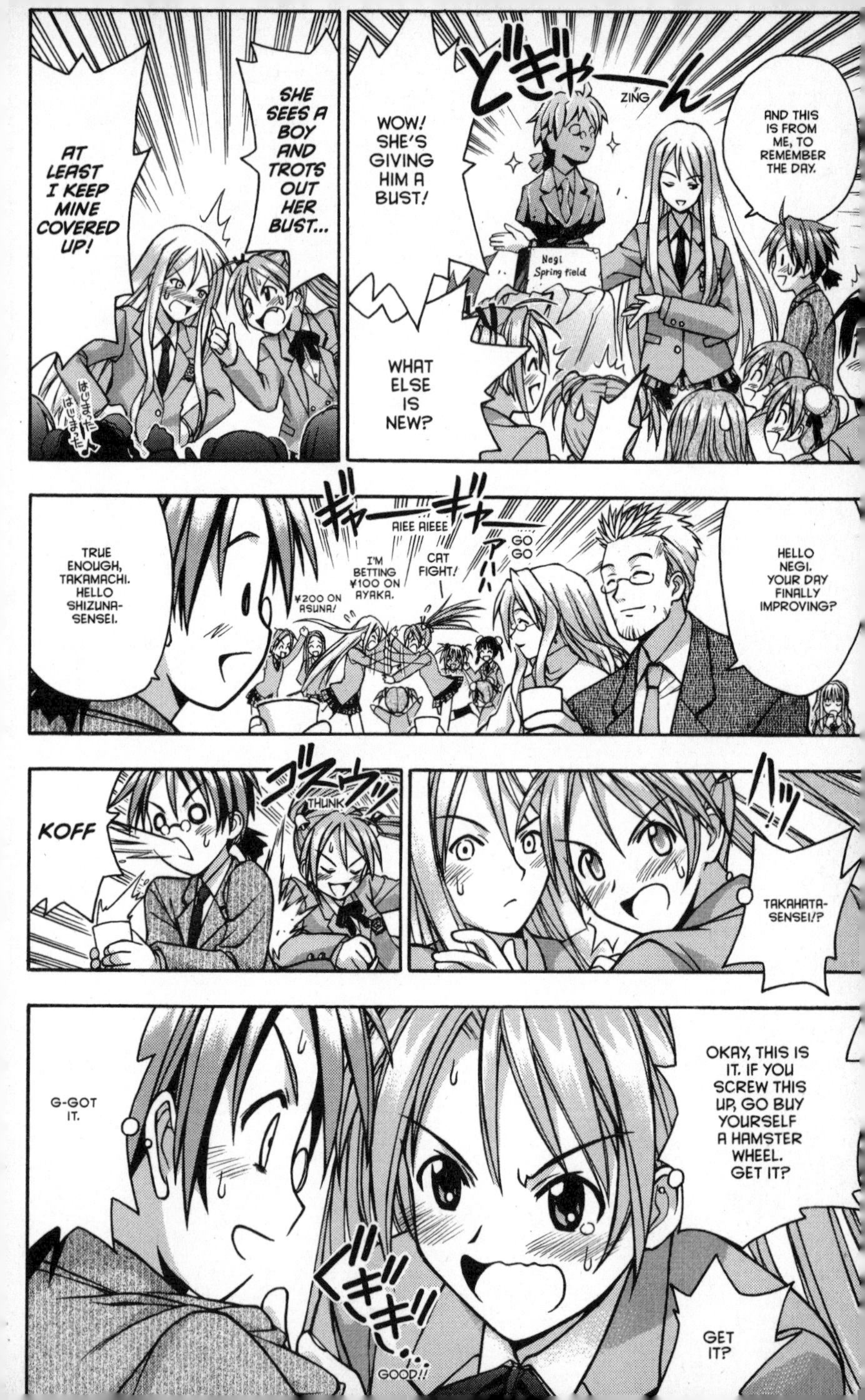

AND THIS IS FROM ME, TO REMEMBER THE DAY.
どぎゃーん
ZING
Negi Spring field
WOW! SHE'S GIVING HIM A BUST!
WHAT ELSE IS NEW?
SHE SEES A BOY AND TROTS OUT HER BUST...
AT LEAST I KEEP MINE COVERED UP!
はじまった はじまった♪
HELLO NEGI. YOUR DAY FINALLY IMPROVING?
GO GO
アハハ
CAT FIGHT!
I'M BETTING ¥100 ON AYAKA.
¥200 ON ASUNA!
ギャーギャー
AIEE AIEEE
TRUE ENOUGH, TAKAMACHI. HELLO SHIZUNA-SENSEI.
ハッ
TAKAHATA-SENSEI!?
ゴスッ
THUNK
KOFF
OKAY, THIS IS IT. IF YOU SCREW THIS UP, GO BUY YOURSELF A HAMSTER WHEEL. GET IT?
GET IT?
G-GOT IT.
ぐぎぎ
GOOD!!

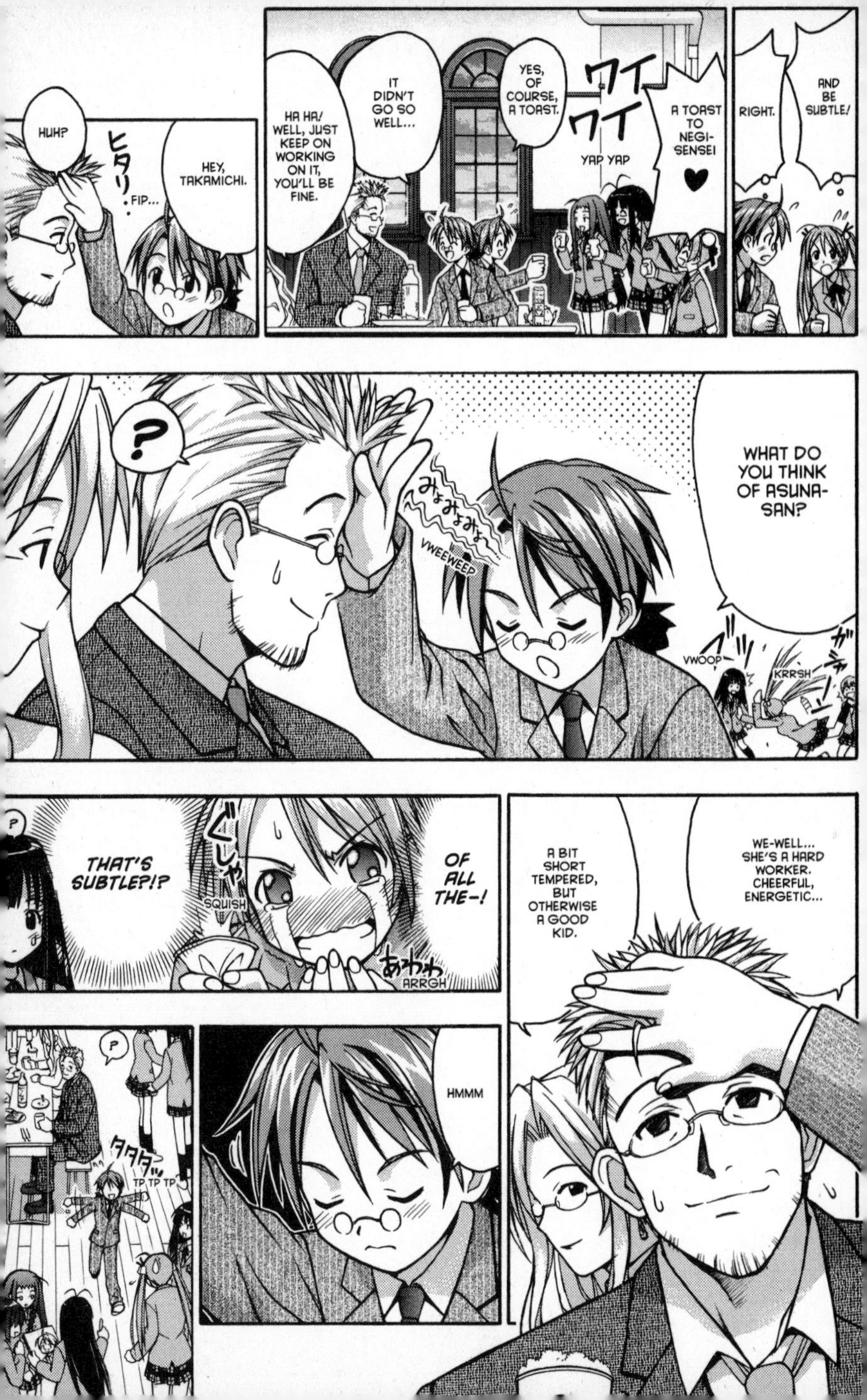

AND BE SUBTLE!
RIGHT.
A TOAST TO NEGI-SENSEI
ワイワイ
YAP YAP
YES, OF COURSE, A TOAST.
IT DIDN'T GO SO WELL...
HA HA! WELL, JUST KEEP ON WORKING ON IT, YOU'LL BE FINE.
HEY, TAKAMICHI.
ヒタリ
FIP...
HUH?
WHAT DO YOU THINK OF ASUNA-SAN?
VWOOP
KRRSH
みょみょみょ
VWEEWEEP
?
WE-WELL... SHE'S A HARD WORKER. CHEERFUL, ENERGETIC...
A BIT SHORT TEMPERED, BUT OTHERWISE A GOOD KID.
OF ALL THE-!
ぐしゃ
SQUISH
あわわ
ARRGH
THAT'S SUBTLE?!?
HMMM
タタタ
TP TP TP

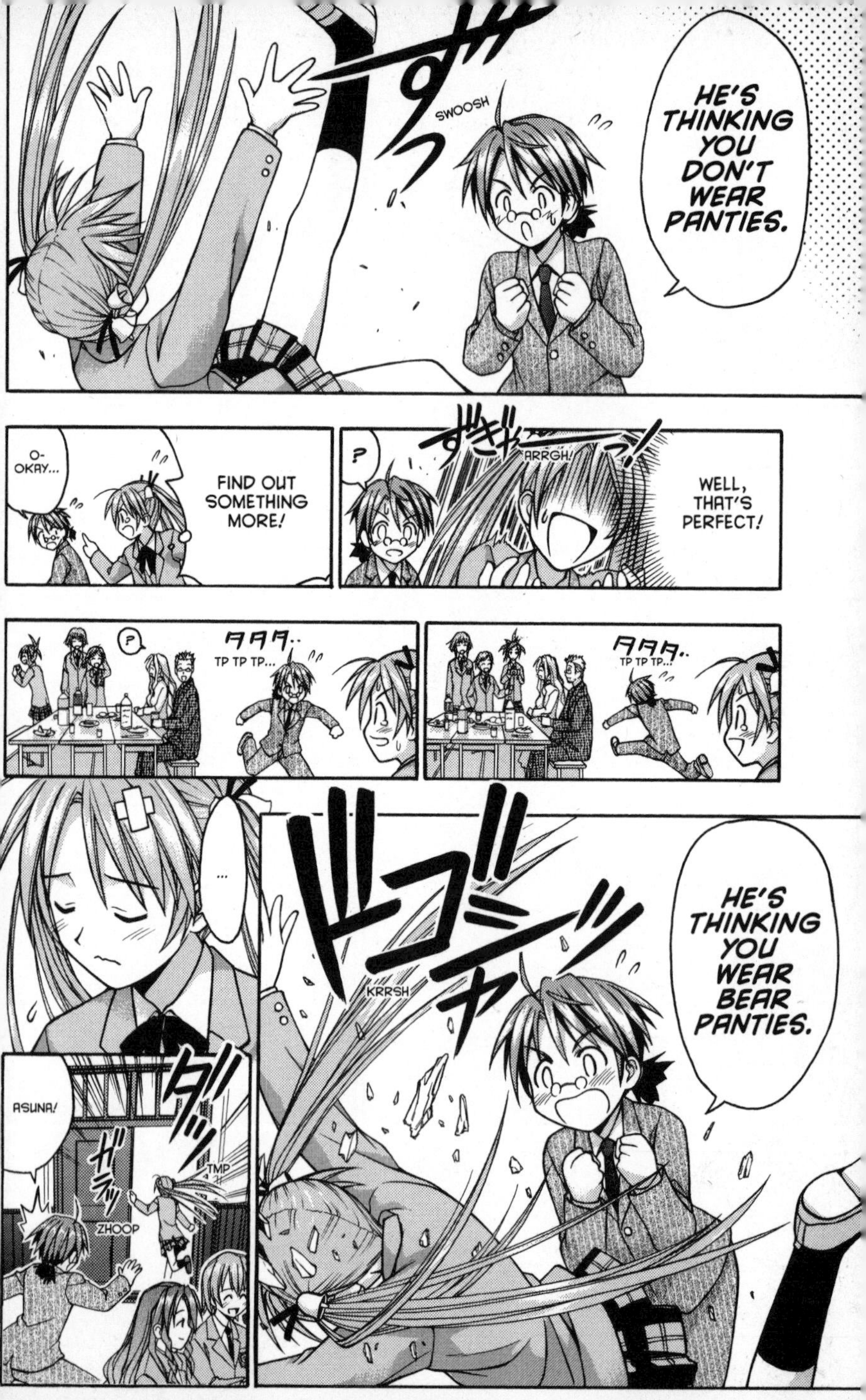
SWOOSH
HE'S THINKING YOU DON'T WEAR PANTIES.
WELL, THAT'S PERFECT!
ARRGH!
?
FIND OUT SOMETHING MORE!
O-OKAY...
タタタ..
TP TP TP...
タタタ..
TP TP TP...
?
HE'S THINKING YOU WEAR BEAR PANTIES.
KRRSH
...
TMP
ZHOOP
ASUNA!

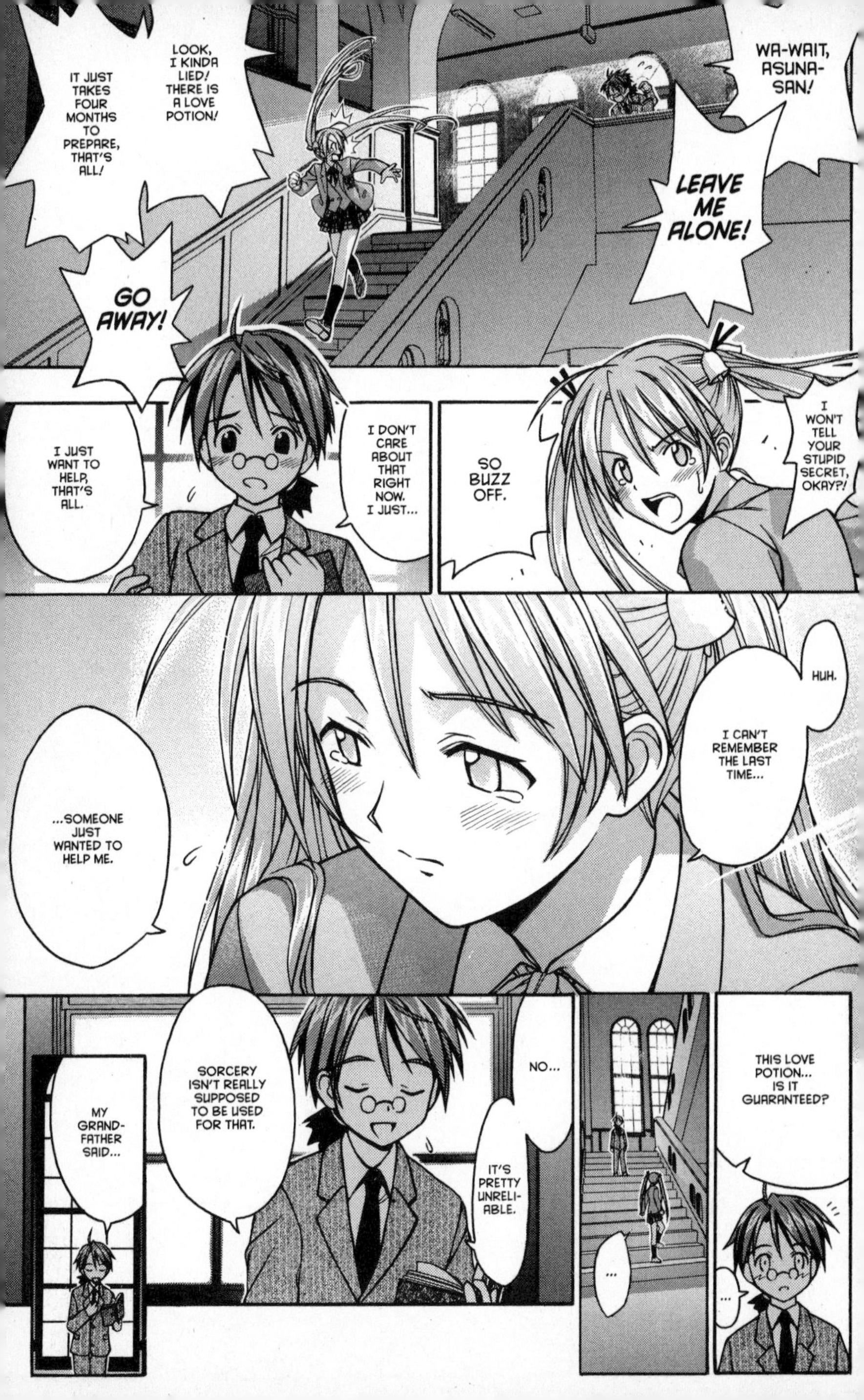
WA-WAIT, ASUNA-SAN!
LEAVE ME ALONE!
LOOK, I KINDA LIED! THERE IS A LOVE POTION!
IT JUST TAKES FOUR MONTHS TO PREPARE, THAT'S ALL!
GO AWAY!
I WON'T TELL YOUR STUPID SECRET, OKAY?!
SO BUZZ OFF.
I DON'T CARE ABOUT THAT RIGHT NOW. I JUST...
I JUST WANT TO HELP, THAT'S ALL.
HUH.
I CAN'T REMEMBER THE LAST TIME...
...SOMEONE JUST WANTED TO HELP ME.
...
THIS LOVE POTION... IS IT GUARANTEED?
...
NO...
IT'S PRETTY UNRELI-ABLE.
SORCERY ISN'T REALLY SUPPOSED TO BE USED FOR THAT.
MY GRAND-FATHER SAID...

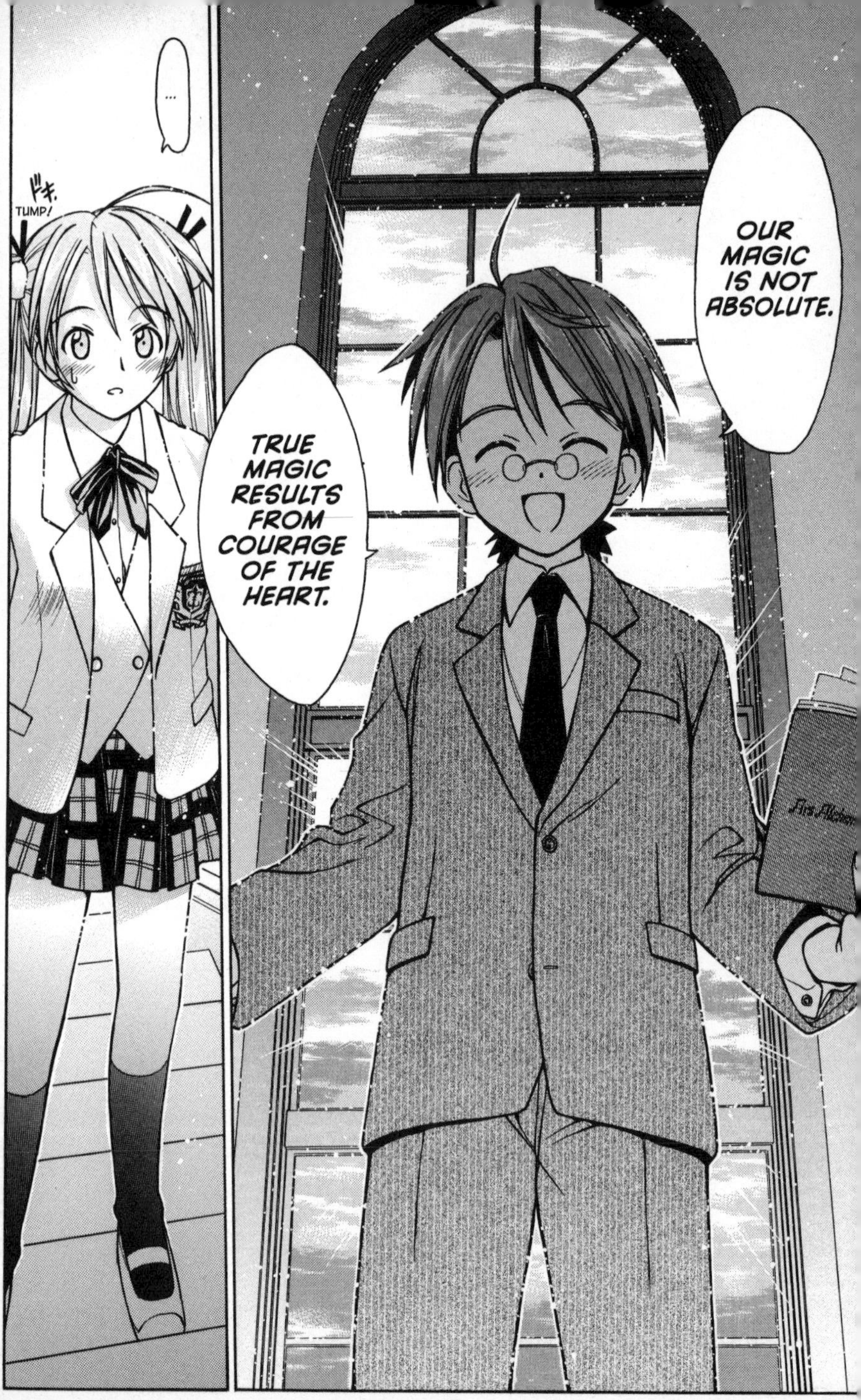
OUR MAGIC IS NOT ABSOLUTE.
TRUE MAGIC RESULTS FROM COURAGE OF THE HEART.
...
ドキ.
TUMP!

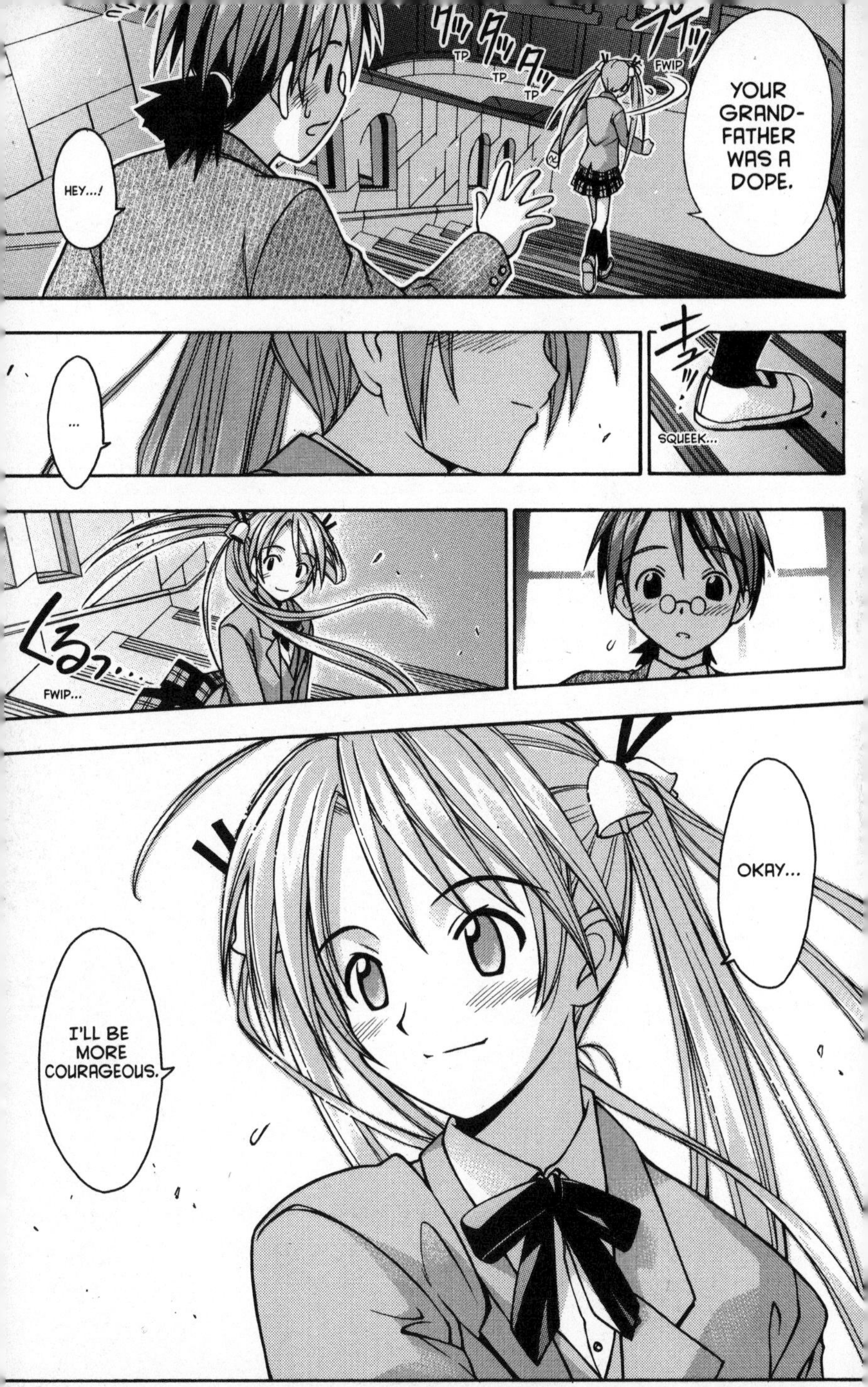
FWIP
TP
TP
TP
YOUR GRANDFATHER WAS A DOPE.
HEY...!
SQUEEK...
...
FWIP...
OKAY...
I'LL BE MORE COURAGEOUS.

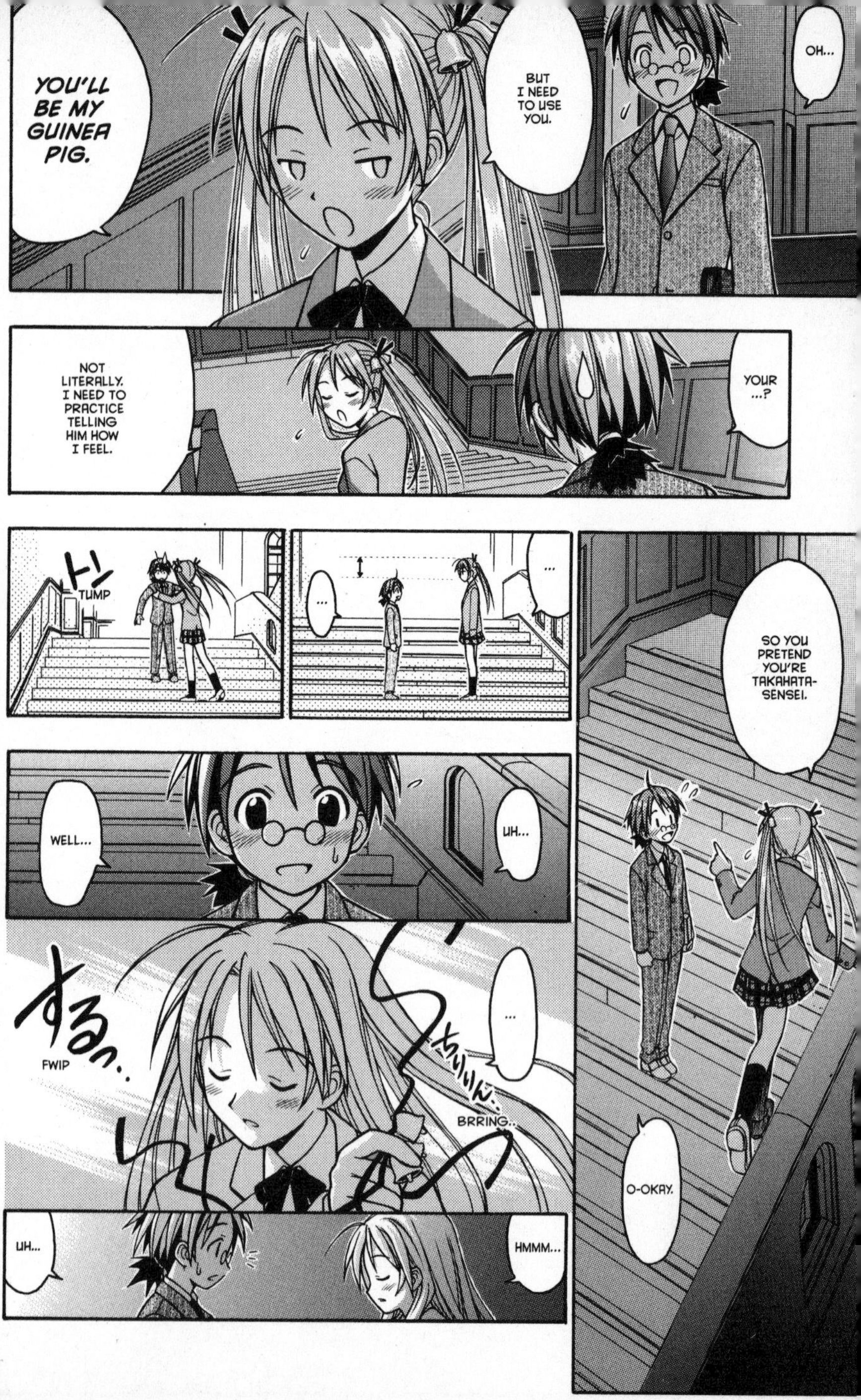
OH...
BUT I NEED TO USE YOU.
YOU'LL BE MY GUINEA PIG.
YOUR ...?
NOT LITERALLY. I NEED TO PRACTICE TELLING HIM HOW I FEEL.
SO YOU PRETEND YOU'RE TAKAHATA-SENSEI.
O-OKAY.
...
...
トン
TUMP
UH...
WELL...
...
ちりりん..
BRRING..
するっ..
FWIP
HMMM...
UH...

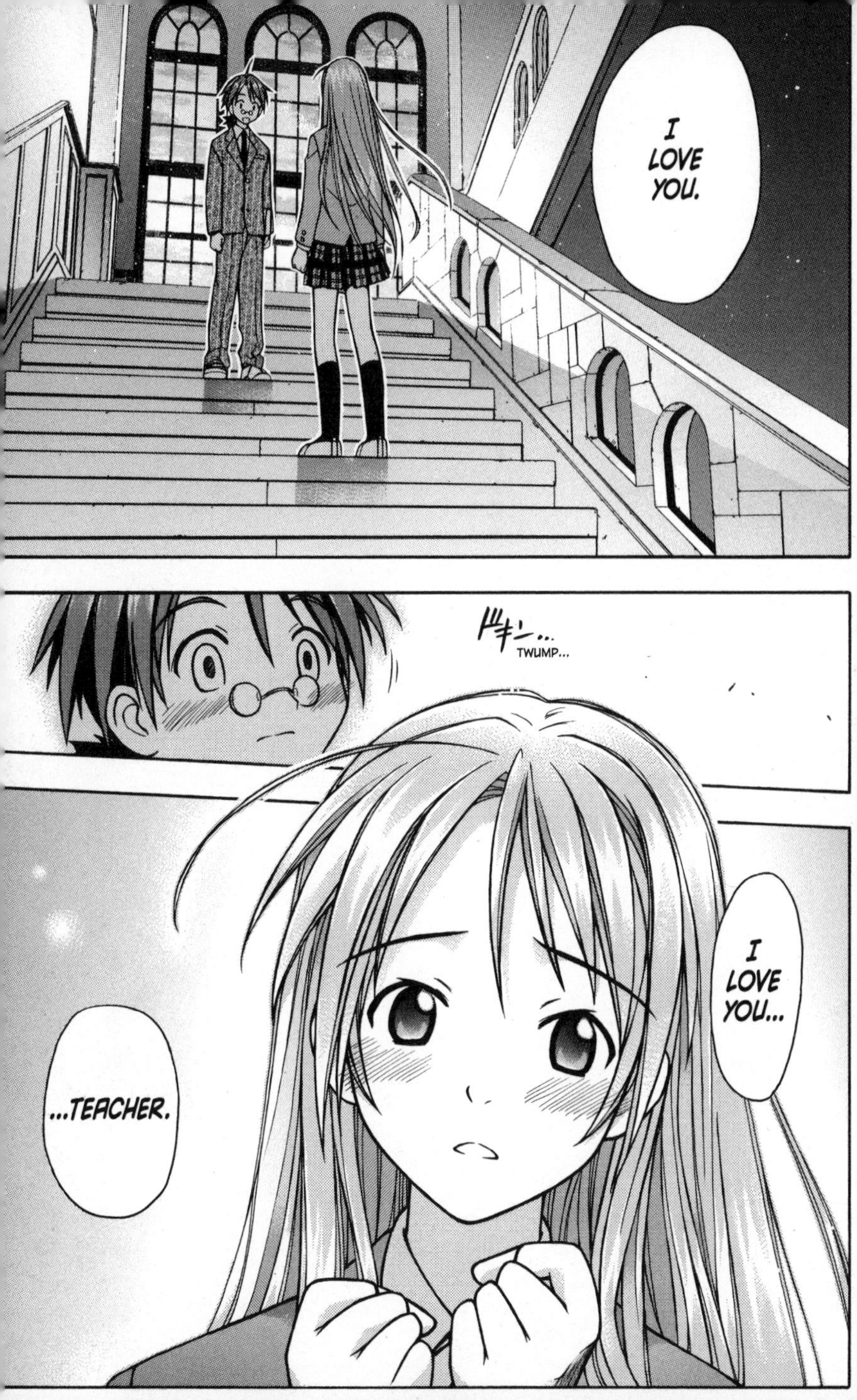
I LOVE YOU.
TWUMP...
I LOVE YOU...
...TEACHER.

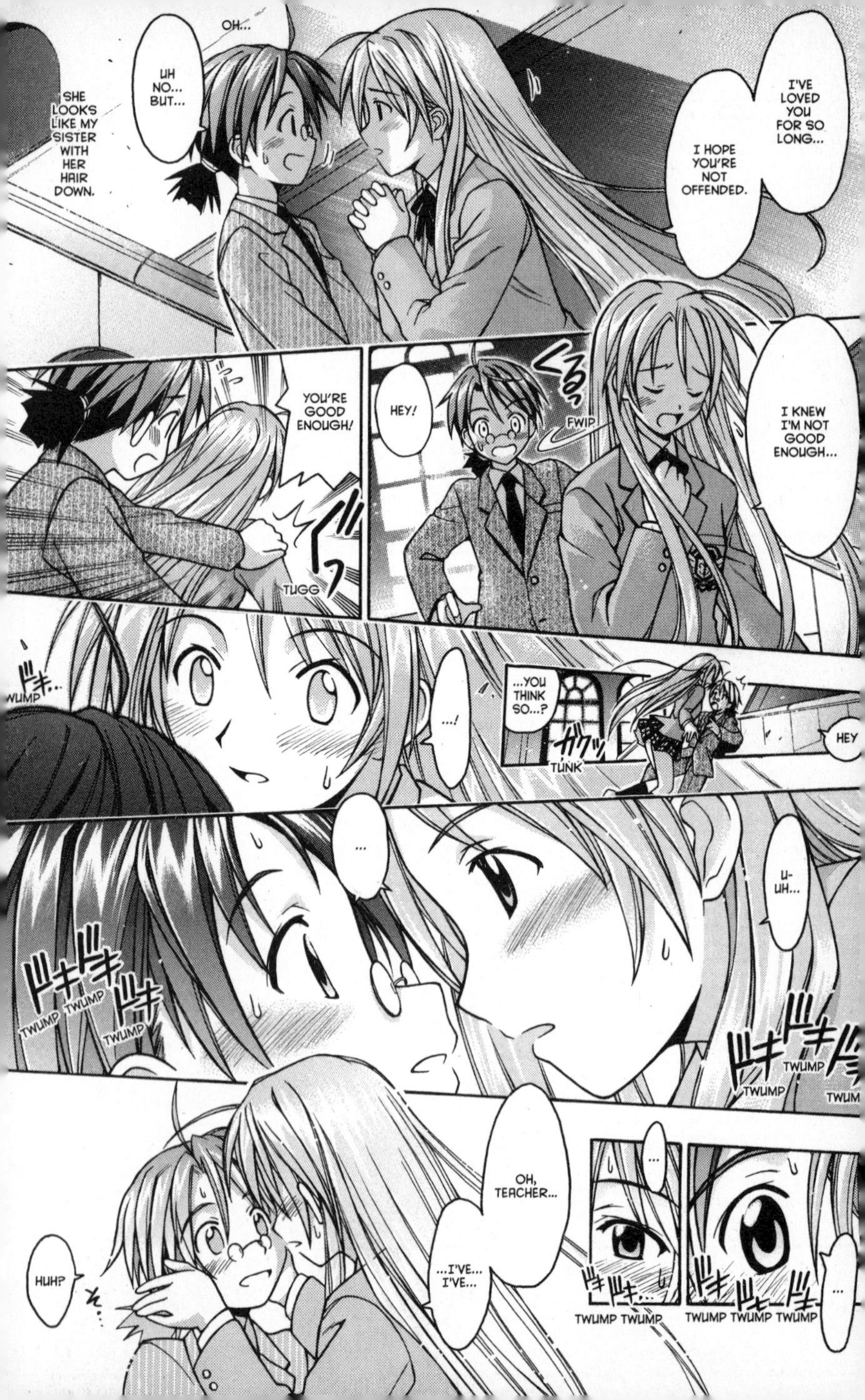
I'VE LOVED YOU FOR SO LONG...
I HOPE YOU'RE NOT OFFENDED.
OH...
UH NO... BUT...
SHE LOOKS LIKE MY SISTER WITH HER HAIR DOWN.
I KNEW I'M NOT GOOD ENOUGH...
FWIP
HEY!
YOU'RE GOOD ENOUGH!
TUGG
HEY
...YOU THINK SO...?
TUNK
...!
WUMP
U-UH...
TWUMP
TWUMP
TWUM
...
TWUMP TWUMP
TWUMP
...
TWUMP TWUMP TWUMP
...
TWUMP TWUMP
OH, TEACHER...
...I'VE... I'VE...
HUH?

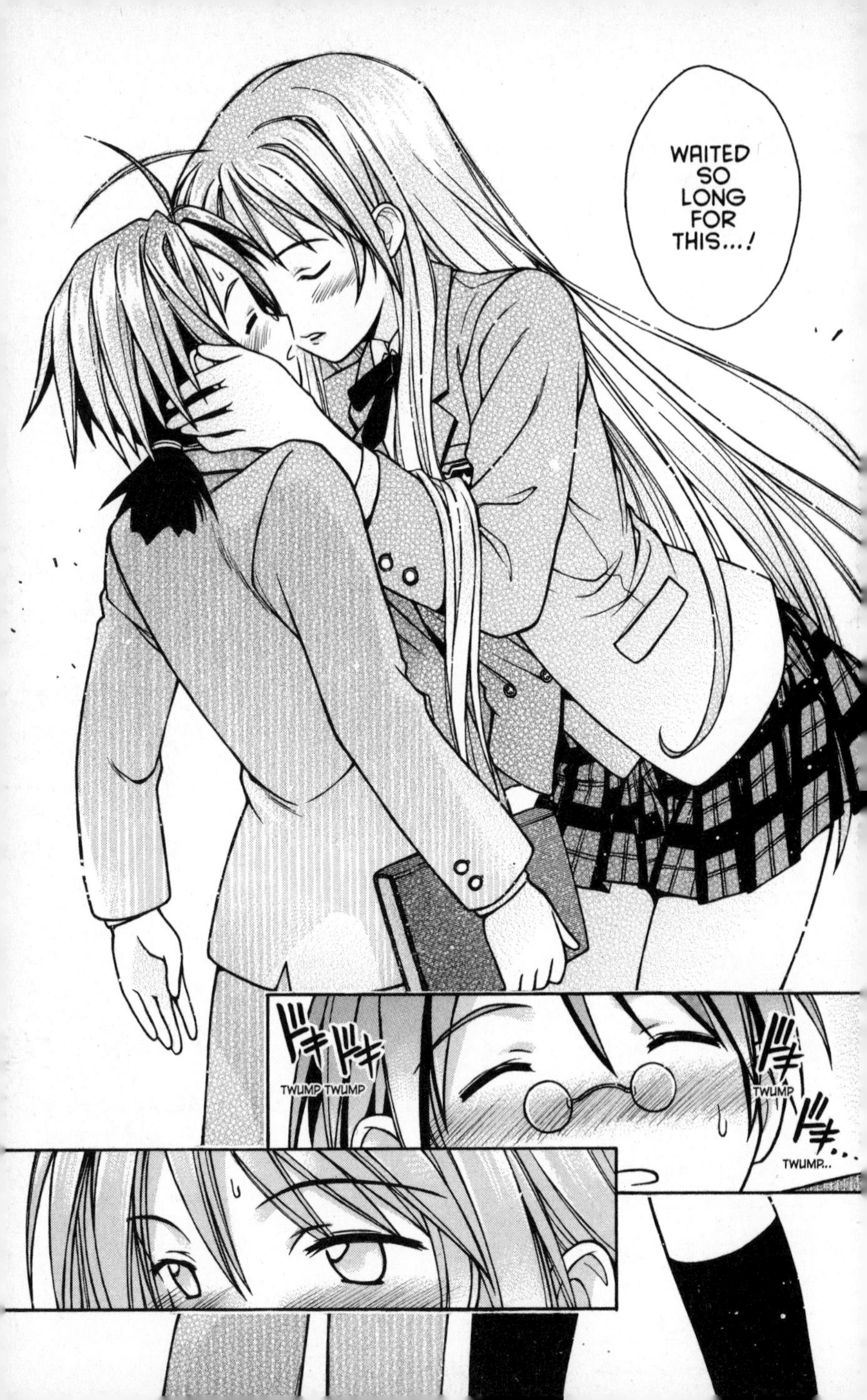
WAITED SO LONG FOR THIS...!
ドキ
TWUMP
ドキ...
TWUMP...
ドキドキ
TWUMP TWUMP

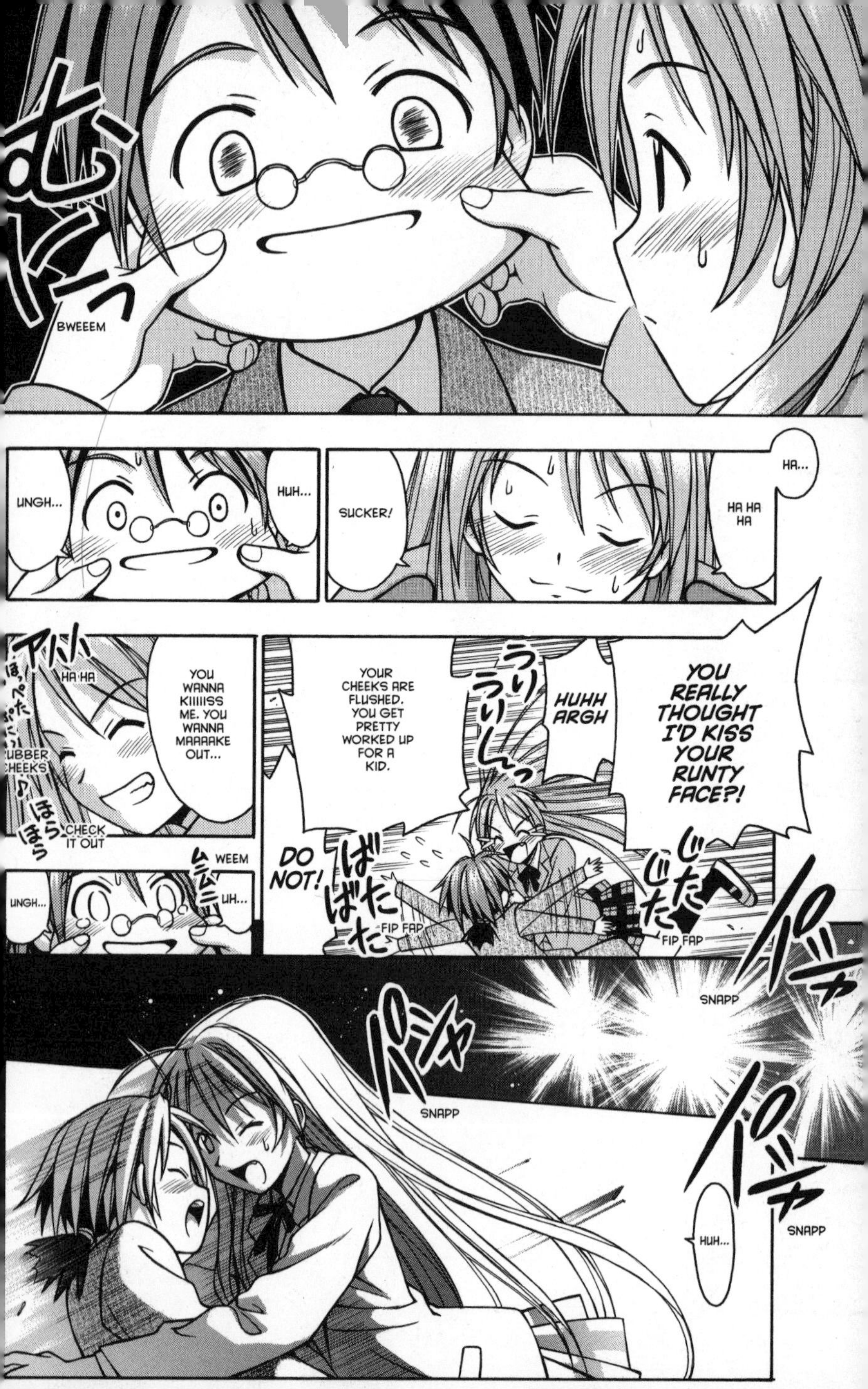

むにーっ
BWEEEM
HA...
HA HA HA
SUCKER!
HUH...
UNGH...
YOU REALLY THOUGHT I'D KISS YOUR RUNTY FACE?!
HUHH ARGH
うりうりんっ
YOUR CHEEKS ARE FLUSHED. YOU GET PRETTY WORKED UP FOR A KID.
YOU WANNA KIIIIISS ME. YOU WANNA MAAAAKE OUT...
アハハ
HA HA
ほっぺたぷにぷに
RUBBER CHEEKS ♪
ほらほら
CHECK IT OUT
じたじた
FIP FAP
DO NOT!
ばたばた
FIP FAP
ムニ
WEEM
UH...
UNGH...
パシャ
SNAPP
パシャ
SNAPP
パシャ
SNAPP
HUH...

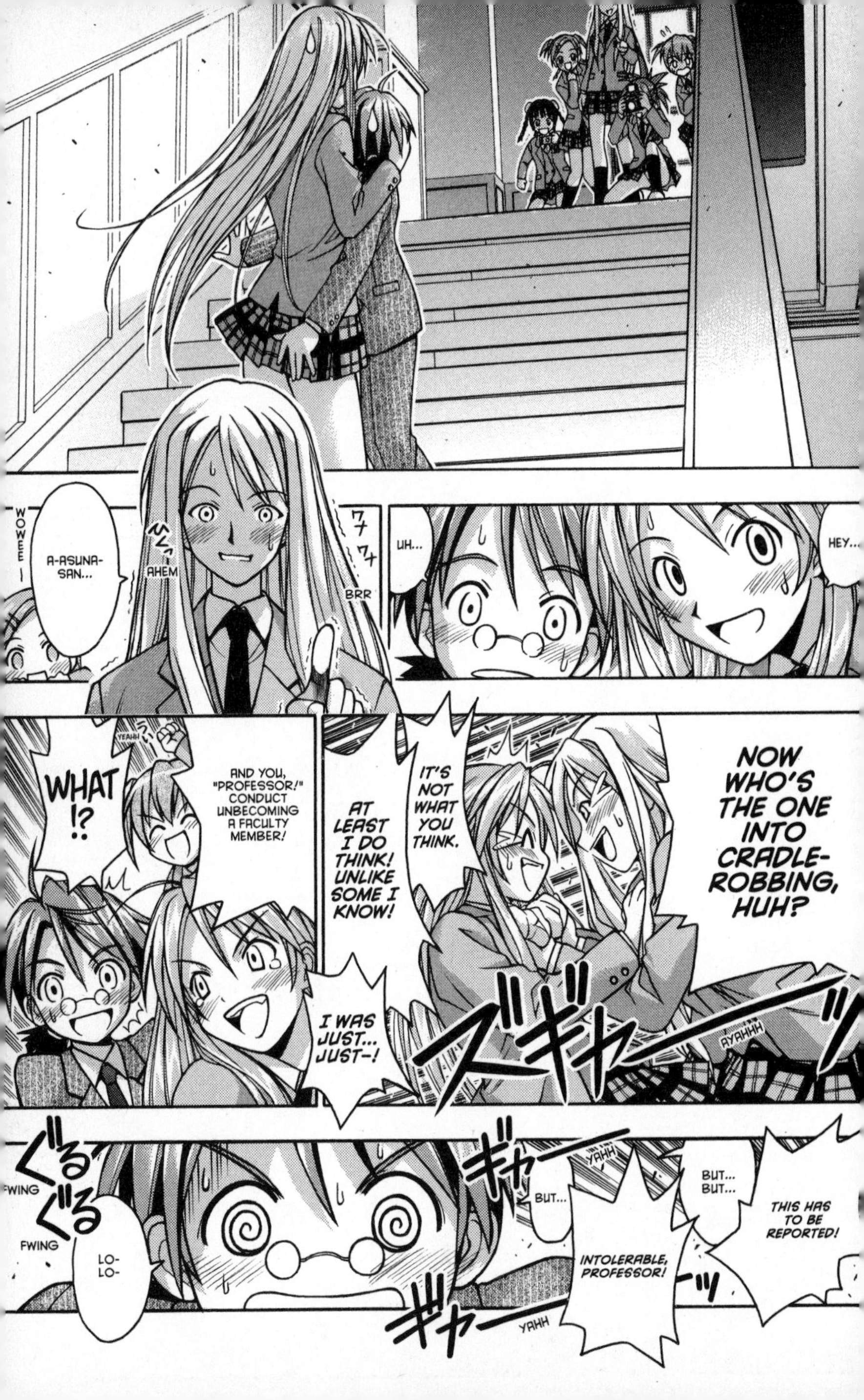
HEY...
UH...
BRR
AHEM
A-ASUNA-SAN...
WOWEE
NOW WHO'S THE ONE INTO CRADLE-ROBBING, HUH?
AYAHHH
IT'S NOT WHAT YOU THINK.
AT LEAST I DO THINK! UNLIKE SOME I KNOW!
I WAS JUST... JUST-!
AND YOU, "PROFESSOR!" CONDUCT UNBECOMING A FACULTY MEMBER!
WHAT!?
YEAHH
THIS HAS TO BE REPORTED!
BUT... BUT...
INTOLERABLE, PROFESSOR!
YAHH
BUT...
YAHH
LO-LO-
FWING
FWING

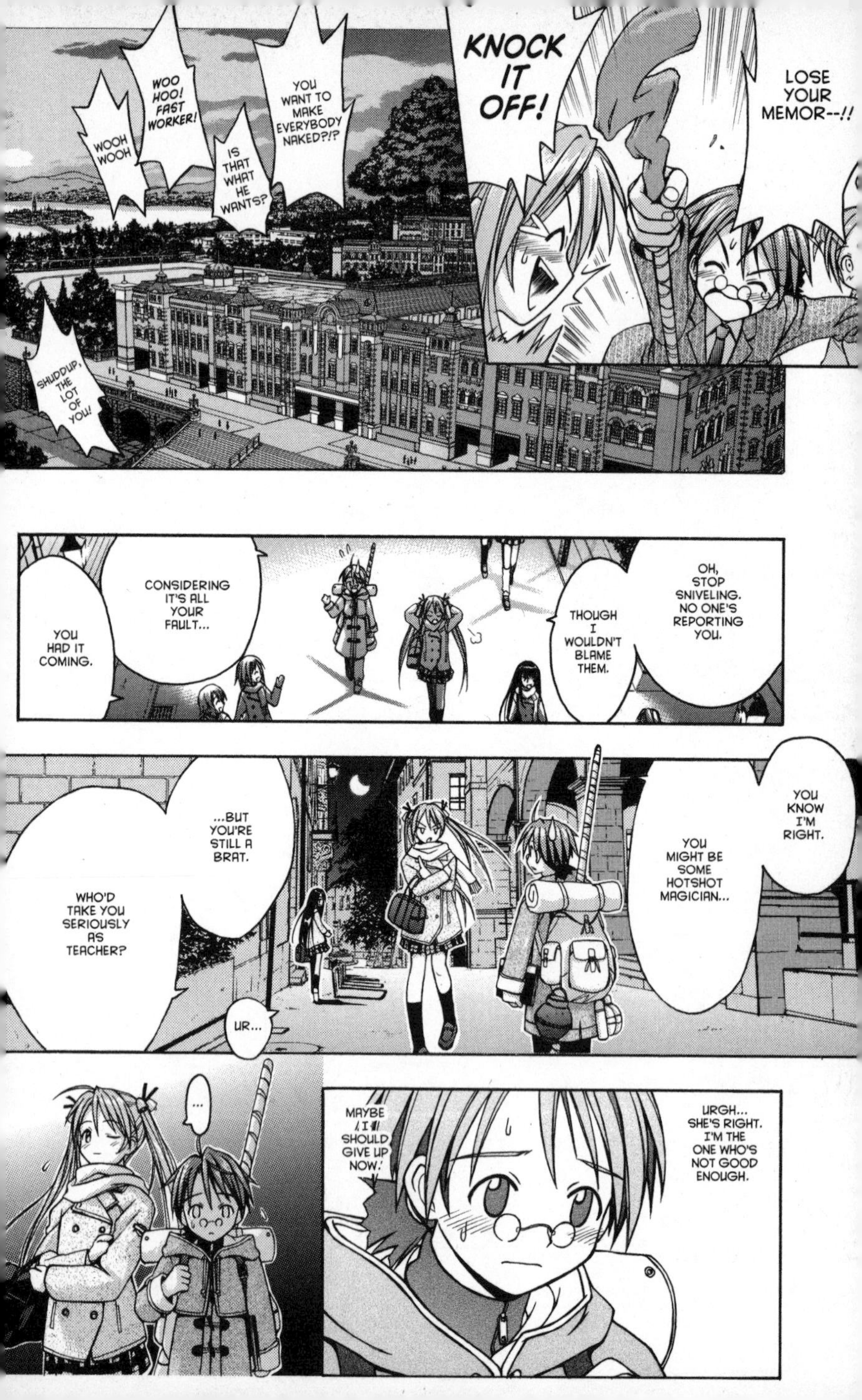

LOSE YOUR MEMOR--!!
KNOCK IT OFF!
YOU WANT TO MAKE EVERYBODY NAKED?!?
IS THAT WHAT HE WANTS?
WOO HOO! FAST WORKER!
WOOH WOOH
SHUDDUP, THE LOT OF YOU!
OH, STOP SNIVELING. NO ONE'S REPORTING YOU.
THOUGH I WOULDN'T BLAME THEM.
CONSIDERING IT'S ALL YOUR FAULT...
YOU HAD IT COMING.
YOU KNOW I'M RIGHT.
YOU MIGHT BE SOME HOTSHOT MAGICIAN...
...BUT YOU'RE STILL A BRAT.
WHO'D TAKE YOU SERIOUSLY AS TEACHER?
UR...
URGH... SHE'S RIGHT. I'M THE ONE WHO'S NOT GOOD ENOUGH.
MAYBE I SHOULD GIVE UP NOW.
...

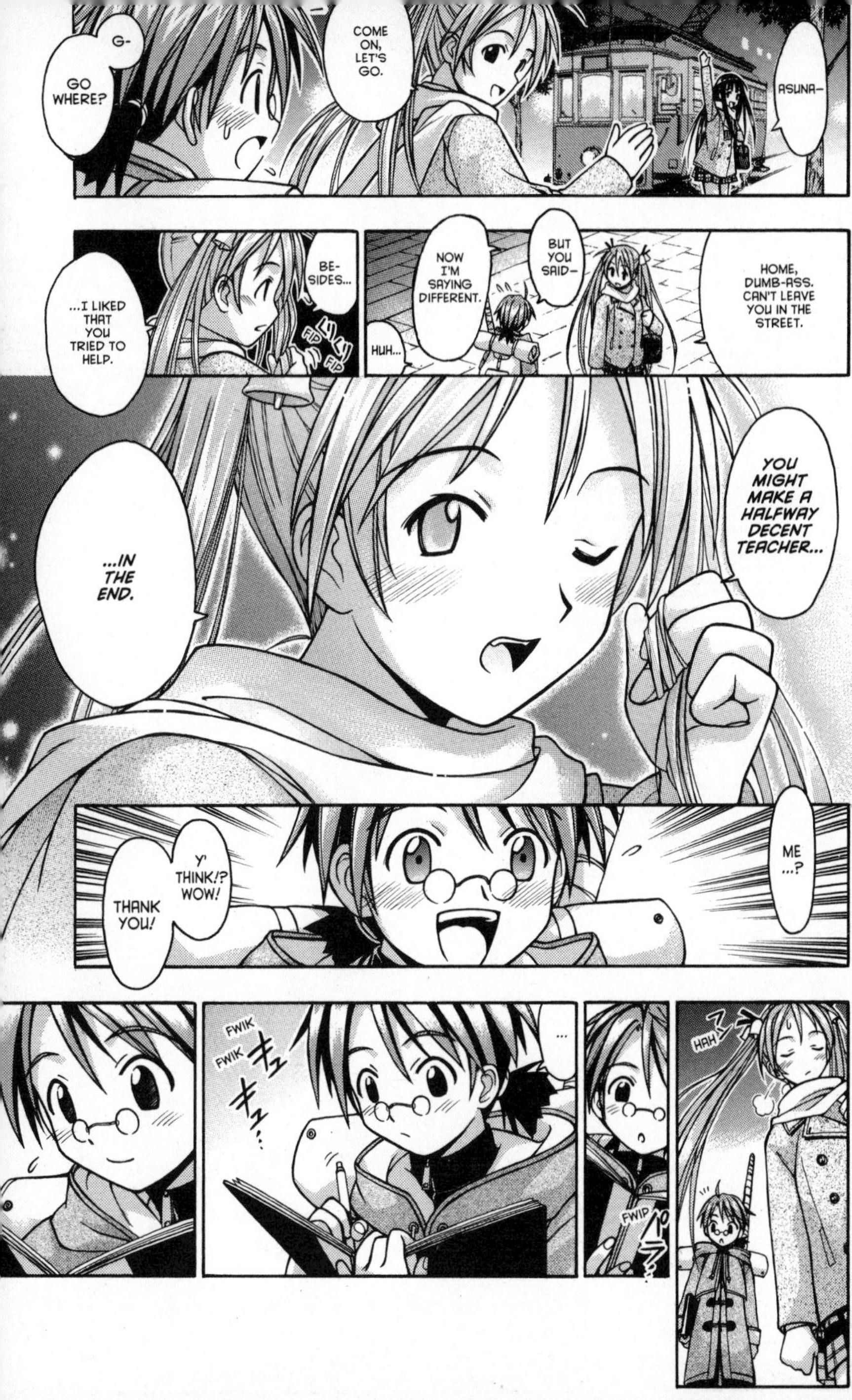
ASUNA—
COME ON, LET'S GO.
G-
GO WHERE?
HOME, DUMB-ASS. CAN'T LEAVE YOU IN THE STREET.
BUT YOU SAID—
HUH...
NOW I'M SAYING DIFFERENT.
BE-SIDES...
...I LIKED THAT YOU TRIED TO HELP.
FIP
FIP
YOU MIGHT MAKE A HALFWAY DECENT TEACHER...
...IN THE END.
ME ...?
Y' THINK!? WOW!
THANK YOU!
HAH
FWIP
...
FWIK
FWIK

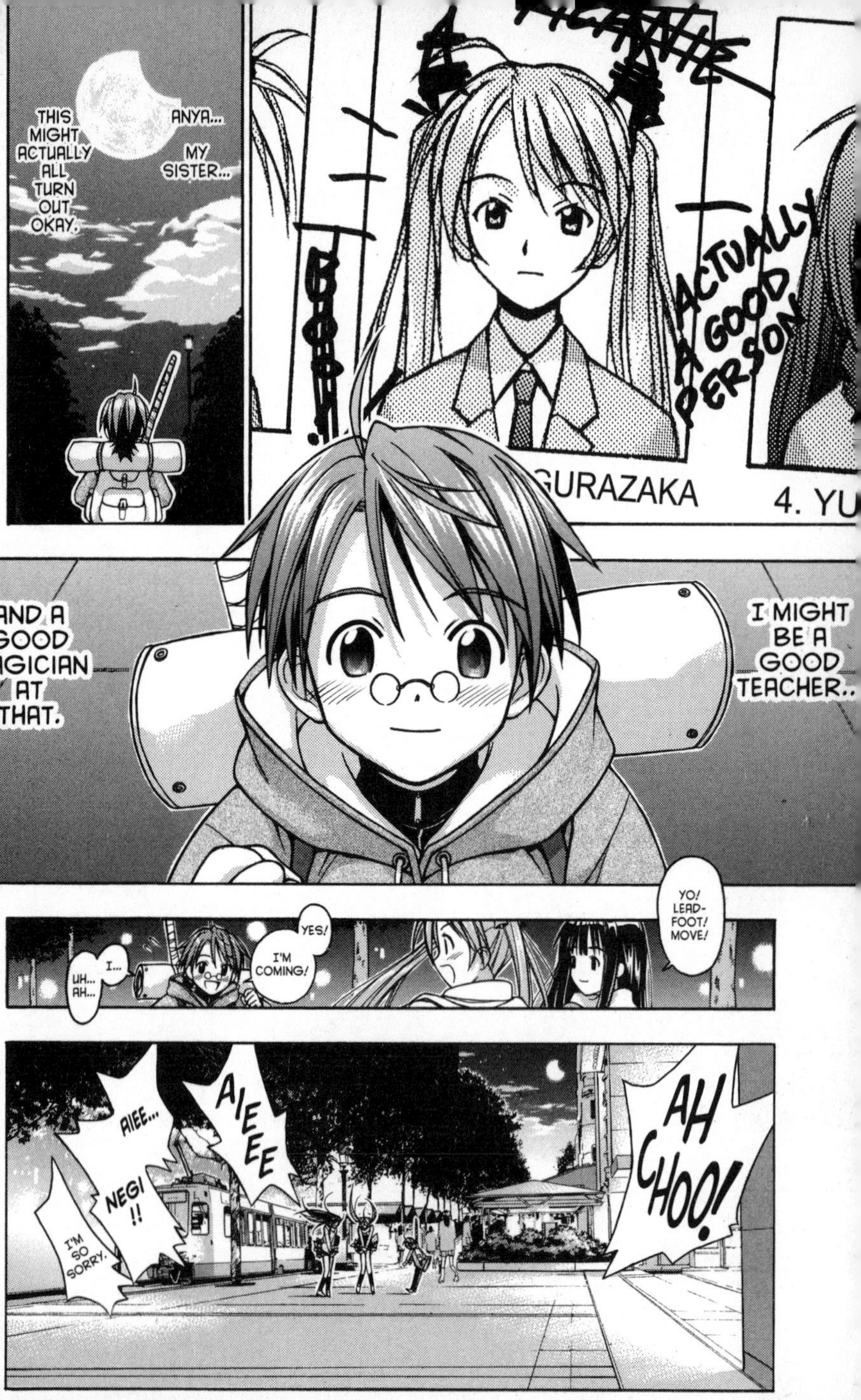
ACTUALLY A GOOD PERSON
GURAZAKA
4. YU
ANYA... MY SISTER...
THIS MIGHT ACTUALLY ALL TURN OUT OKAY.
I MIGHT BE A GOOD TEACHER..
AND A GOOD MAGICIAN AT THAT.
YO! LEAD-FOOT! MOVE!
YES! I'M COMING!
I...
UH... AH...
AH CHOO!
AIEEE
AIEE...
NEGI !!
I'M SO SORRY.

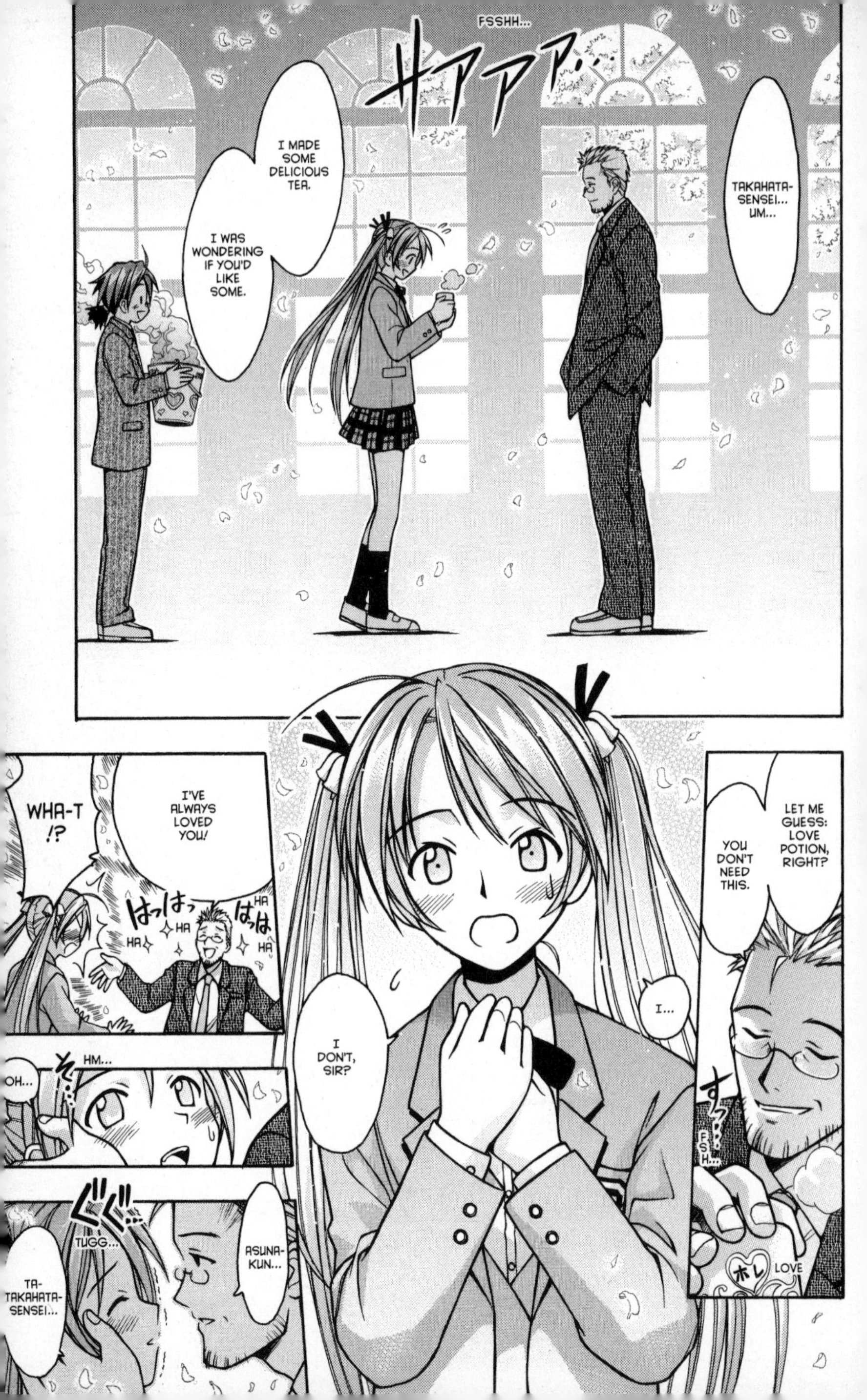
FSSHH...
TAKAHATA-SENSEI... UM...
I MADE SOME DELICIOUS TEA.
I WAS WONDERING IF YOU'D LIKE SOME.
LET ME GUESS: LOVE POTION, RIGHT?
YOU DON'T NEED THIS.
FSH...
LOVE
I...
I DON'T, SIR?
I'VE ALWAYS LOVED YOU!
WHA-T!?
HA HA HA HA HA HA
HM...
OH...
TUGG...
ASUNA-KUN...
TA-TAKAHATA-SENSEI...

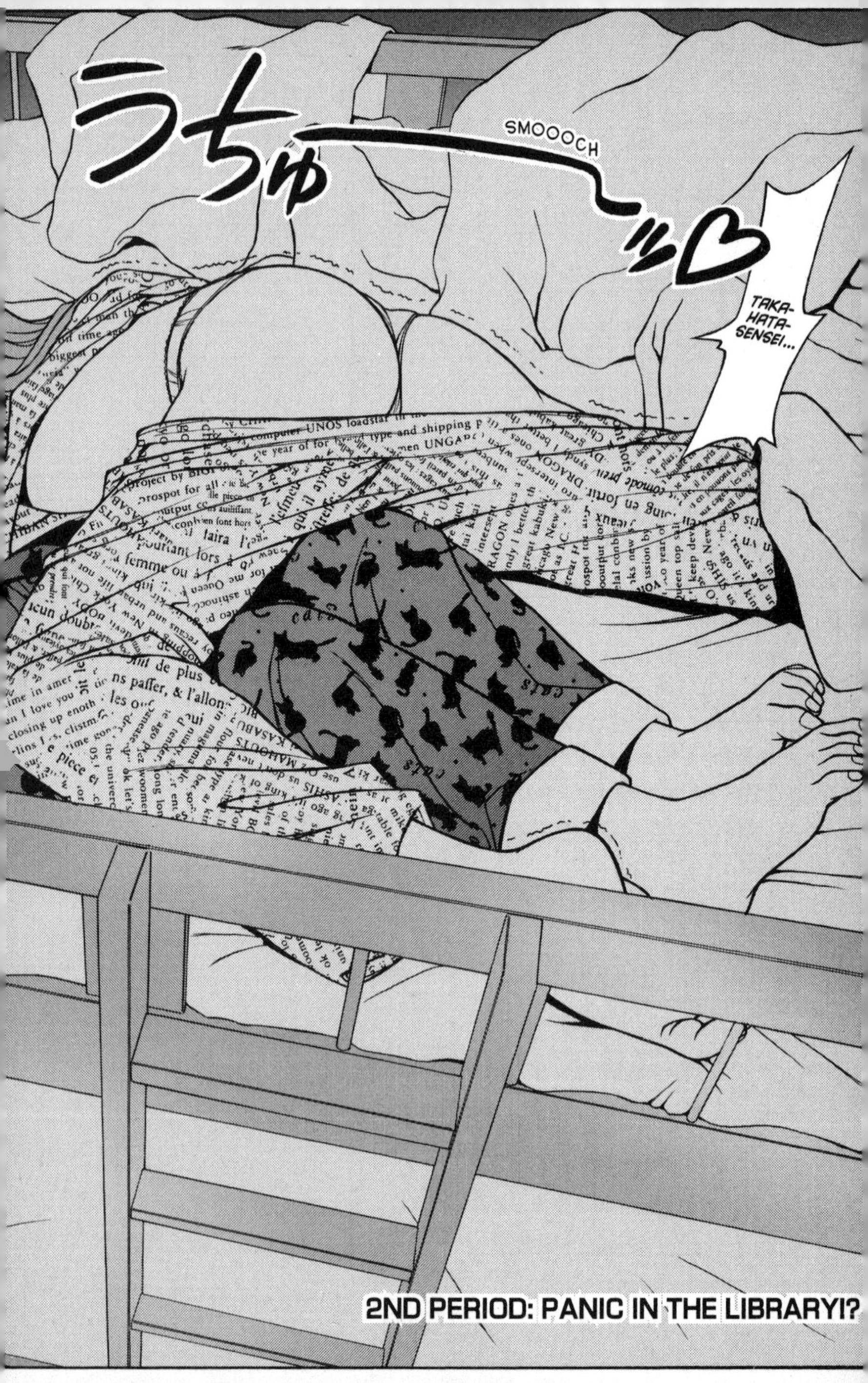
TAKA-HATA-SENSEI...
うちゅ～～ッ♥
SMOOOCH

2ND PERIOD: PANIC IN THE LIBRARY!?

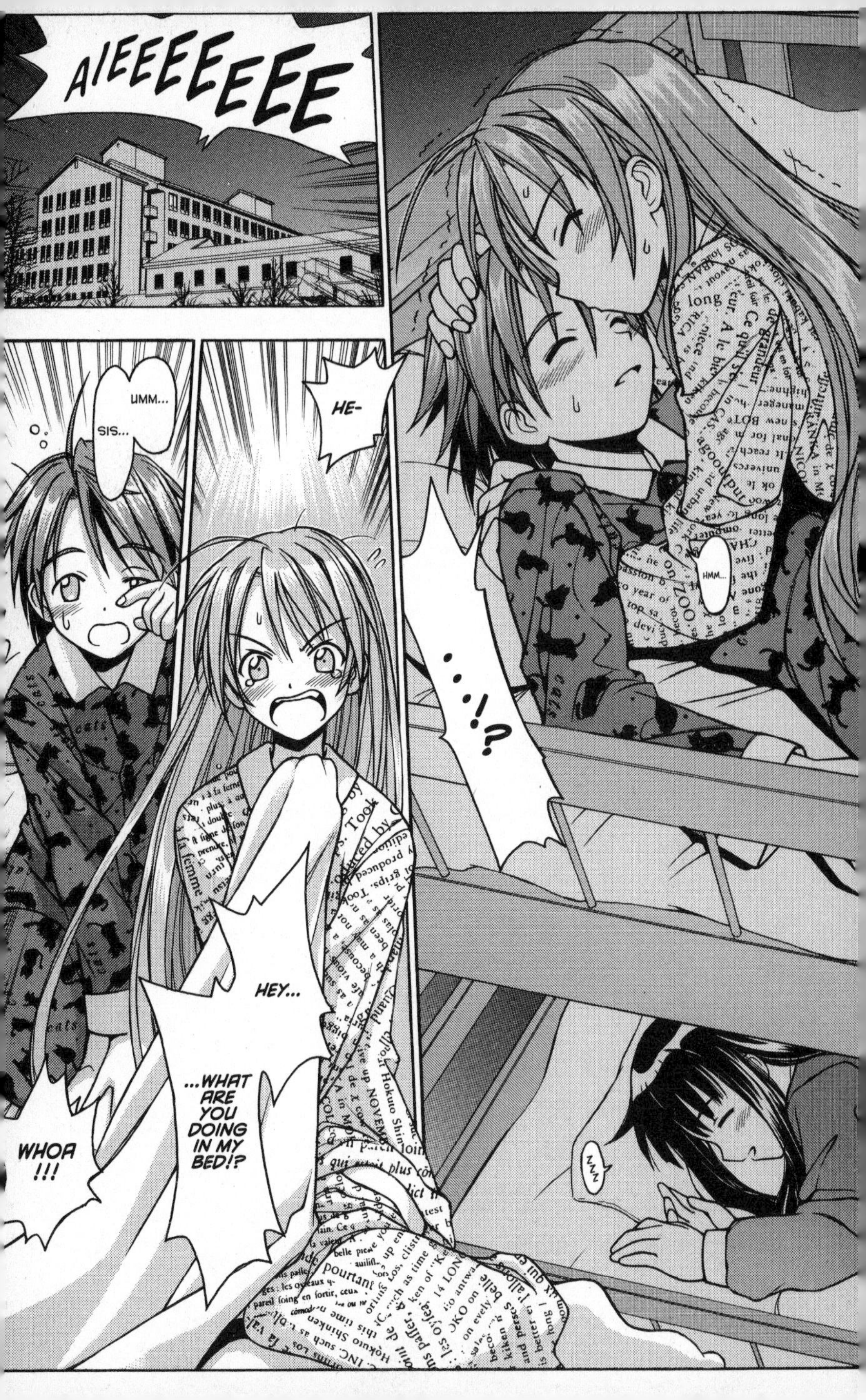
AIEEEEEEE
UMM... SIS...
HE-
HEY...
...WHAT ARE YOU DOING IN MY BED!?
WHOA !!!
HMM...
...!?
NNN

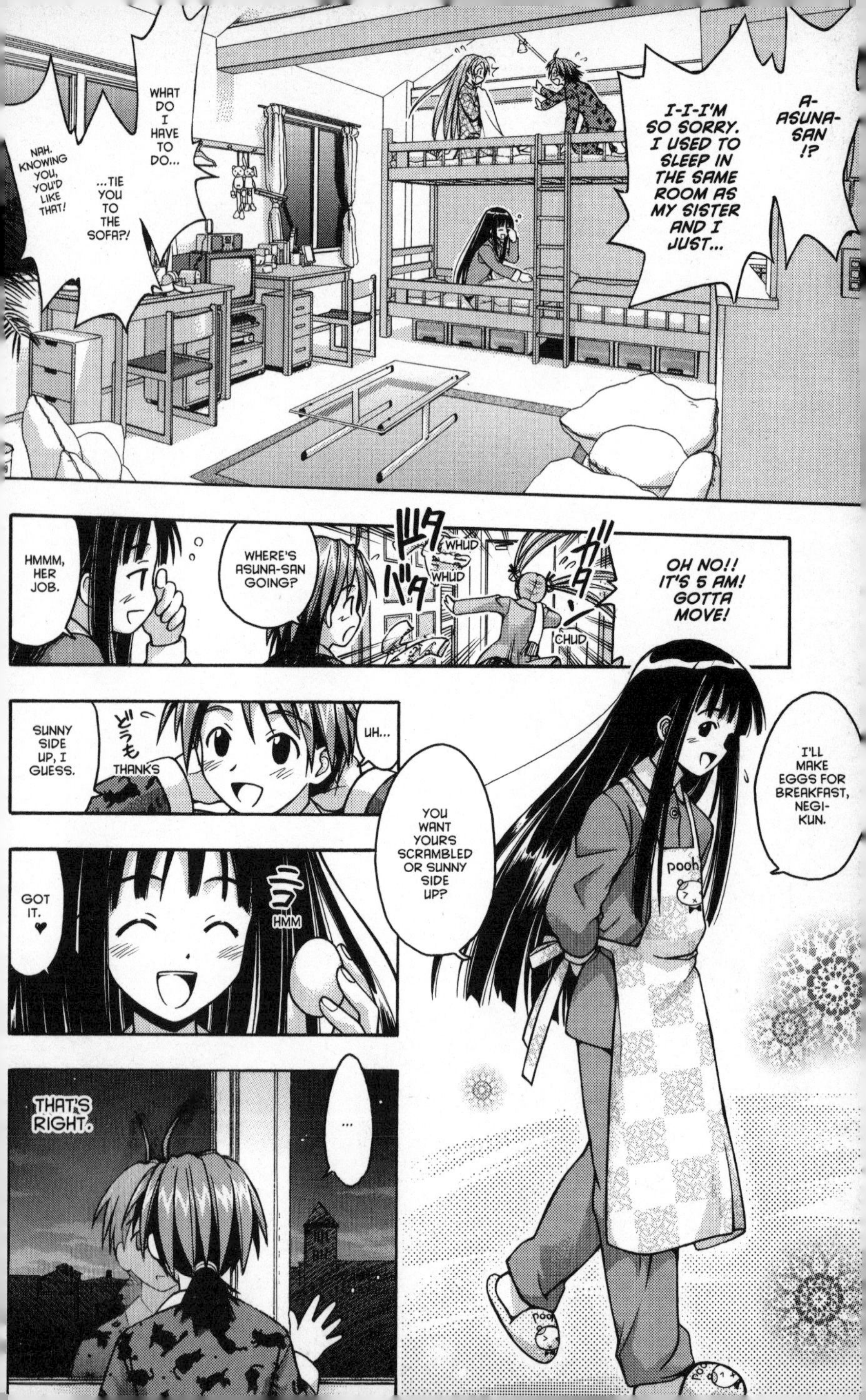

A-ASUNA-SAN!?
I-I-I'M SO SORRY. I USED TO SLEEP IN THE SAME ROOM AS MY SISTER AND I JUST...
WHAT DO I HAVE TO DO...
...TIE YOU TO THE SOFA?!
NAH. KNOWING YOU, YOU'D LIKE THAT!
OH NO!! IT'S 5 AM! GOTTA MOVE!
CHUD
WHUD
WHUD
WHERE'S ASUNA-SAN GOING?
HMMM, HER JOB.
I'LL MAKE EGGS FOR BREAKFAST, NEGI-KUN.
pooh
YOU WANT YOURS SCRAMBLED OR SUNNY SIDE UP?
UH...
THANKS
SUNNY SIDE UP, I GUESS.
HMM
GOT IT. ♥
...
THAT'S RIGHT.

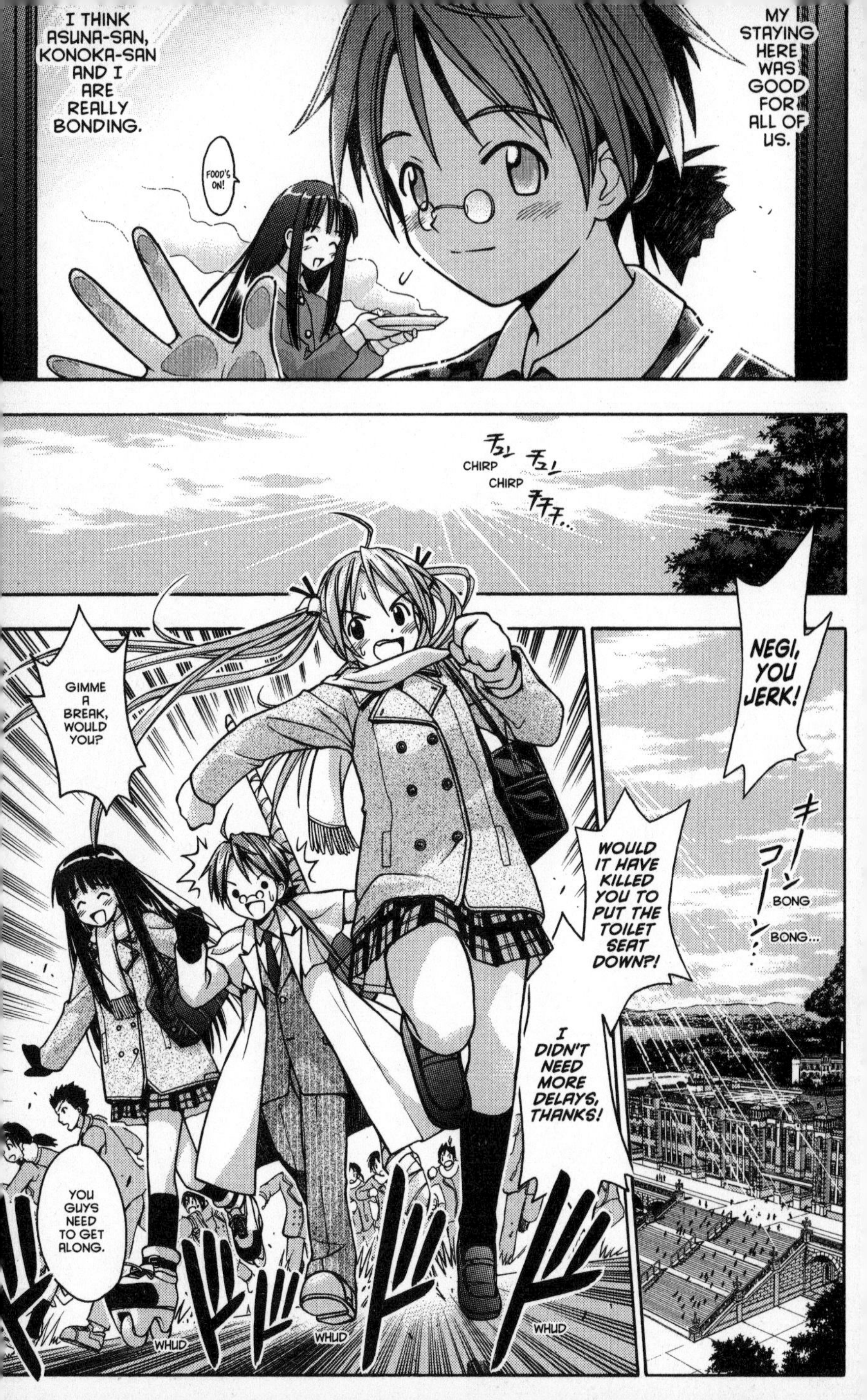
MY STAYING HERE WAS GOOD FOR ALL OF US.
I THINK ASUNA-SAN, KONOKA-SAN AND I ARE REALLY BONDING.
FOOD'S ON!
CHIRP
CHIRP
NEGI, YOU JERK!
BONG
BONG...
WOULD IT HAVE KILLED YOU TO PUT THE TOILET SEAT DOWN?!
I DIDN'T NEED MORE DELAYS, THANKS!
GIMME A BREAK, WOULD YOU?
YOU GUYS NEED TO GET ALONG.
WHUD
WHUD
WHUD

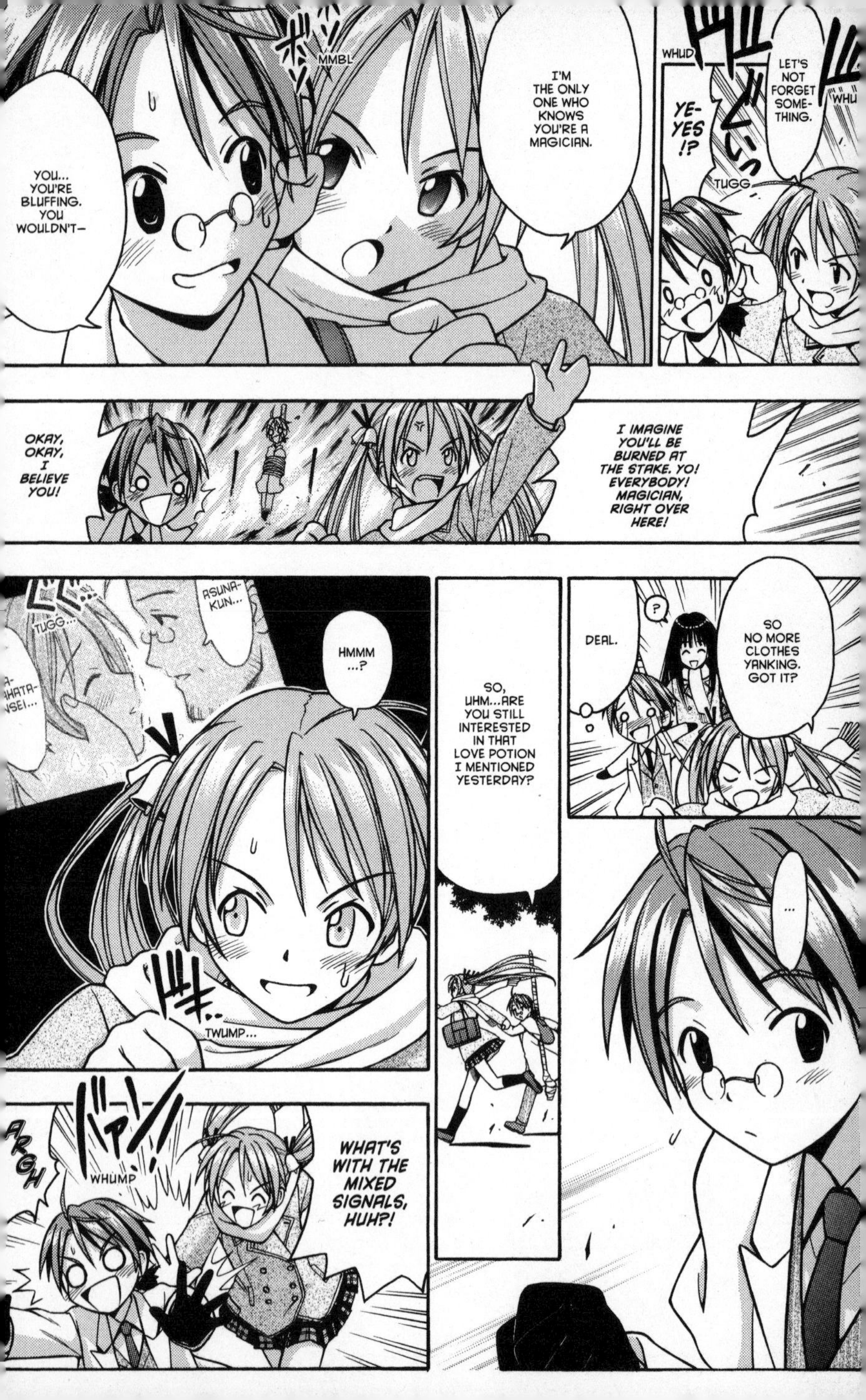
LET'S NOT FORGET SOME-THING.
WHUD
WHU
YE-YES!?
TUGG
I'M THE ONLY ONE WHO KNOWS YOU'RE A MAGICIAN.
MMBL
YOU... YOU'RE BLUFFING. YOU WOULDN'T—
I IMAGINE YOU'LL BE BURNED AT THE STAKE. YO! EVERYBODY! MAGICIAN, RIGHT OVER HERE!
OKAY, OKAY, I BELIEVE YOU!
SO NO MORE CLOTHES YANKING. GOT IT?
?
DEAL.
SO, UHM...ARE YOU STILL INTERESTED IN THAT LOVE POTION I MENTIONED YESTERDAY?
...
ASUNA-KUN...
TUGG...
HMMM...?
TWUMP...
WHAT'S WITH THE MIXED SIGNALS, HUH?!
WHUMP
ARGH

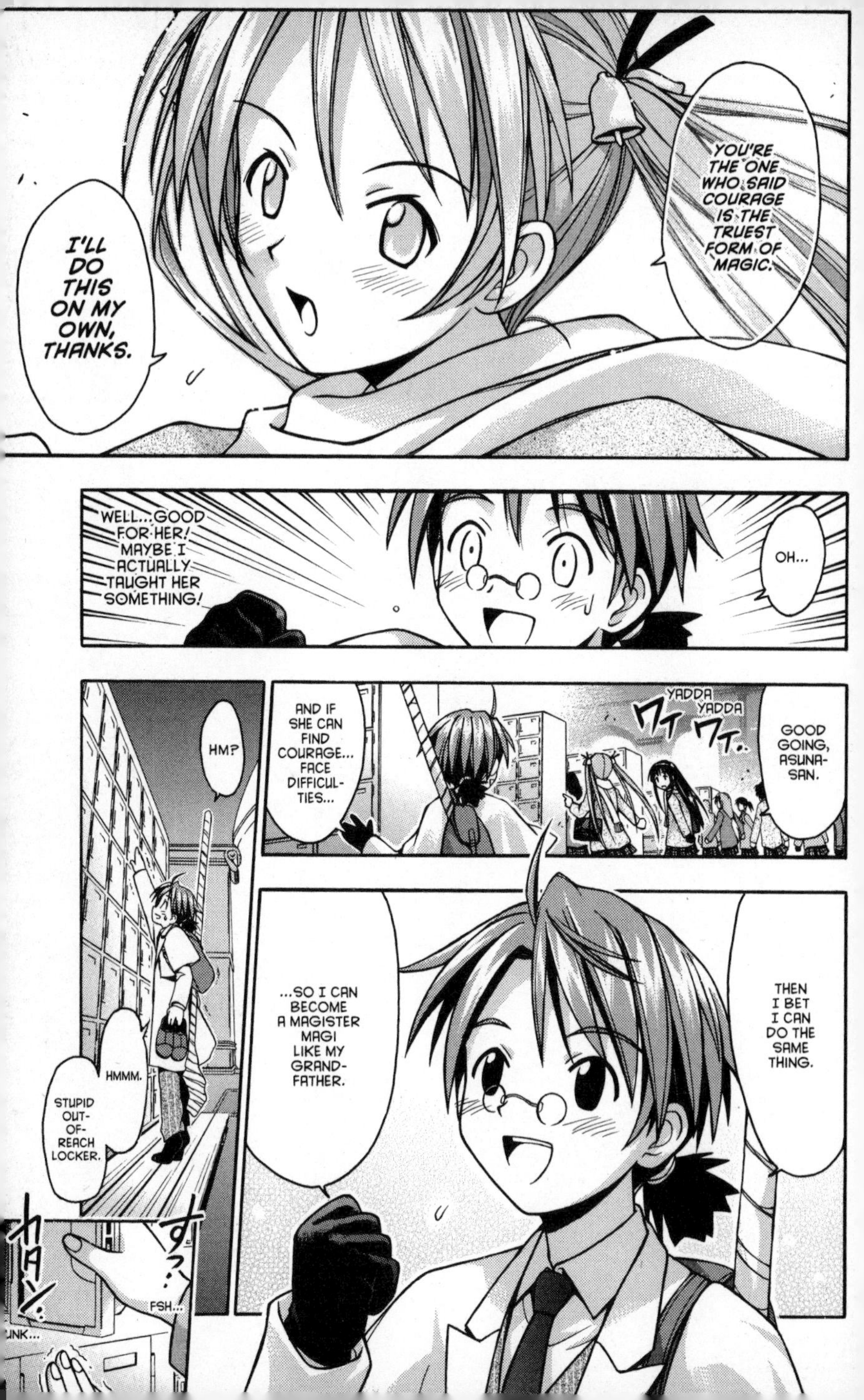
YOU'RE THE ONE WHO SAID COURAGE IS THE TRUEST FORM OF MAGIC.
I'LL DO THIS ON MY OWN, THANKS.
OH...
WELL... GOOD FOR HER! MAYBE I ACTUALLY TAUGHT HER SOMETHING!
GOOD GOING, ASUNA-SAN.
YADDA YADDA
AND IF SHE CAN FIND COURAGE... FACE DIFFICULTIES...
HM?
THEN I BET I CAN DO THE SAME THING.
...SO I CAN BECOME A MAGISTER MAGI LIKE MY GRANDFATHER.
HMMM.
STUPID OUT-OF-REACH LOCKER.
FSH...

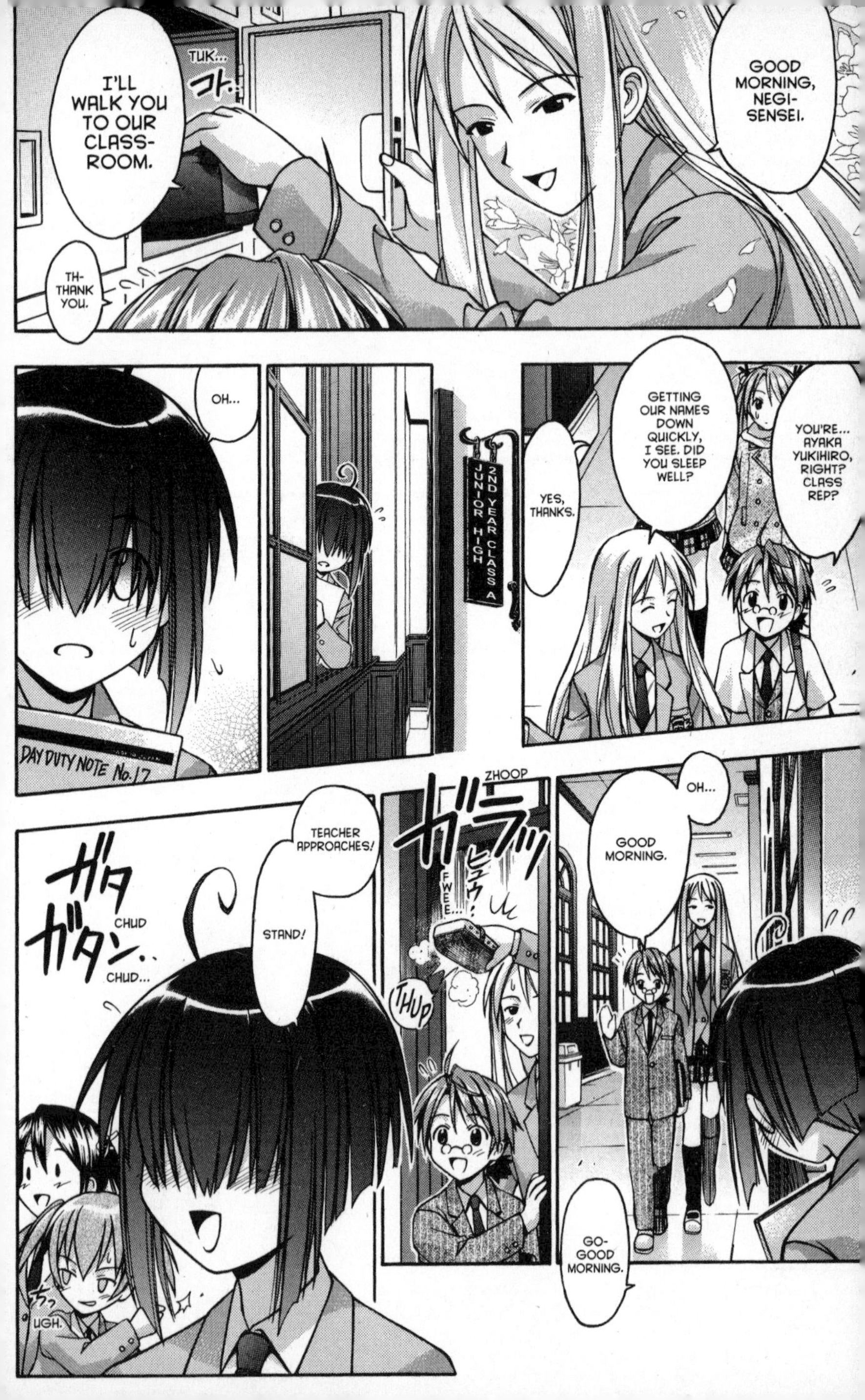
GOOD MORNING, NEGI-SENSEI.
TUK...
コト..
I'LL WALK YOU TO OUR CLASS-ROOM.
TH-THANK YOU.
YOU'RE... AYAKA YUKIHIRO, RIGHT? CLASS REP?
GETTING OUR NAMES DOWN QUICKLY, I SEE. DID YOU SLEEP WELL?
YES, THANKS.
2ND YEAR CLASS A
JUNIOR HIGH
OH...
DAY DUTY NOTE No.17
OH...
GOOD MORNING.
GO-GOOD MORNING.
ガラッ
ZHOOP
ヒュウ
FWEE...
THUP
TEACHER APPROACHES!
STAND!
ガタ
CHUD
ガタン..
CHUD...
UGH.

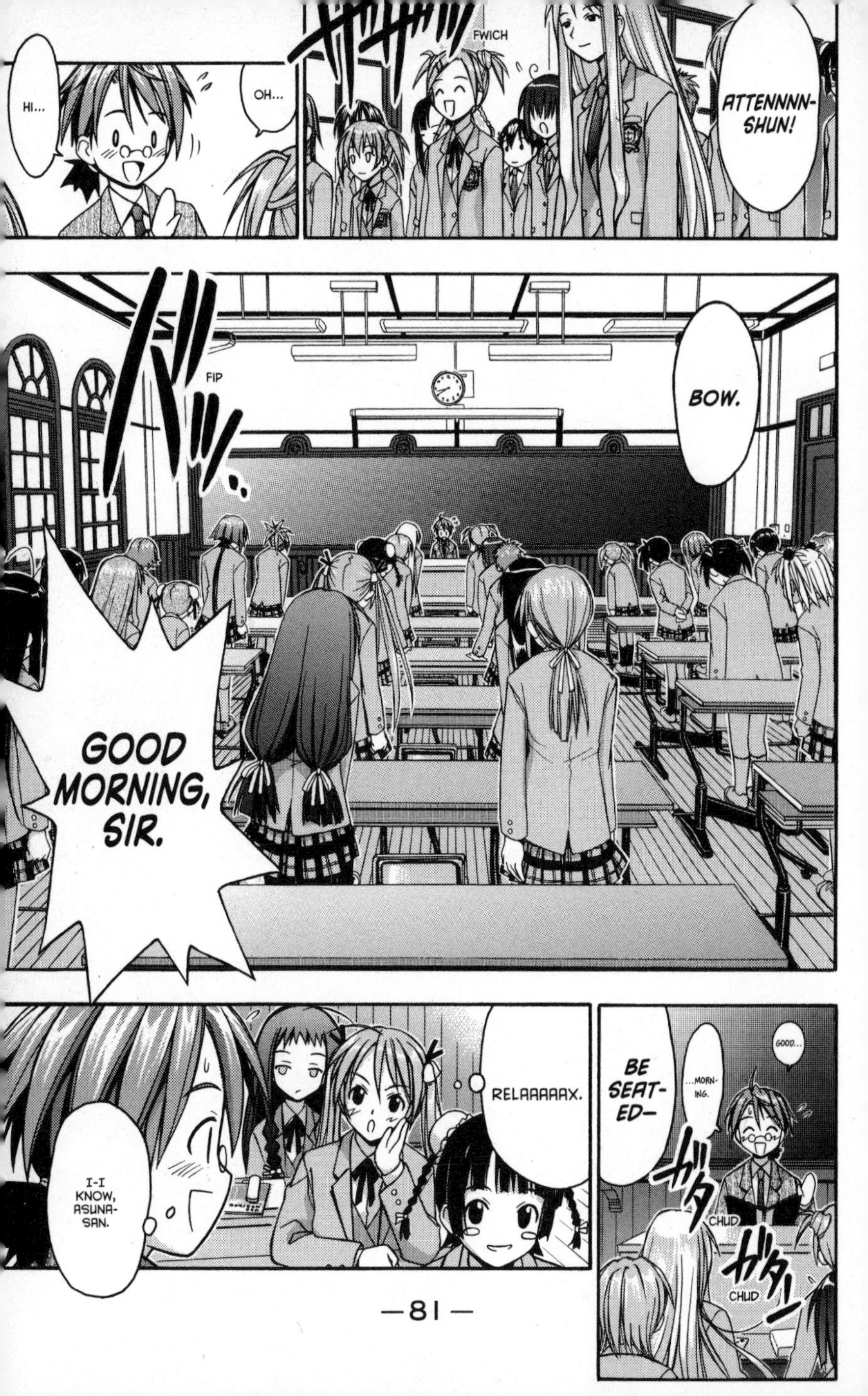
ATTENNNN-SHUN!
FWICH
OH...
HI...
BOW.
FIP
GOOD MORNING, SIR.
GOOD...
...MORNING.
BE SEAT-ED—
CHUD
CHUD
RELAAAAAAX.
I-I KNOW, ASUNA-SAN.

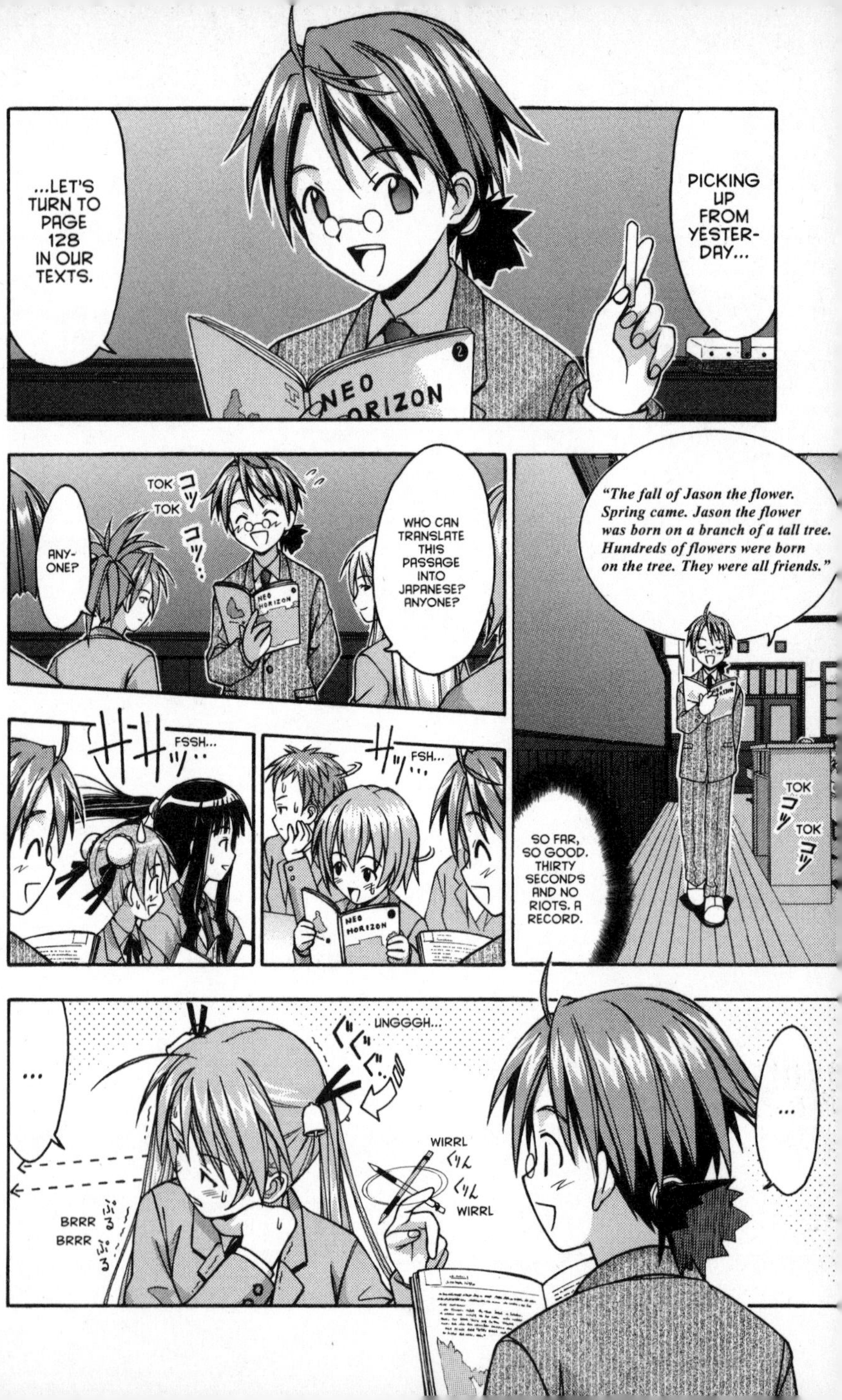
PICKING UP FROM YESTER-DAY...
...LET'S TURN TO PAGE 128 IN OUR TEXTS.
"The fall of Jason the flower. Spring came. Jason the flower was born on a branch of a tall tree. Hundreds of flowers were born on the tree. They were all friends."
TOK コッ TOK コッ
SO FAR, SO GOOD. THIRTY SECONDS AND NO RIOTS. A RECORD.
WHO CAN TRANSLATE THIS PASSAGE INTO JAPANESE? ANYONE?
TOK コッ TOK コッ...
ANY-ONE?
FSH... サッ...
FSSH... サーサッ...
...
UNGGGH... ぐぐぐ...
WIRRL くりん くりん WIRRL
BRRR ぷる BRRR ぷる
...

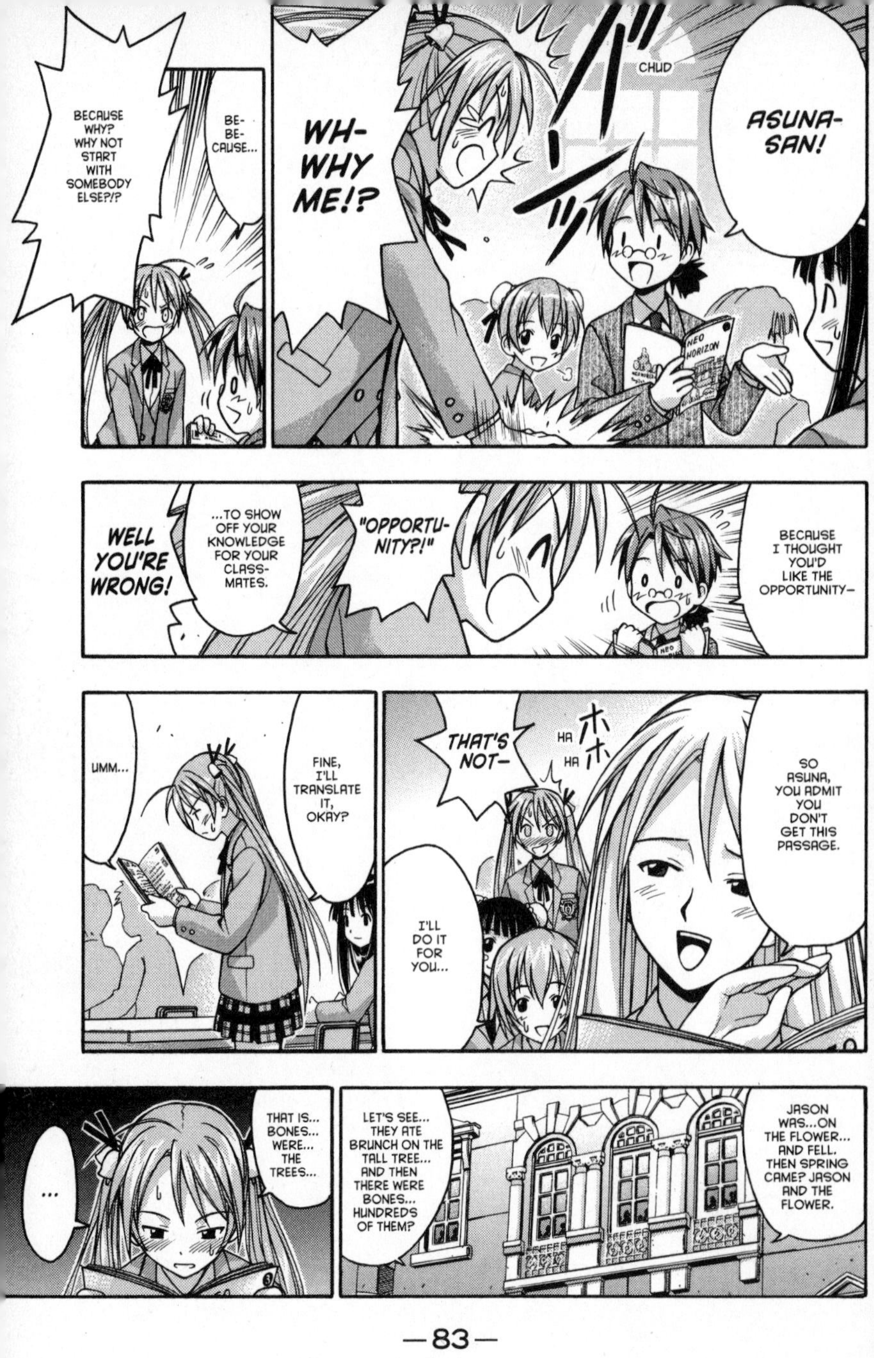
ASUNA-SAN!
CHUD
WH- WHY ME!?
BE- BE- CAUSE...
BECAUSE WHY? WHY NOT START WITH SOMEBODY ELSE?!?
BECAUSE I THOUGHT YOU'D LIKE THE OPPORTUNITY—
"OPPORTU-NITY?!"
...TO SHOW OFF YOUR KNOWLEDGE FOR YOUR CLASS-MATES.
WELL YOU'RE WRONG!
SO ASUNA, YOU ADMIT YOU DON'T GET THIS PASSAGE.
HA HA
I'LL DO IT FOR YOU...
THAT'S NOT—
FINE, I'LL TRANSLATE IT, OKAY?
UMM...
JASON WAS...ON THE FLOWER... AND FELL. THEN SPRING CAME? JASON AND THE FLOWER.
LET'S SEE... THEY ATE BRUNCH ON THE TALL TREE... AND THEN THERE WERE BONES... HUNDREDS OF THEM?
THAT IS... BONES... WERE... THE TREES...
...

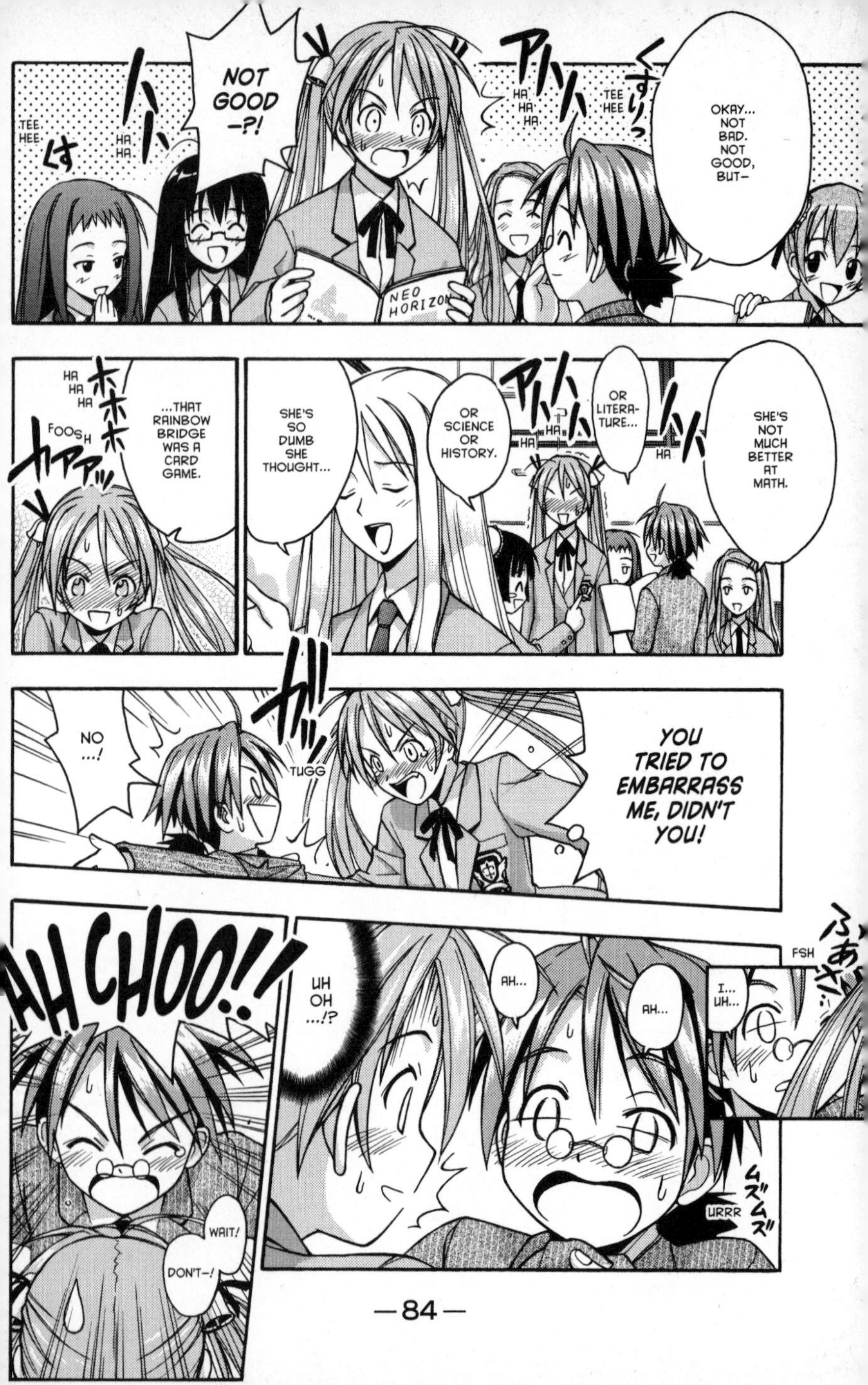

OKAY... NOT BAD. NOT GOOD, BUT—
TEE HEE
HA HA HA
NOT GOOD —?!
HA HA
TEE HEE
SHE'S NOT MUCH BETTER AT MATH.
HA
OR LITERA- TURE...
HA
HA
OR SCIENCE OR HISTORY.
SHE'S SO DUMB SHE THOUGHT...
...THAT RAINBOW BRIDGE WAS A CARD GAME.
HA HA HA
FOOSH
YOU TRIED TO EMBARRASS ME, DIDN'T YOU!
TUGG
NO ...!
FSH
I... UH...
AH...
AH...
UH OH ...!?
URRR
AH CHOO!!
WAIT!
DON'T—!

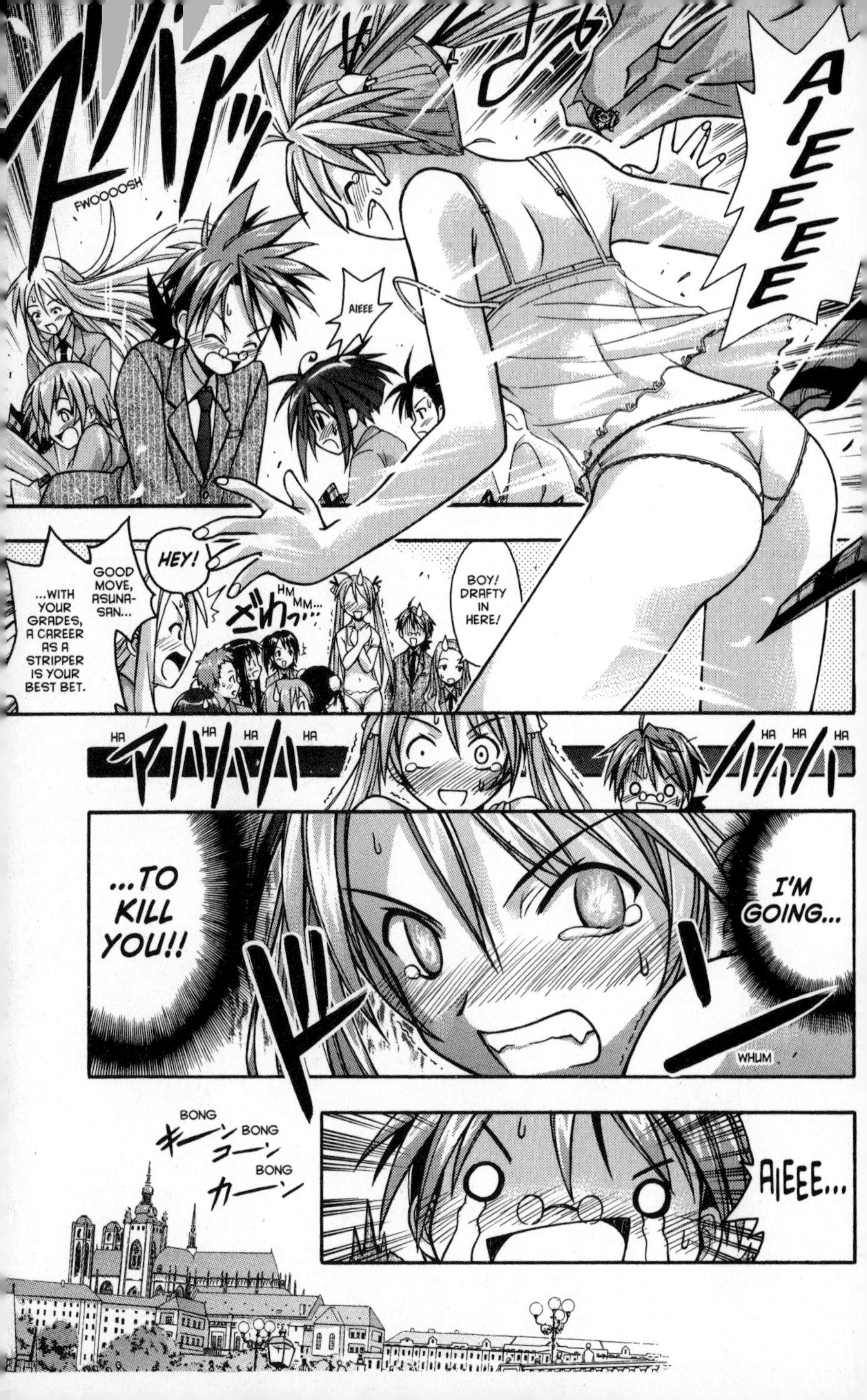
AIEEEEE
AIEEE
FWOOOOSH
BOY! DRAFTY IN HERE!
HM MM...
ざわっ
HEY!
GOOD MOVE, ASUNA-SAN...
...WITH YOUR GRADES, A CAREER AS A STRIPPER IS YOUR BEST BET.
HA HA HA
ハハハハ
アハハハハ
HA HA HA HA
I'M GOING...
...TO KILL YOU!!
ド
WHUM
AIEEE...
キーン BONG
コーン BONG
カーン BONG

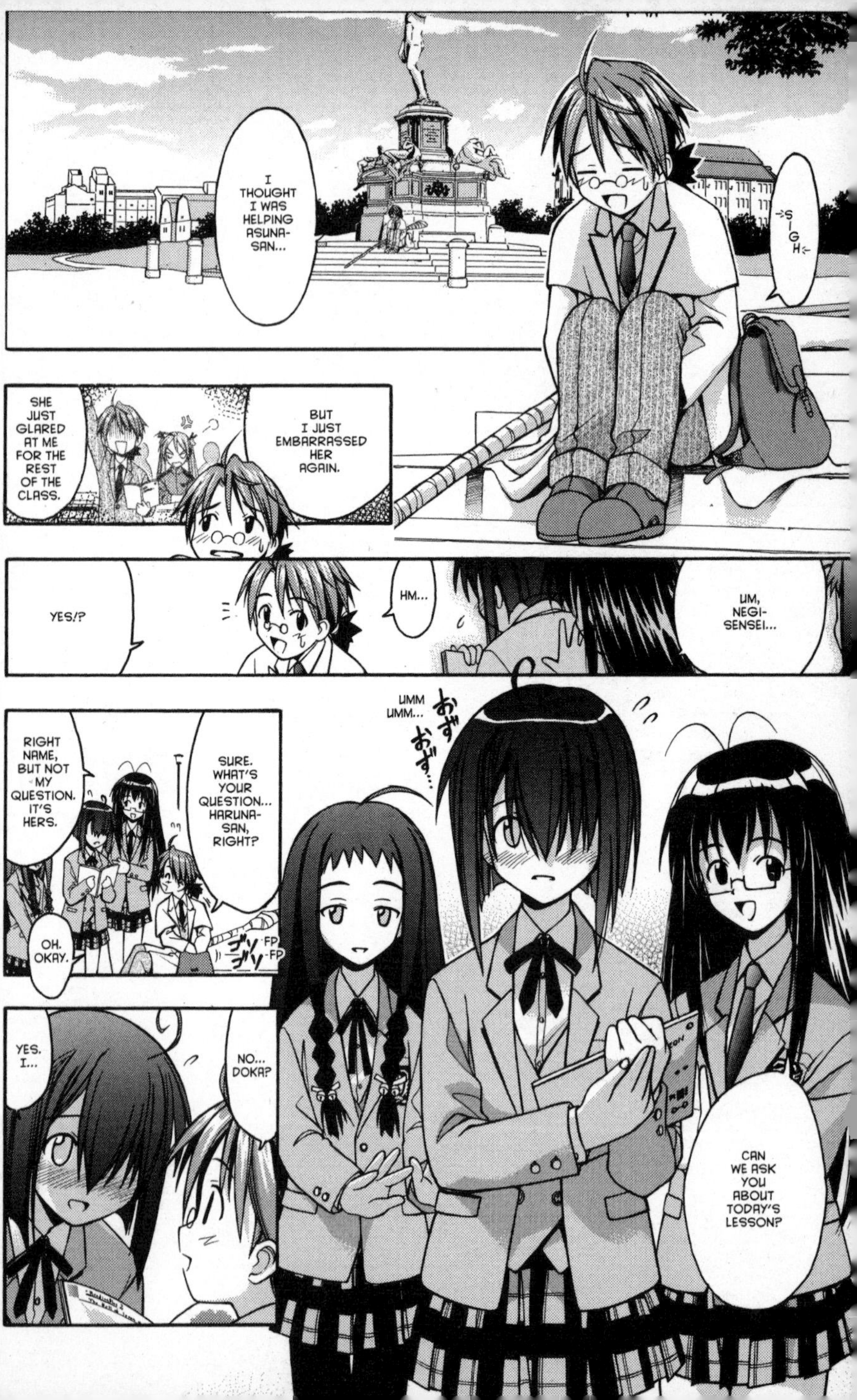
SIGH
I THOUGHT I WAS HELPING ASUNA-SAN...
BUT I JUST EMBARRASSED HER AGAIN.
SHE JUST GLARED AT ME FOR THE REST OF THE CLASS.
UM, NEGI-SENSEI...
HM...
YES!?
UMM UMM...
おずおず...
CAN WE ASK YOU ABOUT TODAY'S LESSON?
SURE. WHAT'S YOUR QUESTION... HARUNA-SAN, RIGHT?
RIGHT NAME, BUT NOT MY QUESTION. IT'S HERS.
FP FP
OH. OKAY.
NO... DOKA?
YES. I...

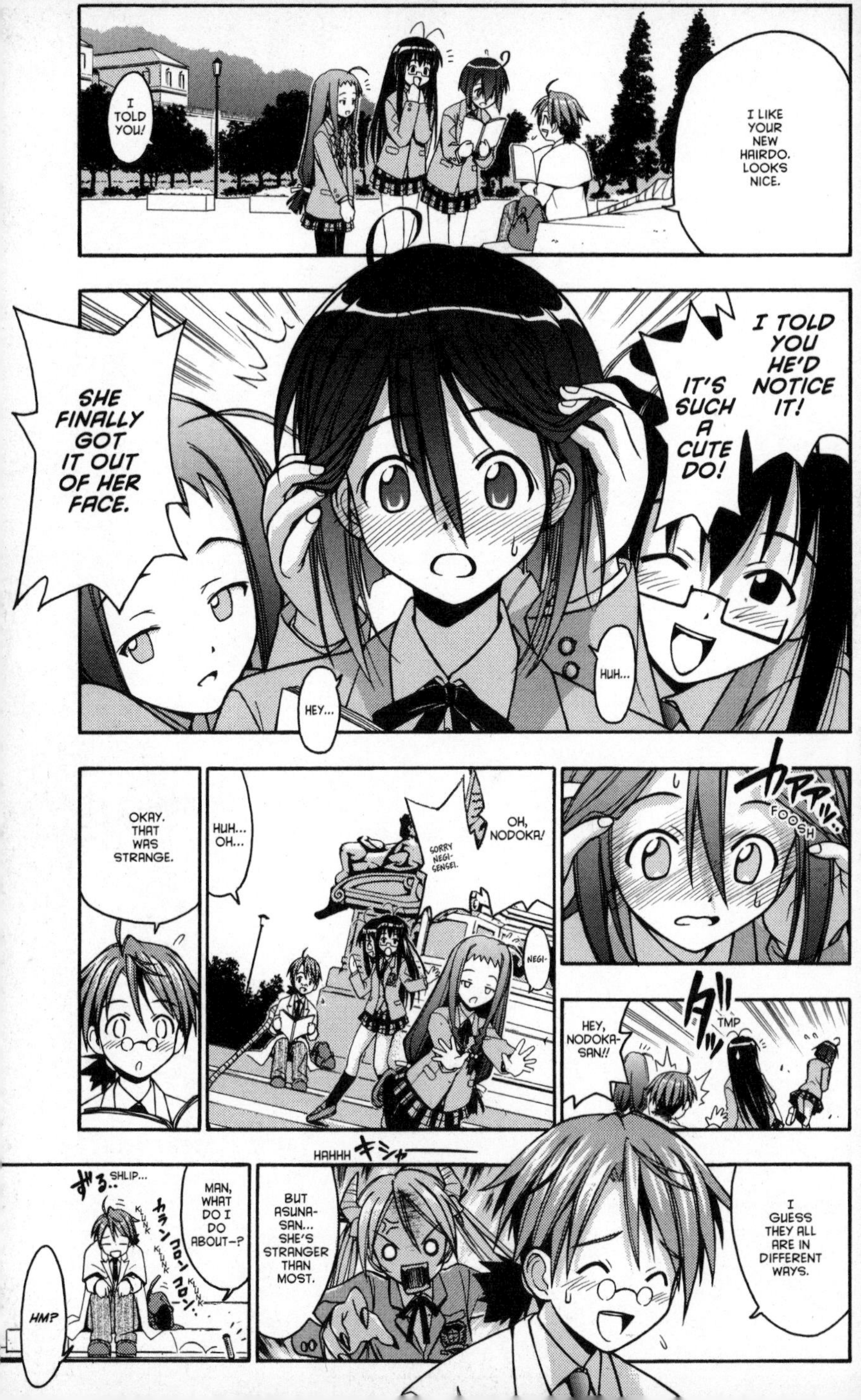
I LIKE YOUR NEW HAIRDO. LOOKS NICE.
I TOLD YOU!
I TOLD YOU HE'D NOTICE IT!
IT'S SUCH A CUTE DO!
SHE FINALLY GOT IT OUT OF HER FACE.
HUH...
HEY...
FOOSH
OH, NODOKA!
SORRY NEGI-SENSEI.
HUH... OH...
NEGI-
HEY, NODOKA-SAN!!
TMP
OKAY. THAT WAS STRANGE.
I GUESS THEY ALL ARE IN DIFFERENT WAYS.
BUT ASUNA-SAN... SHE'S STRANGER THAN MOST.
HAHHH
MAN, WHAT DO I DO ABOUT—?
SHLIP...
KLUNK
KLUNK
KLUNK
HM?

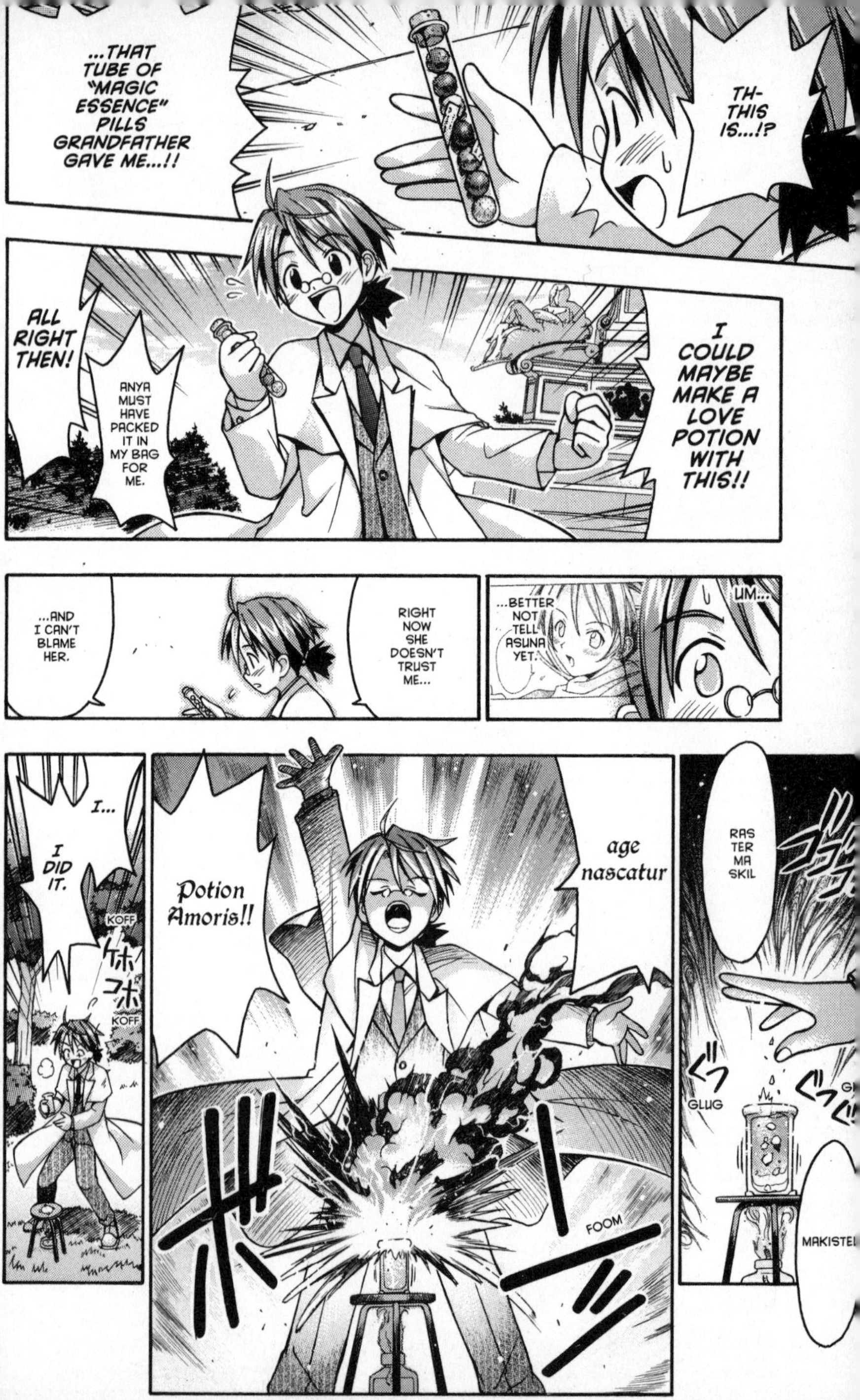
TH-THIS IS...!?
...THAT TUBE OF "MAGIC ESSENCE" PILLS GRANDFATHER GAVE ME...!!
I COULD MAYBE MAKE A LOVE POTION WITH THIS!!
ALL RIGHT THEN!
ANYA MUST HAVE PACKED IT IN MY BAG FOR ME.
UM...
...BETTER NOT TELL ASUNA YET.
RIGHT NOW SHE DOESN'T TRUST ME...
...AND I CAN'T BLAME HER.
RAS TER MA SKIL
MAKISTE
GLUG
age nascatur
Potion Amoris!!
FOOM
I...
I DID IT.
KOFF
KOFF

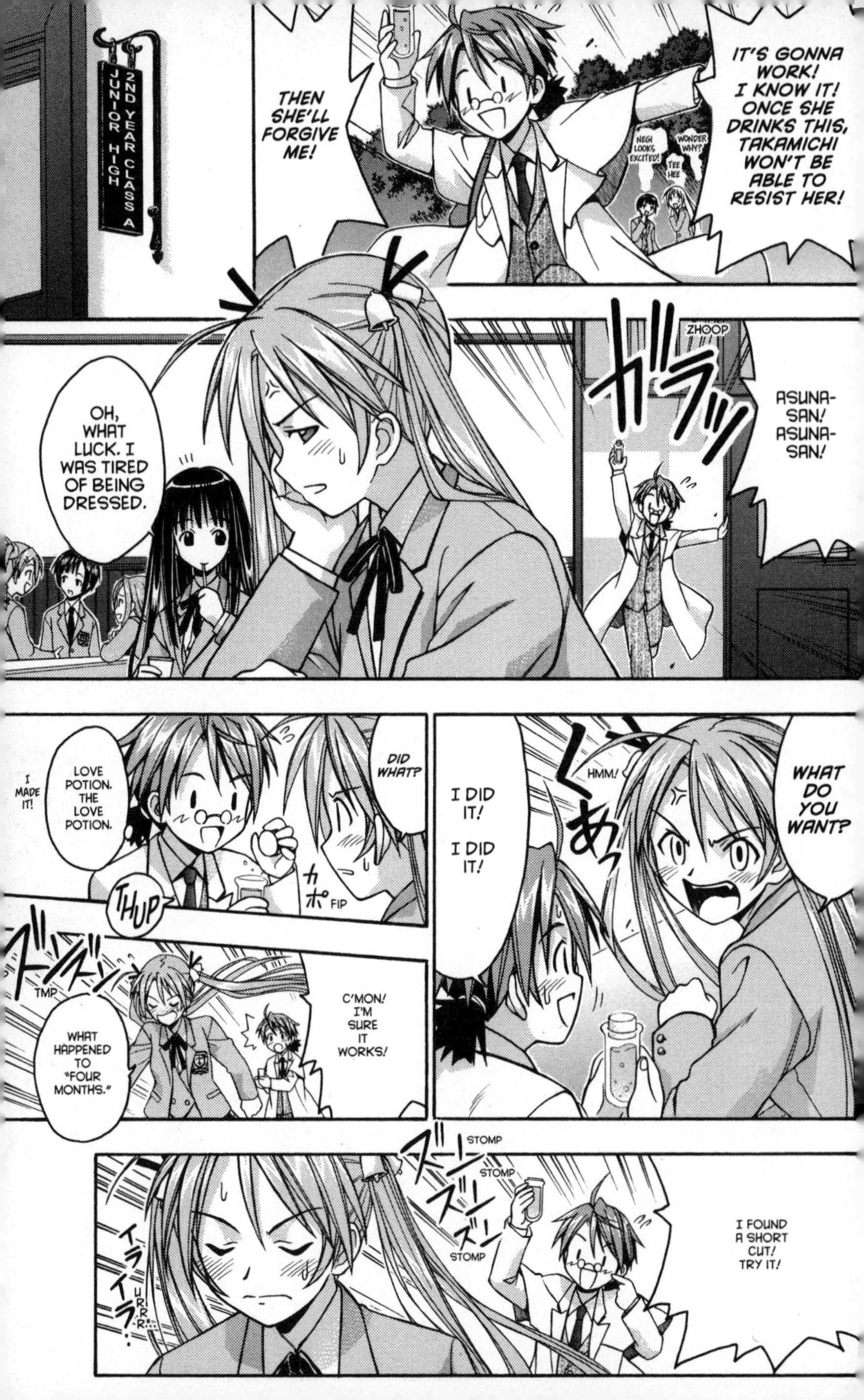
2ND YEAR CLASS A
JUNIOR HIGH
IT'S GONNA WORK! I KNOW IT! ONCE SHE DRINKS THIS, TAKAMICHI WON'T BE ABLE TO RESIST HER!
WONDER WHY?
NEGI LOOKS EXCITED!
TEE HEE
THEN SHE'LL FORGIVE ME!
ZHOOP
ASUNA-SAN! ASUNA-SAN!
OH, WHAT LUCK. I WAS TIRED OF BEING DRESSED.
WHAT DO YOU WANT?
HMM!
I DID IT!
I DID IT!
DID WHAT?
LOVE POTION. THE LOVE POTION.
I MADE IT!
FIP
THUP
C'MON! I'M SURE IT WORKS!
TMP
WHAT HAPPENED TO "FOUR MONTHS."
I FOUND A SHORT CUT! TRY IT!
STOMP
STOMP
STOMP
URRR...

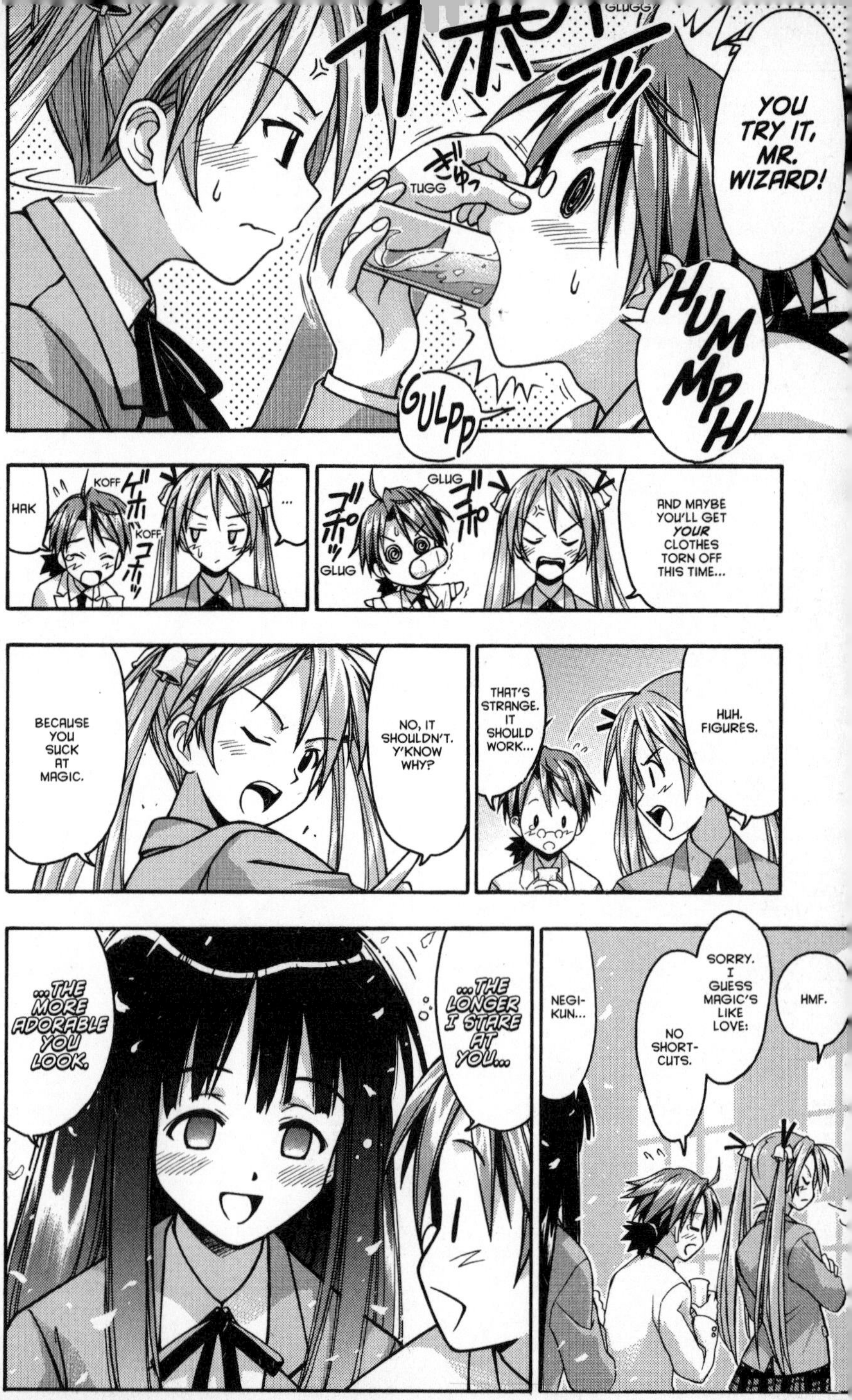
YOU TRY IT, MR. WIZARD!
GLUGG
ぎゅっ
TUGG
HUMMPH
GULPP
AND MAYBE YOU'LL GET *YOUR* CLOTHES TORN OFF THIS TIME...
GLUG
GLUG
...
KOFF
KOFF
HAK
HUH. FIGURES.
THAT'S STRANGE. IT SHOULD WORK...
NO, IT SHOULDN'T. Y'KNOW WHY?
BECAUSE YOU SUCK AT MAGIC.
HMF.
SORRY. I GUESS MAGIC'S LIKE LOVE:
NO SHORT-CUTS.
NEGI-KUN...
...THE LONGER I STARE AT YOU...
...THE MORE ADORABLE YOU LOOK.

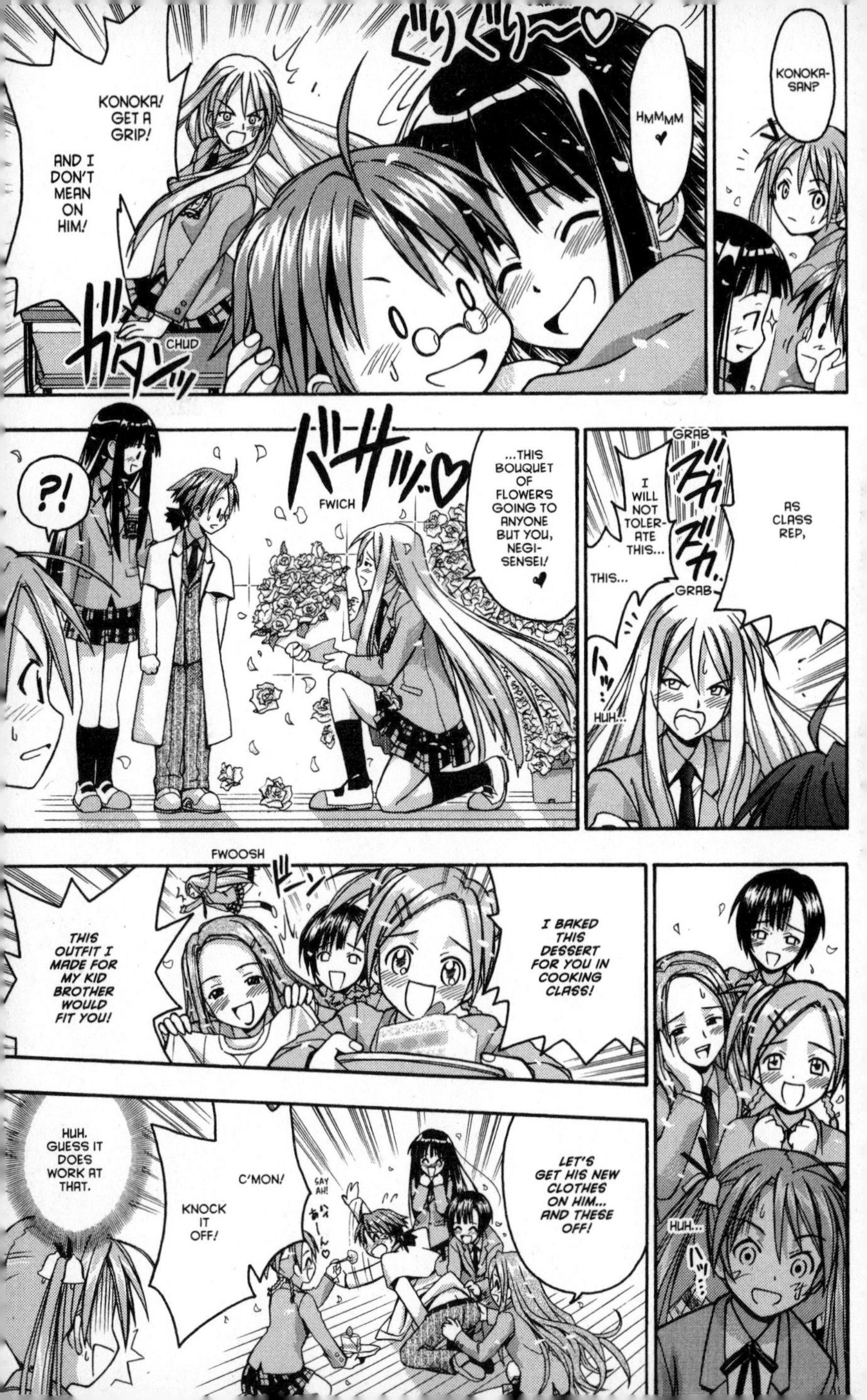
KONOKA-SAN?
HMMMM ♥
ぐりぐり〜♡
KONOKA! GET A GRIP!
AND I DON'T MEAN ON HIM!
CHUD
AS CLASS REP,
GRAB
I WILL NOT TOLERATE THIS...
THIS...
GRAB
HUH...
...THIS BOUQUET OF FLOWERS GOING TO ANYONE BUT YOU, NEGI-SENSEI! ♥
FWICH
?!
HUH...
I BAKED THIS DESSERT FOR YOU IN COOKING CLASS!
FWOOSH
THIS OUTFIT I MADE FOR MY KID BROTHER WOULD FIT YOU!
LET'S GET HIS NEW CLOTHES ON HIM... AND THESE OFF!
SAY AH!
KNOCK IT OFF!
C'MON!
HUH. GUESS IT DOES WORK AT THAT.

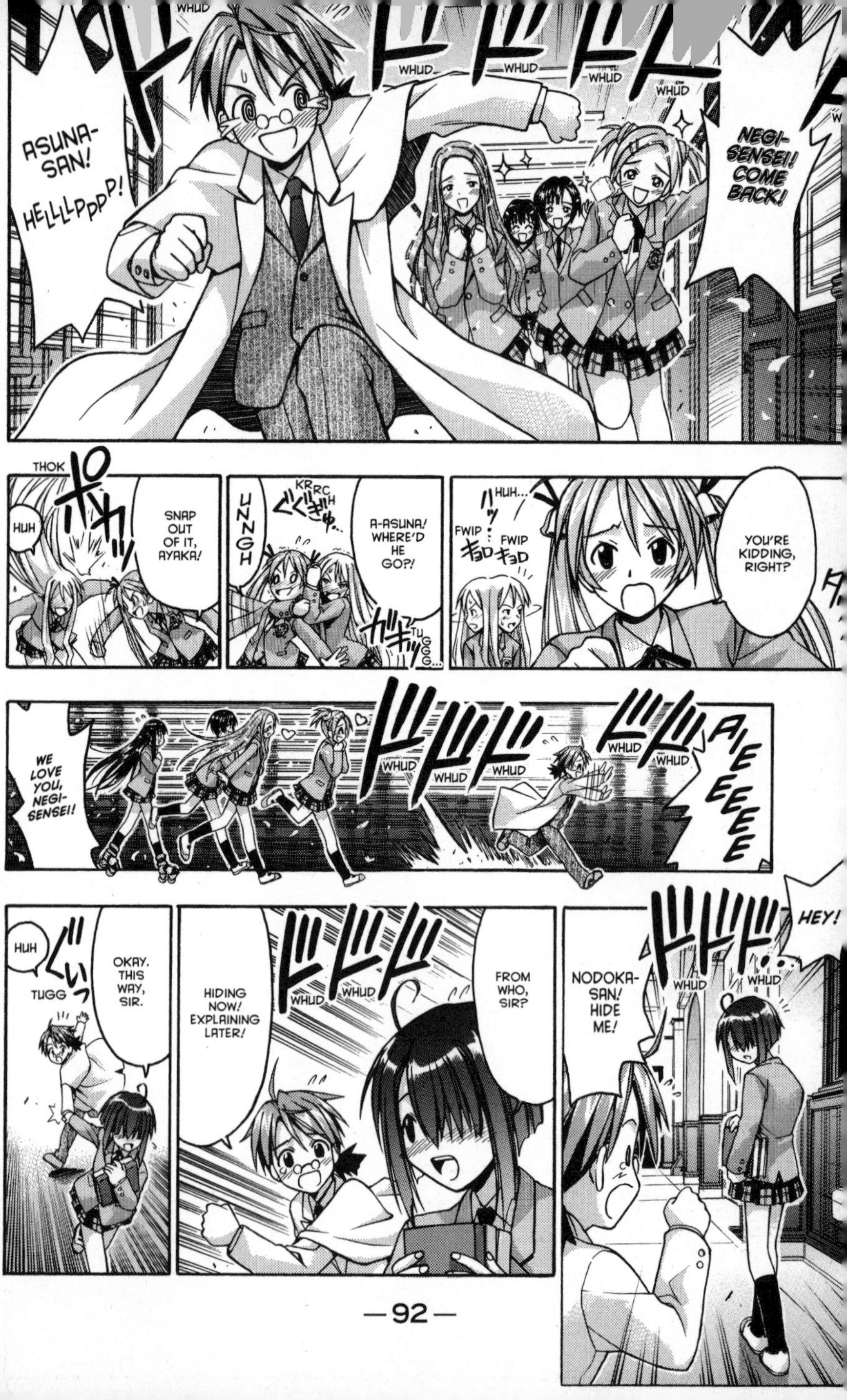
WHUD
WHUD
WHUD
WHUD
WHUD
NEGI-SENSEI! COME BACK!
ASUNA-SAN!
HELLLLPPPP!
YOU'RE KIDDING, RIGHT?
HUH...
FWIP
FWIP
A-ASUNA! WHERE'D HE GO?!
KRRCH
UNNGH
TUGGG...
SNAP OUT OF IT, AYAKA!
THOK
HUH
AIEEEEEE
WHUD
WHUD
WHUD
WHUD
WHUD
WE LOVE YOU, NEGI-SENSEI!
HEY!
WHUD
WHUD
NODOKA-SAN! HIDE ME!
FROM WHO, SIR?
WHUD
WHUD
HIDING NOW! EXPLAINING LATER!
OKAY. THIS WAY, SIR.
HUH
TUGG

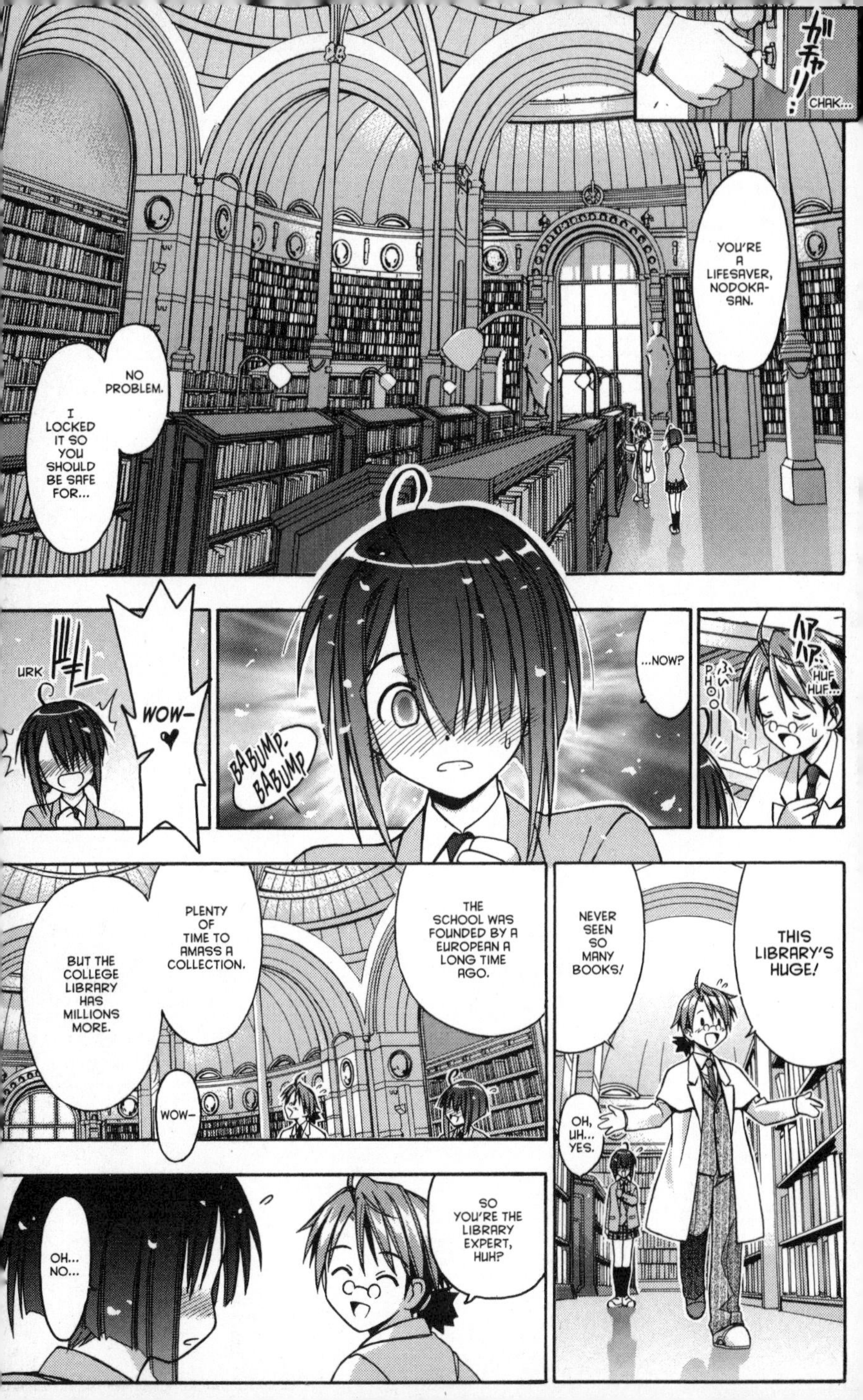
CHAK...
YOU'RE A LIFESAVER, NODOKA-SAN.
NO PROBLEM.
I LOCKED IT SO YOU SHOULD BE SAFE FOR...
...NOW?
HUF HUF...
BABUMP. BABUMP
WOW-♥
URK
THIS LIBRARY'S HUGE!
NEVER SEEN SO MANY BOOKS!
OH, UH... YES.
THE SCHOOL WAS FOUNDED BY A EUROPEAN A LONG TIME AGO.
PLENTY OF TIME TO AMASS A COLLECTION.
BUT THE COLLEGE LIBRARY HAS MILLIONS MORE.
WOW-
SO YOU'RE THE LIBRARY EXPERT, HUH?
OH... NO...

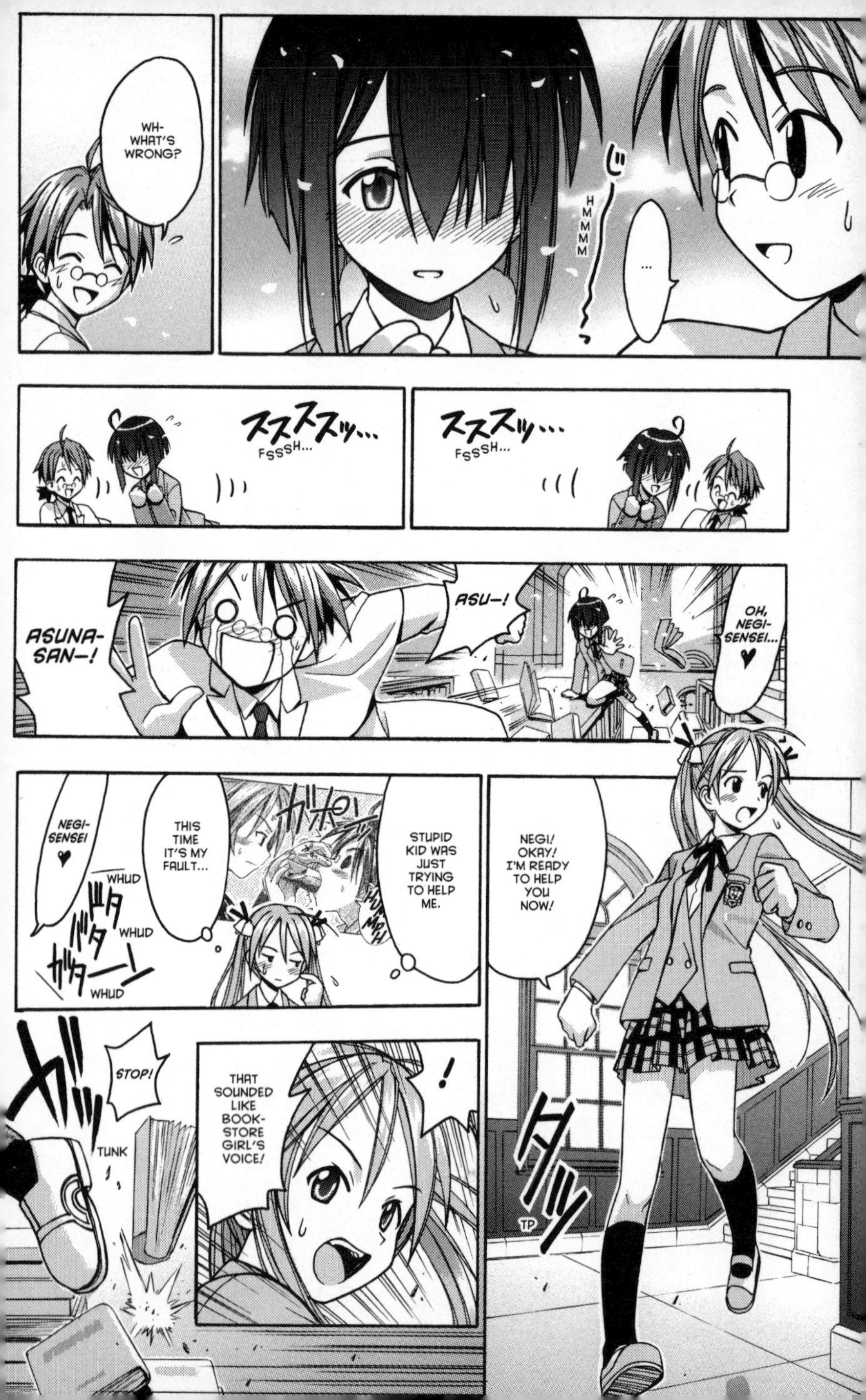

HMMMM
...
WH- WHAT'S WRONG?
スススッ...
FSSSH...
ススススッ...
FSSSH...
OH, NEGI-SENSEI... ♥
ASU-!
ASUNA-SAN-!
NEGI! OKAY! I'M READY TO HELP YOU NOW!
TP
STUPID KID WAS JUST TRYING TO HELP ME.
THIS TIME IT'S MY FAULT...
NEGI-SENSEI ♥
WHUD
WHUD
WHUD
!
THAT SOUNDED LIKE BOOK-STORE GIRL'S VOICE!
STOP!
TUNK

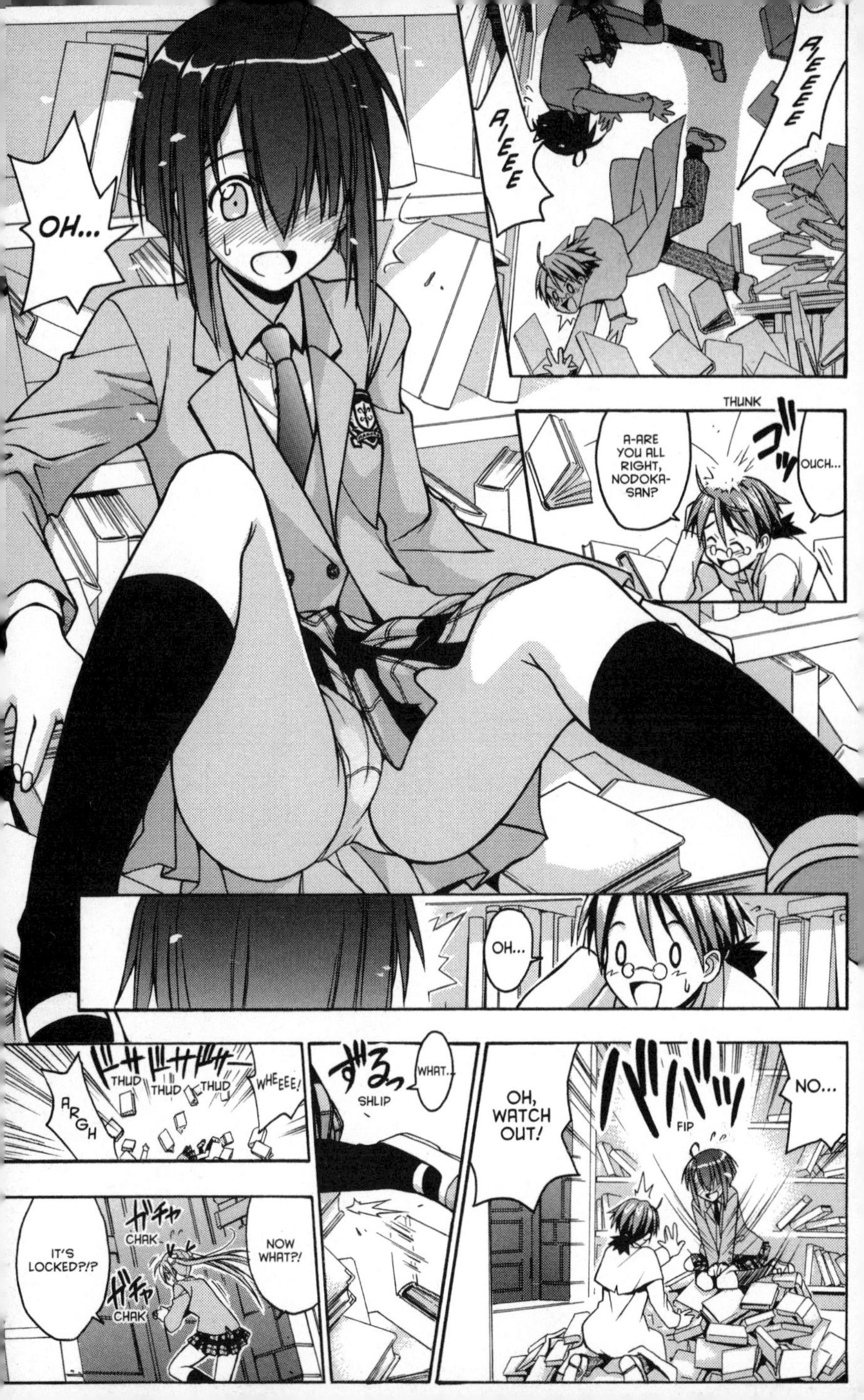
AEEEEE
AIEEE
THUNK
ゴッ
OUCH...
A-ARE YOU ALL RIGHT, NODOKA-SAN?
OH...
OH...
NO...
FIP
OH, WATCH OUT!
WHAT...
ずるっ
SHLIP
WHEEEE!
THUD THUD THUD
ARGH
NOW WHAT?!
ガチャ
CHAK
ガチャ
CHAK
IT'S LOCKED?!?

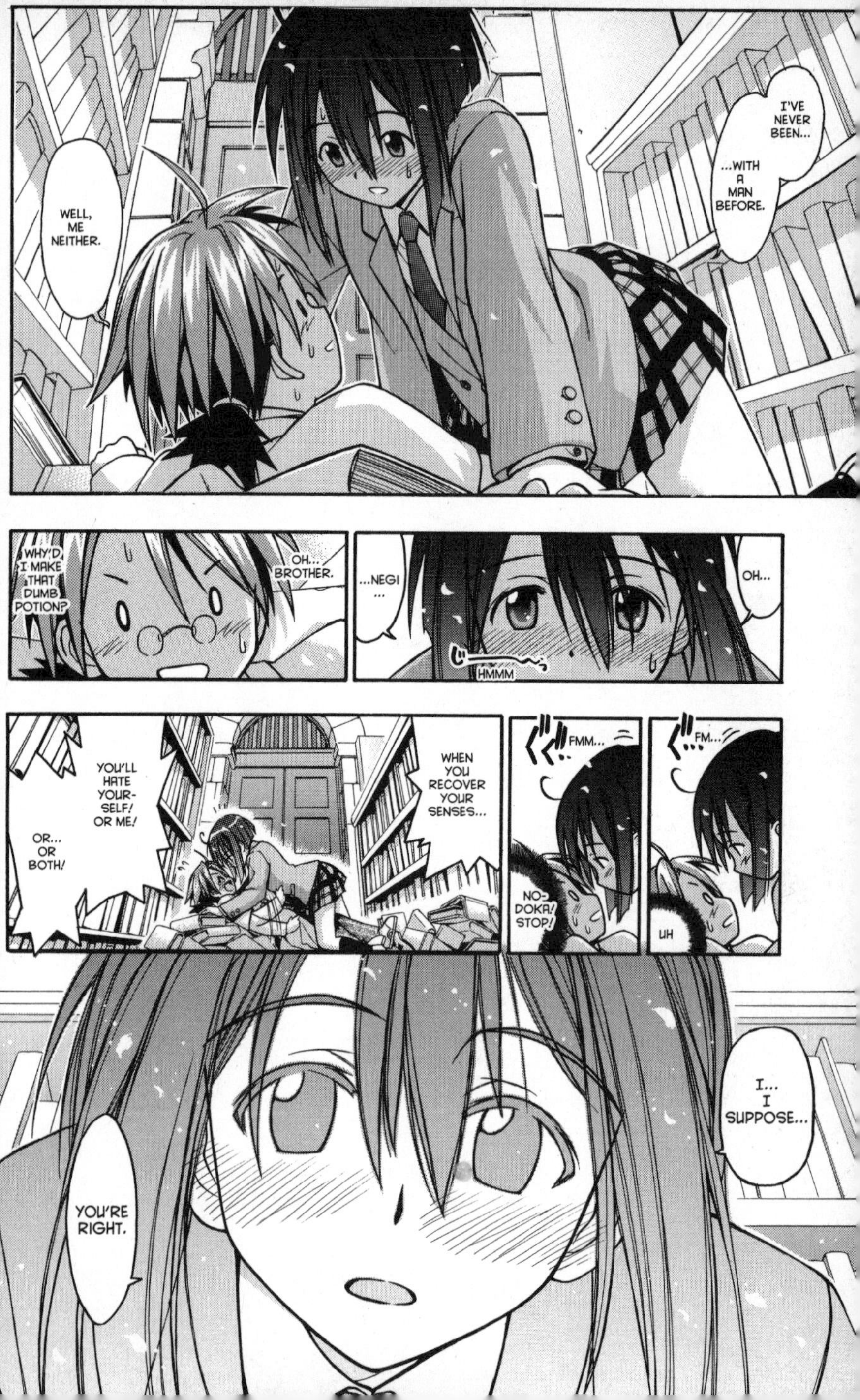
I'VE NEVER BEEN...
...WITH A MAN BEFORE.
WELL, ME NEITHER.
OH...
...NEGI ...
HMMM
OH... BROTHER.
WHY'D I MAKE THAT DUMB POTION?
FM...
UH
FMM...
NO-DOKA! STOP!
WHEN YOU RECOVER YOUR SENSES...
YOU'LL HATE YOUR-SELF! OR ME!
OR... OR BOTH!
I... I SUPPOSE...
YOU'RE RIGHT.

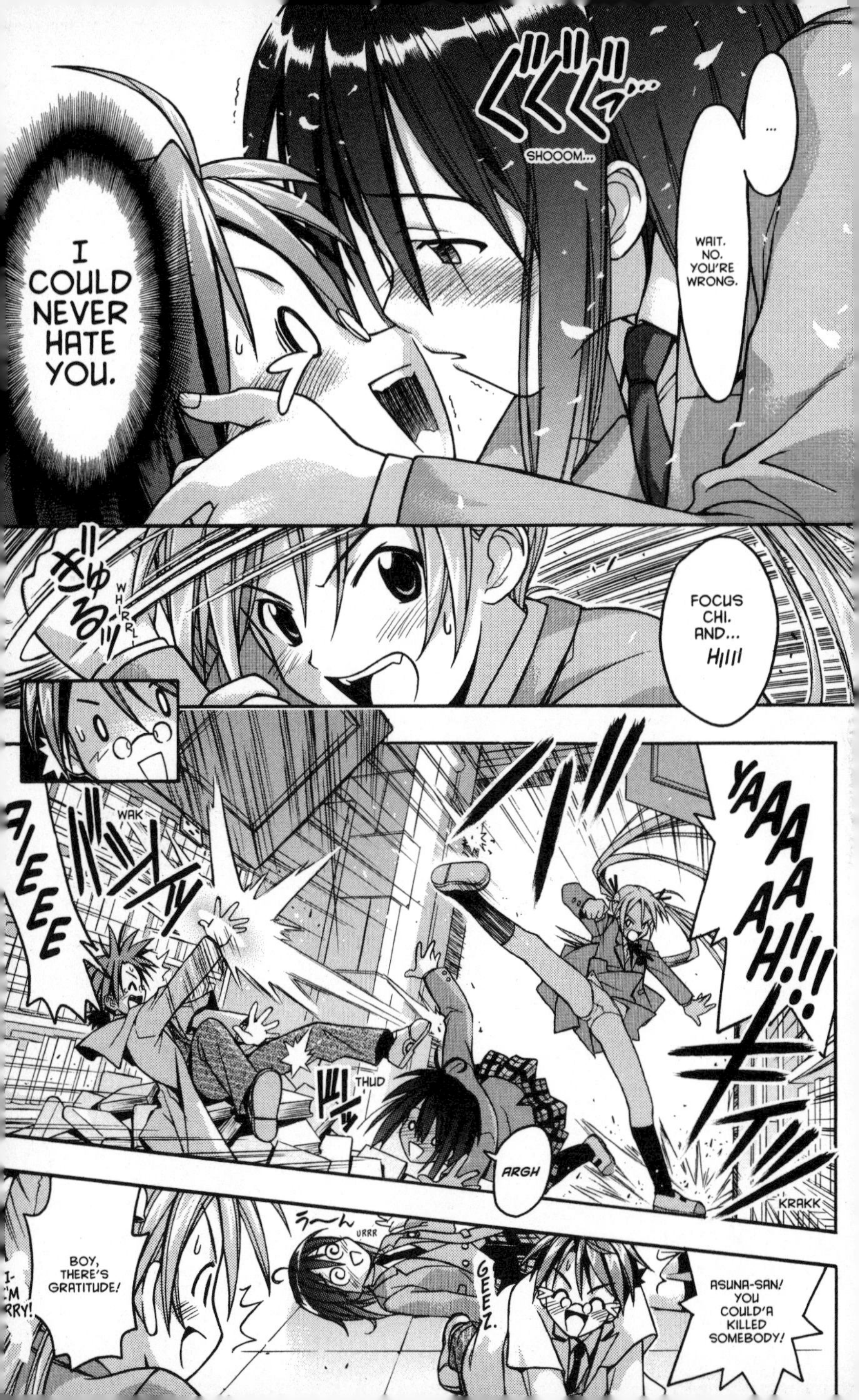

...
WAIT. NO. YOU'RE WRONG.
SHOOOM...
I COULD NEVER HATE YOU.
FOCUS CHI. AND... HIIII
WHIRRL
YAAAAAH!!!!
WAK
THUD
ARGH
KRAKK
ASUNA-SAN! YOU COULD'A KILLED SOMEBODY!
GEEZ.
URRR
BOY, THERE'S GRATITUDE!

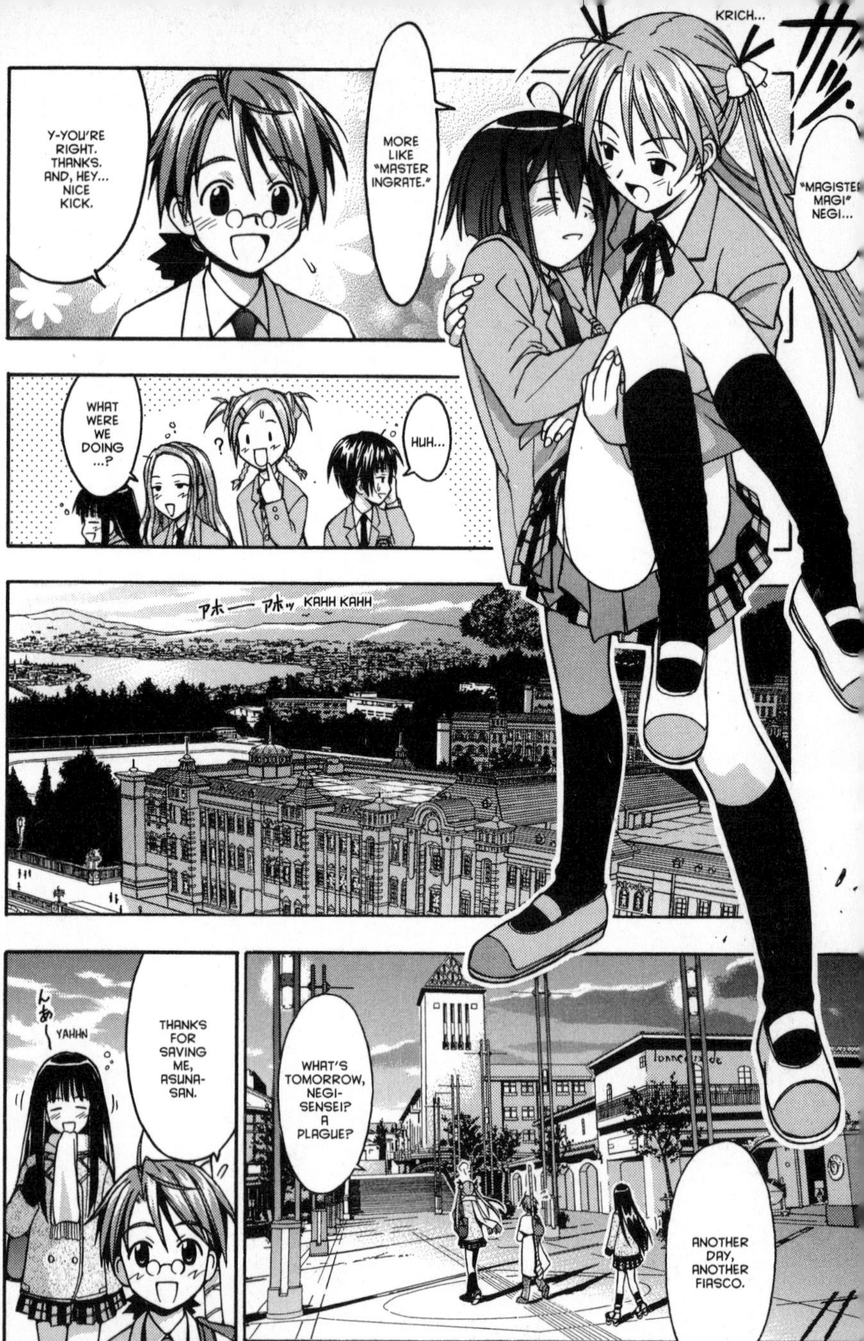
KRICH...
"MAGISTER MAGI" NEGI...
MORE LIKE "MASTER INGRATE."
Y-YOU'RE RIGHT. THANKS. AND, HEY... NICE KICK.
HUH...
WHAT WERE WE DOING ...?
アホー アホッ KAHH KAHH
ANOTHER DAY, ANOTHER FIASCO.
WHAT'S TOMORROW, NEGI-SENSEI? A PLAGUE?
THANKS FOR SAVING ME, ASUNA-SAN.
んあ～ YAHHN

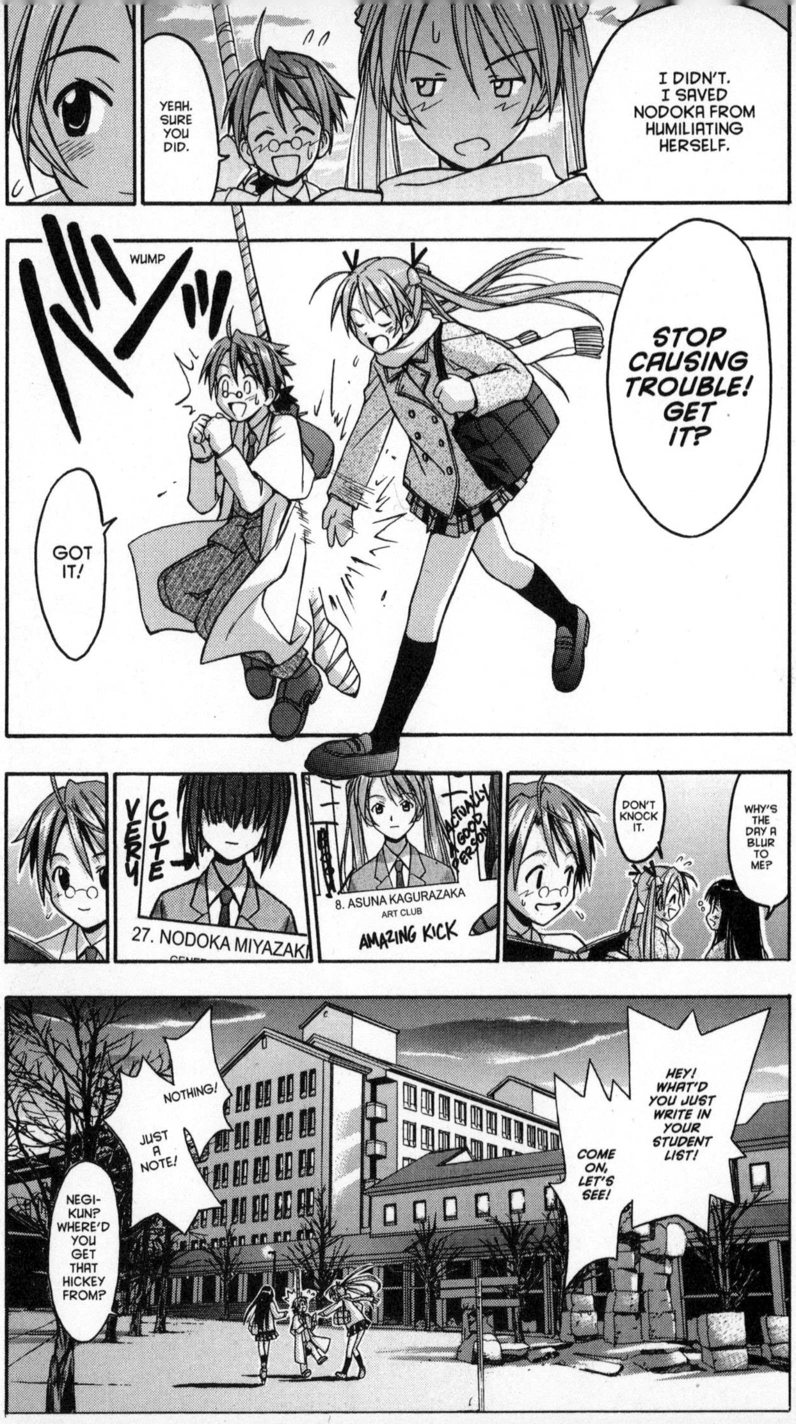
I DIDN'T. I SAVED NODOKA FROM HUMILIATING HERSELF.
YEAH. SURE YOU DID.
STOP CAUSING TROUBLE! GET IT?
WUMP
GOT IT!
WHY'S THE DAY A BLUR TO ME?
DON'T KNOCK IT.
ACTUALLY A GOOD PERSON
8. ASUNA KAGURAZAKA
ART CLUB
AMAZING KICK
VERY CUTE
27. NODOKA MIYAZAKI
HEY! WHAT'D YOU JUST WRITE IN YOUR STUDENT LIST!
COME ON, LET'S SEE!
NOTHING!
JUST A NOTE!
NEGI-KUN? WHERE'D YOU GET THAT HICKEY FROM?

2-A STUDENT PROFILE

STUDENT NUMBER 8
ASUNA KAGURAZAKA (LEFT)

BIRTHDATE: APRIL 21, 1988
BLOODTYPE: B
FAVORITE THINGS: TAKAHATA-SENSEI, COOL MEN
DISLIKES: KIDS, STUDYING
CLUB ACTIVITIES: ART CLUB

STUDENT NUMBER 13
KONOKA KONOE (RIGHT)
BIRTHDATE: MARCH 18, 1989
BLOODTYPE: AB
FAVORITE THINGS: FORTUNE-TELLING,
                    THE SUPERNATURAL, COOKING
DISLIKES: ALMOST NONE
CLUB ACTIVITIES: FORTUNE-TELLING CLUB,
                    LIBRARY EXPLORATION CLUB
REMARKS: SCHOOL DEAN'S GRANDDAUGHTER

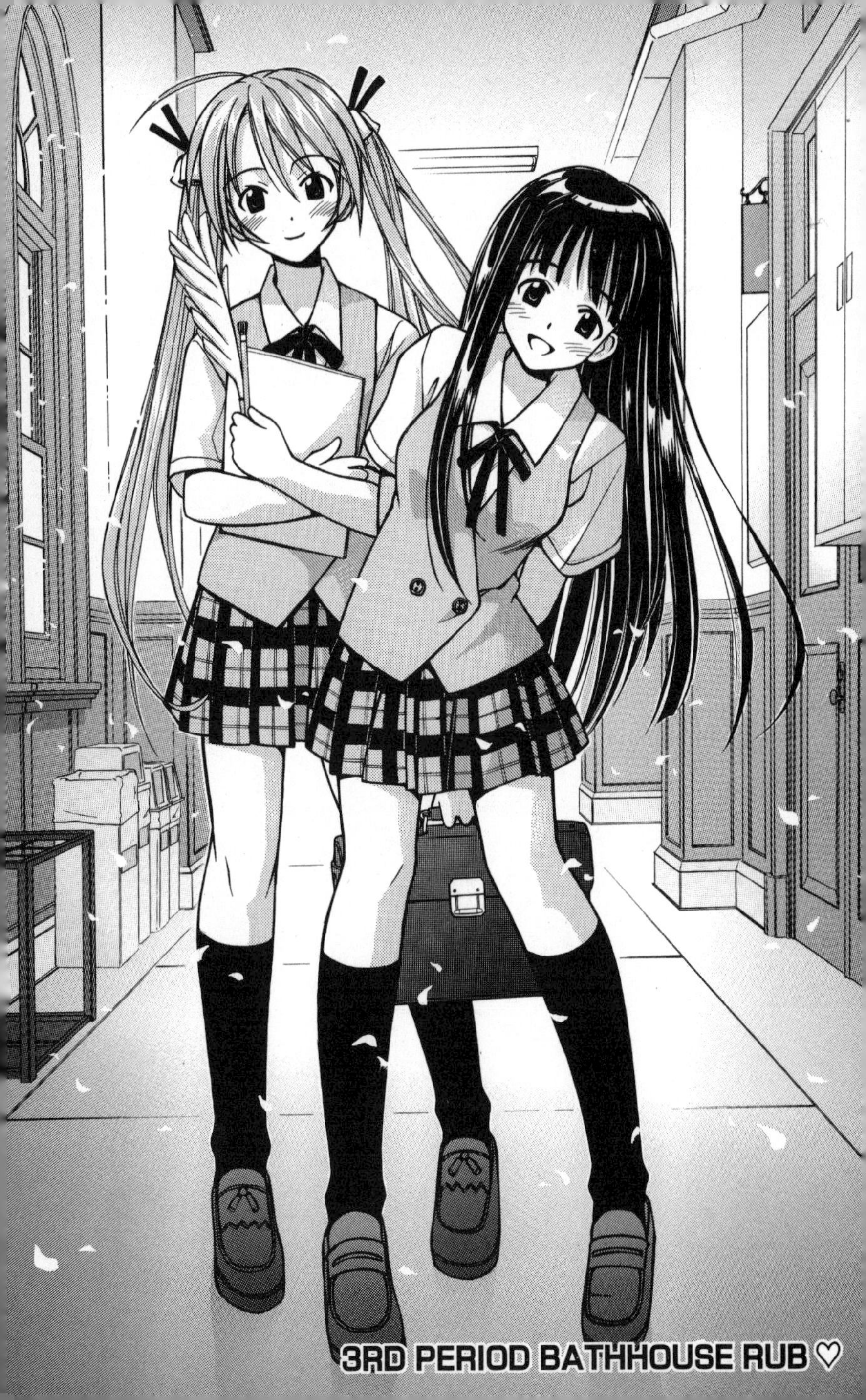
3RD PERIOD BATHHOUSE RUB ♡

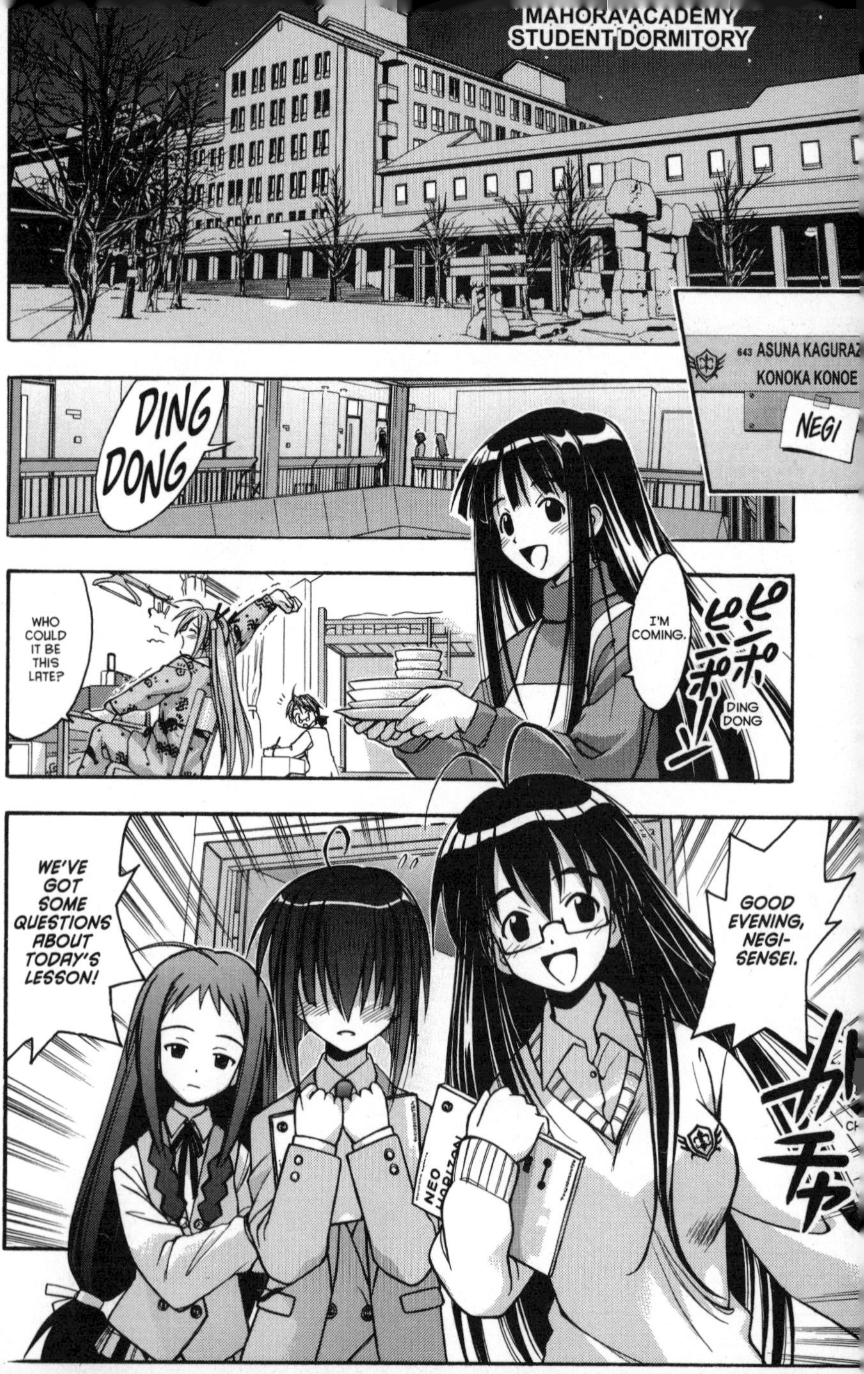
MAHORA ACADEMY
STUDENT DORMITORY
643 ASUNA KAGURAZ
KONOKA KONOE
NEGI
DING DONG
I'M COMING.
DING DONG
WHO COULD IT BE THIS LATE?
GOOD EVENING, NEGI-SENSEI.
WE'VE GOT SOME QUESTIONS ABOUT TODAY'S LESSON!
NEO HORIZON

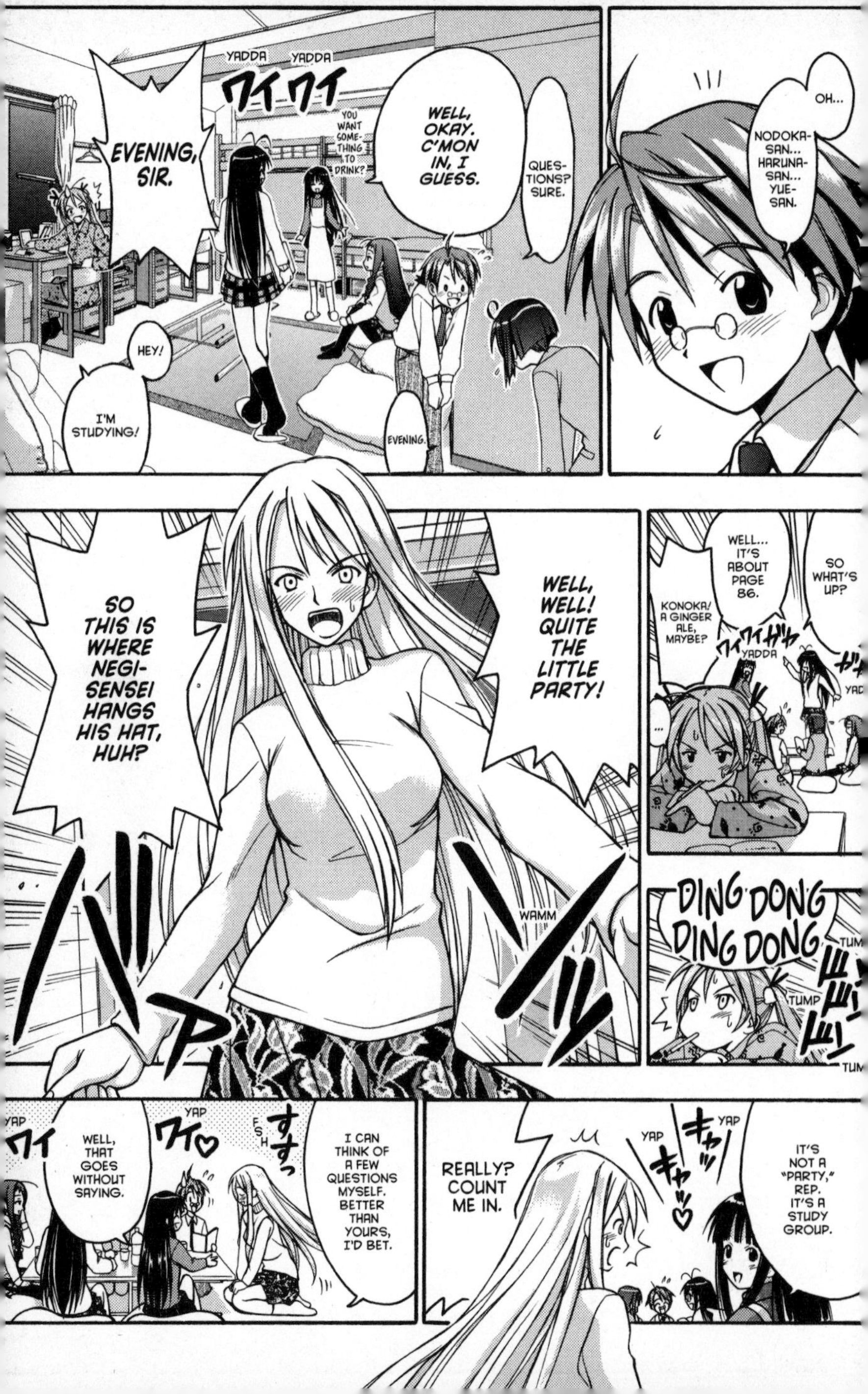
OH...
NODOKA-SAN... HARUNA-SAN... YUE-SAN.
QUESTIONS? SURE.
WELL, OKAY. C'MON IN, I GUESS.
YOU WANT SOME-THING TO DRINK?
YADDA YADDA
ワイワイ
EVENING, SIR.
HEY!
I'M STUDYING!
EVENING.
SO WHAT'S UP?
WELL... IT'S ABOUT PAGE 86.
KONOKA! A GINGER ALE, MAYBE?
YADDA
...
DING DONG DING DONG
TUMP
TUMP
WELL, WELL! QUITE THE LITTLE PARTY!
SO THIS IS WHERE NEGI-SENSEI HANGS HIS HAT, HUH?
WAMM
IT'S NOT A "PARTY," REP. IT'S A STUDY GROUP.
YAP
YAP
REALLY? COUNT ME IN.
I CAN THINK OF A FEW QUESTIONS MYSELF. BETTER THAN YOURS, I'D BET.
FSH
WELL, THAT GOES WITHOUT SAYING.
YAP
YAP

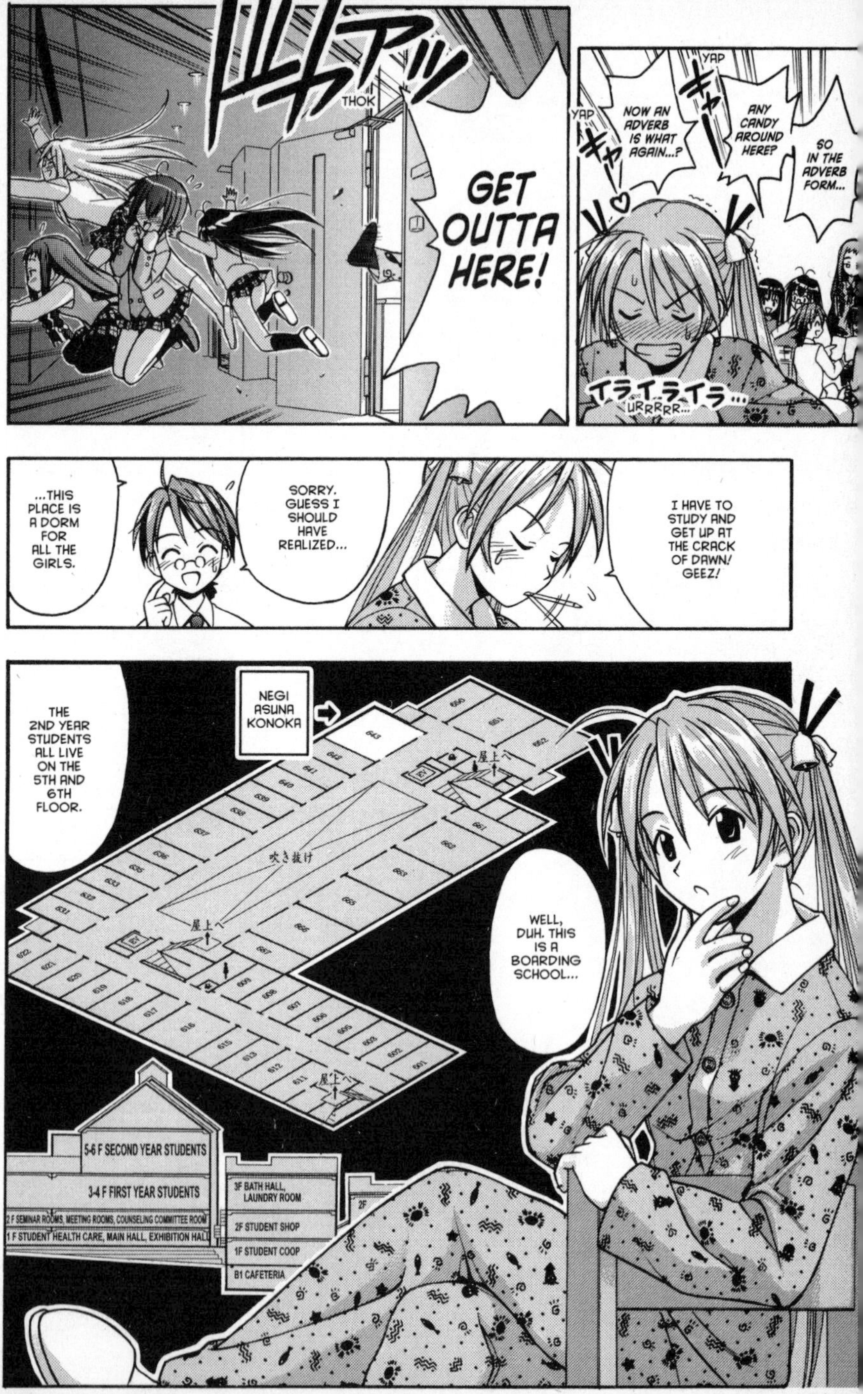
SO IN THE ADVERB FORM...
ANY CANDY AROUND HERE?
YAP
NOW AN ADVERB IS WHAT AGAIN...?
YAP
URRRRR...
THOK
GET OUTTA HERE!
I HAVE TO STUDY AND GET UP AT THE CRACK OF DAWN! GEEZ!
SORRY. GUESS I SHOULD HAVE REALIZED...
...THIS PLACE IS A DORM FOR ALL THE GIRLS.
WELL, DUH. THIS IS A BOARDING SCHOOL...
THE 2ND YEAR STUDENTS ALL LIVE ON THE 5TH AND 6TH FLOOR.
NEGI
ASUNA
KONOKA
5-6 F SECOND YEAR STUDENTS
3-4 F FIRST YEAR STUDENTS
2 F SEMINAR ROOMS, MEETING ROOMS, COUNSELING COMMITTEE ROOM
1 F STUDENT HEALTH CARE, MAIN HALL, EXHIBITION HALL
3F BATH HALL, LAUNDRY ROOM
2F STUDENT SHOP
1F STUDENT COOP
B1 CAFETERIA

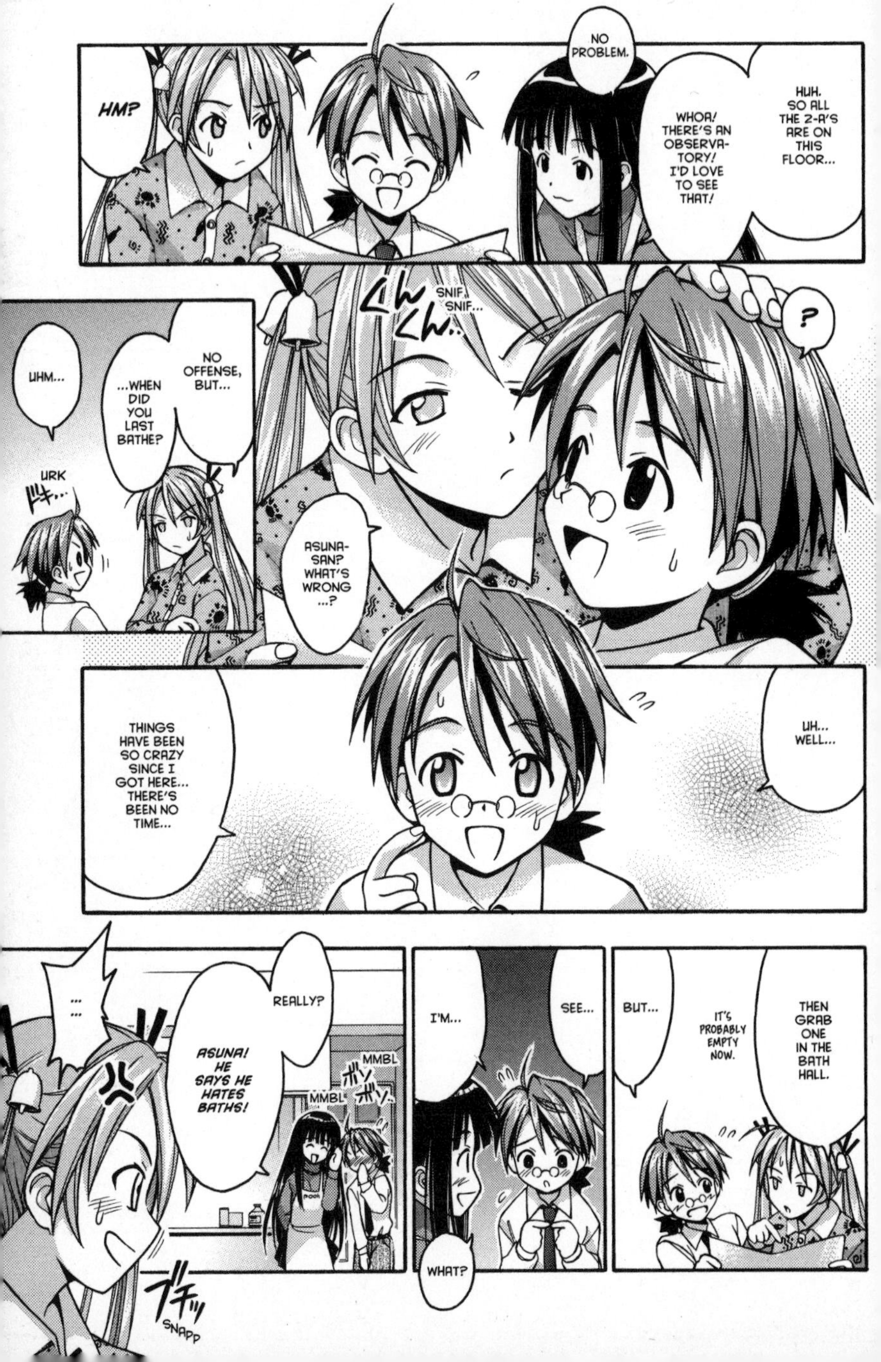
HUH. SO ALL THE 2-A'S ARE ON THIS FLOOR...
WHOA! THERE'S AN OBSERVA-TORY! I'D LOVE TO SEE THAT!
NO PROBLEM.
HM?
?
くんくん
SNIF, SNIF...
ASUNA-SAN? WHAT'S WRONG ...?
NO OFFENSE, BUT...
...WHEN DID YOU LAST BATHE?
UHM...
ドキ...
URK
UH... WELL...
THINGS HAVE BEEN SO CRAZY SINCE I GOT HERE... THERE'S BEEN NO TIME...
THEN GRAB ONE IN THE BATH HALL.
IT'S PROBABLY EMPTY NOW.
BUT...
SEE...
I'M...
WHAT?
REALLY?
ASUNA! HE SAYS HE HATES BATHS!
ボソ ボソ
MMBL MMBL
......
ブチッ
SNAPP

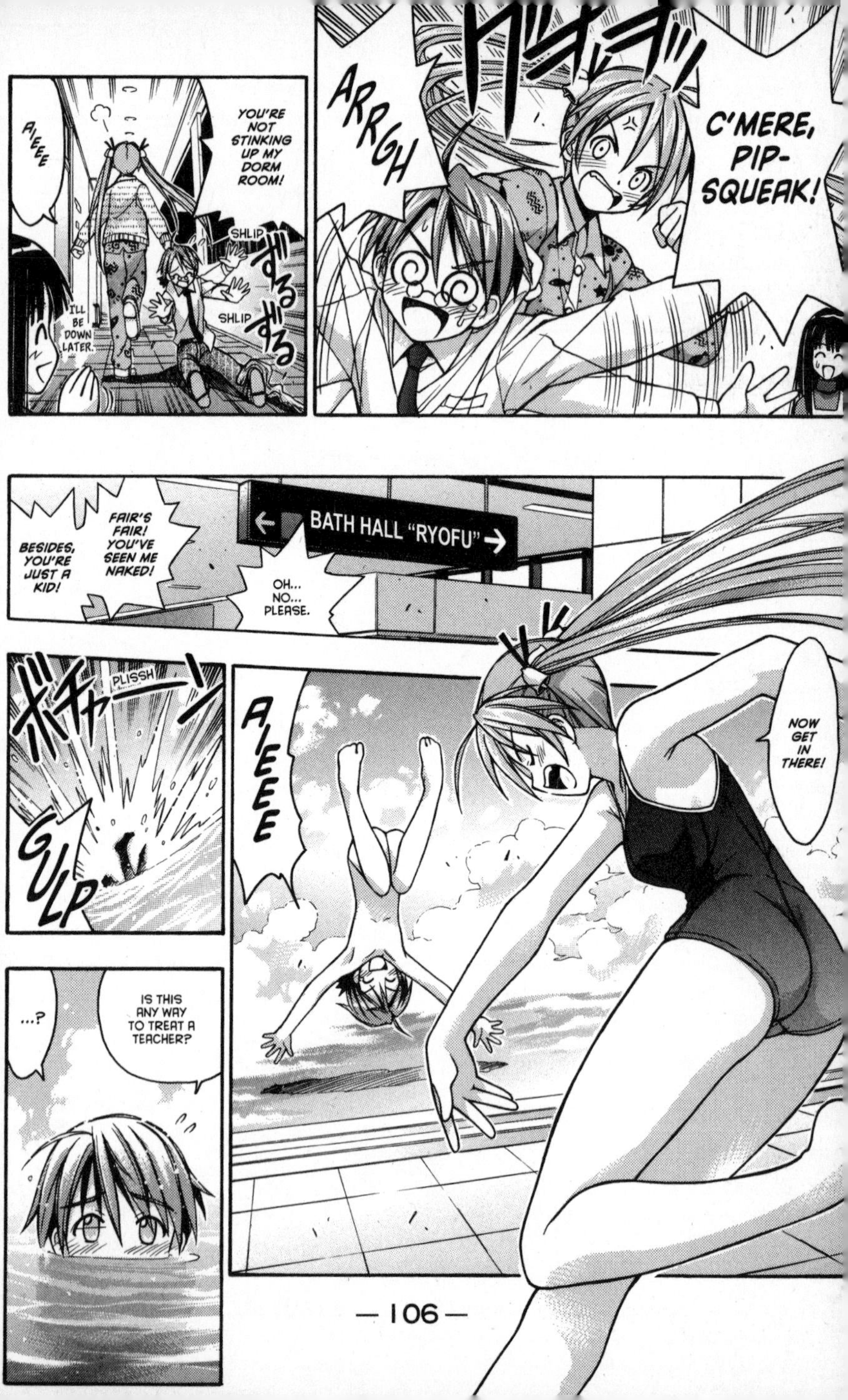
ARRGH
C'MERE, PIP-SQUEAK!
YOU'RE NOT STINKING UP MY DORM ROOM!
AIEEE
SHLIP
ずる
SHLIP
ずる
I'LL BE DOWN LATER.
BATH HALL "RYOFU"
FAIR'S FAIR! YOU'VE SEEN ME NAKED!
BESIDES, YOU'RE JUST A KID!
OH... NO... PLEASE.
NOW GET IN THERE!
AIEEE
PLISSH
GULP
IS THIS ANY WAY TO TREAT A TEACHER?
...?

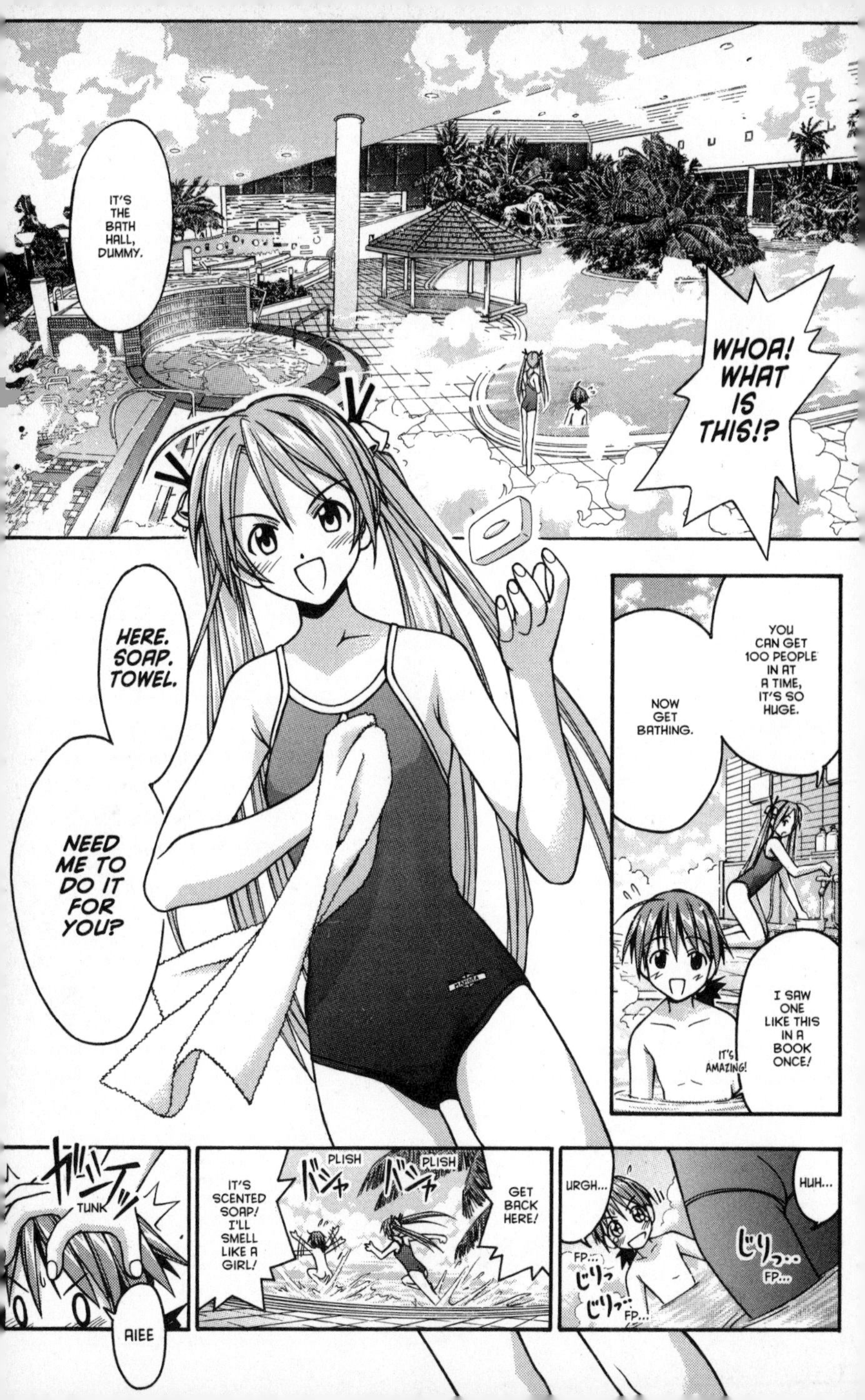

WHOA! WHAT IS THIS!?
IT'S THE BATH HALL, DUMMY.
YOU CAN GET 100 PEOPLE IN AT A TIME, IT'S SO HUGE.
NOW GET BATHING.
I SAW ONE LIKE THIS IN A BOOK ONCE!
IT'S AMAZING!
HERE. SOAP. TOWEL.
NEED ME TO DO IT FOR YOU?
HUH...
URGH...
FP...
FP...
FP...
GET BACK HERE!
PLISH
PLISH
IT'S SCENTED SOAP! I'LL SMELL LIKE A GIRL!
TUNK
AIEE

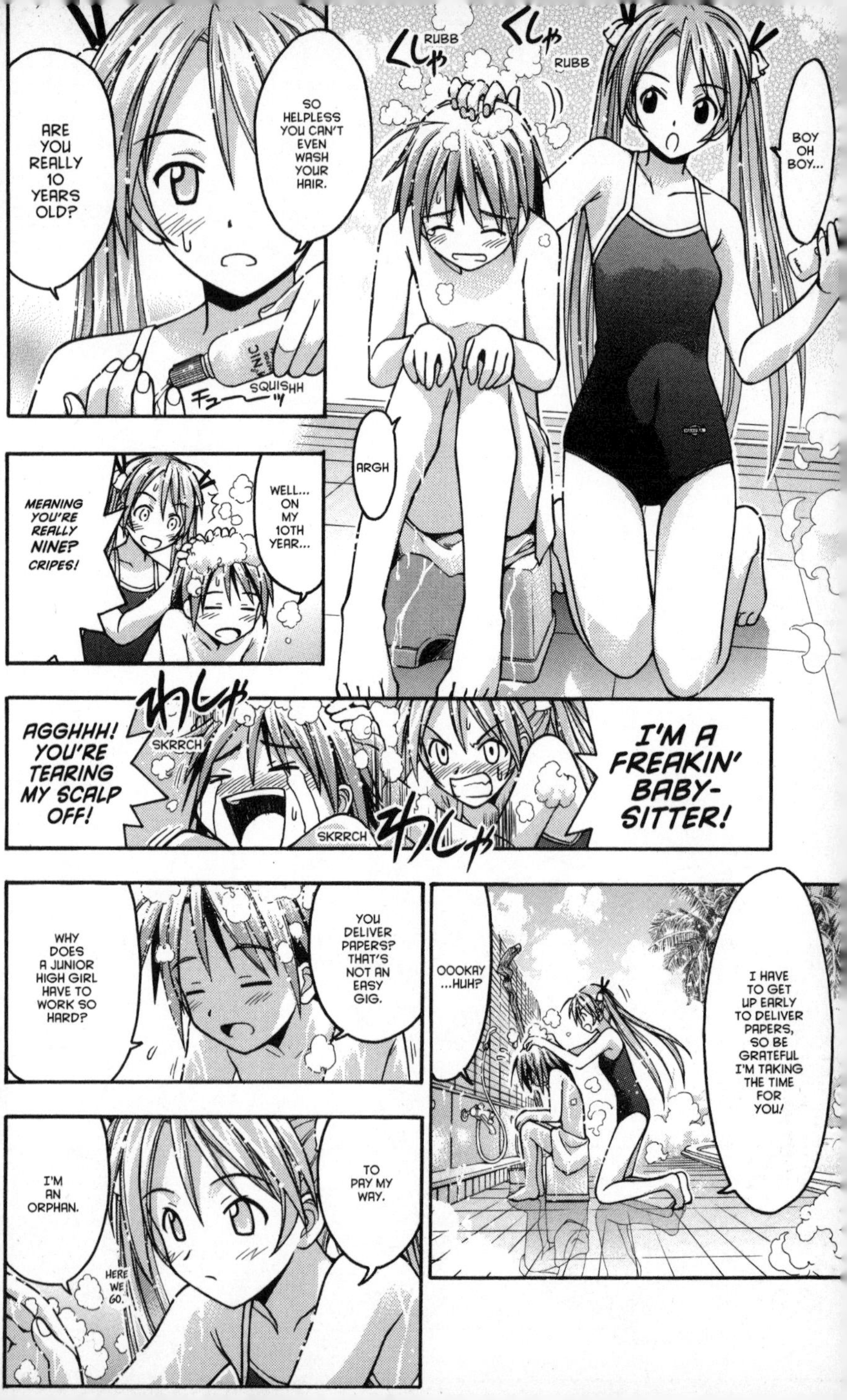

くしゃ
RUBB
くしゃ
RUBB
BOY OH BOY...
SO HELPLESS YOU CAN'T EVEN WASH YOUR HAIR.
ARE YOU REALLY 10 YEARS OLD?
チュ〜〜ッ
SQUISHH
ARGH
WELL... ON MY 10TH YEAR...
MEANING YOU'RE REALLY NINE? CRIPES!
I'M A FREAKIN' BABY-SITTER!
わしゃ
SKRRCH
わしゃ
SKRRCH
AGGHHH! YOU'RE TEARING MY SCALP OFF!
I HAVE TO GET UP EARLY TO DELIVER PAPERS, SO BE GRATEFUL I'M TAKING THE TIME FOR YOU!
OOOKAY ...HUH?
YOU DELIVER PAPERS? THAT'S NOT AN EASY GIG.
WHY DOES A JUNIOR HIGH GIRL HAVE TO WORK SO HARD?
TO PAY MY WAY.
I'M AN ORPHAN.
HERE WE GO.

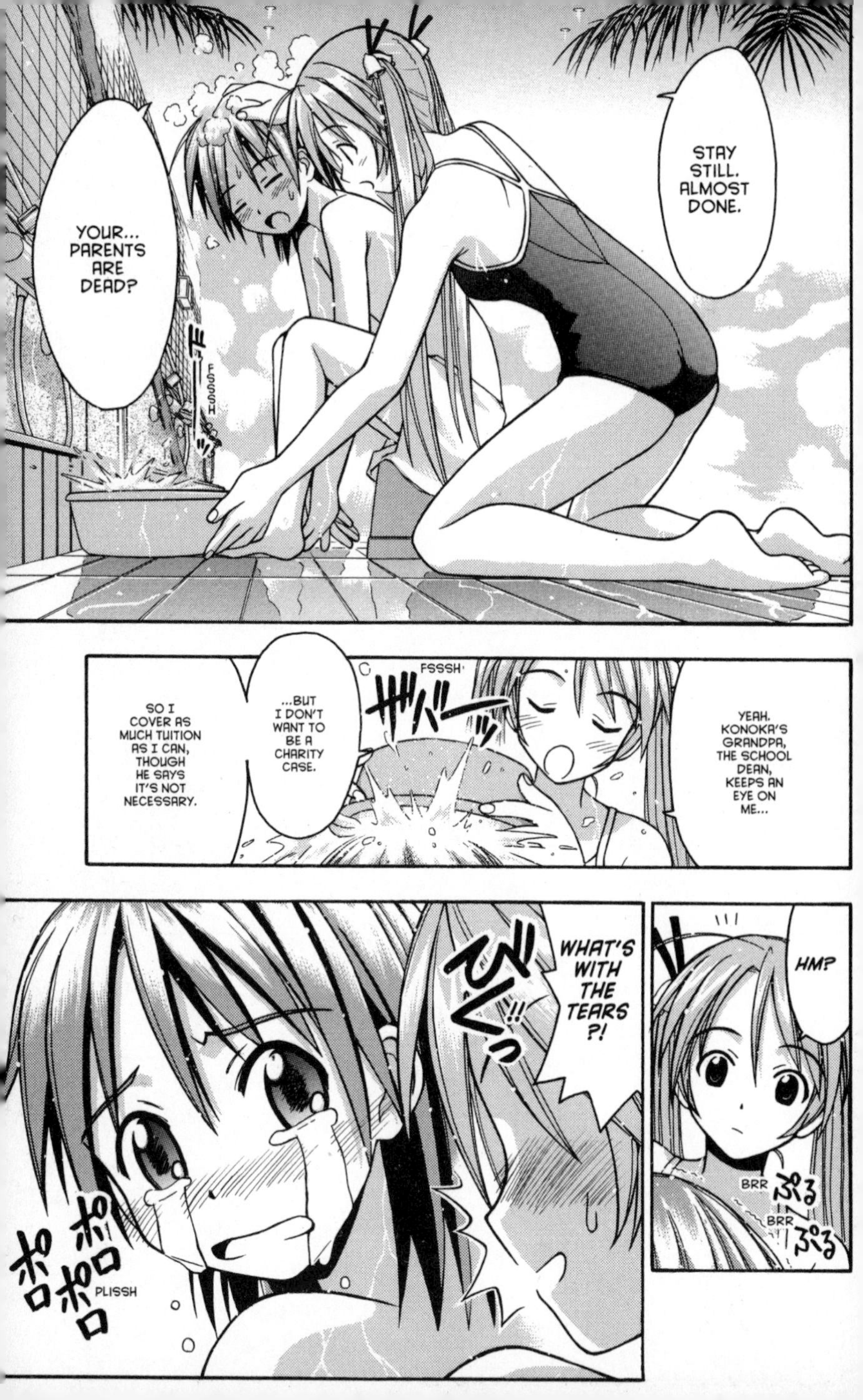
STAY STILL. ALMOST DONE.
YOUR... PARENTS ARE DEAD?
FSSSH
YEAH. KONOKA'S GRANDPA, THE SCHOOL DEAN, KEEPS AN EYE ON ME...
...BUT I DON'T WANT TO BE A CHARITY CASE.
SO I COVER AS MUCH TUITION AS I CAN, THOUGH HE SAYS IT'S NOT NECESSARY.
FSSSH
HM?
BRR
BRR
WHAT'S WITH THE TEARS?!
PLISSH

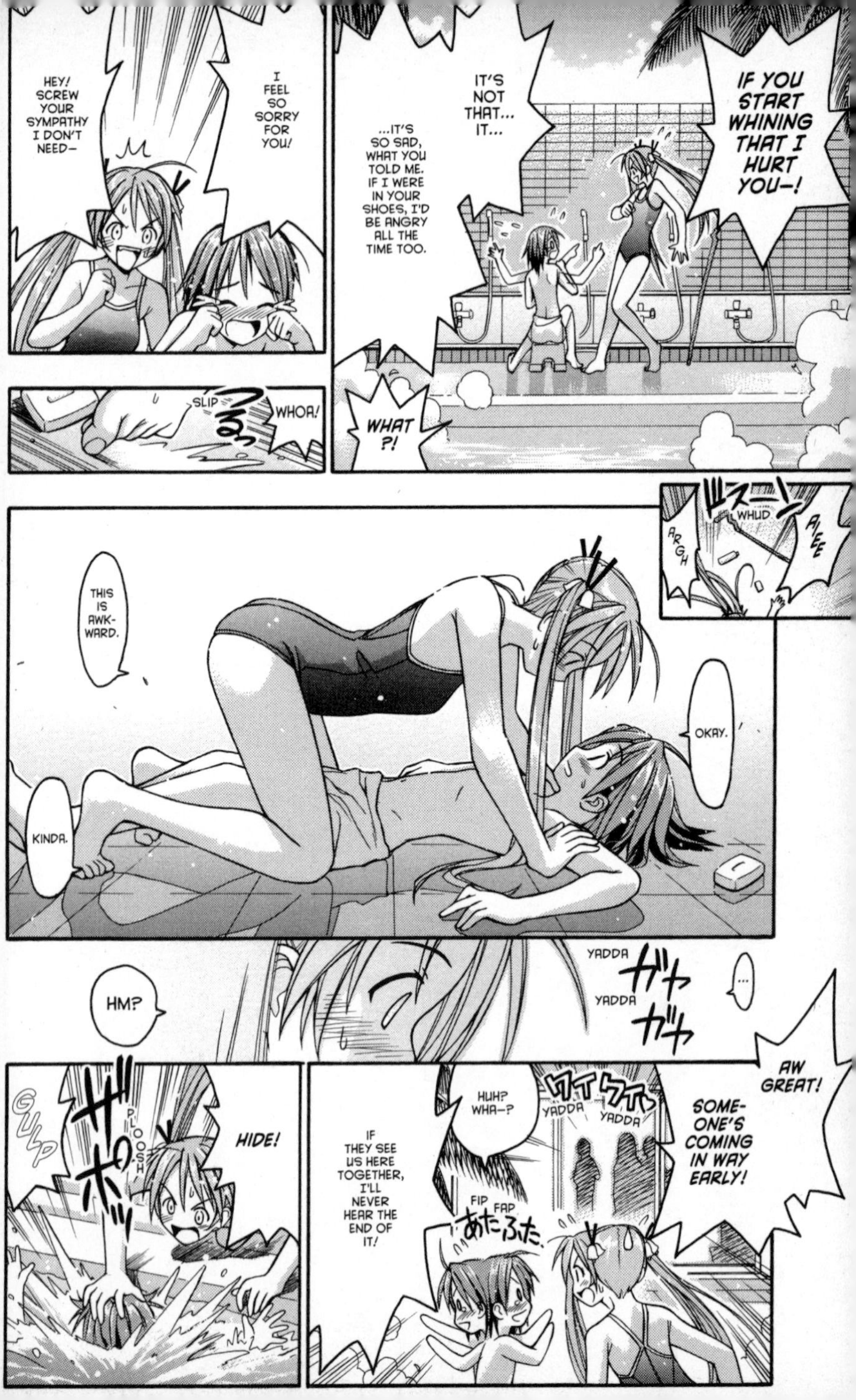
IF YOU START WHINING THAT I HURT YOU—!
IT'S NOT THAT... IT...
...IT'S SO SAD, WHAT YOU TOLD ME. IF I WERE IN YOUR SHOES, I'D BE ANGRY ALL THE TIME TOO.
I FEEL SO SORRY FOR YOU!
HEY! SCREW YOUR SYMPATHY I DON'T NEED—
WHAT ?!
WHOA!
SLIP
つるっ
ドスーン
WHUD
AIEE
ARGH
OKAY.
THIS IS AWK-WARD.
KINDA.
...
YADDA
ガヤ
YADDA
ガヤ
HM?
AW GREAT!
SOME-ONE'S COMING IN WAY EARLY!
HUH? WHA—?
ワイワイ
YADDA
YADDA
IF THEY SEE US HERE TOGETHER, I'LL NEVER HEAR THE END OF IT!
FIP
FAP
あたふた
HIDE!
PLOOSH
GULP

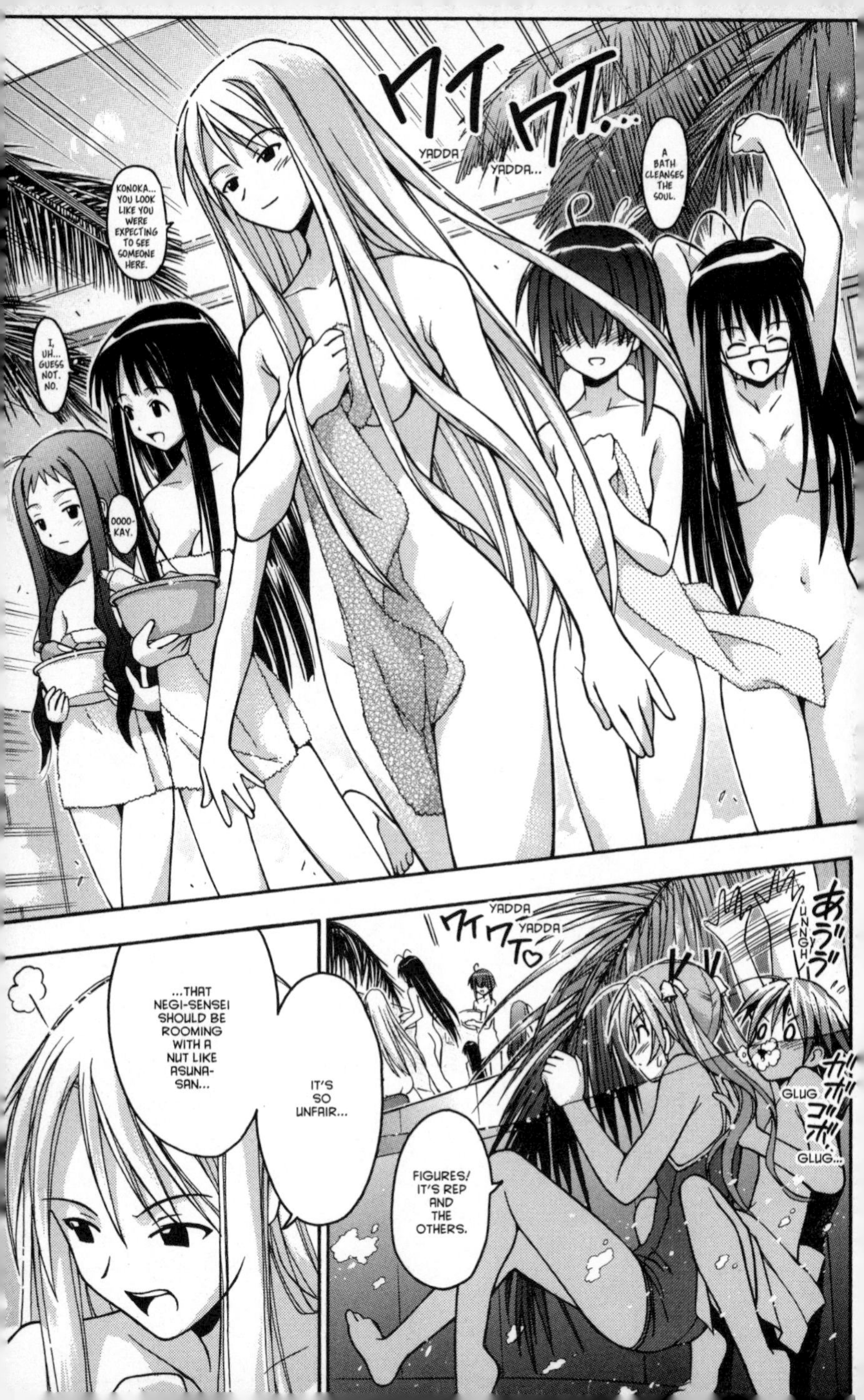
YADDA YADDA...
A BATH CLEANSES THE SOUL.
KONOKA... YOU LOOK LIKE YOU WERE EXPECTING TO SEE SOMEONE HERE.
I, UH... GUESS NOT, NO.
OOOO-KAY.
UNGH!
YADDA YADDA
GLUG GLUG...
FIGURES! IT'S REP AND THE OTHERS.
...THAT NEGI-SENSEI SHOULD BE ROOMING WITH A NUT LIKE ASUNA-SAN...
IT'S SO UNFAIR...

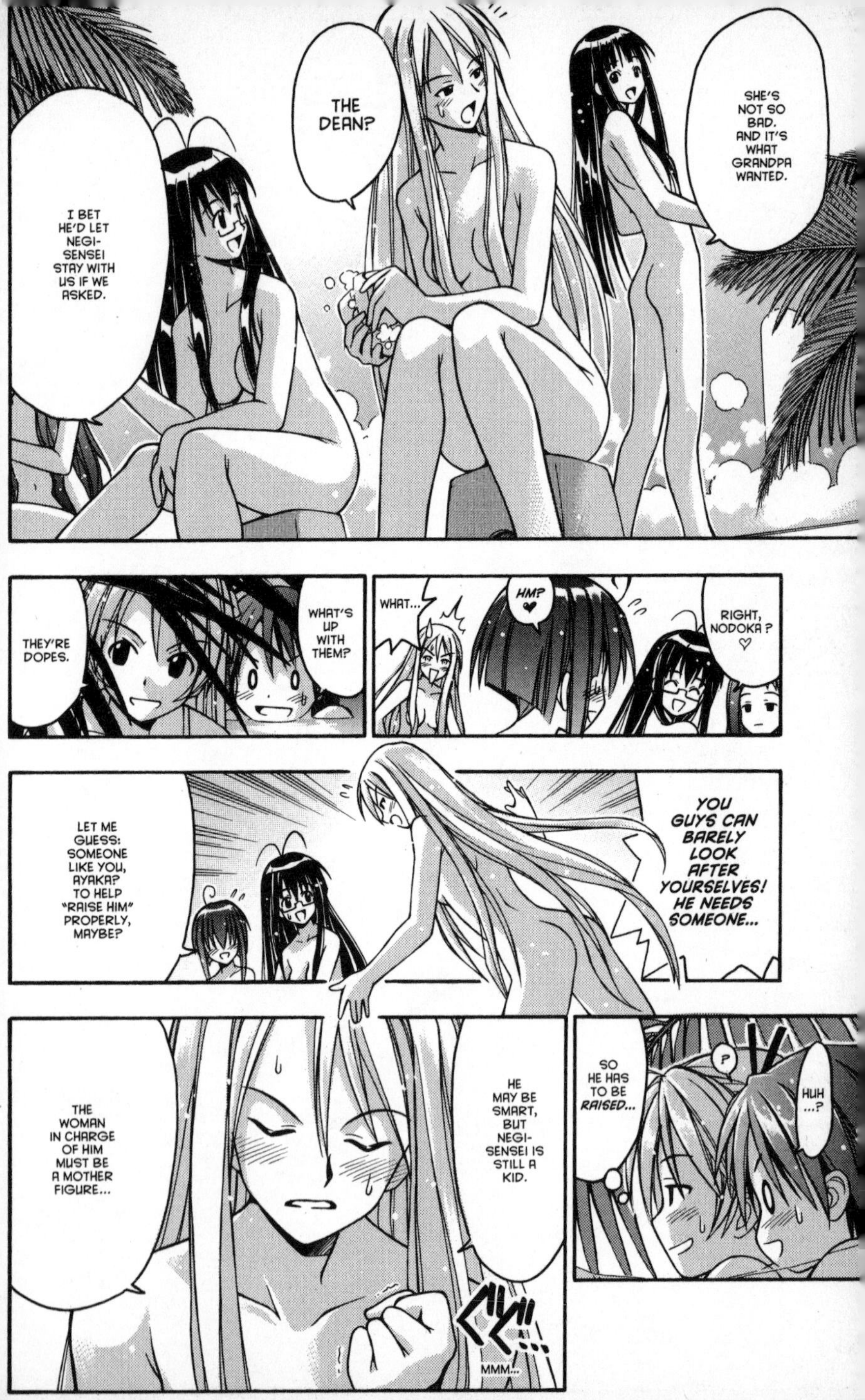
SHE'S NOT SO BAD. AND IT'S WHAT GRANDPA WANTED.
THE DEAN?
I BET HE'D LET NEGI-SENSEI STAY WITH US IF WE ASKED.
RIGHT, NODOKA? ♡
HM? ♥
WHAT...
WHAT'S UP WITH THEM?
THEY'RE DOPES.
YOU GUYS CAN BARELY LOOK AFTER YOURSELVES! HE NEEDS SOMEONE...
LET ME GUESS: SOMEONE LIKE YOU, AYAKA? TO HELP "RAISE HIM" PROPERLY, MAYBE?
HUH ...?
?
SO HE HAS TO BE *RAISED*...
HE MAY BE SMART, BUT NEGI-SENSEI IS STILL A KID.
THE WOMAN IN CHARGE OF HIM MUST BE A MOTHER FIGURE...
MMM...

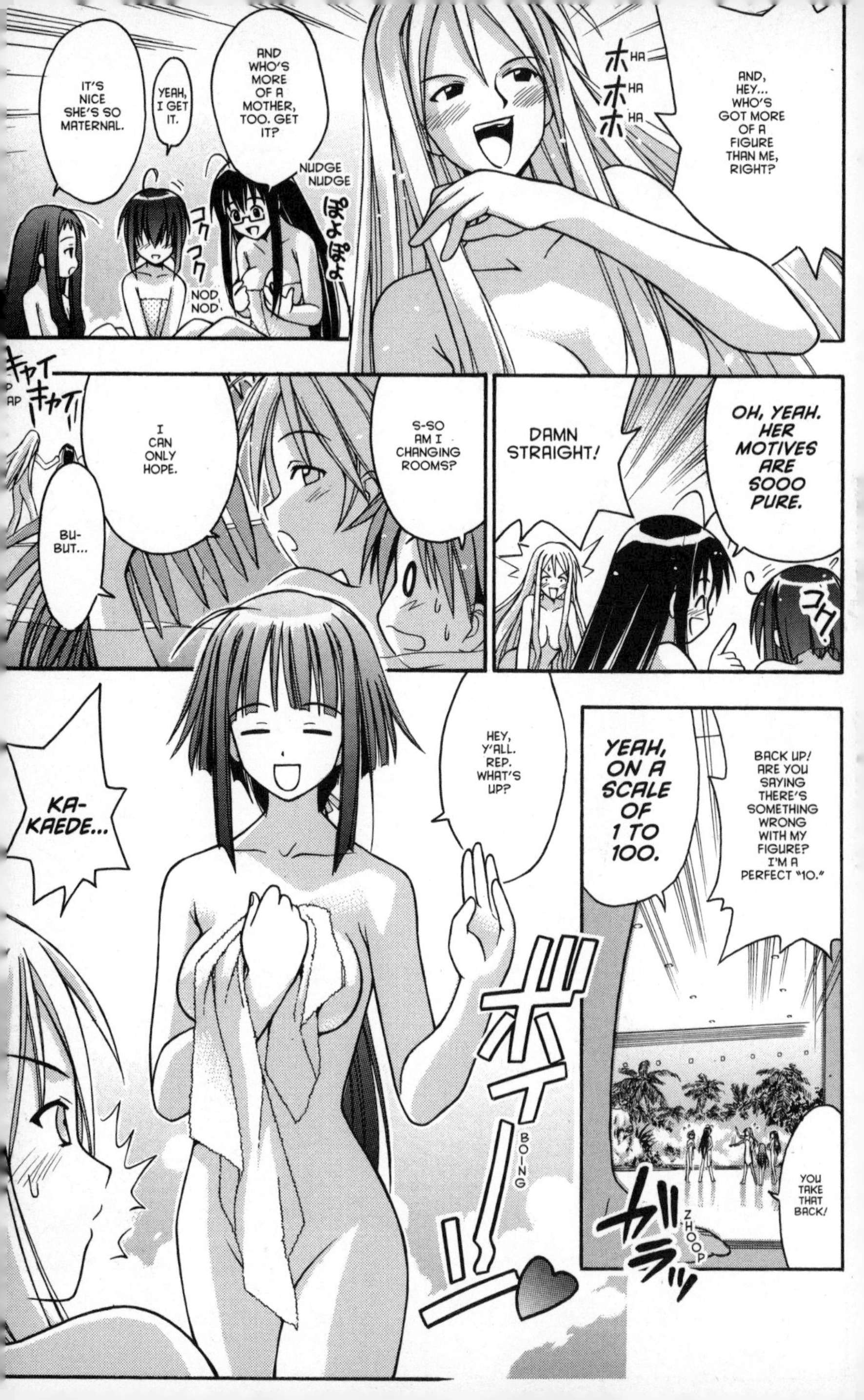
AND, HEY... WHO'S GOT MORE OF A FIGURE THAN ME, RIGHT?
ホホホ
HA HA HA
AND WHO'S MORE OF A MOTHER, TOO. GET IT?
NUDGE NUDGE
ぽよぽよ
YEAH, I GET IT.
IT'S NICE SHE'S SO MATERNAL.
コクコク
NOD NOD
OH, YEAH. HER MOTIVES ARE SOOO PURE.
DAMN STRAIGHT!
コク
S-SO AM I CHANGING ROOMS?
I CAN ONLY HOPE.
キャイキャイ
BU-BUT...
BACK UP! ARE YOU SAYING THERE'S SOMETHING WRONG WITH MY FIGURE? I'M A PERFECT "10."
YEAH, ON A SCALE OF 1 TO 100.
YOU TAKE THAT BACK!
ガラッ
ZHOOP
HEY, Y'ALL. REP. WHAT'S UP?
ボイーン
BOING
KA-KAEDE...

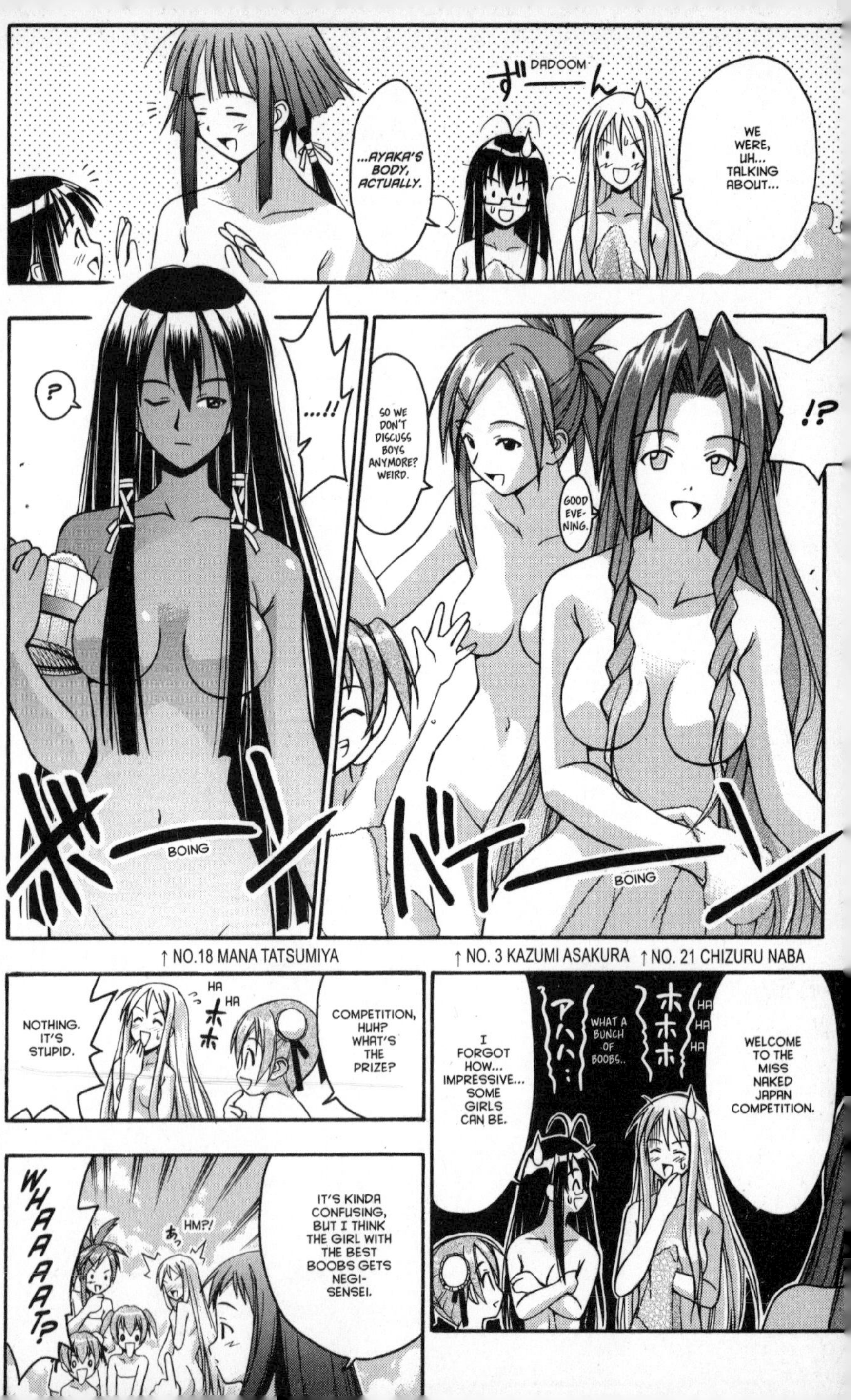
WE WERE, UH... TALKING ABOUT...
DADOOM
...AYAKA'S BODY, ACTUALLY.
!?
GOOD EVE-NING.
SO WE DON'T DISCUSS BOYS ANYMORE? WEIRD.
BOING
...!!
?
BOING
↑ NO.18 MANA TATSUMIYA
↑ NO. 3 KAZUMI ASAKURA
↑ NO. 21 CHIZURU NABA
WELCOME TO THE MISS NAKED JAPAN COMPETITION.
HA HA HA
WHAT A BUNCH OF BOOBS..
I FORGOT HOW... IMPRESSIVE... SOME GIRLS CAN BE.
COMPETITION, HUH? WHAT'S THE PRIZE?
HA HA
NOTHING. IT'S STUPID.
IT'S KINDA CONFUSING, BUT I THINK THE GIRL WITH THE BEST BOOBS GETS NEGI-SENSEI.
HM?!
WHAAAAAT?

NO. 12
FEI KU

NO. 19
LINGSHEN CHAO

NO. 17
SAKURAKO SHIINA

NO. 11
MADOKA KUGIMIYA

NO. 7
MISA KAKIZAKI

15
"SUNA SAKURAZAKI

NO. 26
EVANGELINE A.K. MCDOWELL

NO. 23
FUMIKA NARUTAKI

NO. 22
FUKA NARUTAKI

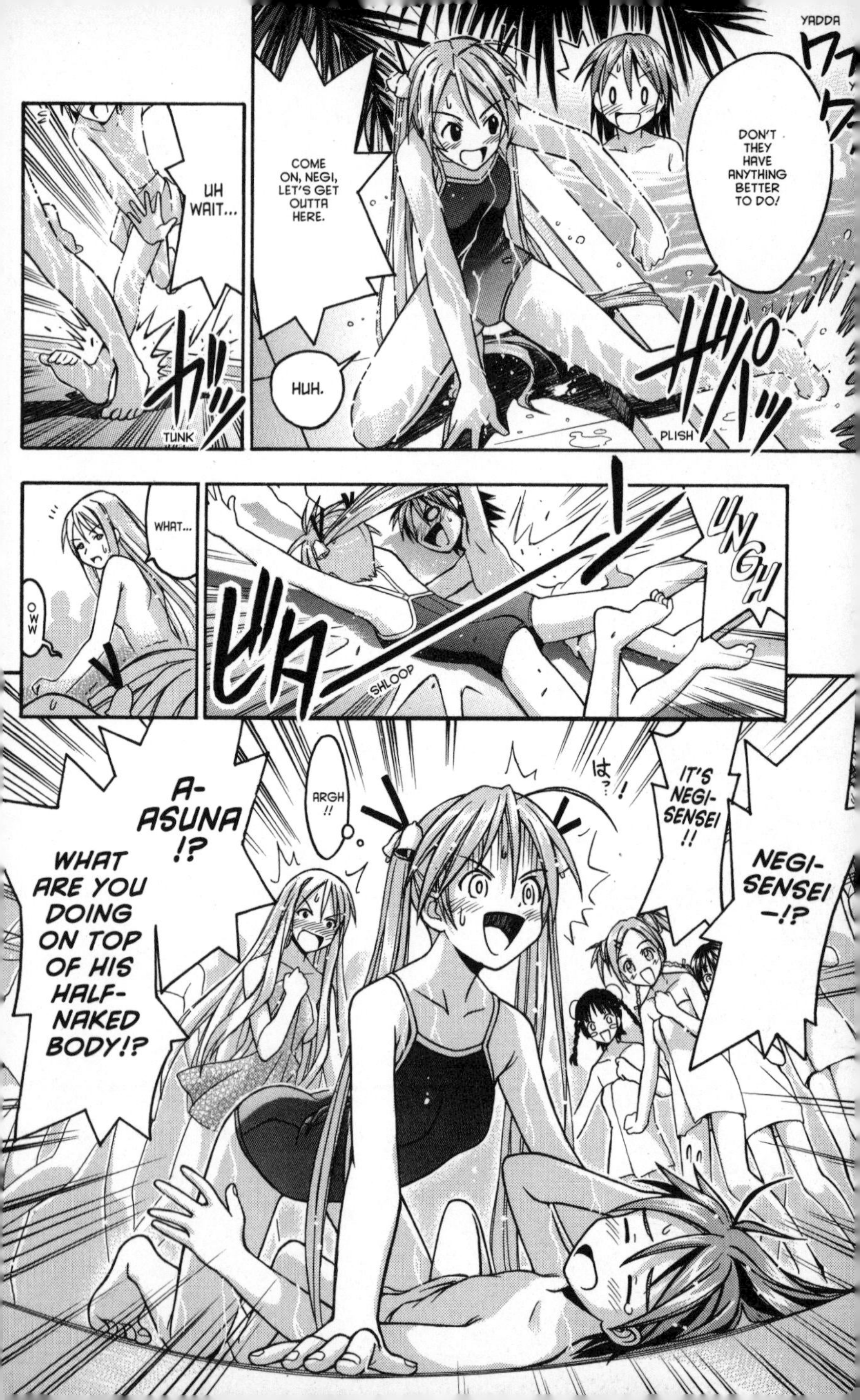
YADDA
DON'T THEY HAVE ANYTHING BETTER TO DO!
COME ON, NEGI, LET'S GET OUTTA HERE.
HUH.
PLISH
UH WAIT...
TUNK
UNGH
SHLOOP
WHAT...
OWW
NEGI-SENSEI—!?
IT'S NEGI-SENSEI!!
ARGH!!
A-ASUNA!?
WHAT ARE YOU DOING ON TOP OF HIS HALF-NAKED BODY!?

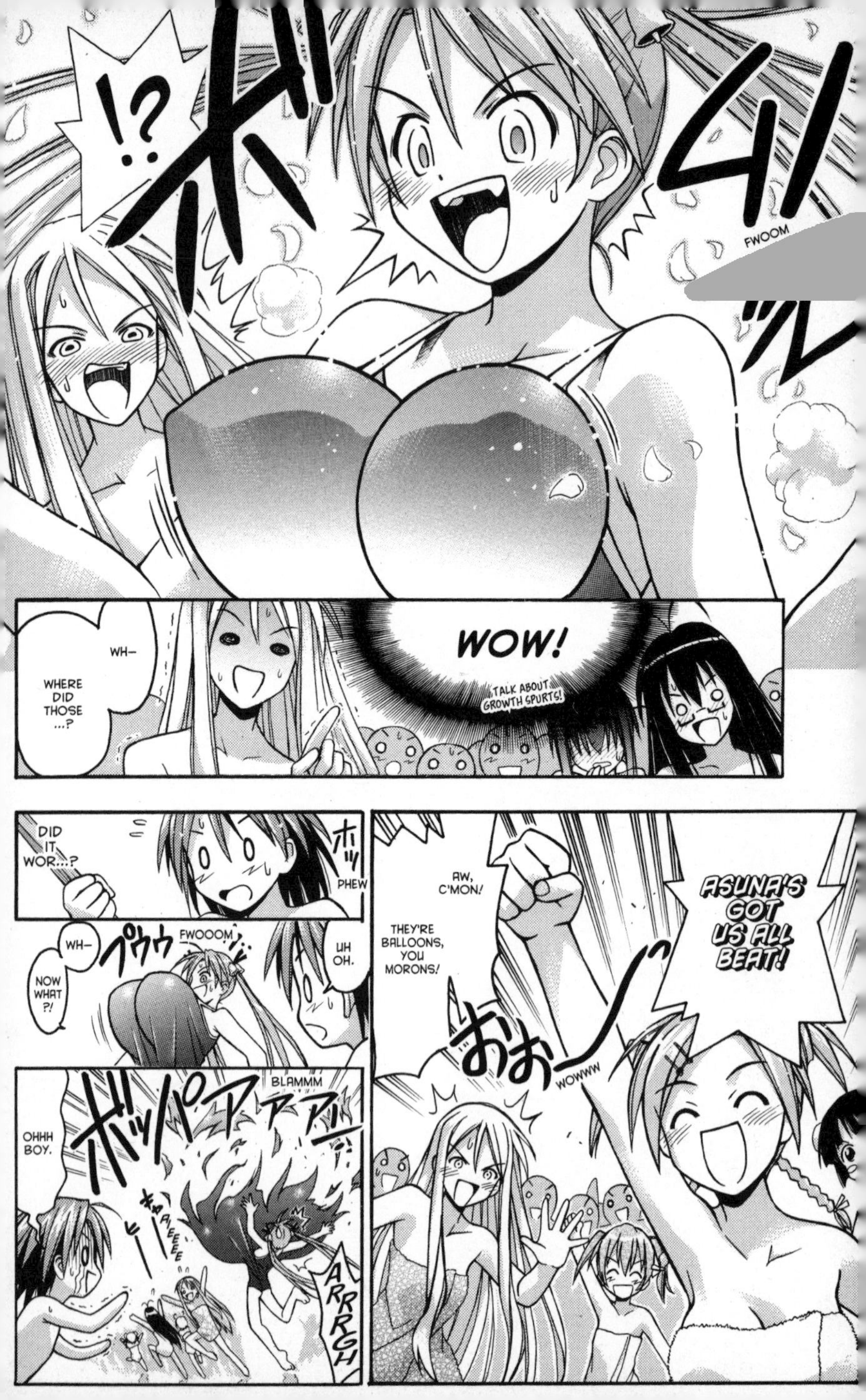
!?
FWOOM
WOW!
TALK ABOUT GROWTH SPURTS!
WH—
WHERE DID THOSE ...?
ASUNA'S GOT US ALL BEAT!
AW, C'MON!
THEY'RE BALLOONS, YOU MORONS!
おお〜
WOWWW
PHEW
DID IT WOR...?
UH OH.
FWOOOM
WH—
NOW WHAT?!
BLAMMM
OHHH BOY.
AIEEEE
ARRRGH

STUDENT NUMBER 4
YUE AYASE (LEFT)
BIRTHDATE: NOVEMBER 16, 1988
BLOODTYPE: AB
FAVORITE THINGS: READING
DISLIKES: STUDYING FOR SCHOOL
CLUB ACTIVITIES: CHILDREN'S LITERATURE STUDY GROUP,
                 PHILOSOPHY STUDY GROUP,
                 LIBRARY CLUB

STUDENT NUMBER 14
HARUNA SAOTOME (RIGHT)
BIRTHDATE: AUGUST 18, 1988
BLOODTYPE: B
FAVORITE THINGS: TEA CEREMONY;
                 LOTS OF TROUBLE
DISLIKES: REPTILES, DEADLINES
CLUB ACTIVITIES: MANGA CLUB,
                 LIBRARY EXPLORATION
                 GROUP
REMARKS: PSEUDONYM "PAL"

STUDENT NUMBER 27
NODOKA MIYAZAKI (MIDDLE)
BIRTHDATE: MAY 10, 1988
BLOODTYPE: O
FAVORITE THINGS: TO BE SURROUNDED BY BOOKS,
                 ORGANIZING BOOKS
DISLIKES: GUYS
CLUB ACTIVITIES: GENERAL LIBRARY COMMITTEE MEMBER,
                 LIBRARY REPRESENTATIVE,
                 LIBRARY CLUB

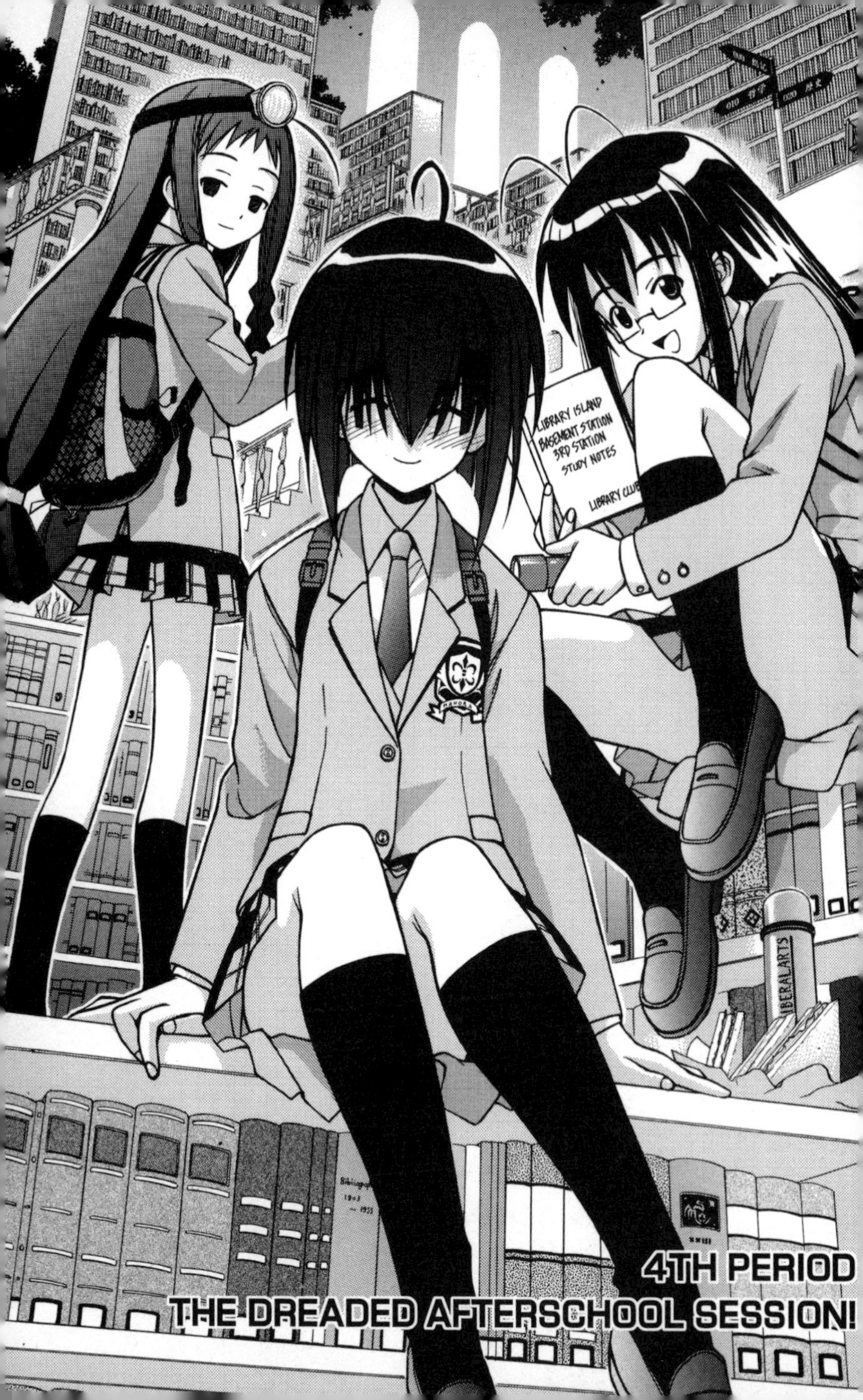
LIBRARY ISLAND
BASEMENT STATION
3RD STATION
STUDY NOTES
LIBRARY CLUB
LIBERAL ARTS
4TH PERIOD
THE DREADED AFTERSCHOOL SESSION!

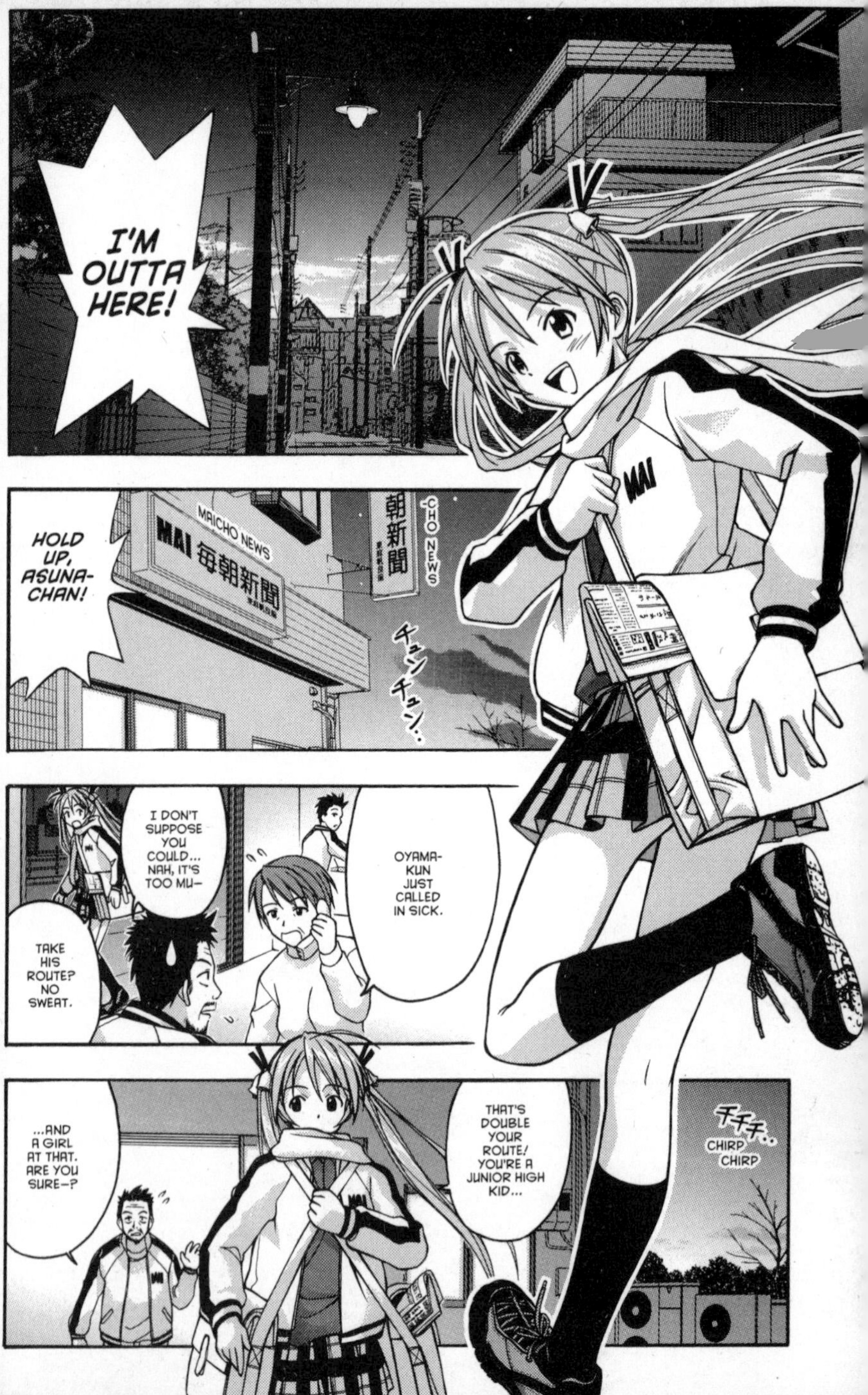
I'M OUTTA HERE!
-CHO NEWS
チュンチュン..
MAICHO NEWS
MAI 毎朝新聞
HOLD UP, ASUNA-CHAN!
OYAMA-KUN JUST CALLED IN SICK.
I DON'T SUPPOSE YOU COULD... NAH, IT'S TOO MU–
TAKE HIS ROUTE? NO SWEAT.
チチチ..
CHIRP CHIRP
THAT'S DOUBLE YOUR ROUTE! YOU'RE A JUNIOR HIGH KID...
...AND A GIRL AT THAT. ARE YOU SURE–?

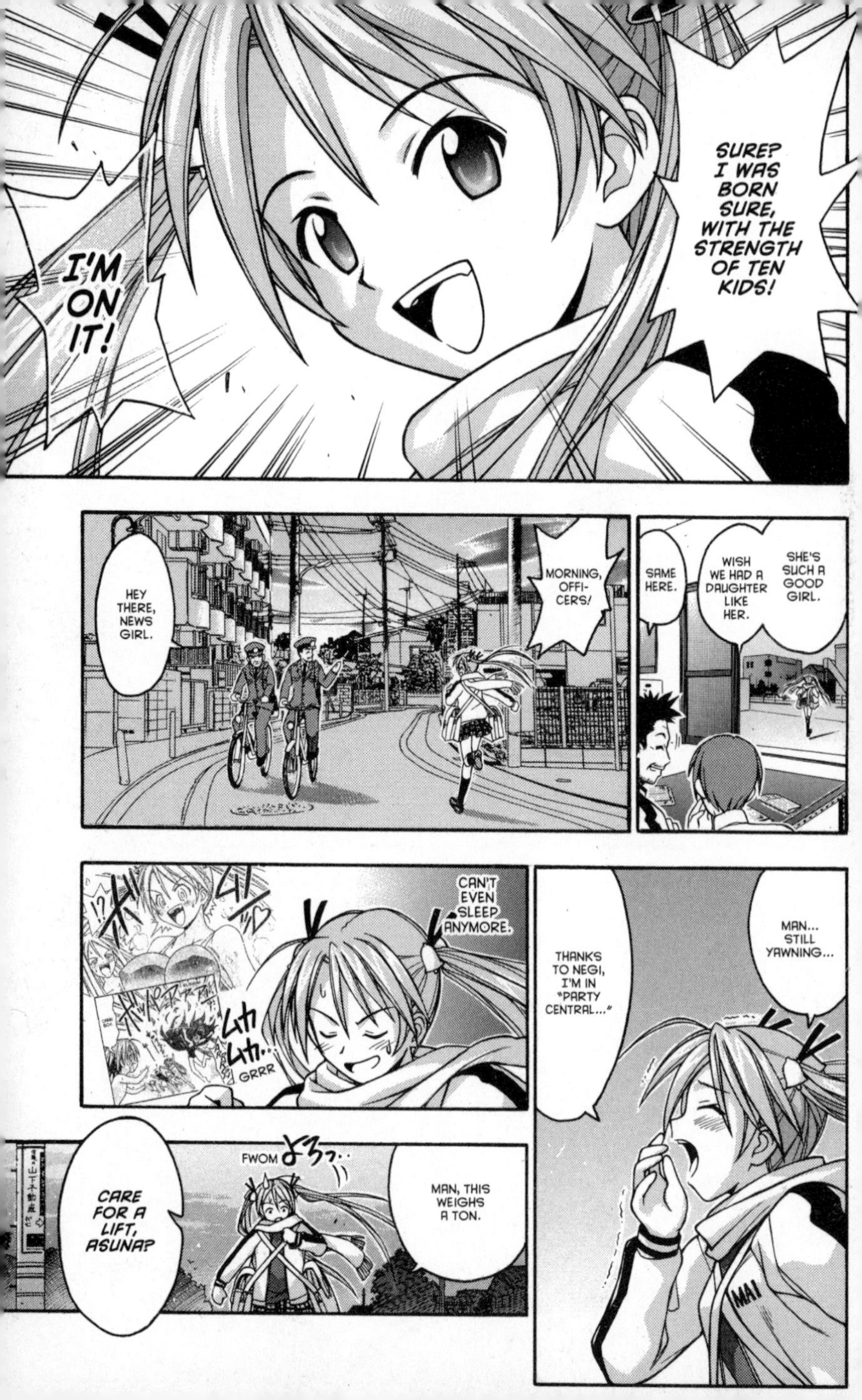
SURE? I WAS BORN SURE, WITH THE STRENGTH OF TEN KIDS!
I'M ON IT!
SHE'S SUCH A GOOD GIRL.
WISH WE HAD A DAUGHTER LIKE HER.
SAME HERE.
MORNING, OFFI-CERS!
HEY THERE, NEWS GIRL.
MAN... STILL YAWNING...
THANKS TO NEGI, I'M IN "PARTY CENTRAL..."
MAI
CAN'T EVEN SLEEP ANYMORE.
GRRR
MAN, THIS WEIGHS A TON.
FWOM
CARE FOR A LIFT, ASUNA?

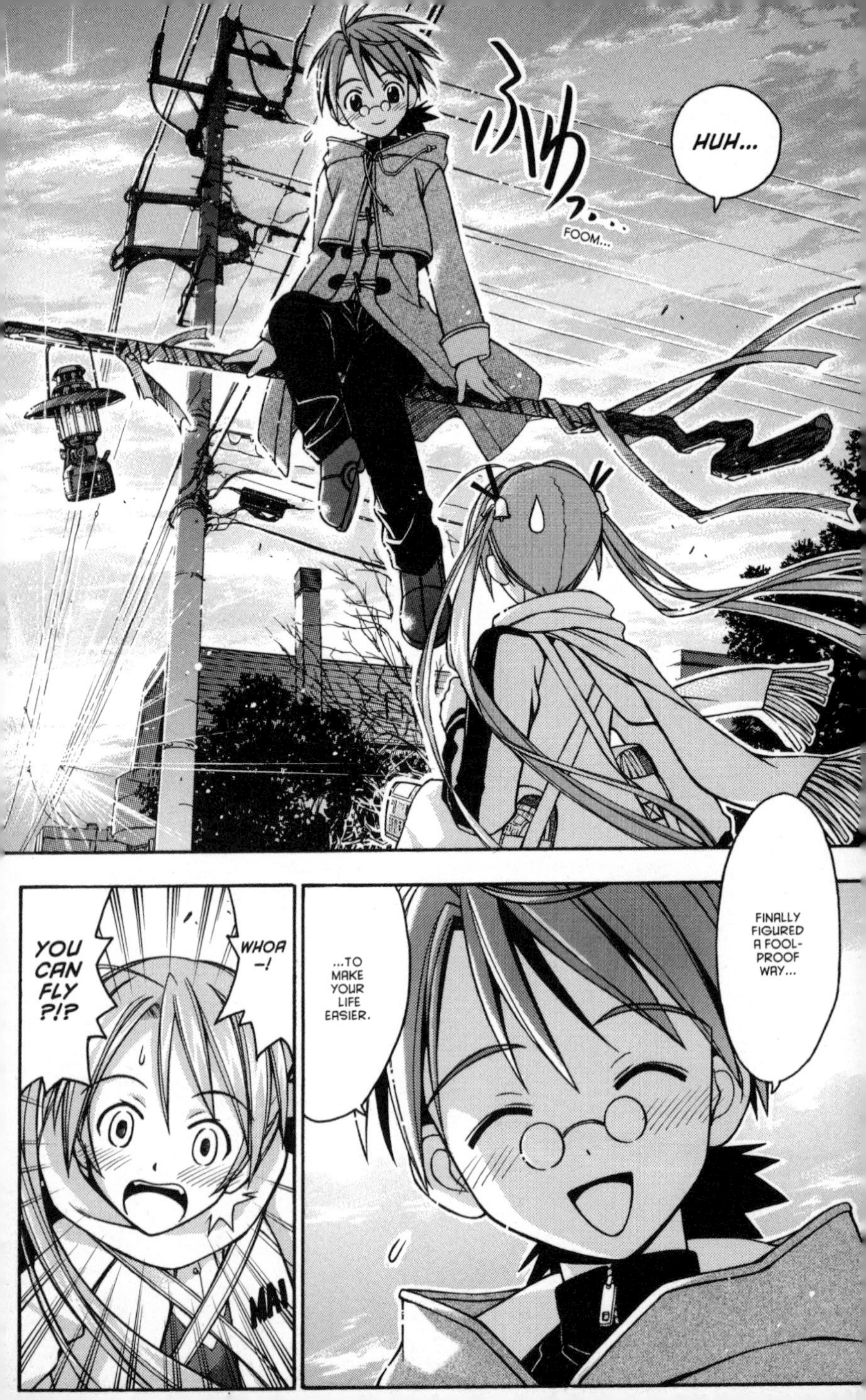

ふわっ...
FOOM...
HUH...
FINALLY FIGURED A FOOL-PROOF WAY...
...TO MAKE YOUR LIFE EASIER.
WHOA—!
YOU CAN FLY?!?

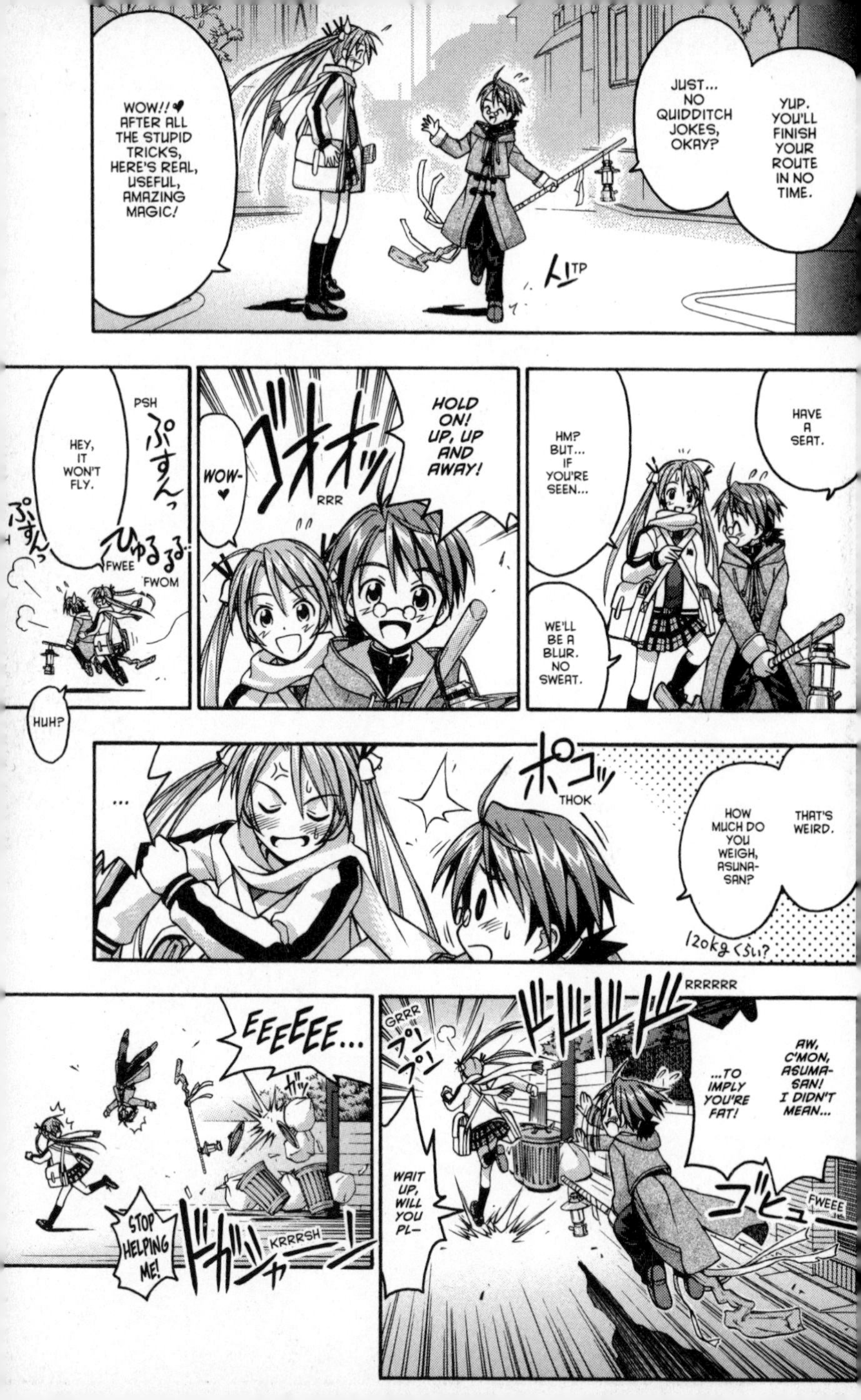
YUP. YOU'LL FINISH YOUR ROUTE IN NO TIME.
JUST... NO QUIDDITCH JOKES, OKAY?
WOW!! ♥ AFTER ALL THE STUPID TRICKS, HERE'S REAL, USEFUL, AMAZING MAGIC!
TP
HAVE A SEAT.
HM? BUT... IF YOU'RE SEEN...
WE'LL BE A BLUR. NO SWEAT.
HOLD ON! UP, UP AND AWAY!
ゴオオッ
RRR
WOW-♥
PSH
ぷすんっ
HEY, IT WON'T FLY.
ぷすんっ
ひゅるるる
FWEE
FWOM
HUH?
THAT'S WEIRD.
HOW MUCH DO YOU WEIGH, ASUNA-SAN?
120kgくらい?
ポコッ
THOK
...
AW, C'MON, ASUNA-SAN! I DIDN'T MEAN...
...TO IMPLY YOU'RE FAT!
ドドドドド
RRRRRR
ゴヒュー
FWEEE
GRRR
WAIT UP, WILL YOU PL—
EEEEEEE...
STOP HELPING ME!
ドガシャー
KRRRSH

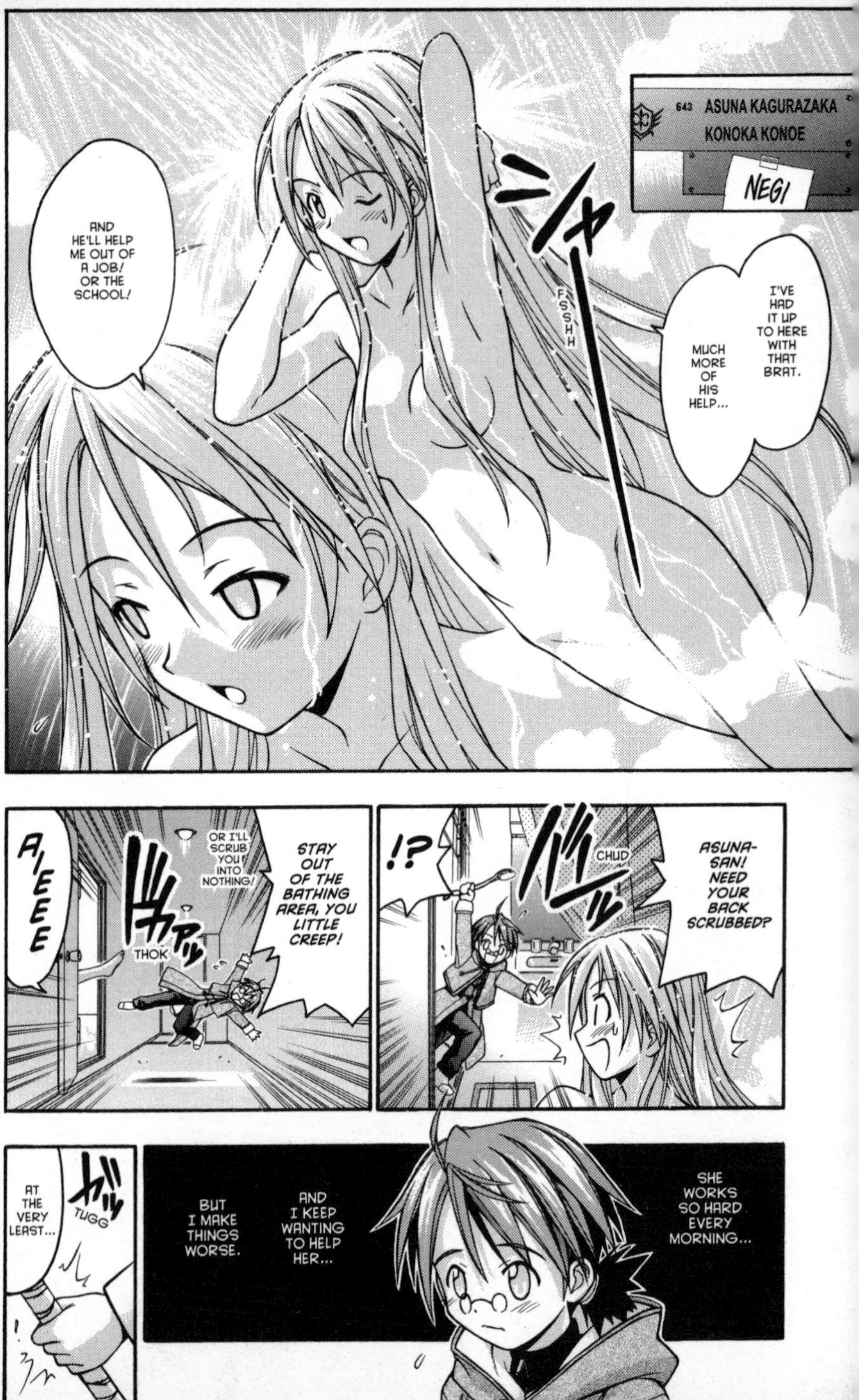
643 ASUNA KAGURAZAKA
KONOKA KONOE
NEGI
I'VE HAD IT UP TO HERE WITH THAT BRAT.
MUCH MORE OF HIS HELP...
FSSHH
AND HE'LL HELP ME OUT OF A JOB! OR THE SCHOOL!
ASUNA-SAN! NEED YOUR BACK SCRUBBED?
CHUD
!?
STAY OUT OF THE BATHING AREA, YOU LITTLE CREEP!
OR I'LL SCRUB YOU INTO NOTHING!
THOK
AIEEE
SHE WORKS SO HARD EVERY MORNING...
AND I KEEP WANTING TO HELP HER...
BUT I MAKE THINGS WORSE.
TUGG
AT THE VERY LEAST...

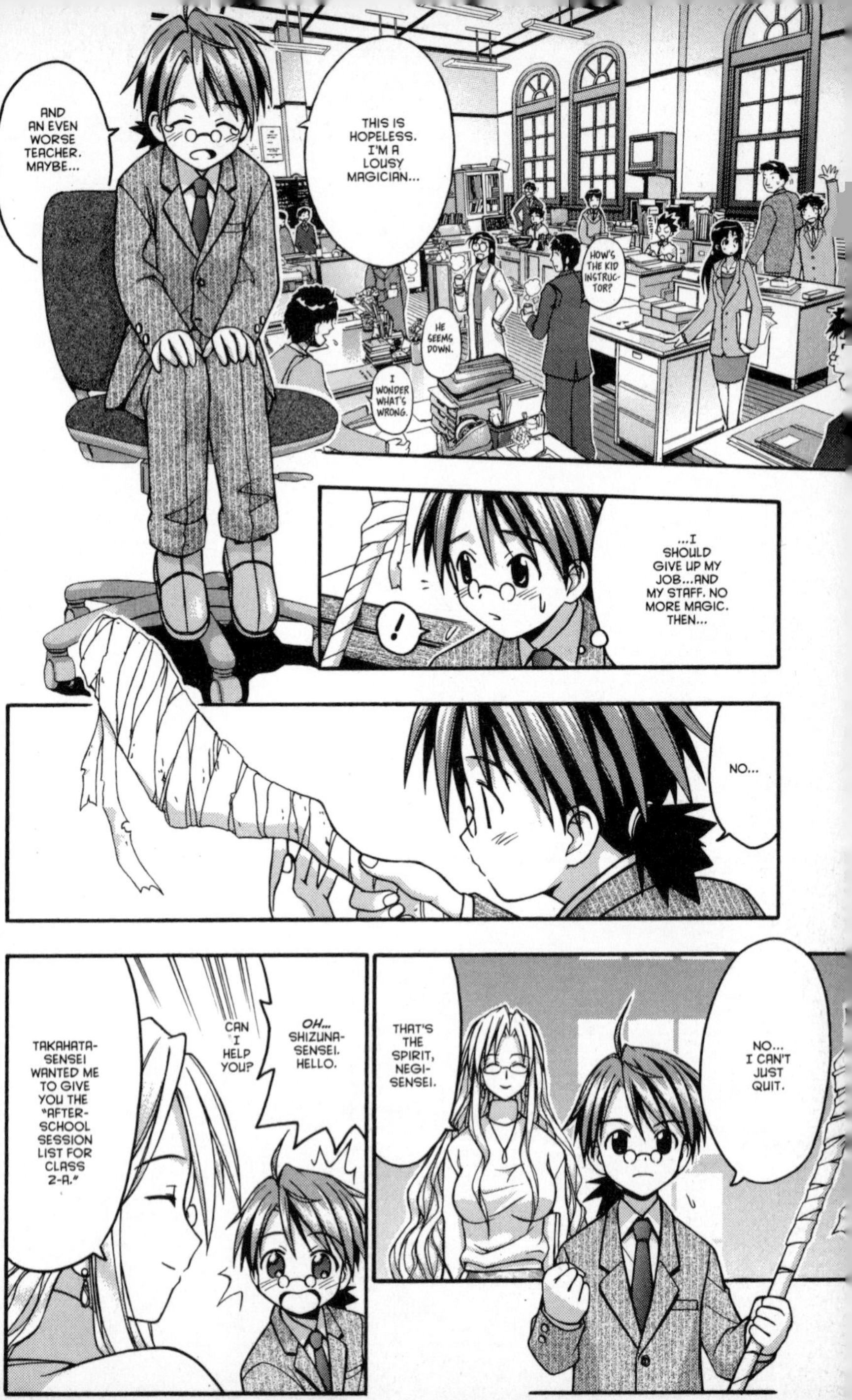

HOW'S THE KID INSTRUCTOR?
HE SEEMS DOWN.
I WONDER WHAT'S WRONG.
THIS IS HOPELESS. I'M A LOUSY MAGICIAN...
AND AN EVEN WORSE TEACHER. MAYBE...
...I SHOULD GIVE UP MY JOB...AND MY STAFF. NO MORE MAGIC. THEN...
!
NO...
NO... I CAN'T JUST QUIT.
THAT'S THE SPIRIT, NEGI-SENSEI.
OH... SHIZUNA-SENSEI. HELLO.
CAN I HELP YOU?
TAKAHATA-SENSEI WANTED ME TO GIVE YOU THE "AFTER-SCHOOL SESSION LIST FOR CLASS 2-A."

...AND LOW SCORERS STAY AFTER SCHOOL FOR TUTORING.

YES, TAKAHATA-SENSEI GIVES POP QUIZZES...

"AFTER-SCHOOL SESSION LIST"?

ACCEPT AFTER SCHOOL HELP? WELL, SHE'S NEVER MINDED BEFORE...

ASUNA-SAN COULD SURE USE ENGLISH HELP. BUT SHE'D NEVER—

LET'S SEE WHO THE LUCKY DEVILS ARE.

IT'S YOUR JOB, IF YOU THINK YOU CAN HANDLE IT.

Afterschool Session List

No. 4 Yue Ayase
Quiz 7 8 Points
Quiz 8 14 Points

No. 8 Asuna Kagurazaka
Quiz 7 6 Points
Quiz 8 8 Points

No. 12 Fei Ku
Quiz 7 12 Points
Quiz 8 14 Points

No. 16 Makie Sasaki
Quiz 7 8 Points
Quiz 8 10 Points

OF COURSE.

YES! PERFECT!

WAAAIT A MINUTE. MAYBE...

YEAH, I GUESS SO.

THEN AGAIN, TAKAMICHI TAUGHT THOSE. YOU, IT'D BE A DIFFERENT STORY.

I'VE FINALLY FOUND A WAY TO HELP ASUNA-SAN!

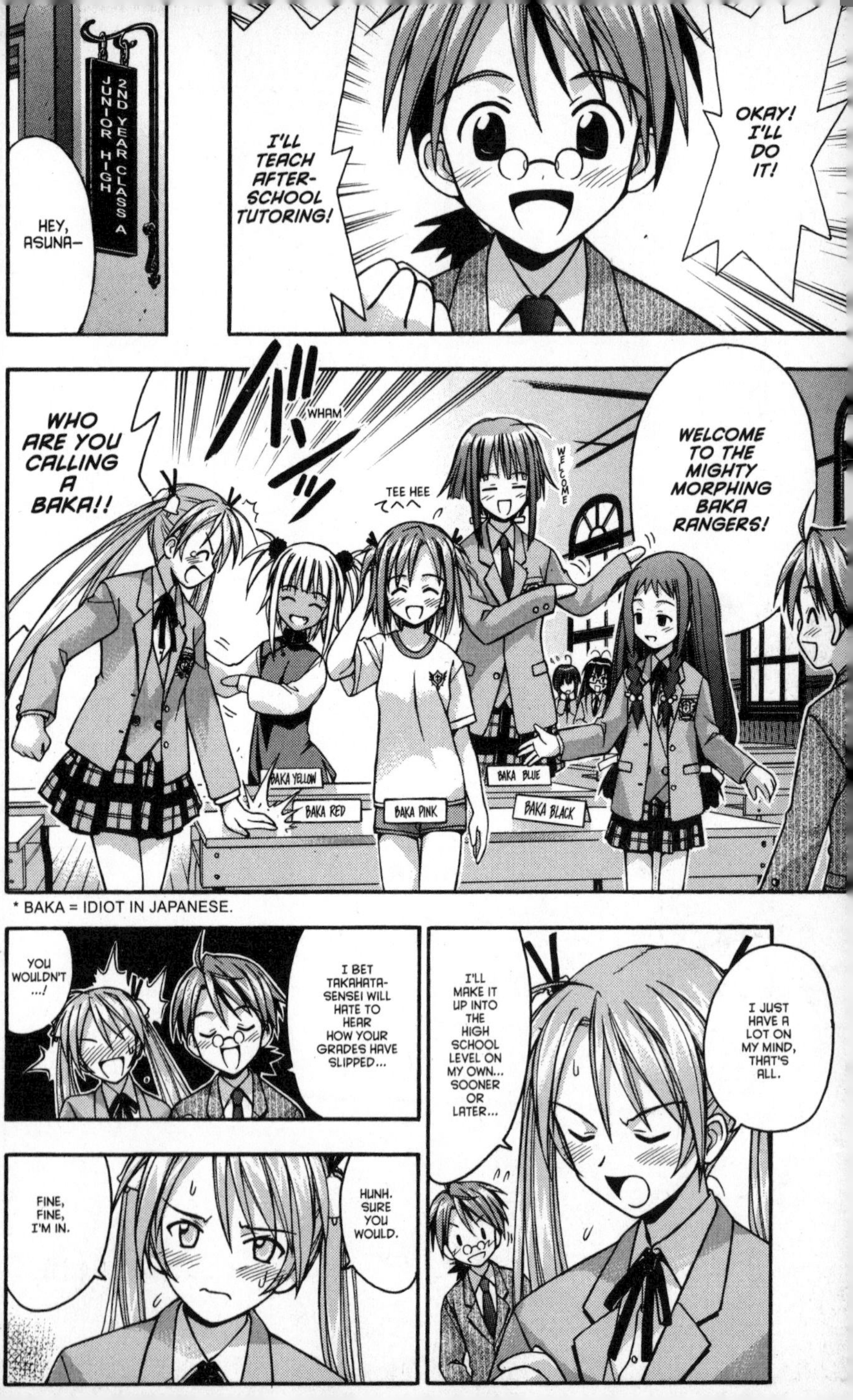
OKAY! I'LL DO IT!
I'LL TEACH AFTER-SCHOOL TUTORING!
2ND YEAR CLASS A JUNIOR HIGH
HEY, ASUNA—
WELCOME TO THE MIGHTY MORPHING BAKA RANGERS!
WELCOME
TEE HEE てへへ
WHAM
WHO ARE YOU CALLING A BAKA!!
BAKA YELLOW
BAKA RED
BAKA PINK
BAKA BLUE
BAKA BLACK
I JUST HAVE A LOT ON MY MIND, THAT'S ALL.
I'LL MAKE IT UP INTO THE HIGH SCHOOL LEVEL ON MY OWN... SOONER OR LATER...
I BET TAKAHATA-SENSEI WILL HATE TO HEAR HOW YOUR GRADES HAVE SLIPPED...
YOU WOULDN'T ...!
HUNH. SURE YOU WOULD.
FINE, FINE, I'M IN.

* BAKA = IDIOT IN JAPANESE.

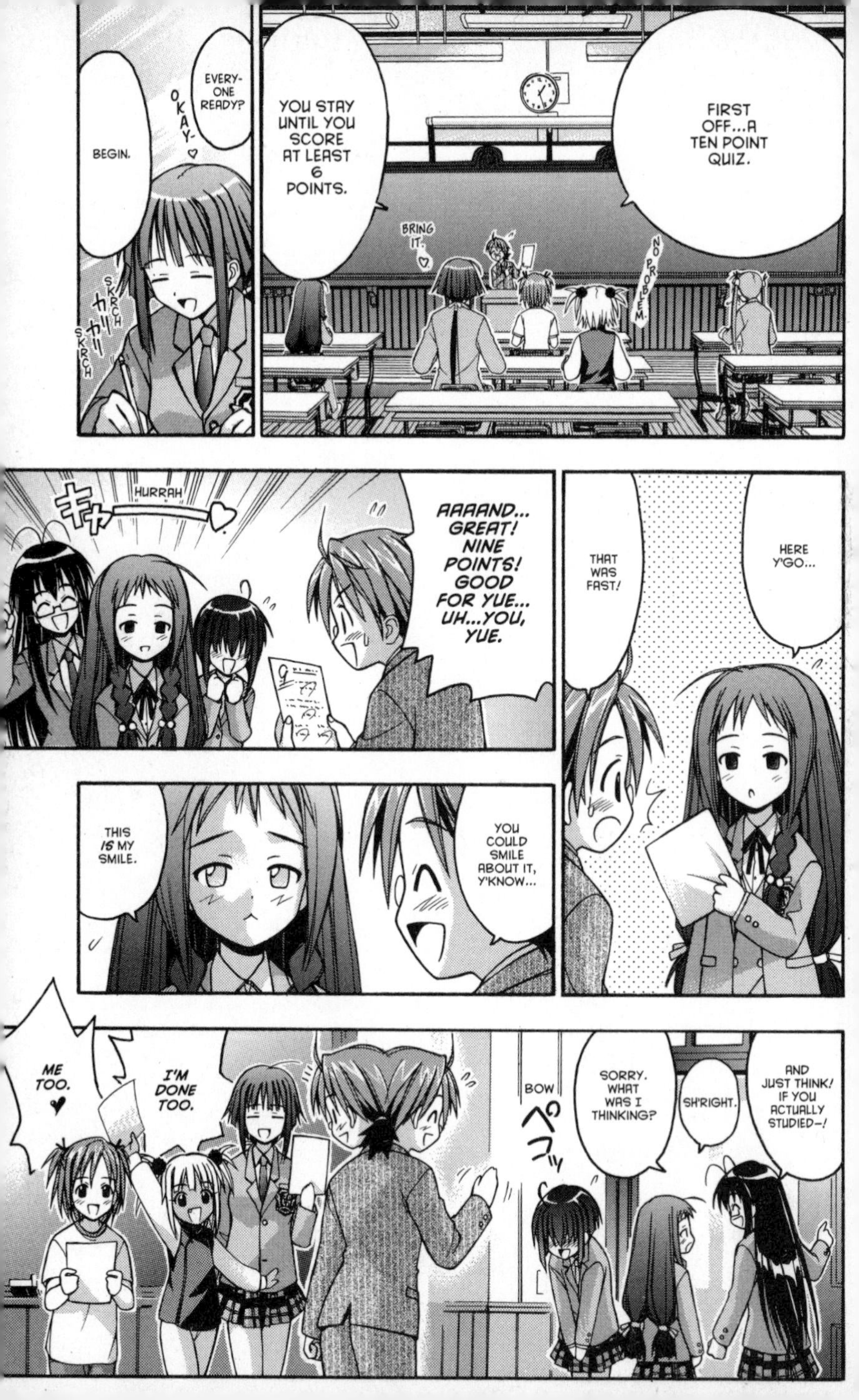

FIRST OFF...A TEN POINT QUIZ.
YOU STAY UNTIL YOU SCORE AT LEAST 6 POINTS.
BRING IT. ♡
NO PROBLEM.
EVERY-ONE READY?
OKAY~ ♡
BEGIN.
SKRCH SKRCH
HERE Y'GO...
THAT WAS FAST!
AAAAND... GREAT! NINE POINTS! GOOD FOR YUE... UH...YOU, YUE.
HURRAH
YOU COULD SMILE ABOUT IT, Y'KNOW...
THIS *IS* MY SMILE.
AND JUST THINK! IF YOU ACTUALLY STUDIED—!
SH'RIGHT.
SORRY. WHAT WAS I THINKING?
BOW
I'M DONE TOO.
ME TOO. ♥

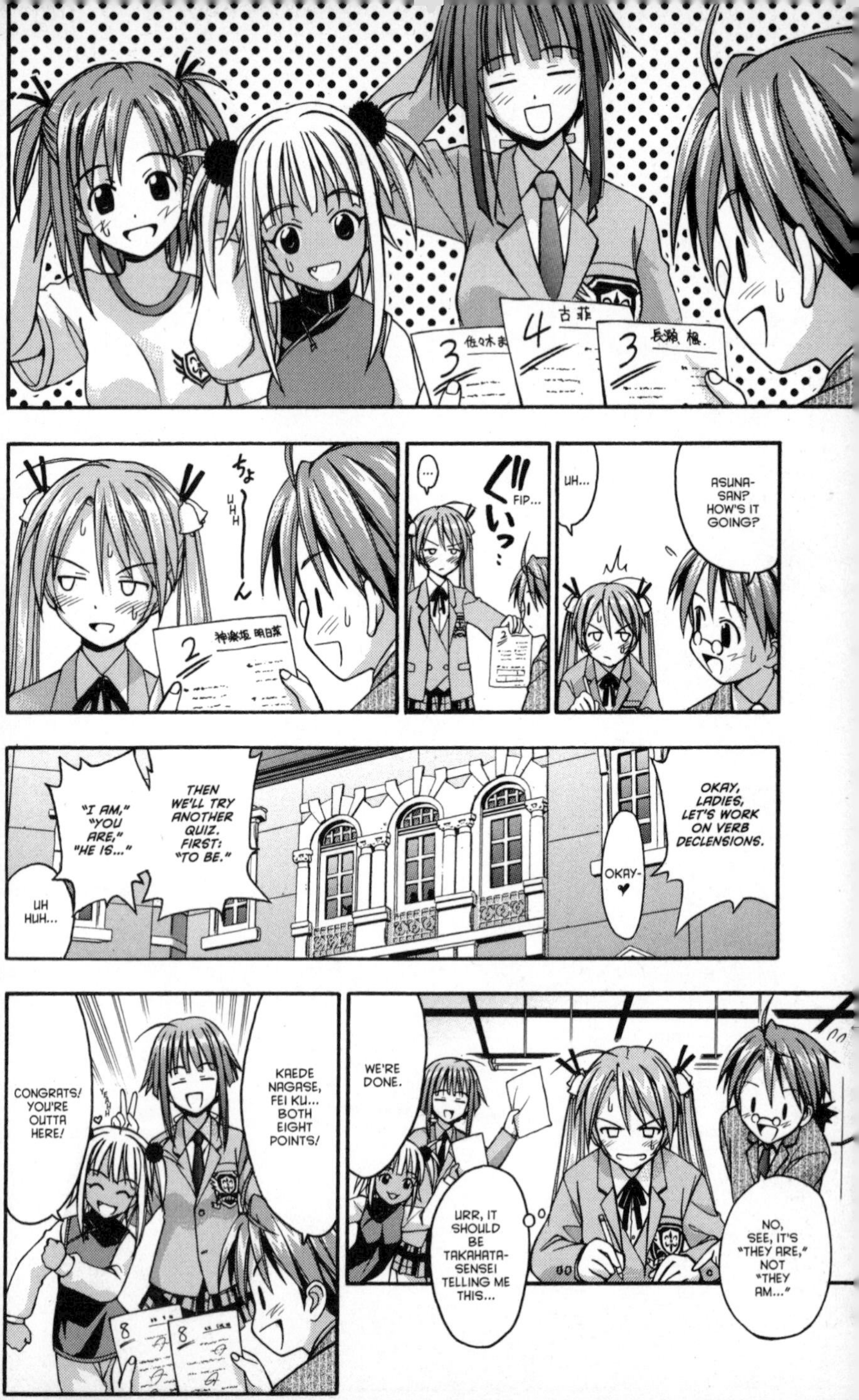

長瀬 楓.
古菲
佐々木ま
ASUNA-SAN? HOW'S IT GOING?
UH...
...
ぐいっ
FIP...
ちょーーーん
UHH
神楽坂 明日菜
OKAY, LADIES, LET'S WORK ON VERB DECLENSIONS.
OKAY-♥
THEN WE'LL TRY ANOTHER QUIZ. FIRST: "TO BE."
"I AM," "YOU ARE," "HE IS..."
UH HUH...
WE'RE DONE.
NO, SEE, IT'S "THEY ARE," NOT "THEY AM..."
URR, IT SHOULD BE TAKAHATA-SENSEI TELLING ME THIS...
KAEDE NAGASE, FEI KU... BOTH EIGHT POINTS!
CONGRATS! YOU'RE OUTTA HERE!
YEAAH

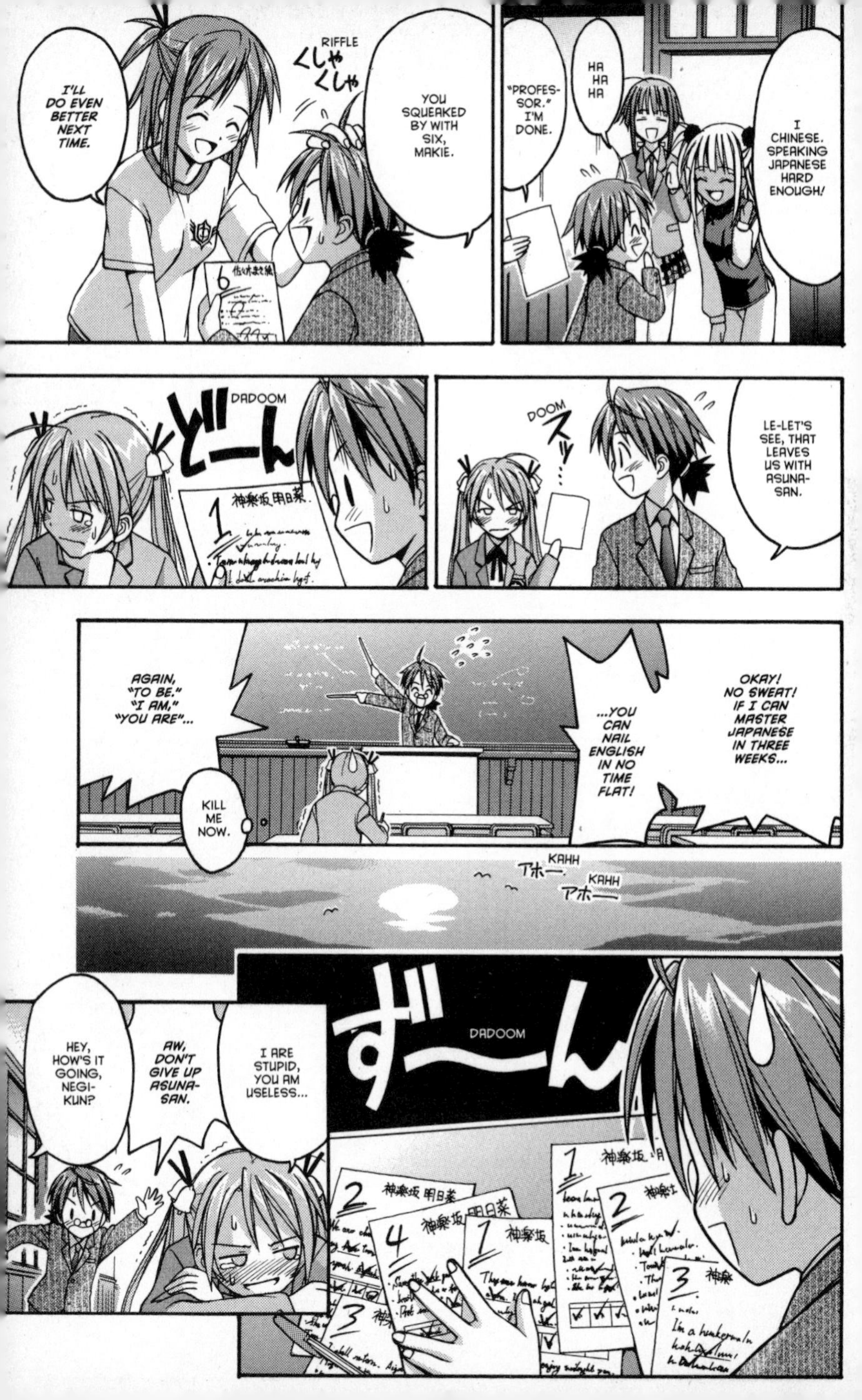
I CHINESE. SPEAKING JAPANESE HARD ENOUGH!
HA HA HA
"PROFES-SOR." I'M DONE.
YOU SQUEAKED BY WITH SIX, MAKIE.
RIFFLE
くしゃくしゃ
I'LL DO EVEN BETTER NEXT TIME.
LE-LET'S SEE, THAT LEAVES US WITH ASUNA-SAN.
DOOM
スッ…
DADOOM
どーん
神楽坂明日菜
OKAY! NO SWEAT! IF I CAN MASTER JAPANESE IN THREE WEEKS...
...YOU CAN NAIL ENGLISH IN NO TIME FLAT!
AGAIN, "TO BE." "I AM," "YOU ARE"...
KILL ME NOW.
KAHH
アホー
KAHH
アホー
DADOOM
ずーん
I ARE STUPID, YOU AM USELESS...
AW, DON'T GIVE UP ASUNA-SAN.
HEY, HOW'S IT GOING, NEGI-KUN?

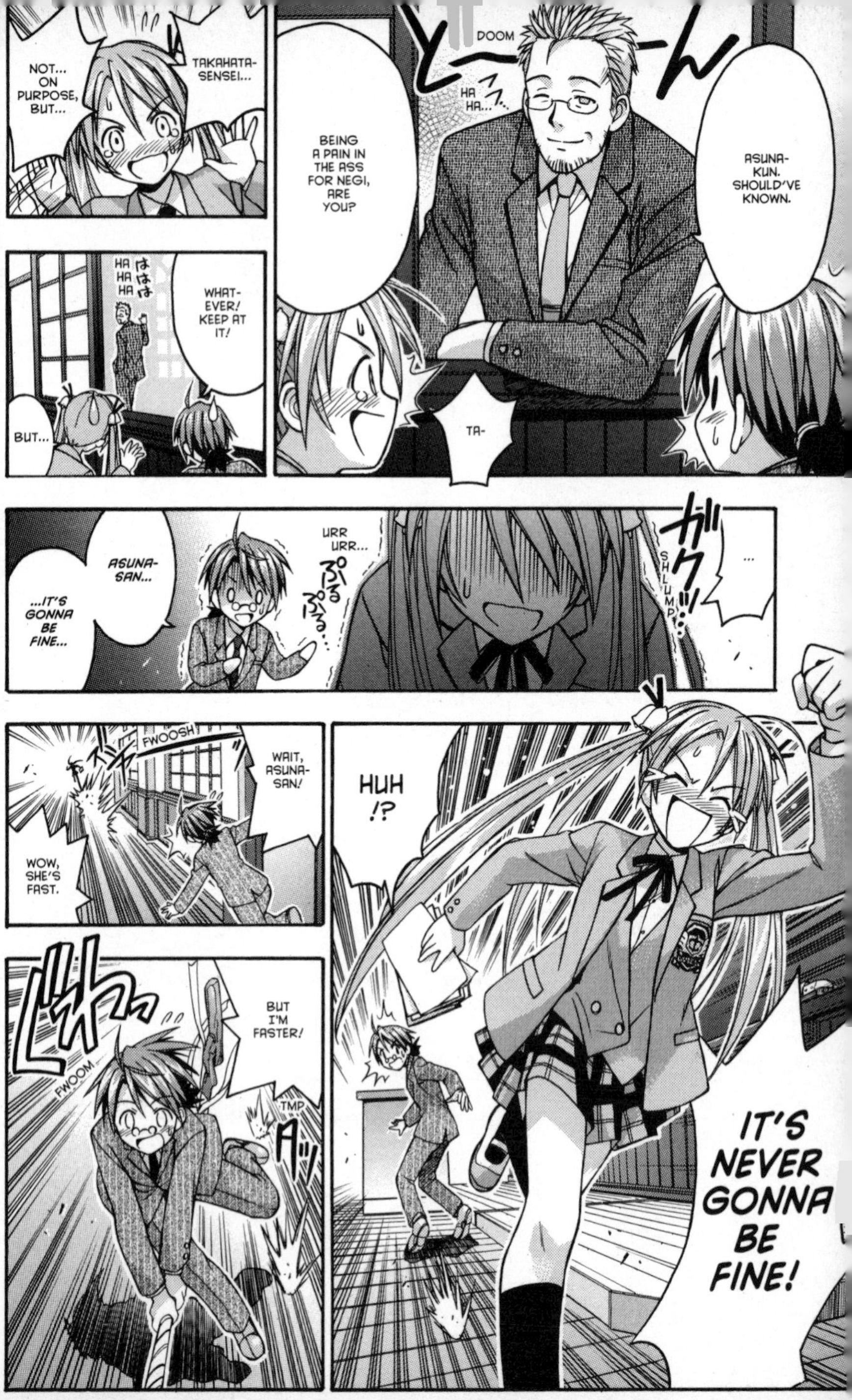
DOOM
ASUNA-KUN. SHOULD'VE KNOWN.
HA HA...
BEING A PAIN IN THE ASS FOR NEGI, ARE YOU?
TA-
TAKAHATA-SENSEI...
NOT... ON PURPOSE, BUT...
WHAT-EVER! KEEP AT IT!
HA HA HA
ははは
BUT...
ガクッ
SHLUMP
...
URR URR...
ぷるぷる
ASUNA-SAN...
...IT'S GONNA BE FINE...
HUH!?
IT'S NEVER GONNA BE FINE!
WAIT, ASUNA-SAN!
FWOOSH
WOW, SHE'S FAST.
BUT I'M FASTER!
FWOOM
TMP

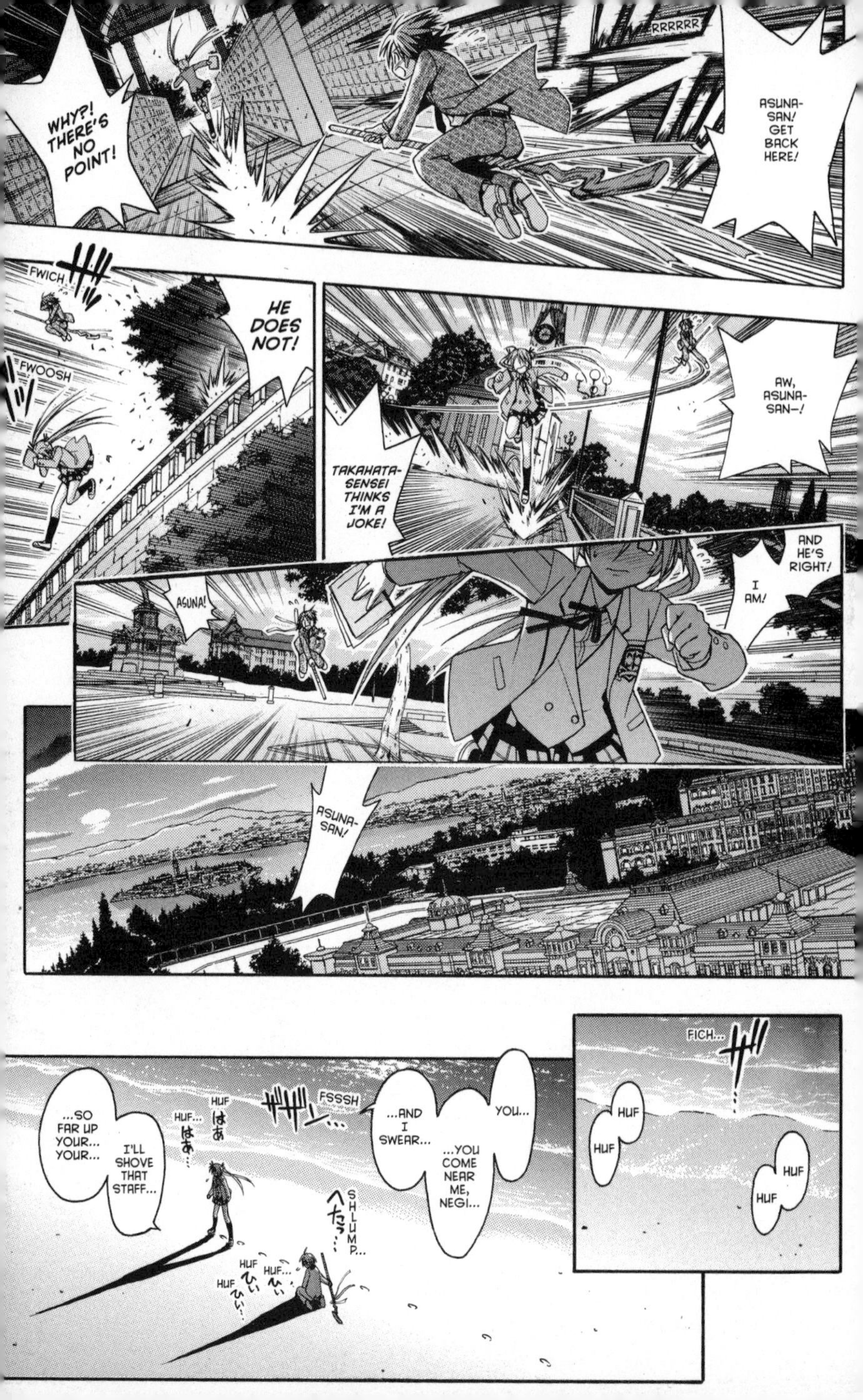
RRRRRR
ASUNA-SAN! GET BACK HERE!
WHY?! THERE'S NO POINT!
AW, ASUNA-SAN—!
TAKAHATA-SENSEI THINKS I'M A JOKE!
FWICH
FWOOSH
HE DOES NOT!
AND HE'S RIGHT!
I AM!
ASUNA!
ASUNA-SAN!
FICH...
HUF
HUF
HUF
HUF
YOU...
...YOU COME NEAR ME, NEGI...
...AND I SWEAR...
FSSSH
I'LL SHOVE THAT STAFF...
...SO FAR UP YOUR... YOUR...
HUF... HUF
はあ はあ...
SHLUMP...
HUF... HUF
HUF

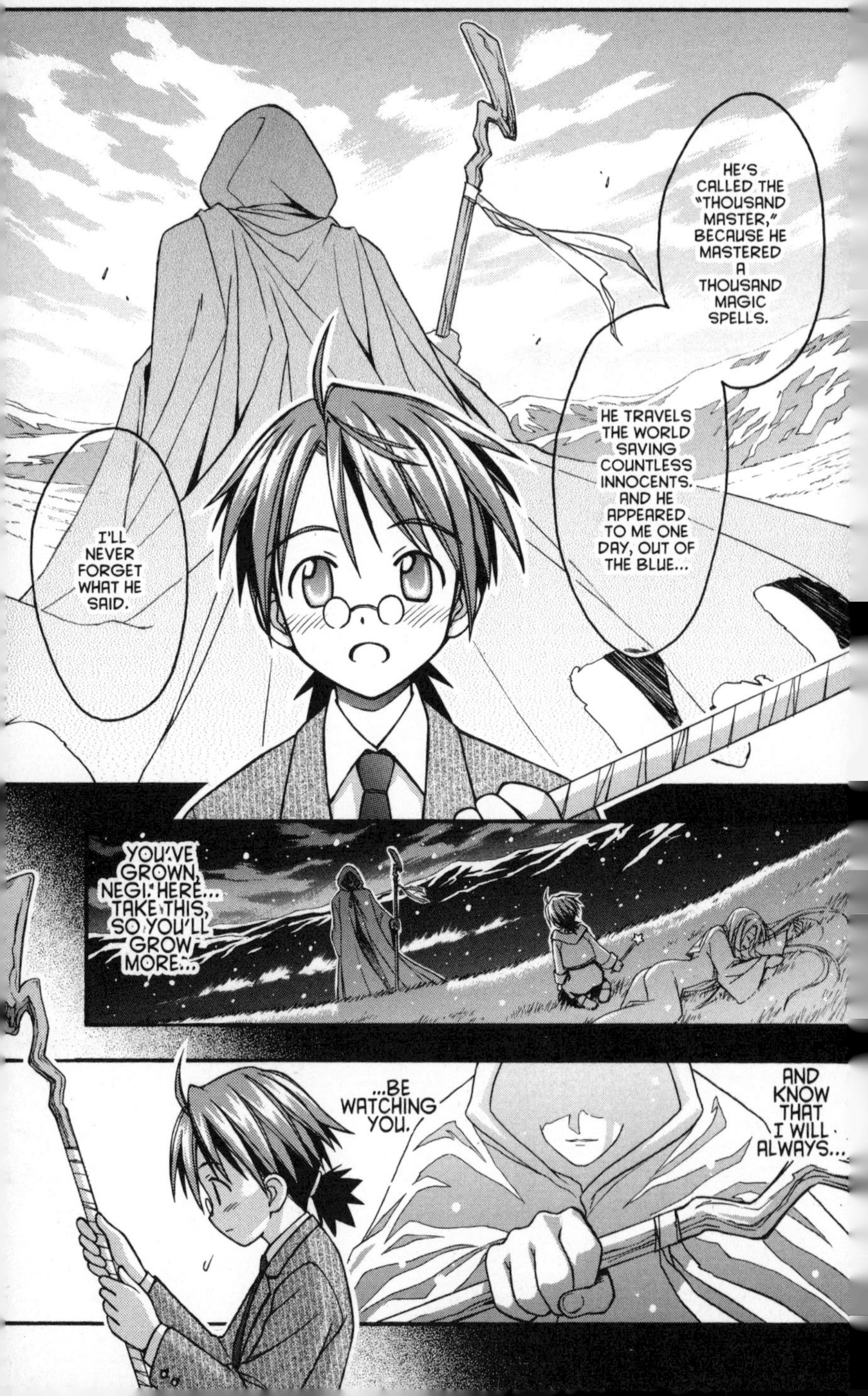
HE'S CALLED THE "THOUSAND MASTER," BECAUSE HE MASTERED A THOUSAND MAGIC SPELLS.
HE TRAVELS THE WORLD SAVING COUNTLESS INNOCENTS. AND HE APPEARED TO ME ONE DAY, OUT OF THE BLUE...
I'LL NEVER FORGET WHAT HE SAID.
YOU'VE GROWN, NEGI. HERE... TAKE THIS, SO YOU'LL GROW MORE...
AND KNOW THAT I WILL ALWAYS...
...BE WATCHING YOU.

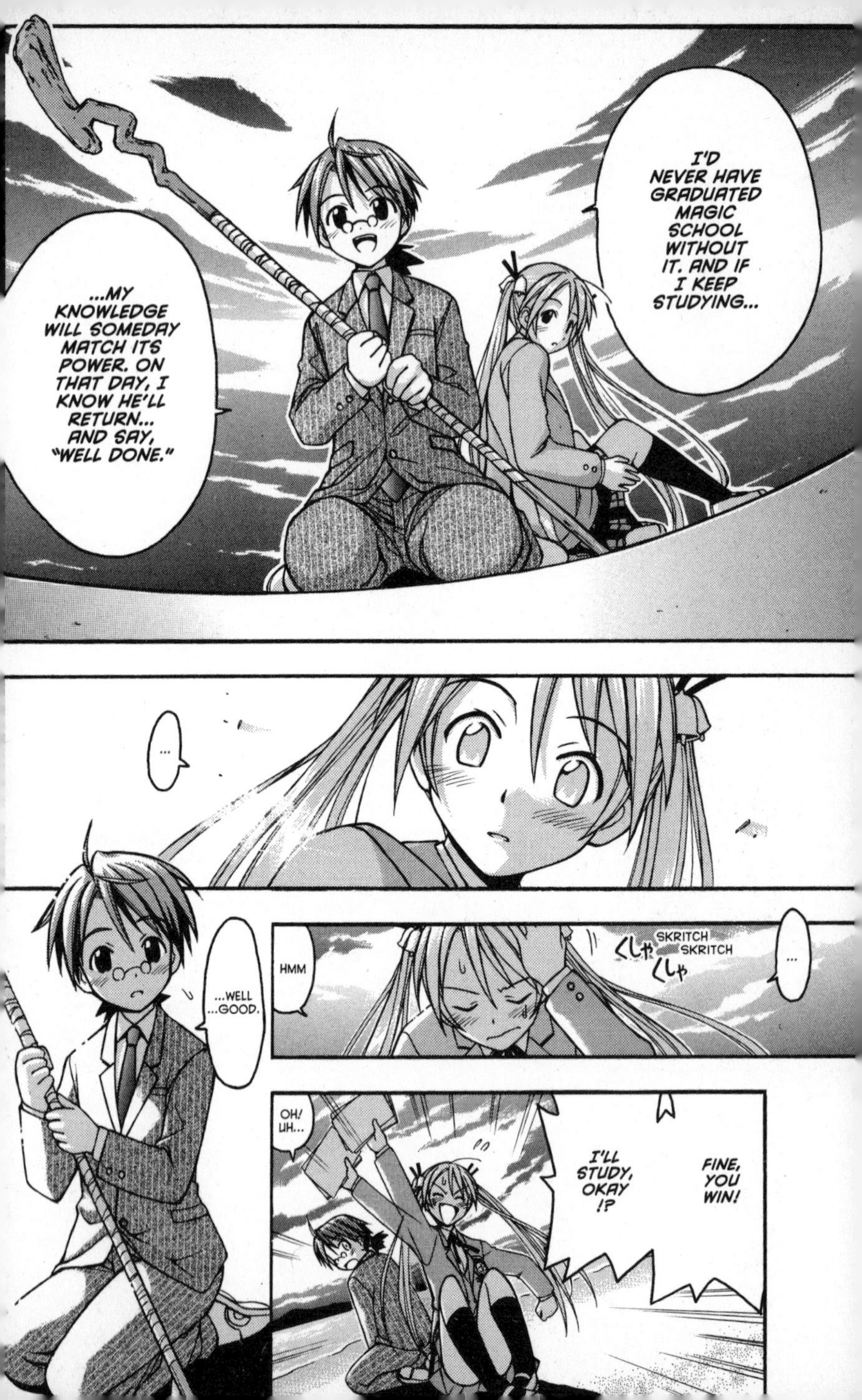
I'D NEVER HAVE GRADUATED MAGIC SCHOOL WITHOUT IT. AND IF I KEEP STUDYING...
...MY KNOWLEDGE WILL SOMEDAY MATCH ITS POWER. ON THAT DAY, I KNOW HE'LL RETURN... AND SAY, "WELL DONE."
...
...
くしゃ SKRITCH
くしゃ SKRITCH
HMM
...WELL ...GOOD.
FINE, YOU WIN!
I'LL STUDY, OKAY !?
OH! UH...

2-A STUDENT PROFILE

STUDENT NUMBER 2
YUNA AKASHI (BOTTOM)

BIRTHDATE: JUNE 1, 1988
BLOODTYPE: A
FAVORITE THINGS: FATHER
DISLIKES: BAD CLOTHES,
        SHIRTS HANGING OUT,
        SLOPPY LIFESTYLE
CLUB ACTIVITIES: BASKETBALL

STUDENT NUMBER 5
AKO IZUMI (RIGHT)

BIRTHDATE: NOVEMBER 21, 1988
BLOODTYPE: A
FAVORITE THINGS: CUTE BANDAIDS,
        DOING LAUNDRY
DISLIKES: BLOOD, FIGHTS
CLUB ACTIVITIES: NURSE'S OFFICE,
        BOYS' SOCCER
        TEAM MANAGER

STUDENT NUMBER 16
MAKIE SASAKI (TOP LEFT)

BIRTHDATE: MARCH 7, 1989
BLOODTYPE: O
FAVORITE THINGS: DEVOTED TO RHYTHMIC GYMNASTICS,
        NEGI, CUTE THINGS
DISLIKES: SLIMY THINGS LIKE NATTO
CLUB ACTIVITIES: RHYTHMIC GYMNASTICS

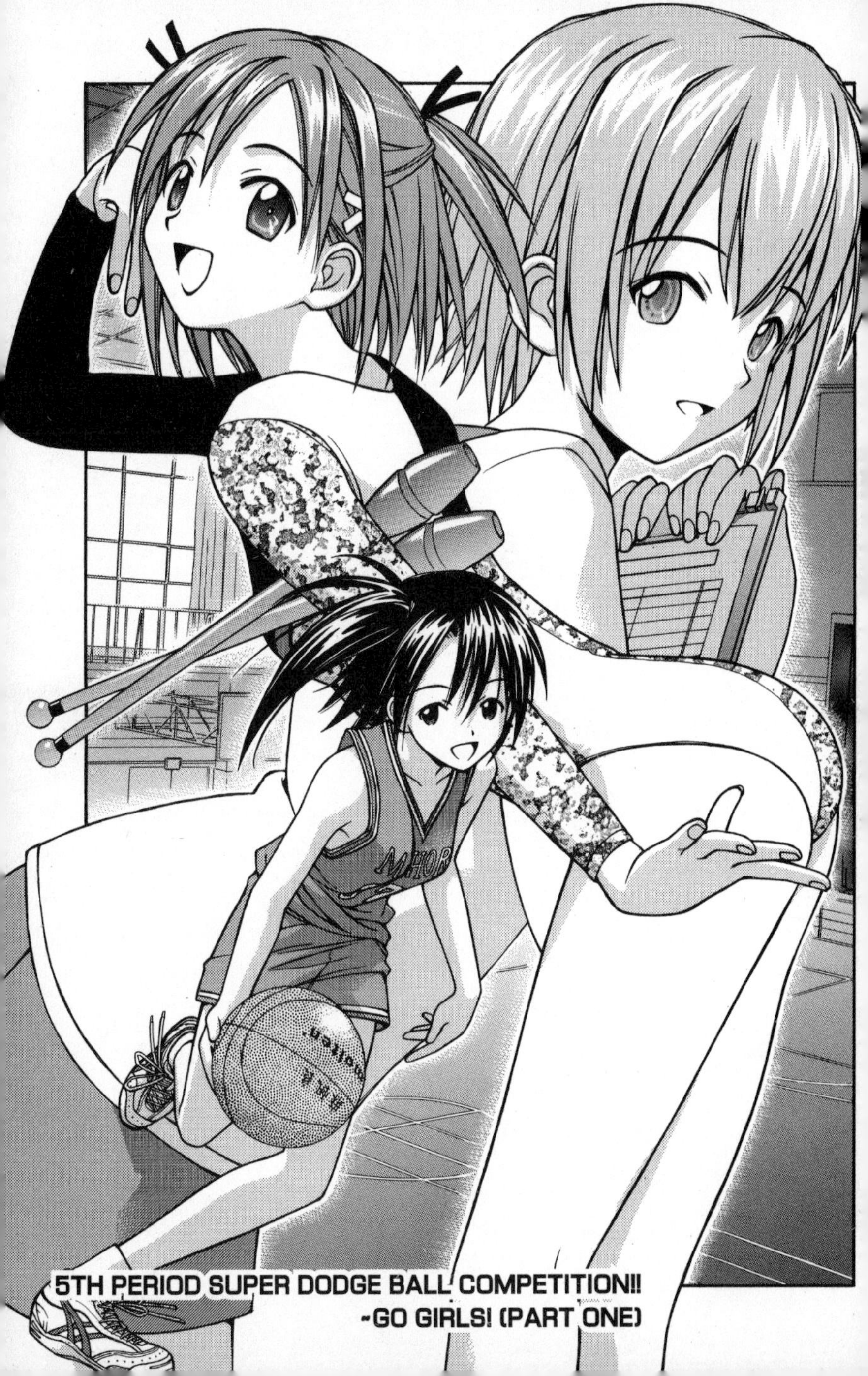

5TH PERIOD SUPER DODGE BALL COMPETITION!! ~GO GIRLS! (PART ONE)

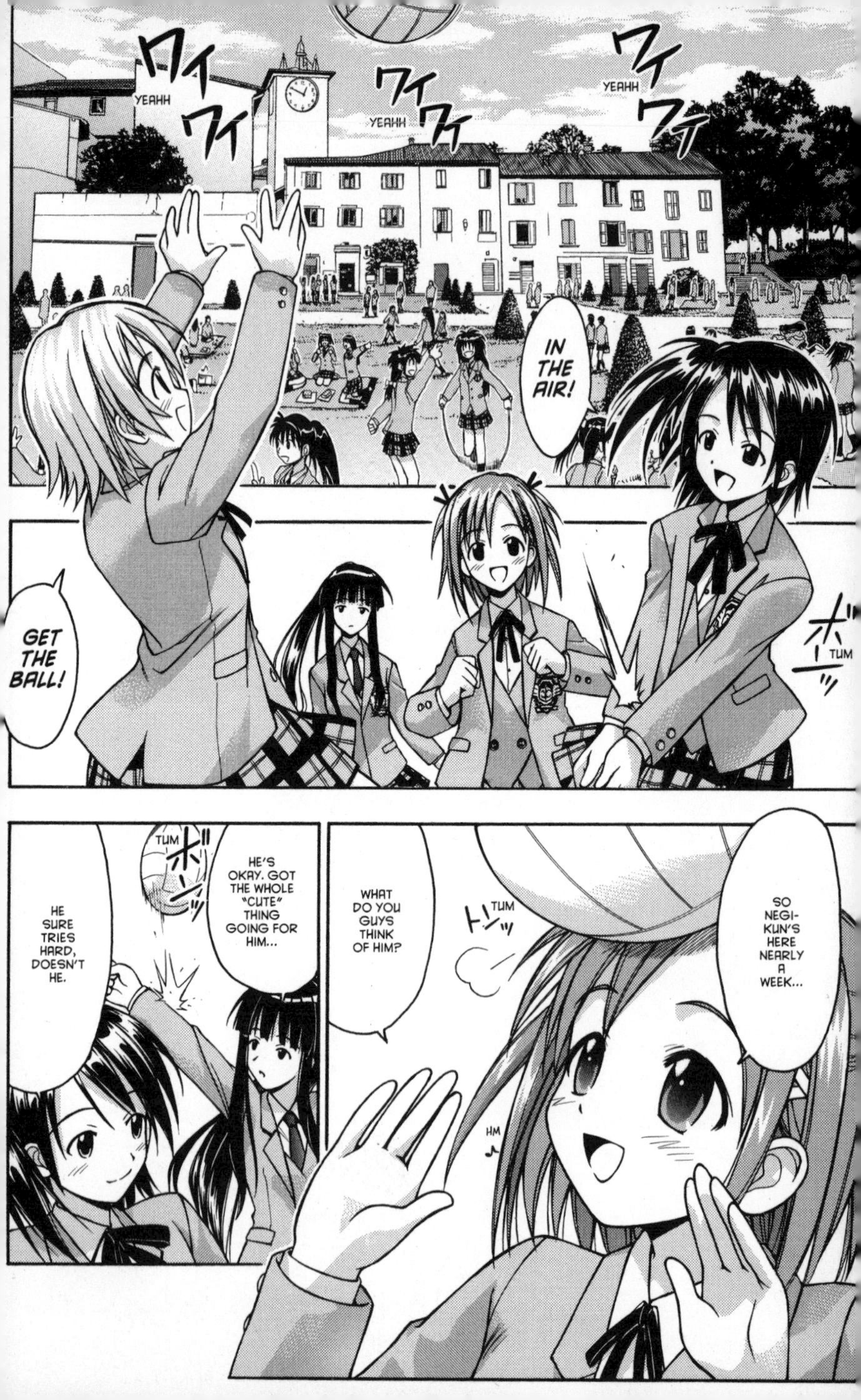
ワイワイ
YEAHH
ワイワイ
YEAHH
ワイワイ
YEAHH
IN THE AIR!
ボッ
TUM
GET THE BALL!
SO NEGI-KUN'S HERE NEARLY A WEEK...
トンッ
TUM
HM
WHAT DO YOU GUYS THINK OF HIM?
ボンッ
TUM
HE'S OKAY. GOT THE WHOLE "CUTE" THING GOING FOR HIM...
HE SURE TRIES HARD, DOESN'T HE.

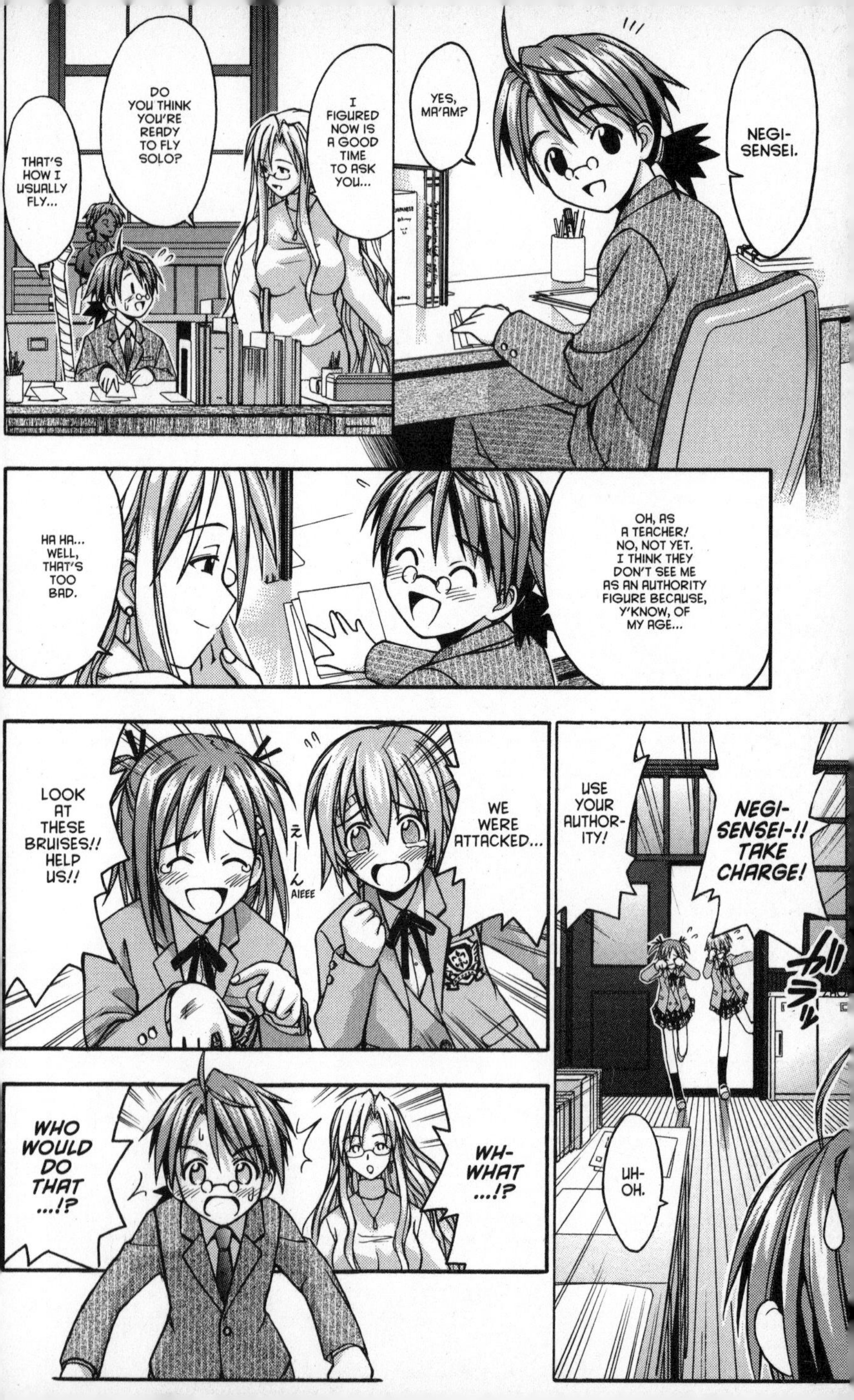

NEGI-SENSEI.
YES, MA'AM?
I FIGURED NOW IS A GOOD TIME TO ASK YOU...
DO YOU THINK YOU'RE READY TO FLY SOLO?
THAT'S HOW I USUALLY FLY...
OH, AS A TEACHER! NO, NOT YET. I THINK THEY DON'T SEE ME AS AN AUTHORITY FIGURE BECAUSE, Y'KNOW, OF MY AGE...
HA HA... WELL, THAT'S TOO BAD.
ガラッ
NEGI-SENSEI-!! TAKE CHARGE!
USE YOUR AUTHOR-ITY!
UH-OH.
WE WERE ATTACKED...
えーん
AIEEE
LOOK AT THESE BRUISES!! HELP US!!
WH-WHAT ...!?
WHO WOULD DO THAT ...!?

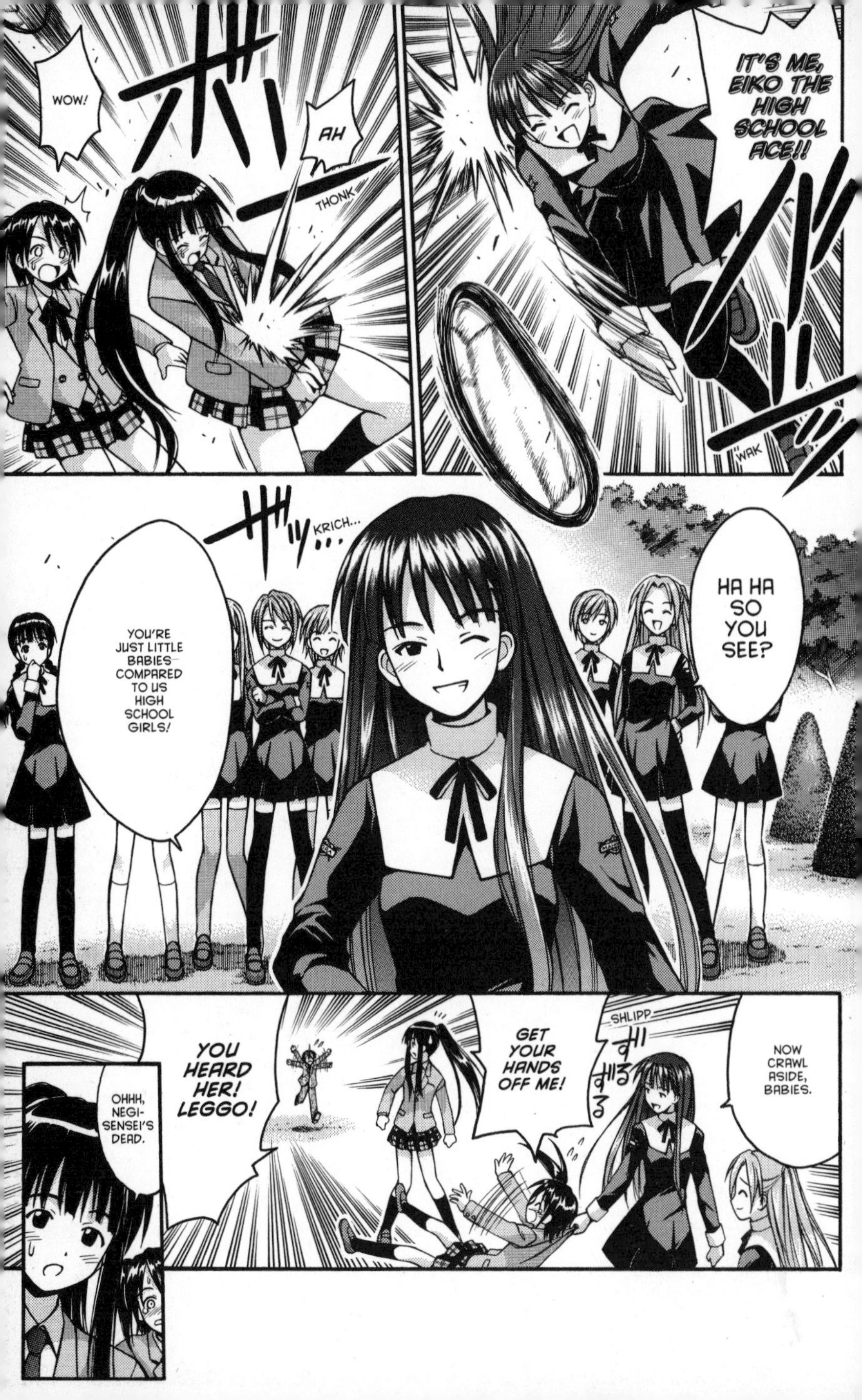

IT'S ME, EIKO THE HIGH SCHOOL ACE!!
WAK
AH
THONK
WOW!
HA HA SO YOU SEE?
KRICH...
YOU'RE JUST LITTLE BABIES— COMPARED TO US HIGH SCHOOL GIRLS!
NOW CRAWL ASIDE, BABIES.
SHLIPP
GET YOUR HANDS OFF ME!
YOU HEARD HER! LEGGO!
OHHH, NEGI-SENSEI'S DEAD.

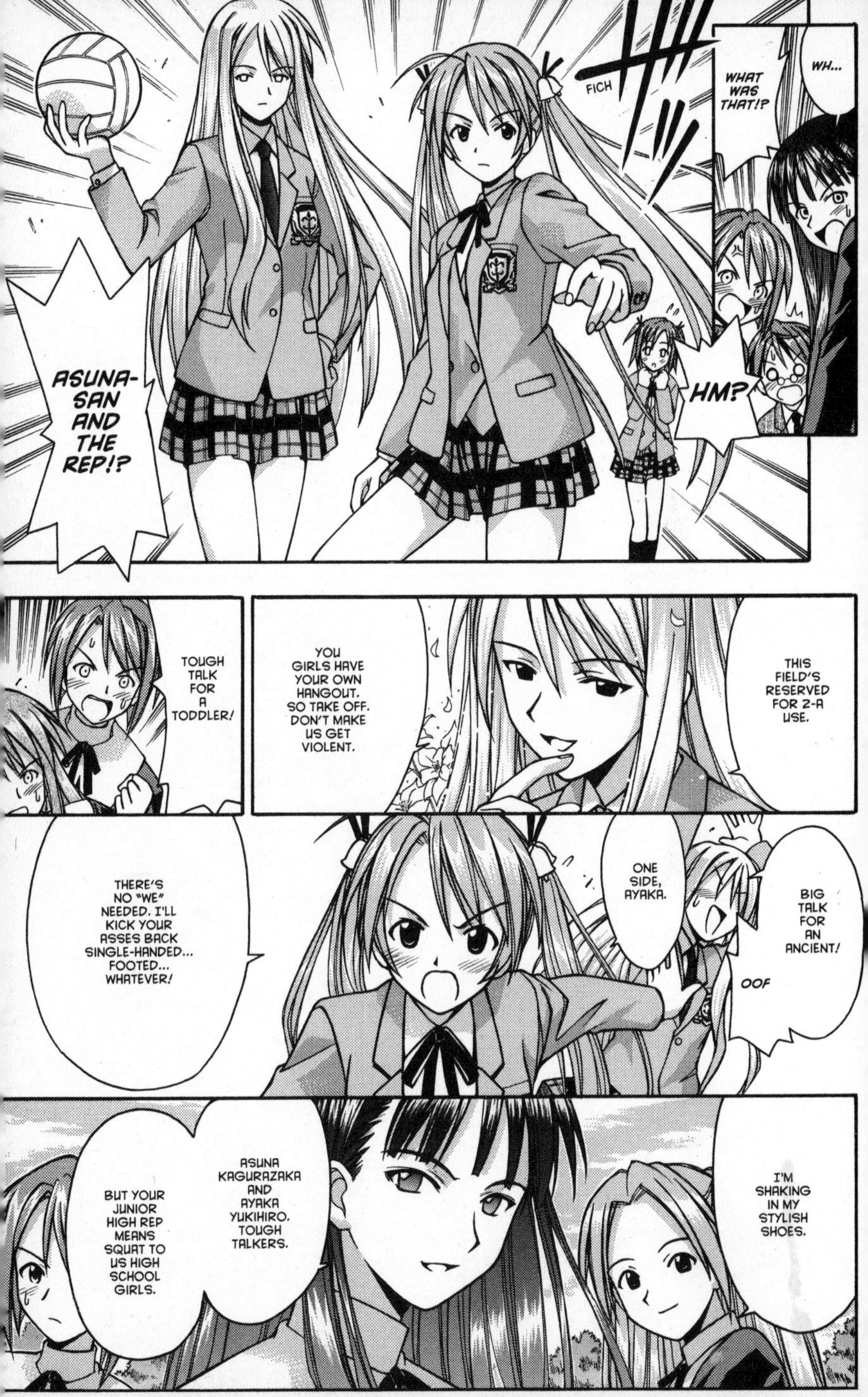
WH...
WHAT WAS THAT!?
FICH
HM?
ASUNA-SAN AND THE REP!?
THIS FIELD'S RESERVED FOR 2-A USE.
YOU GIRLS HAVE YOUR OWN HANGOUT. SO TAKE OFF. DON'T MAKE US GET VIOLENT.
TOUGH TALK FOR A TODDLER!
BIG TALK FOR AN ANCIENT!
OOF
ONE SIDE, AYAKA.
THERE'S NO "WE" NEEDED. I'LL KICK YOUR ASSES BACK SINGLE-HANDED... FOOTED... WHATEVER!
I'M SHAKING IN MY STYLISH SHOES.
ASUNA KAGURAZAKA AND AYAKA YUKIHIRO. TOUGH TALKERS.
BUT YOUR JUNIOR HIGH REP MEANS SQUAT TO US HIGH SCHOOL GIRLS.

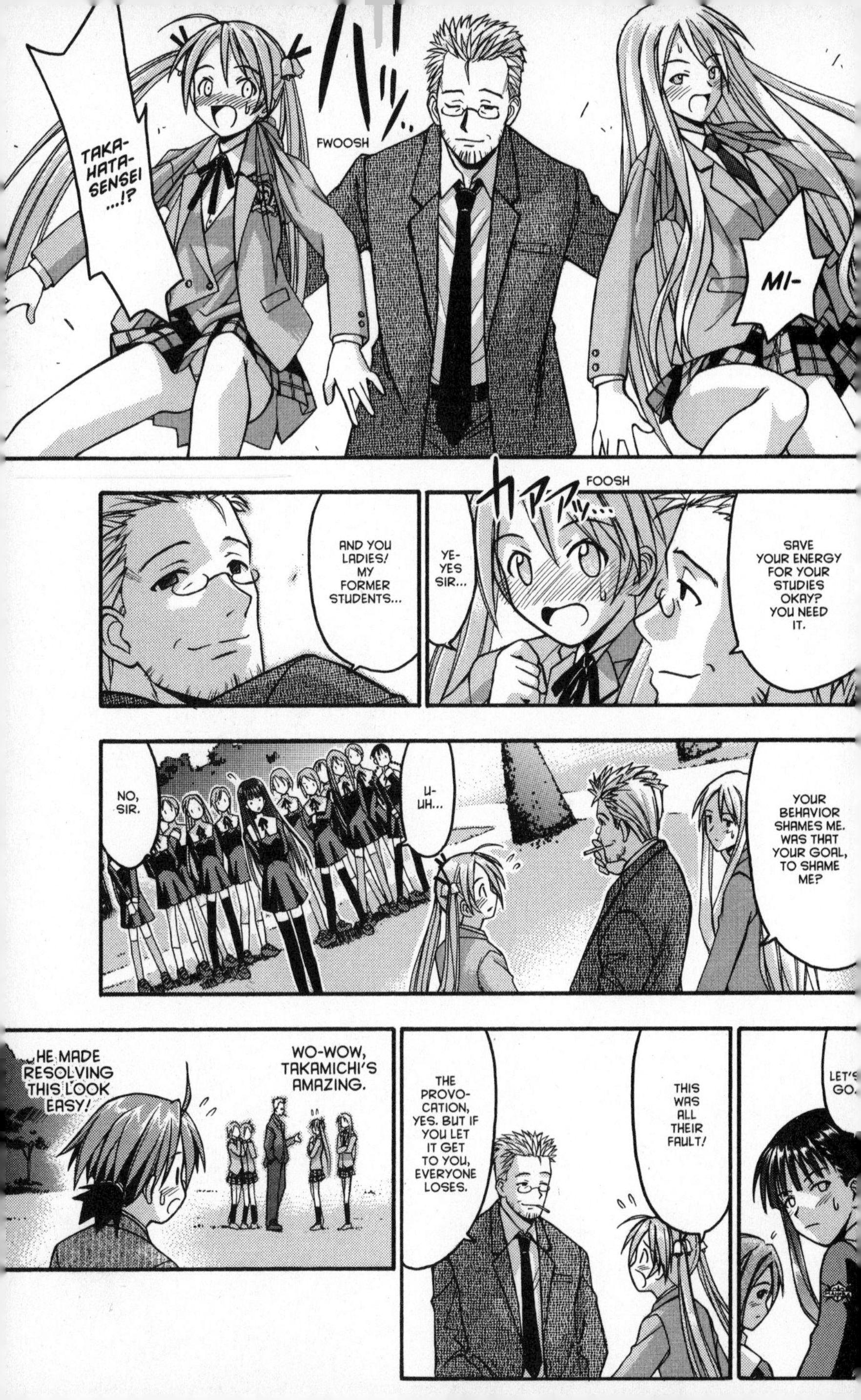
MI-
FWOOSH
TAKA-HATA-SENSEI...!?
FOOSH
SAVE YOUR ENERGY FOR YOUR STUDIES OKAY? YOU NEED IT.
YE-YES SIR...
AND YOU LADIES! MY FORMER STUDENTS...
YOUR BEHAVIOR SHAMES ME. WAS THAT YOUR GOAL, TO SHAME ME?
U-UH...
NO, SIR.
LET'S GO.
THIS WAS ALL THEIR FAULT!
THE PROVOCATION, YES. BUT IF YOU LET IT GET TO YOU, EVERYONE LOSES.
WO-WOW, TAKAMICHI'S AMAZING.
HE MADE RESOLVING THIS LOOK EASY!

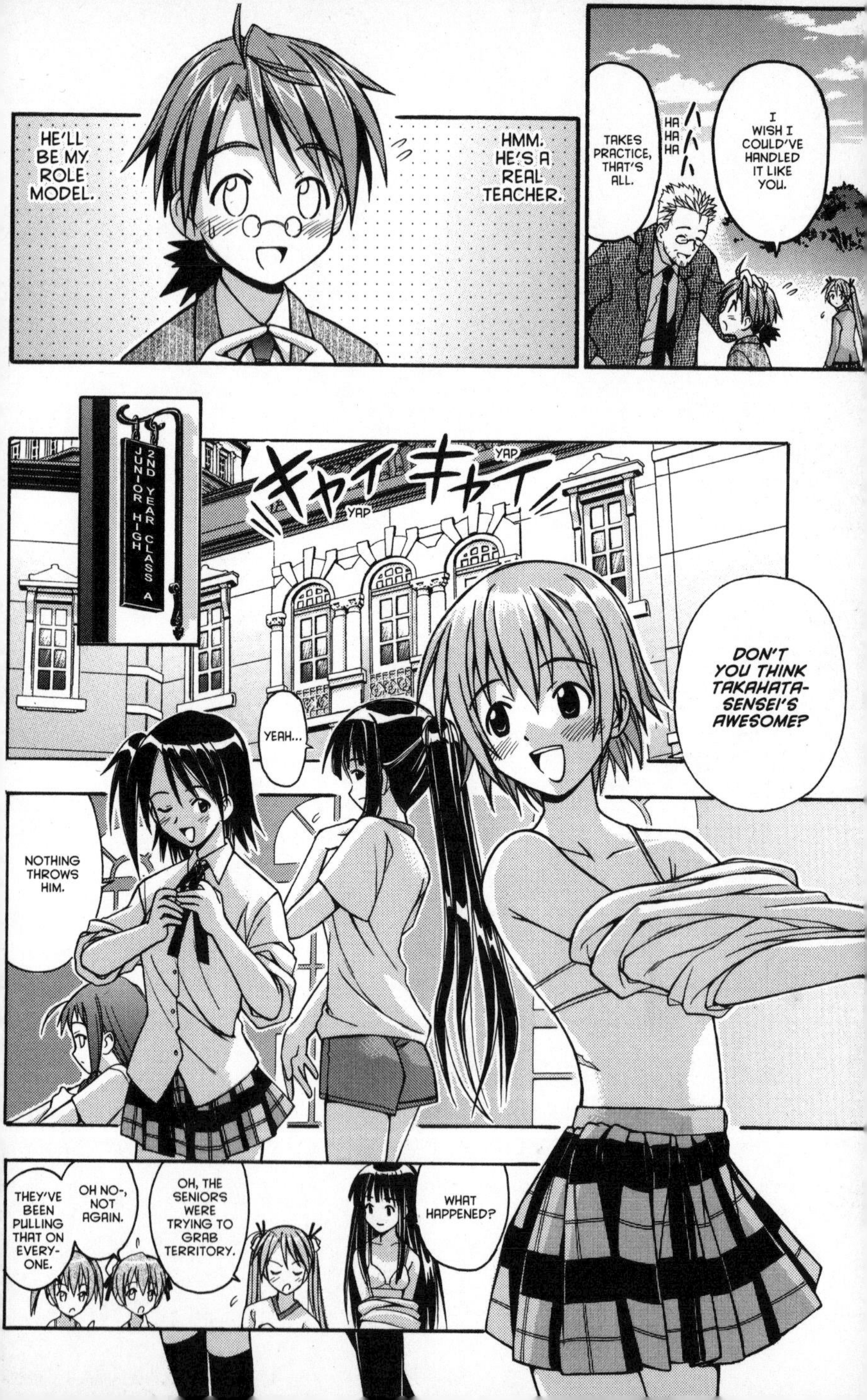
I WISH I COULD'VE HANDLED IT LIKE YOU.
HA HA HA
TAKES PRACTICE, THAT'S ALL.
HMM. HE'S A REAL TEACHER.
HE'LL BE MY ROLE MODEL.
2ND YEAR CLASS A JUNIOR HIGH
キャイ キャイ
YAP
YAP
DON'T YOU THINK TAKAHATA-SENSEI'S AWESOME?
YEAH...
NOTHING THROWS HIM.
WHAT HAPPENED?
OH, THE SENIORS WERE TRYING TO GRAB TERRITORY.
OH NO-, NOT AGAIN.
THEY'VE BEEN PULLING THAT ON EVERY-ONE.

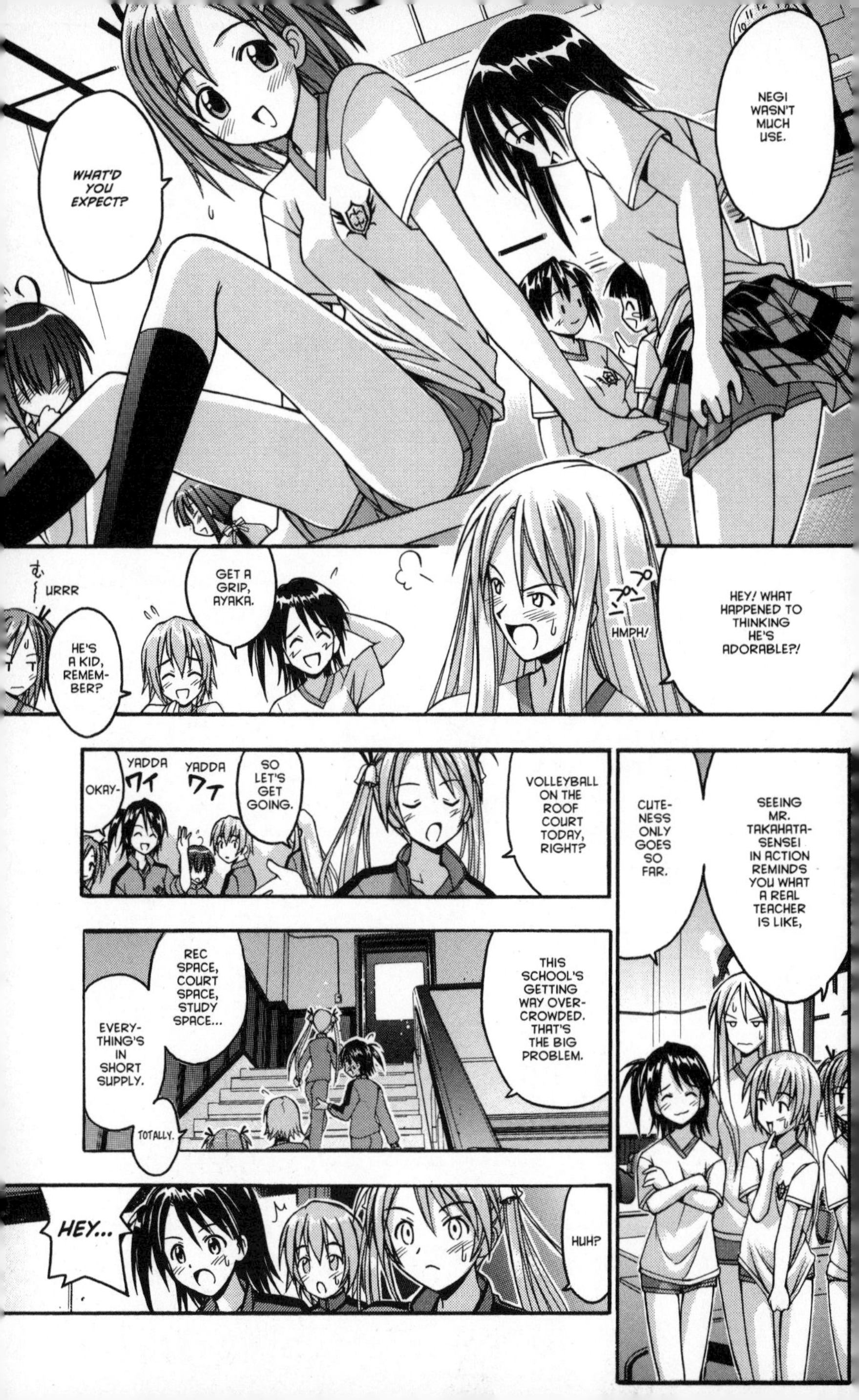
NEGI WASN'T MUCH USE.
WHAT'D YOU EXPECT?
HEY! WHAT HAPPENED TO THINKING HE'S ADORABLE?!
HMPH!
GET A GRIP, AYAKA.
HE'S A KID, REMEMBER?
URRR
SEEING MR. TAKAHATA-SENSEI IN ACTION REMINDS YOU WHAT A REAL TEACHER IS LIKE,
CUTENESS ONLY GOES SO FAR.
VOLLEYBALL ON THE ROOF COURT TODAY, RIGHT?
SO LET'S GET GOING.
YADDA
YADDA
OKAY-
THIS SCHOOL'S GETTING WAY OVERCROWDED. THAT'S THE BIG PROBLEM.
REC SPACE, COURT SPACE, STUDY SPACE...
EVERYTHING'S IN SHORT SUPPLY.
TOTALLY.
HUH?
HEY...

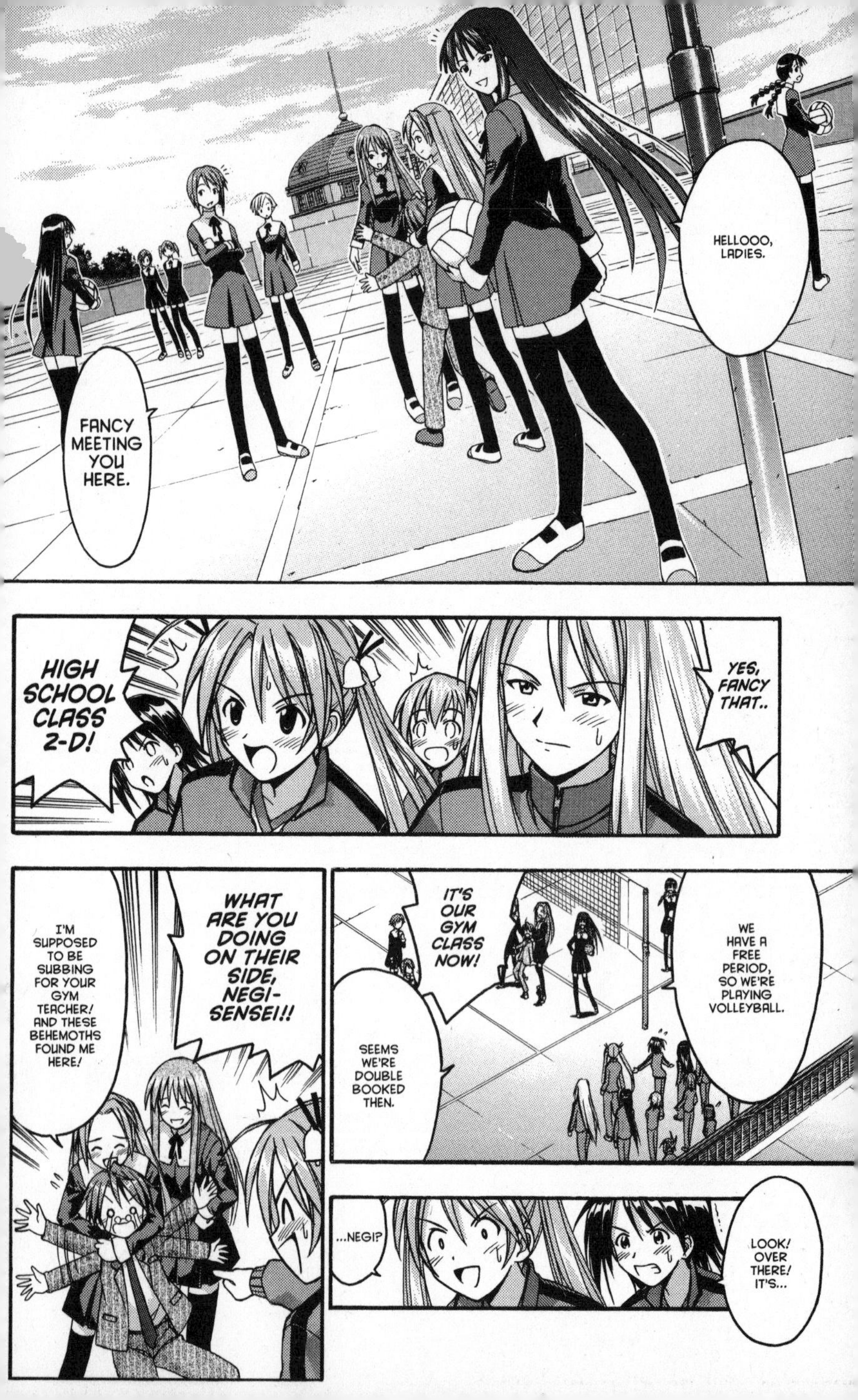
HELLOOO, LADIES.
FANCY MEETING YOU HERE.
YES, FANCY THAT..
HIGH SCHOOL CLASS 2-D!
WE HAVE A FREE PERIOD, SO WE'RE PLAYING VOLLEYBALL.
IT'S OUR GYM CLASS NOW!
SEEMS WE'RE DOUBLE BOOKED THEN.
LOOK! OVER THERE! IT'S...
...NEGI?
WHAT ARE YOU DOING ON THEIR SIDE, NEGI-SENSEI!!
I'M SUPPOSED TO BE SUBBING FOR YOUR GYM TEACHER! AND THESE BEHEMOTHS FOUND ME HERE!

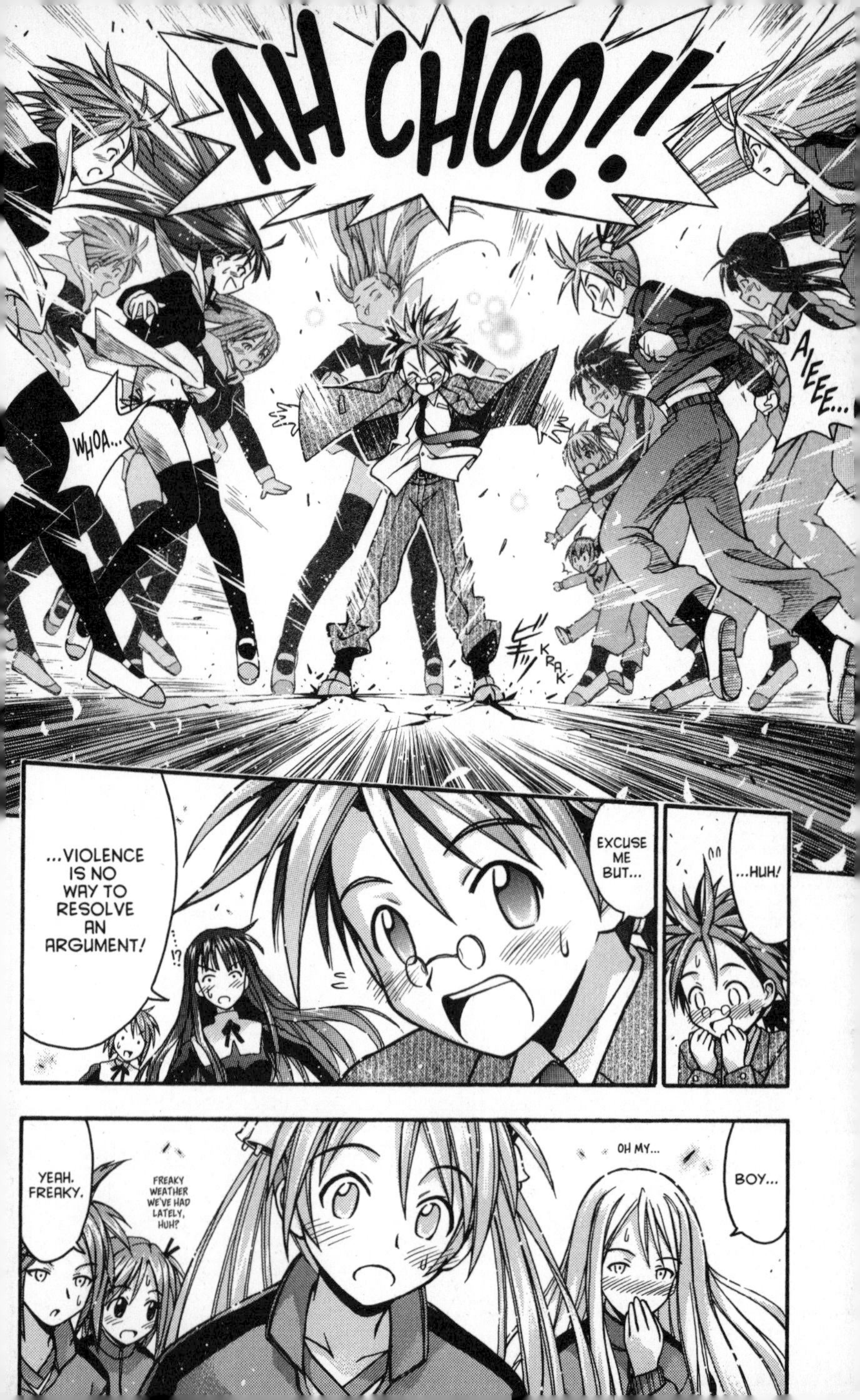
AH CHOO!!
AIEEE...
WHOA...
KRAK
...HUH!
EXCUSE ME BUT...
...VIOLENCE IS NO WAY TO RESOLVE AN ARGUMENT!
!?
BOY...
OH MY...
FREAKY WEATHER WE'VE HAD LATELY, HUH?
YEAH. FREAKY.

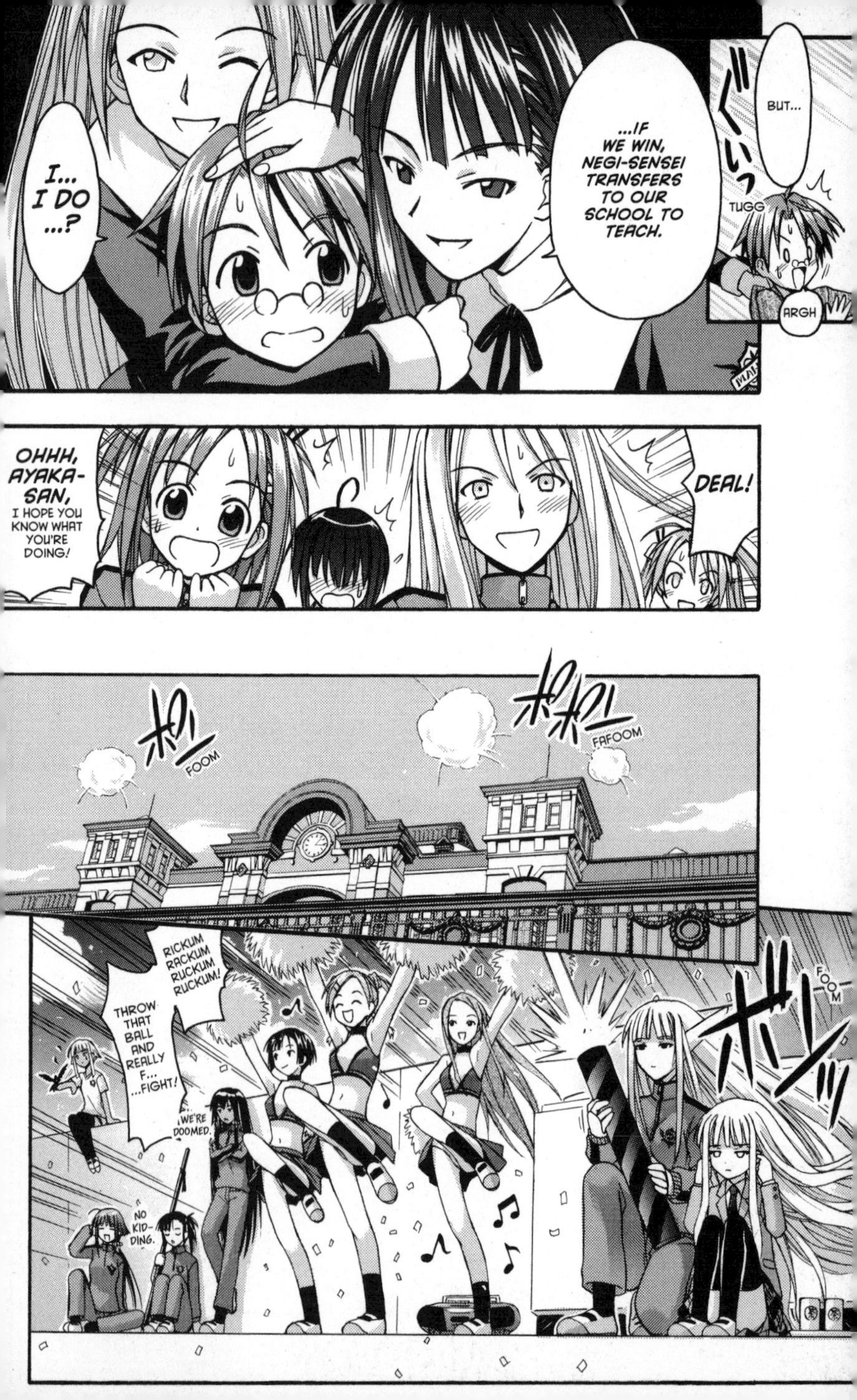
BUT...
TUGG
ARGH
...IF WE WIN, NEGI-SENSEI TRANSFERS TO OUR SCHOOL TO TEACH.
I... I DO ...?
DEAL!
OHHH, AYAKA-SAN, I HOPE YOU KNOW WHAT YOU'RE DOING!
FAFOOM
FOOM
FOOM
RICKUM RACKUM RUCKUM RUCKUM!
THROW THAT BALL AND REALLY F... ...FIGHT!
WE'RE DOOMED.
NO KID-DING.

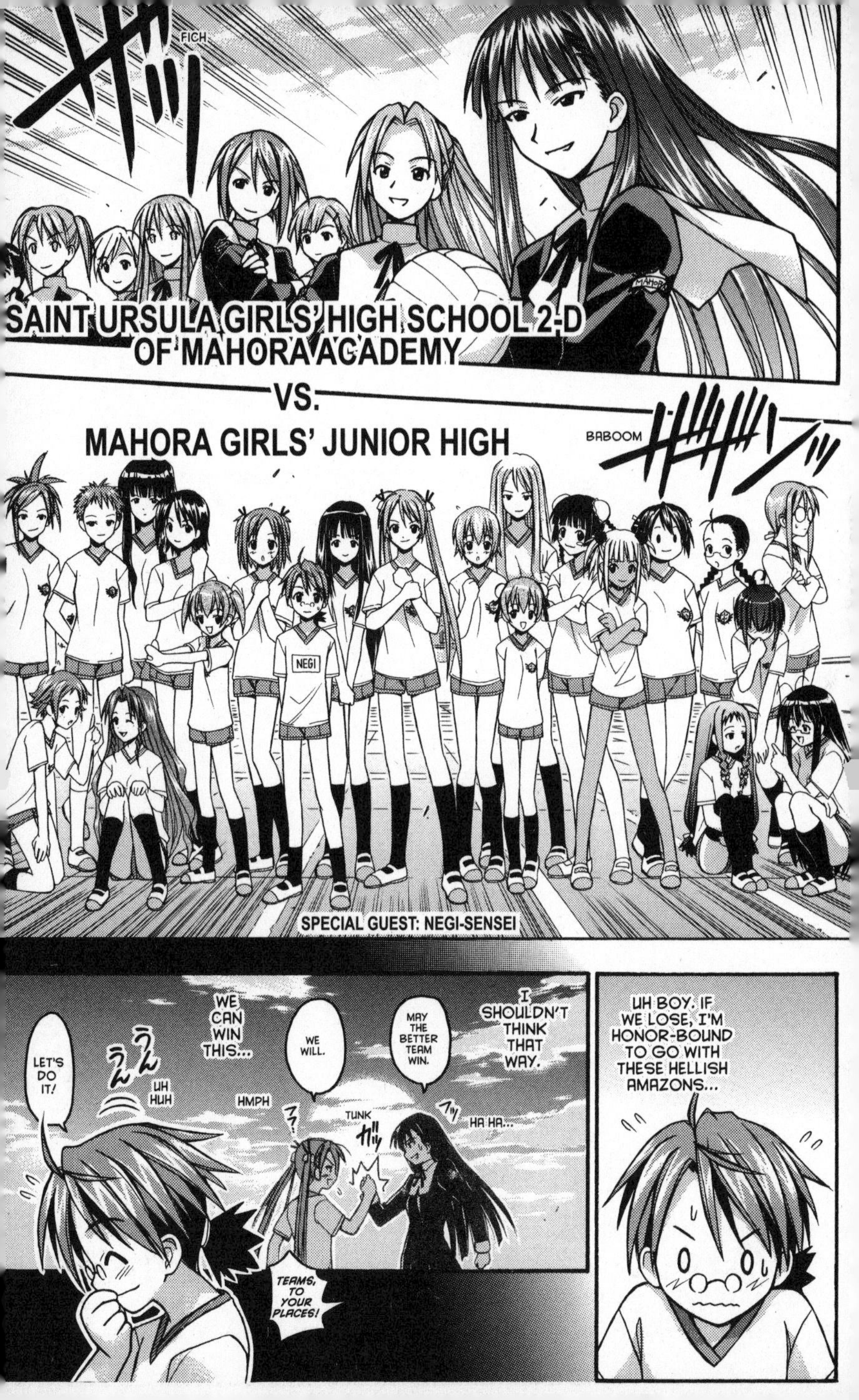
FICH
SAINT URSULA GIRLS' HIGH SCHOOL 2-D
OF MAHORA ACADEMY
VS.
MAHORA GIRLS' JUNIOR HIGH
BABOOM
NEGI
SPECIAL GUEST: NEGI-SENSEI
UH BOY, IF WE LOSE, I'M HONOR-BOUND TO GO WITH THESE HELLISH AMAZONS...
I SHOULDN'T THINK THAT WAY.
HA HA...
MAY THE BETTER TEAM WIN.
TUNK
WE WILL.
HMPH
WE CAN WIN THIS...
UH HUH
LET'S DO IT!
TEAMS, TO YOUR PLACES!

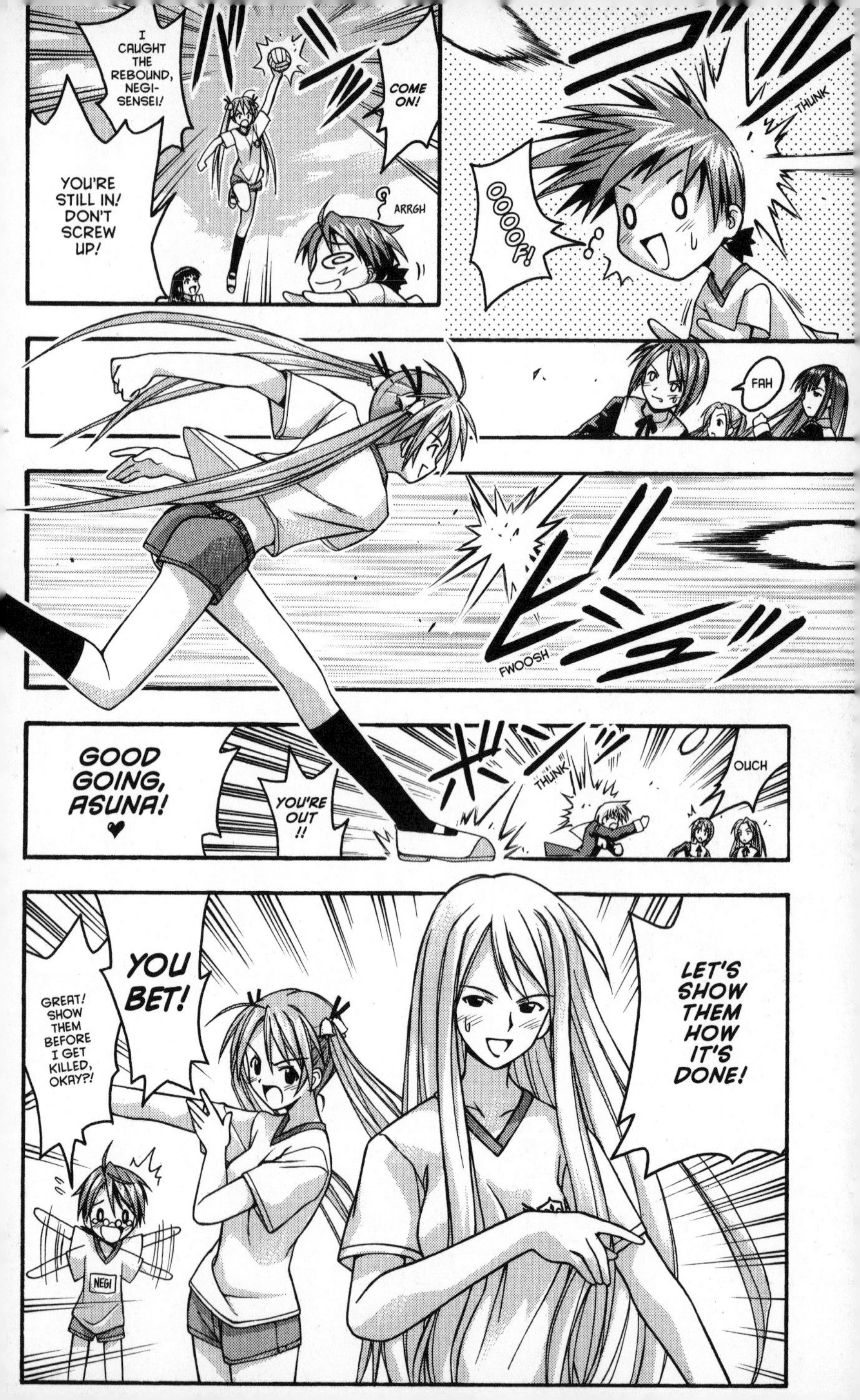
OOOOF!
THUNK
I CAUGHT THE REBOUND, NEGI-SENSEI!
COME ON!
ARRGH
YOU'RE STILL IN! DON'T SCREW UP!
FAH
FWOOSH
OUCH
THUNK
YOU'RE OUT !!
GOOD GOING, ASUNA!
LET'S SHOW THEM HOW IT'S DONE!
YOU BET!
GREAT! SHOW THEM BEFORE I GET KILLED, OKAY?!
NEGI

NEGI TEAM | HIGH SCHOOL GIRLS

WITH 11 TO GO!!

22 | **10**

HIGH SCHOOL TEAM HAS 1 OUT!!

ALL RIGHT!

YEAHH YEAHH YEAHH

IT ISN'T A FIGHT! IT'S WAR! NOW KEEP LOW OR BE A CASUALTY!

THIS ISN'T SUPPOSED TO BE A FIGHT!

WE'LL WIN THIS FIGHT HANDS DOWN!

TIME TO PUT YOUR AGGRESSION TO GOOD USE, ASUNA!

HA HA

6TH PERIOD SUPER DODGE BALL COMPETITION!! ~GO GIRLS! (PART TWO)

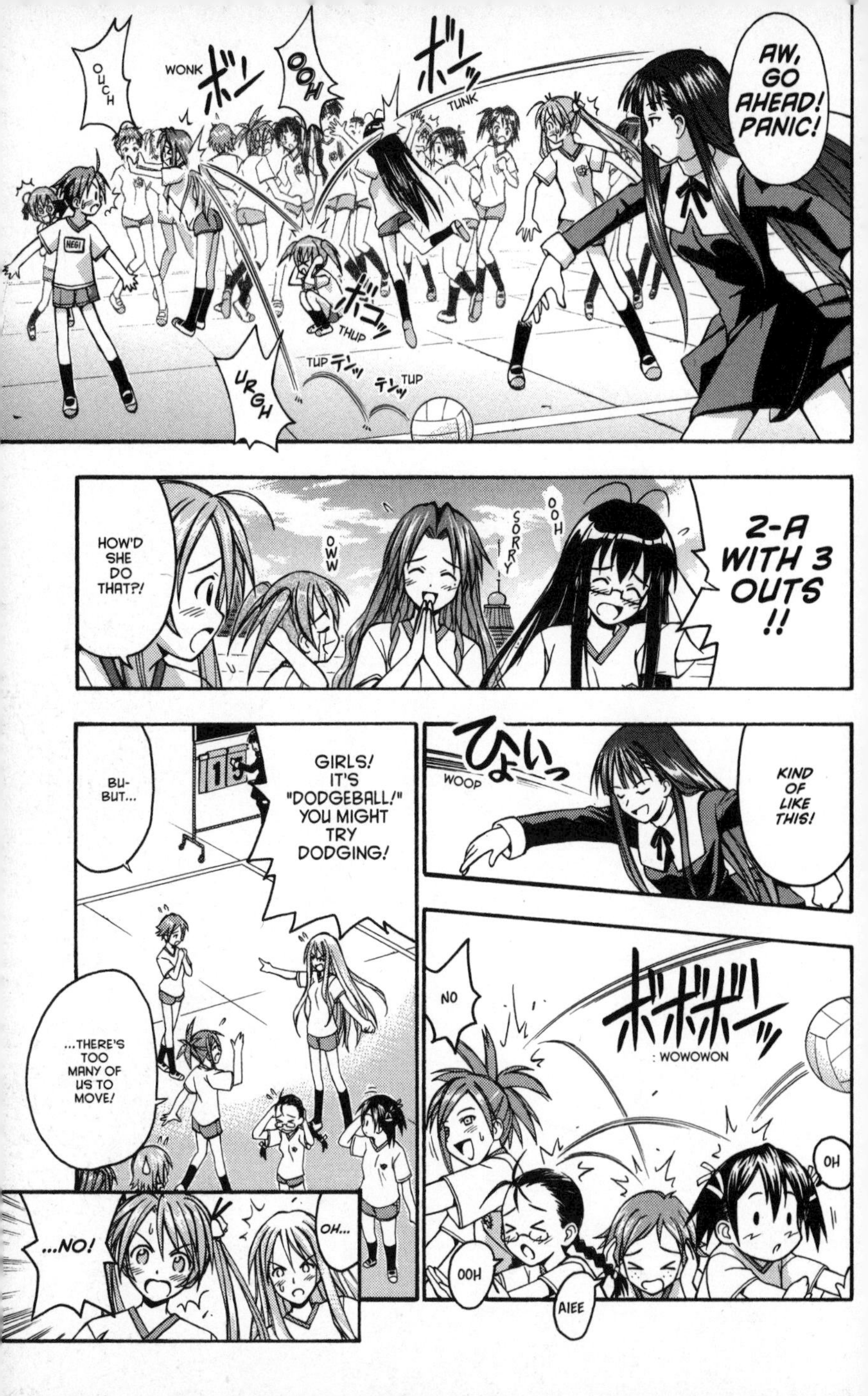
AW, GO AHEAD! PANIC!
ボーッ
TUNK
OOOH
ボン
WONK
OUCH
ボゴッ
THUP
テンッ
TUP
テンッ
TUP
URGH
2-A WITH 3 OUTS !!
OOH
SORRY
OWW
HOW'D SHE DO THAT?!
ひょいっ
WOOP
KIND OF LIKE THIS!
GIRLS! IT'S "DODGEBALL!" YOU MIGHT TRY DODGING!
BU-BUT...
...THERE'S TOO MANY OF US TO MOVE!
ボボボーッ
: WOWOWON
NO
OH
OOH
AIEE
OH...
...NO!

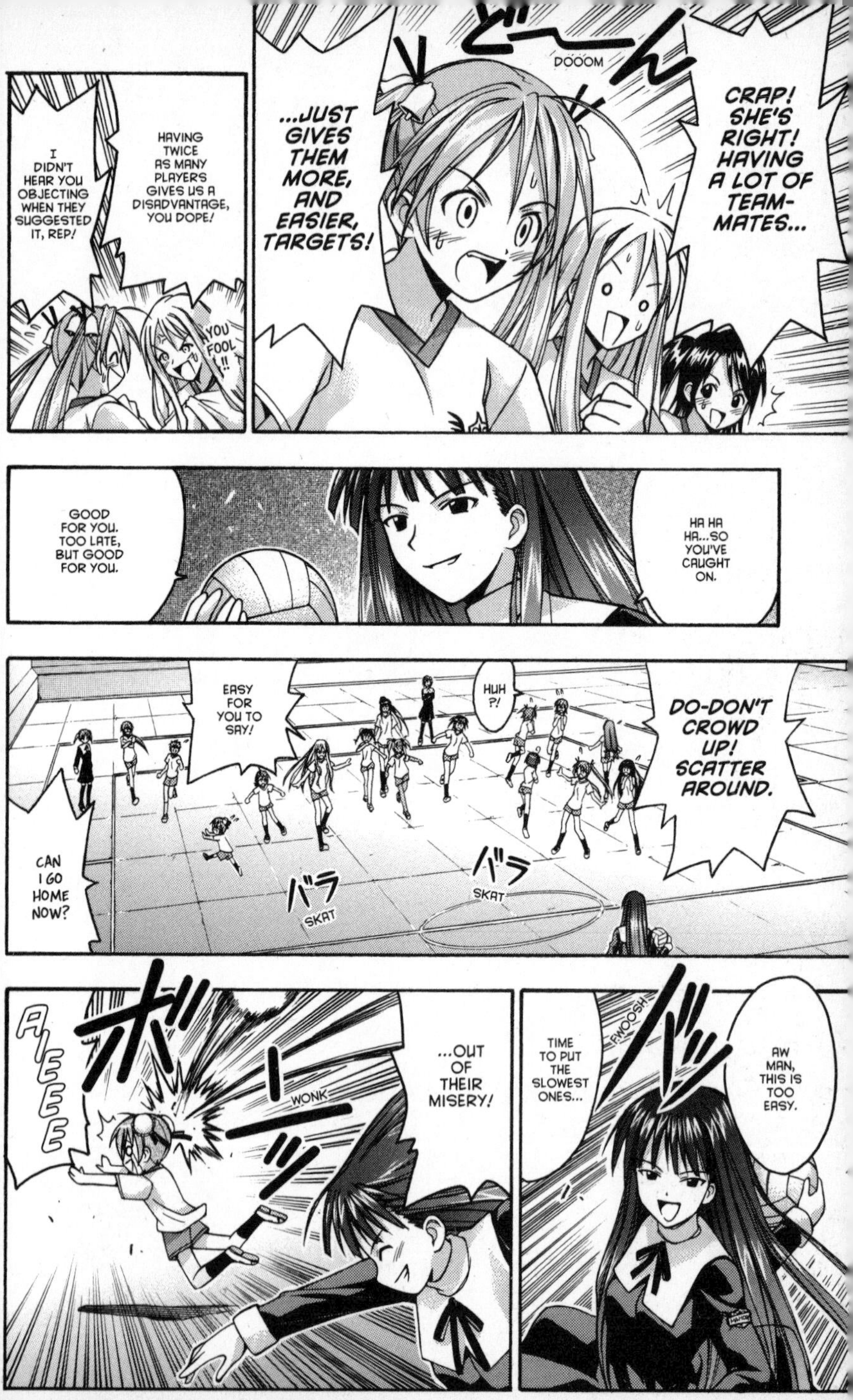
DOOOM
CRAP! SHE'S RIGHT! HAVING A LOT OF TEAM-MATES...
...JUST GIVES THEM MORE, AND EASIER, TARGETS!
HAVING TWICE AS MANY PLAYERS GIVES US A DISADVANTAGE, YOU DOPE!
I DIDN'T HEAR YOU OBJECTING WHEN THEY SUGGESTED IT, REP!
YOU FOOL!!
HA HA HA...SO YOU'VE CAUGHT ON.
GOOD FOR YOU. TOO LATE, BUT GOOD FOR YOU.
DO-DON'T CROWD UP! SCATTER AROUND.
HUH?!
EASY FOR YOU TO SAY!
SKAT
SKAT
CAN I GO HOME NOW?
AW MAN, THIS IS TOO EASY.
FWOOSH
TIME TO PUT THE SLOWEST ONES...
...OUT OF THEIR MISERY!
WONK
AIEEEE

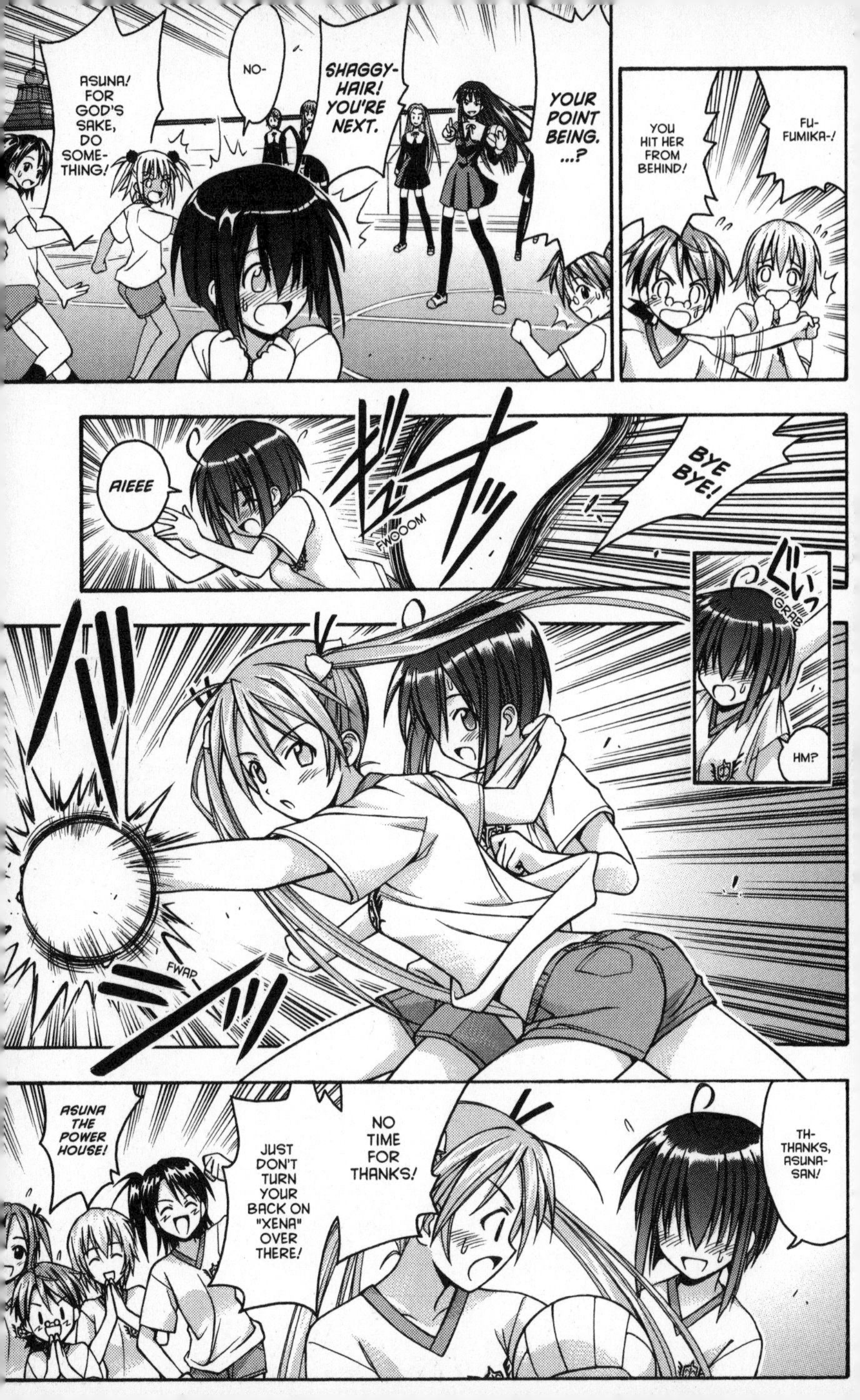
FU-FUMIKA-!
YOU HIT HER FROM BEHIND!
YOUR POINT BEING. ...?
SHAGGY-HAIR! YOU'RE NEXT.
NO-
ASUNA! FOR GOD'S SAKE, DO SOMETHING!
BYE BYE!
FWOOOM
AIEEE
ぐいっ
GRAB
HM?
FWAP
TH-THANKS, ASUNA-SAN!
NO TIME FOR THANKS!
JUST DON'T TURN YOUR BACK ON "XENA" OVER THERE!
ASUNA THE POWER HOUSE!

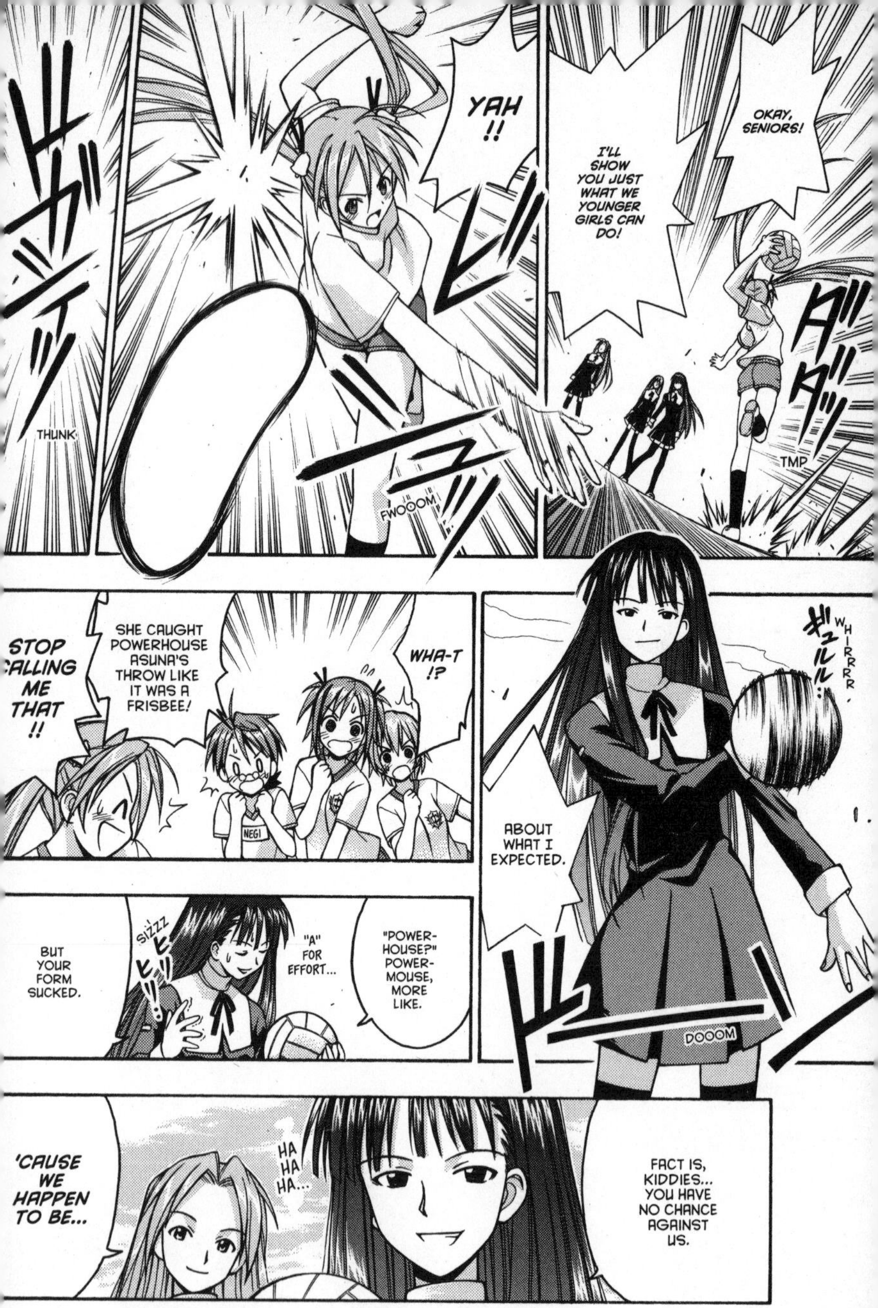
OKAY, SENIORS!
I'LL SHOW YOU JUST WHAT WE YOUNGER GIRLS CAN DO!
TMP
YAH !!
FWOOOM
THUNK
WHIRRRR
ABOUT WHAT I EXPECTED.
DOOOM
WHA-T !?
SHE CAUGHT POWERHOUSE ASUNA'S THROW LIKE IT WAS A FRISBEE!
STOP CALLING ME THAT !!
"POWER-HOUSE?" POWER-MOUSE, MORE LIKE.
"A" FOR EFFORT...
SIZZZ
BUT YOUR FORM SUCKED.
FACT IS, KIDDIES... YOU HAVE NO CHANCE AGAINST US.
HA HA HA...
'CAUSE WE HAPPEN TO BE...

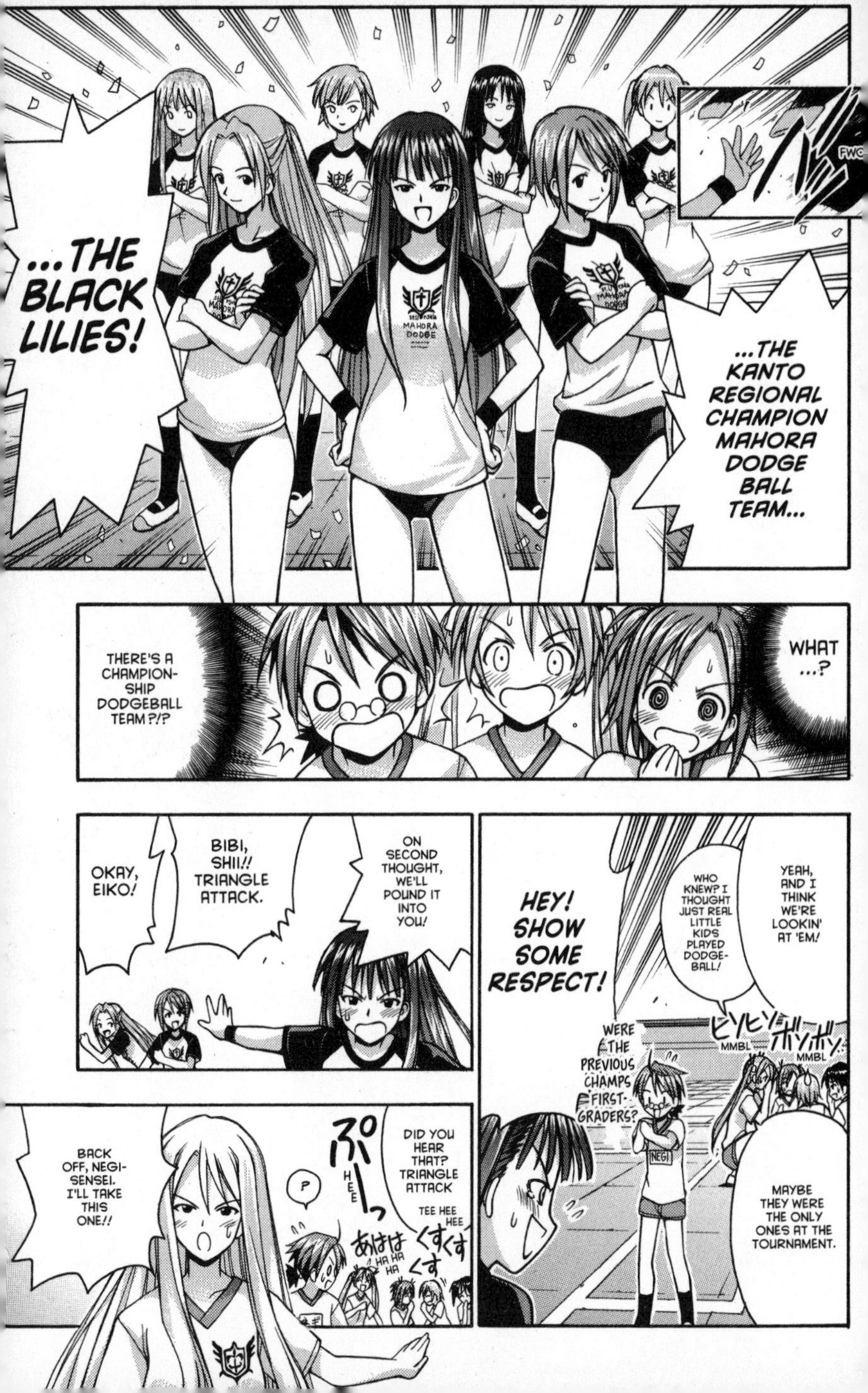
...THE KANTO REGIONAL CHAMPION MAHORA DODGE BALL TEAM...
...THE BLACK LILIES!
MAHORA DODGE
WHAT ...?
THERE'S A CHAMPIONSHIP DODGEBALL TEAM?!?
YEAH, AND I THINK WE'RE LOOKIN' AT 'EM!
WHO KNEW? I THOUGHT JUST REAL LITTLE KIDS PLAYED DODGEBALL!
HEY! SHOW SOME RESPECT!
ヒソヒソ MMBL
ボソボソ MMBL
WERE THE PREVIOUS CHAMPS FIRST-GRADERS?
NEGI
MAYBE THEY WERE THE ONLY ONES AT THE TOURNAMENT.
ON SECOND THOUGHT, WE'LL POUND IT INTO YOU!
BIBI, SHII!! TRIANGLE ATTACK.
OKAY, EIKO!
DID YOU HEAR THAT? TRIANGLE ATTACK
ぷーっ HEE
くすくす TEE HEE HEE
あはは HA HA HA
?
BACK OFF, NEGI-SENSEI. I'LL TAKE THIS ONE!!

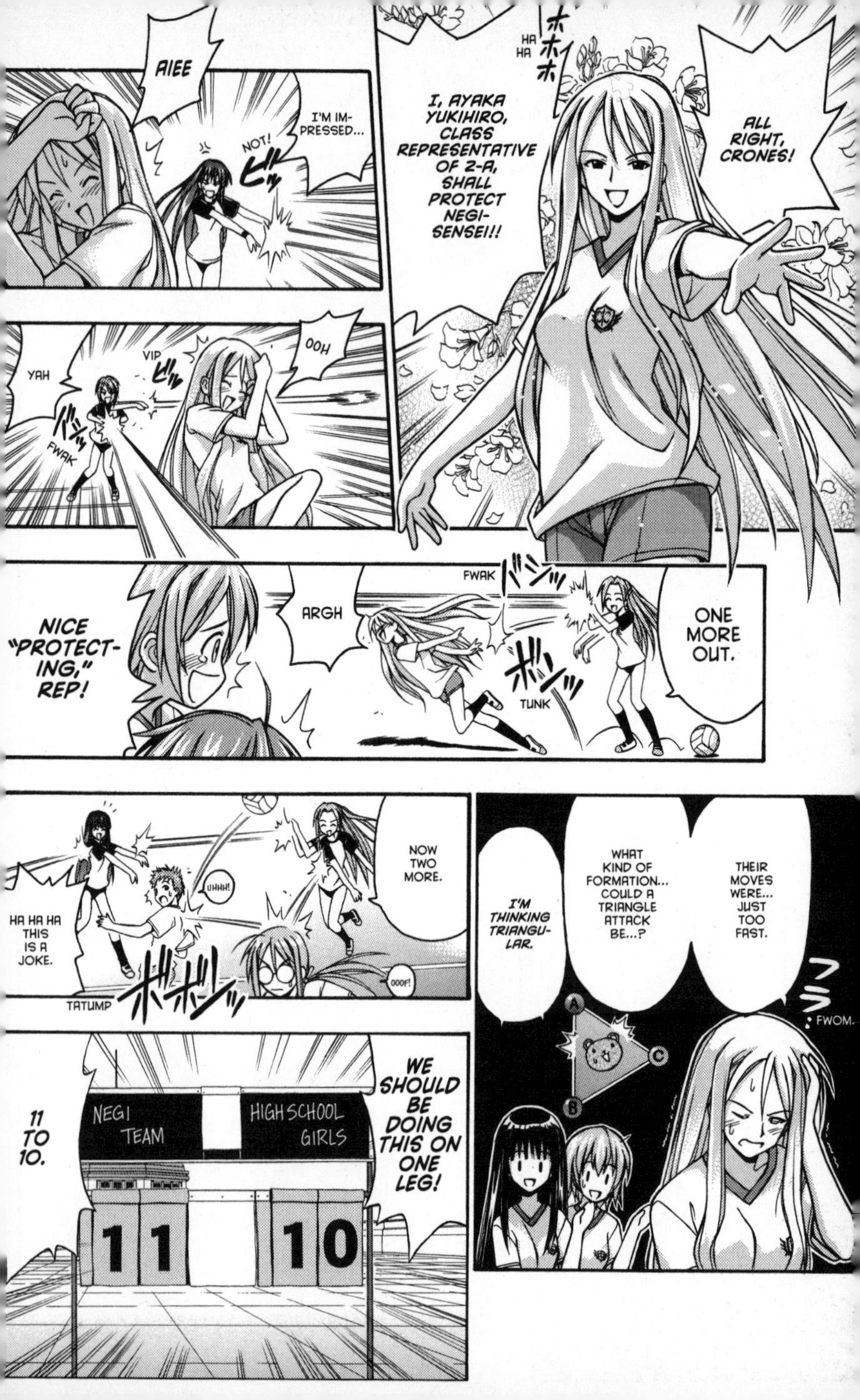
HA HA
ALL RIGHT, CRONES!
I, AYAKA YUKIHIRO, CLASS REPRESENTATIVE OF 2-A, SHALL PROTECT NEGI-SENSEI!!
AIEE
I'M IM-PRESSED...
NOT!
OOH
VIP
YAH
FWAK
ONE MORE OUT.
FWAK
TUNK
ARGH
NICE "PROTECTING," REP!
THEIR MOVES WERE... JUST TOO FAST.
WHAT KIND OF FORMATION... COULD A TRIANGLE ATTACK BE...?
I'M THINKING TRIANGULAR.
FWOM.
NOW TWO MORE.
UHHH!
OOOF!
HA HA HA THIS IS A JOKE.
TATUMP
WE SHOULD BE DOING THIS ON ONE LEG!
NEGI TEAM
HIGH SCHOOL GIRLS
11
10
11 TO 10.

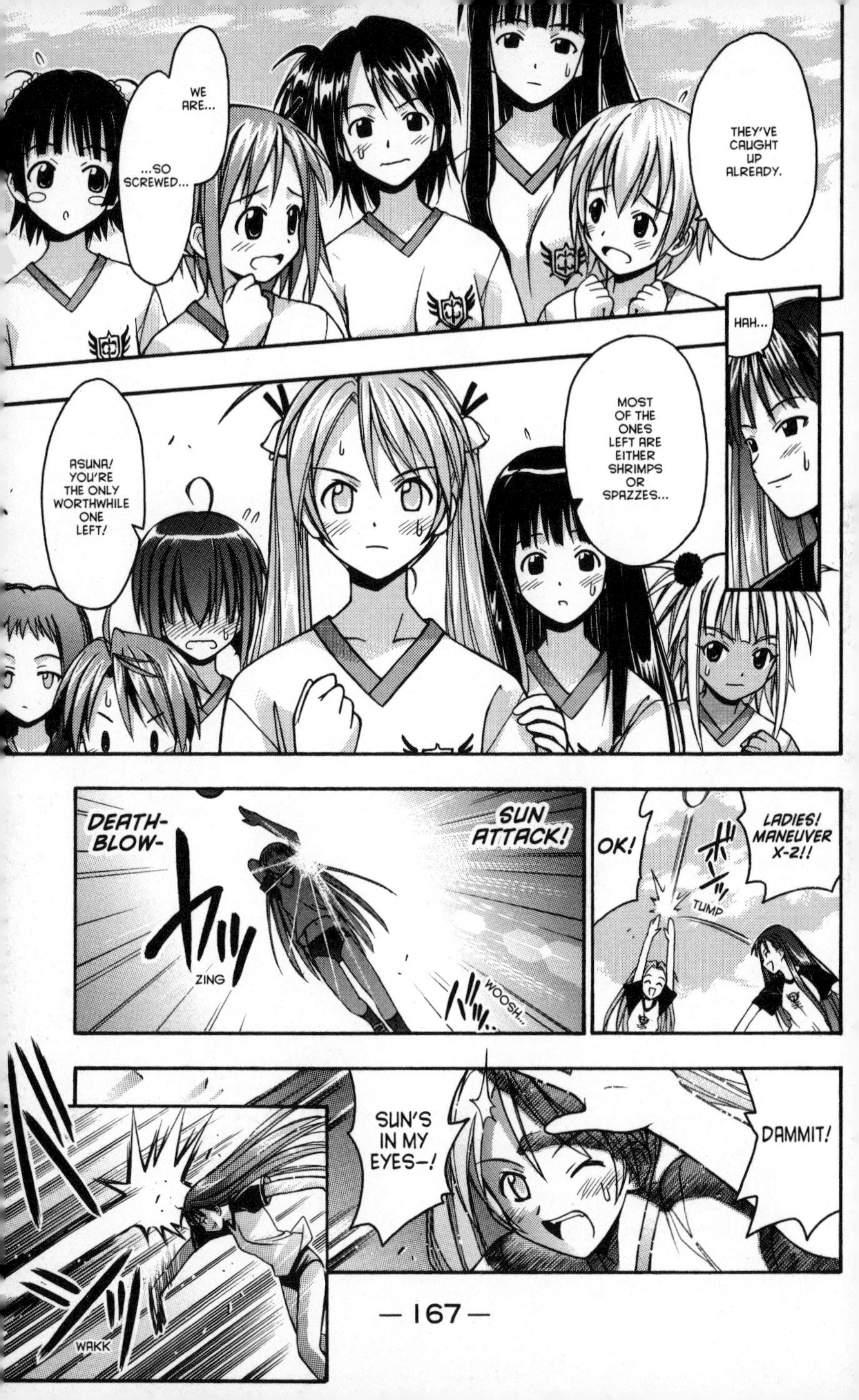
THEY'VE CAUGHT UP ALREADY.
WE ARE...
...SO SCREWED...
HAH...
MOST OF THE ONES LEFT ARE EITHER SHRIMPS OR SPAZZES...
ASUNA! YOU'RE THE ONLY WORTHWHILE ONE LEFT!
LADIES! MANEUVER X-2!!
OK!
TUMP
SUN ATTACK!
DEATH-BLOW-
ZING
WOOSH...
DAMMIT!
SUN'S IN MY EYES—!
WAKK

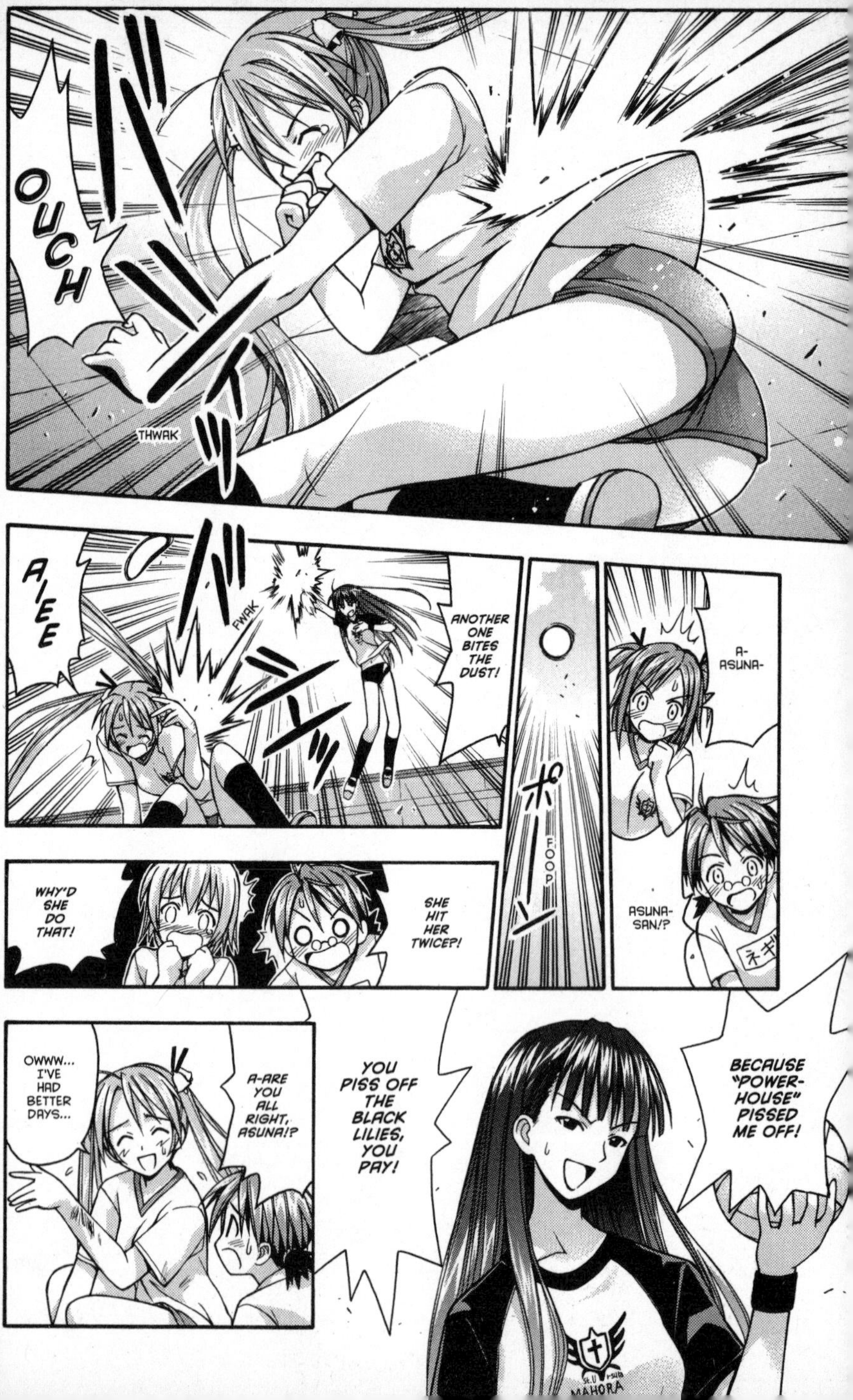
OUCH
THWAK
AIEE
FWAK
ANOTHER ONE BITES THE DUST!
FOOP
A-ASUNA-
ASUNA-SAN!?
SHE HIT HER TWICE?!
WHY'D SHE DO THAT!
BECAUSE "POWER-HOUSE" PISSED ME OFF!
YOU PISS OFF THE BLACK LILIES, YOU PAY!
A-ARE YOU ALL RIGHT, ASUNA!?
OWWW... I'VE HAD BETTER DAYS...

— 170 —

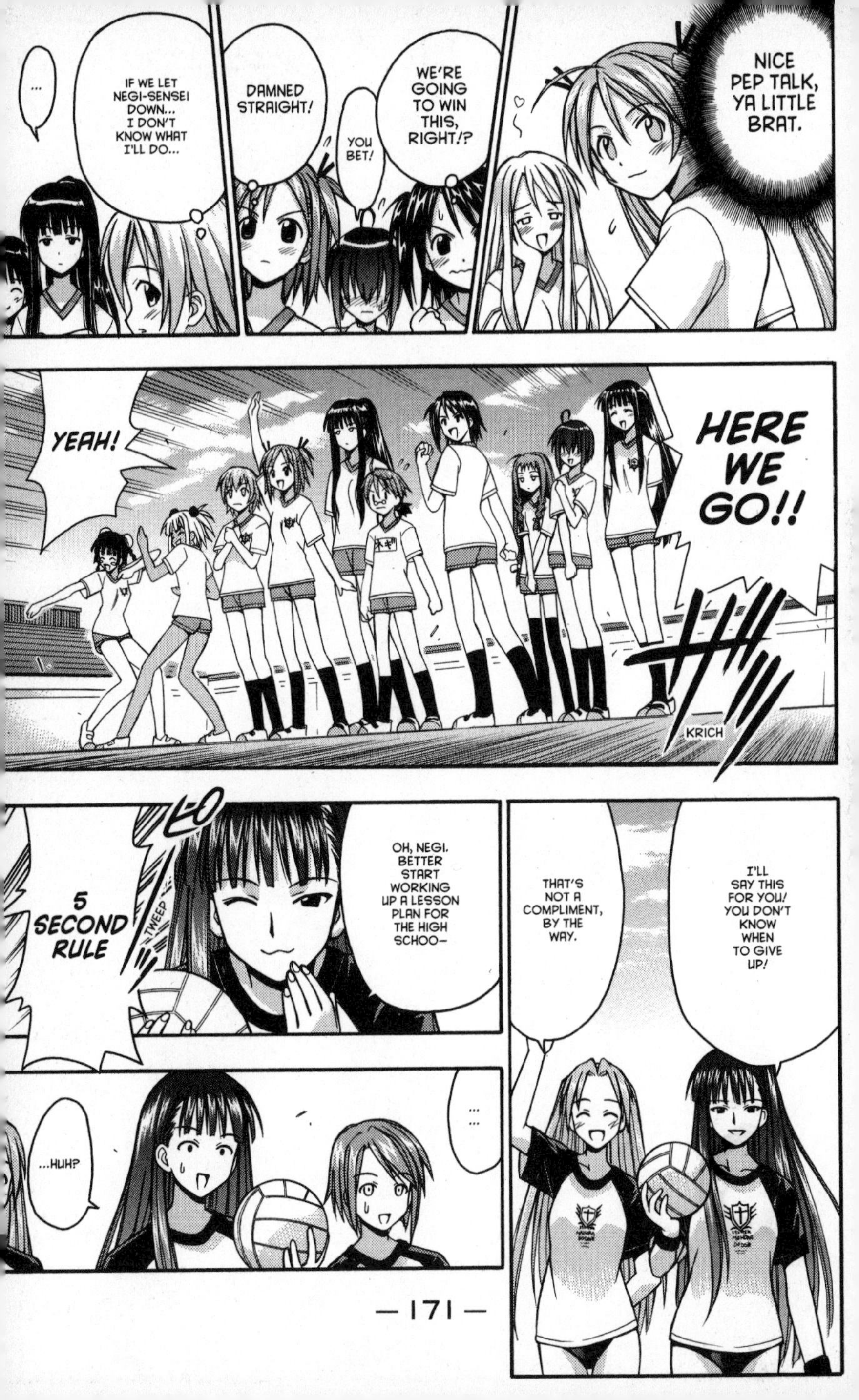
NICE PEP TALK, YA LITTLE BRAT.
WE'RE GOING TO WIN THIS, RIGHT!?
YOU BET!
DAMNED STRAIGHT!
IF WE LET NEGI-SENSEI DOWN... I DON'T KNOW WHAT I'LL DO...
...
HERE WE GO!!
YEAH!
KRICH
I'LL SAY THIS FOR YOU! YOU DON'T KNOW WHEN TO GIVE UP!
THAT'S NOT A COMPLIMENT, BY THE WAY.
OH, NEGI. BETTER START WORKING UP A LESSON PLAN FOR THE HIGH SCHOO–
TWEEP
5 SECOND RULE
... ...
...HUH?

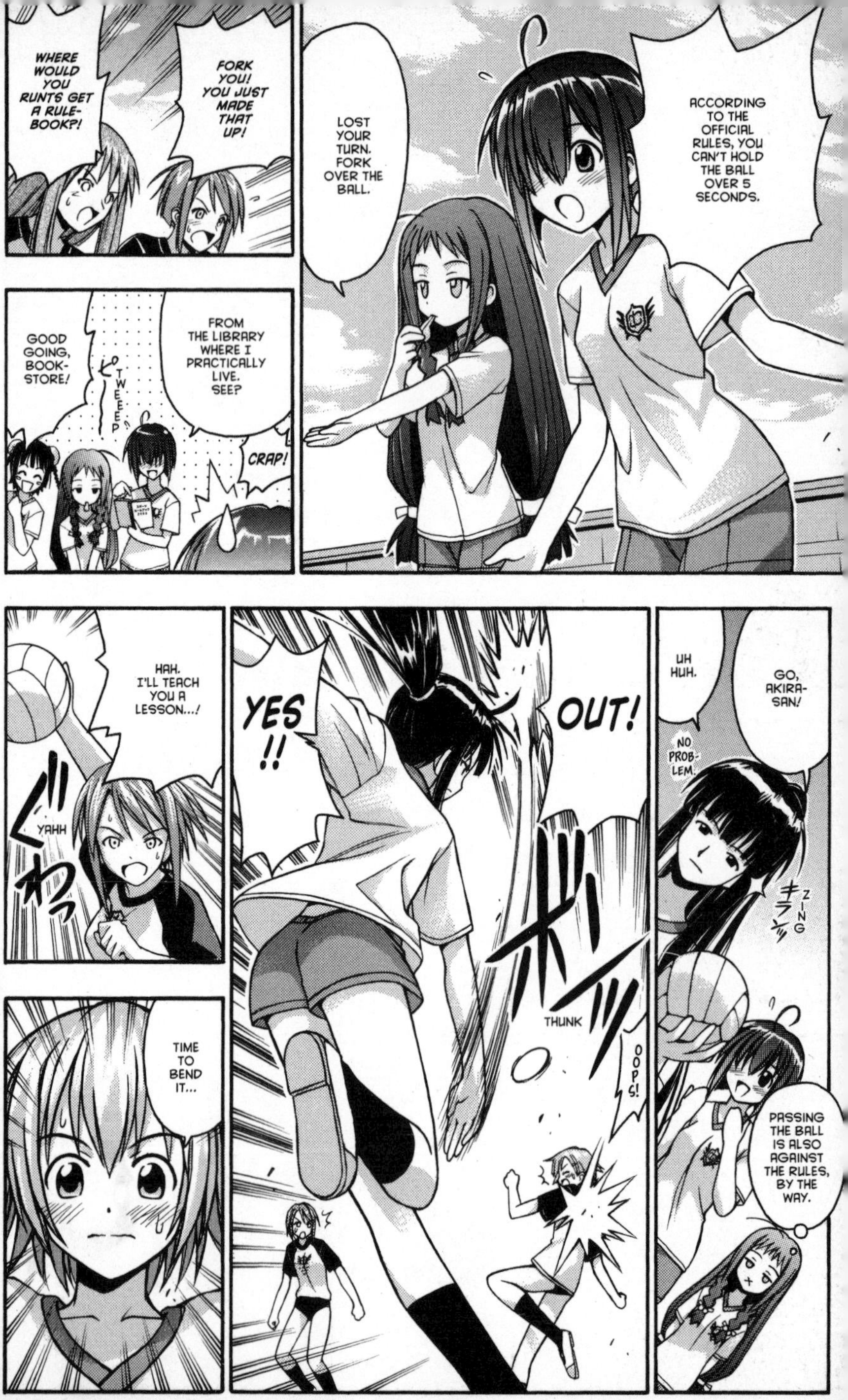
ACCORDING TO THE OFFICIAL RULES, YOU CAN'T HOLD THE BALL OVER 5 SECONDS.
LOST YOUR TURN. FORK OVER THE BALL.
FORK YOU! YOU JUST MADE THAT UP!
WHERE WOULD YOU RUNTS GET A RULE-BOOK?!
FROM THE LIBRARY WHERE I PRACTICALLY LIVE. SEE?
GOOD GOING, BOOKSTORE!
TWEEEP
CRAP!
GO, AKIRA-SAN!
UH HUH.
NO PROBLEM.
ZING
PASSING THE BALL IS ALSO AGAINST THE RULES, BY THE WAY.
OUT!
YES!!
THUNK
OOPS!
HAH. I'LL TEACH YOU A LESSON...!
YAHH
TIME TO BEND IT...

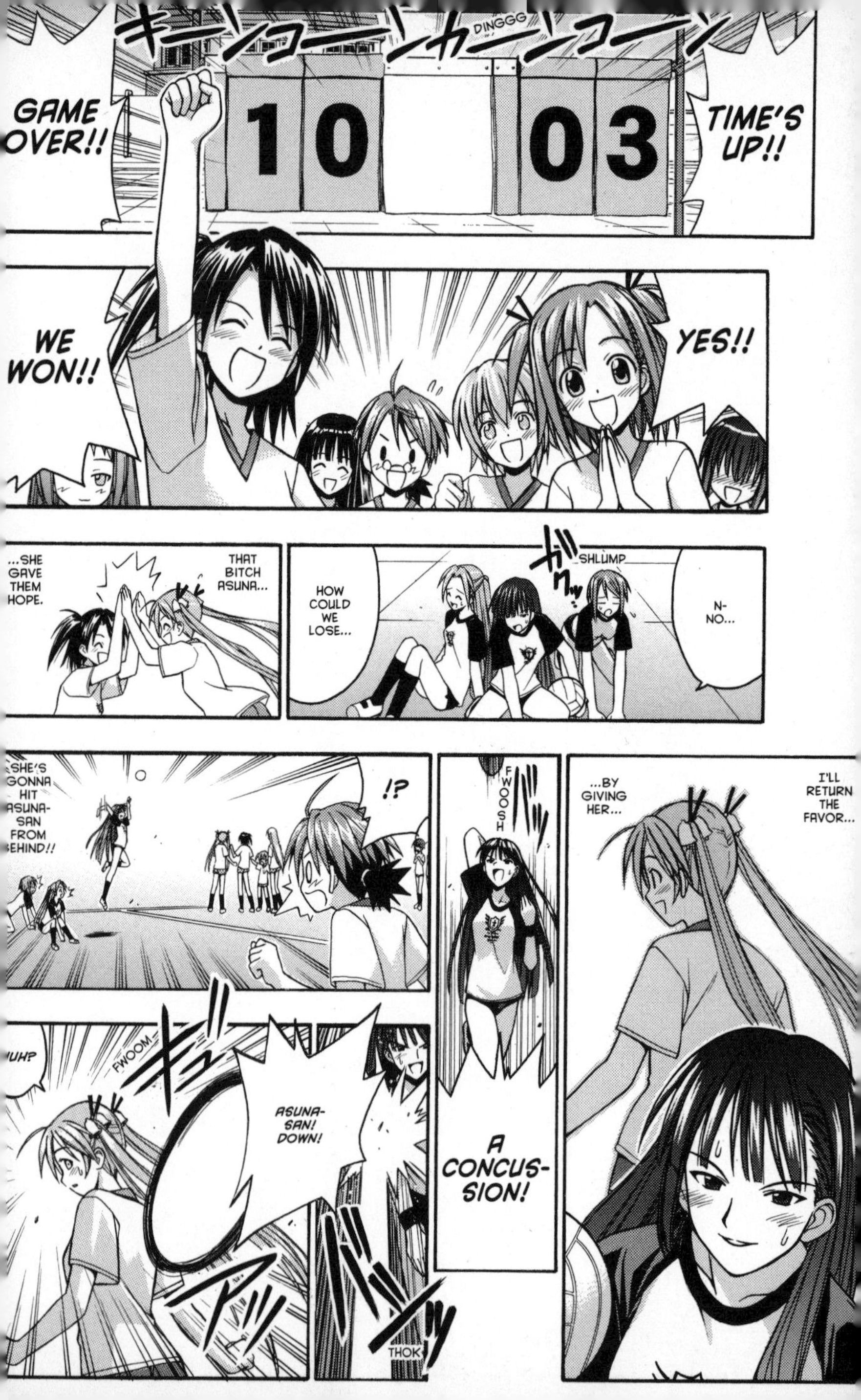
DINGGG
TIME'S UP!!
GAME OVER!!
10 03
YES!!
WE WON!!
N-NO...
SHLUMP
HOW COULD WE LOSE...
THAT BITCH ASUNA...
...SHE GAVE THEM HOPE.
I'LL RETURN THE FAVOR...
...BY GIVING HER...
FWOOSH
A CONCUSSION!
!?
SHE'S GONNA HIT ASUNA-SAN FROM BEHIND!!
ASUNA-SAN! DOWN!
FWOOM
HUH?
THOK

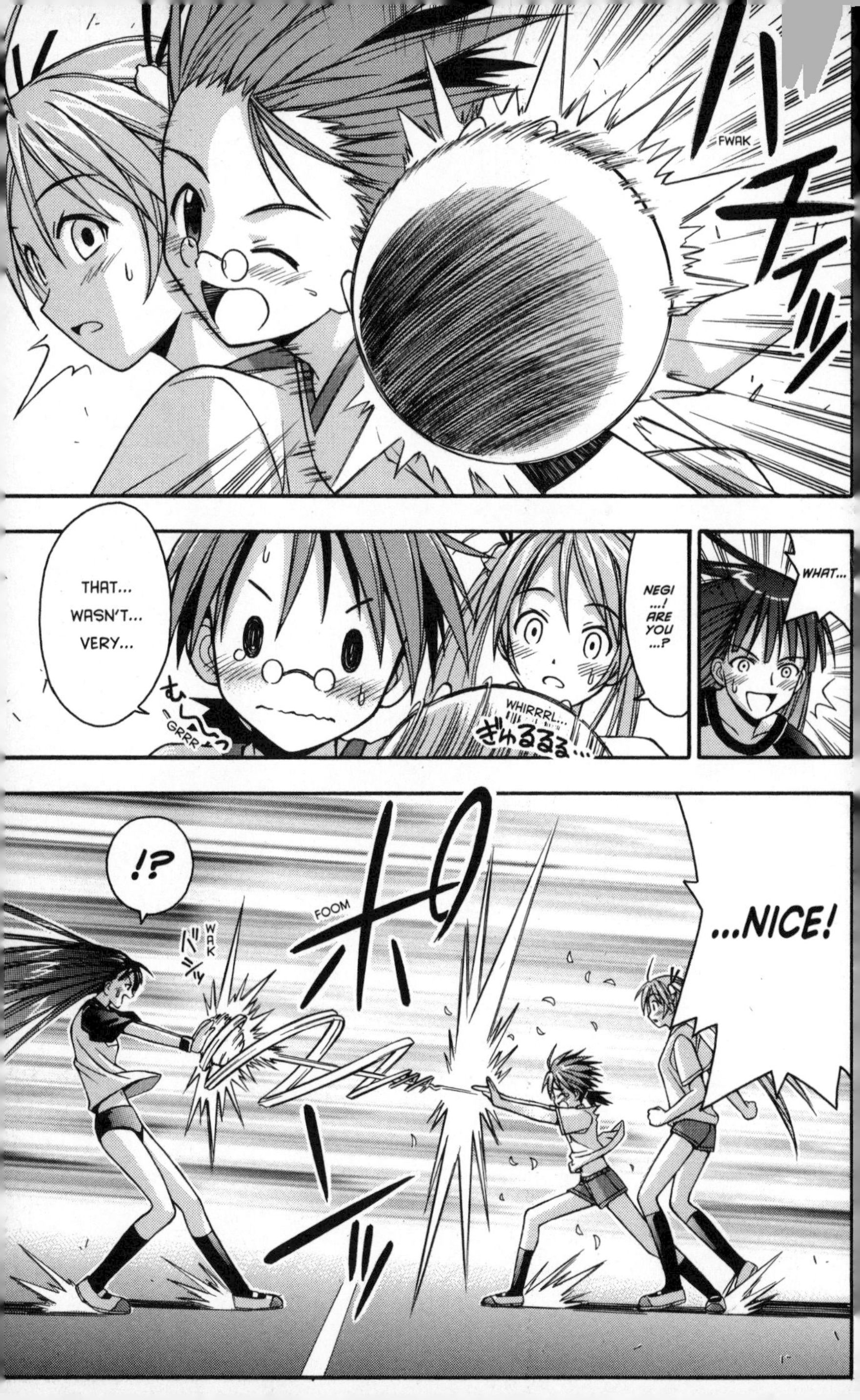
FWAK
WHAT...
NEGI ...! ARE YOU ...?
WHIRRRL...
ぎゅるるる…
THAT... WASN'T... VERY...
GRRR
...NICE!
FOOM
WAK
!?

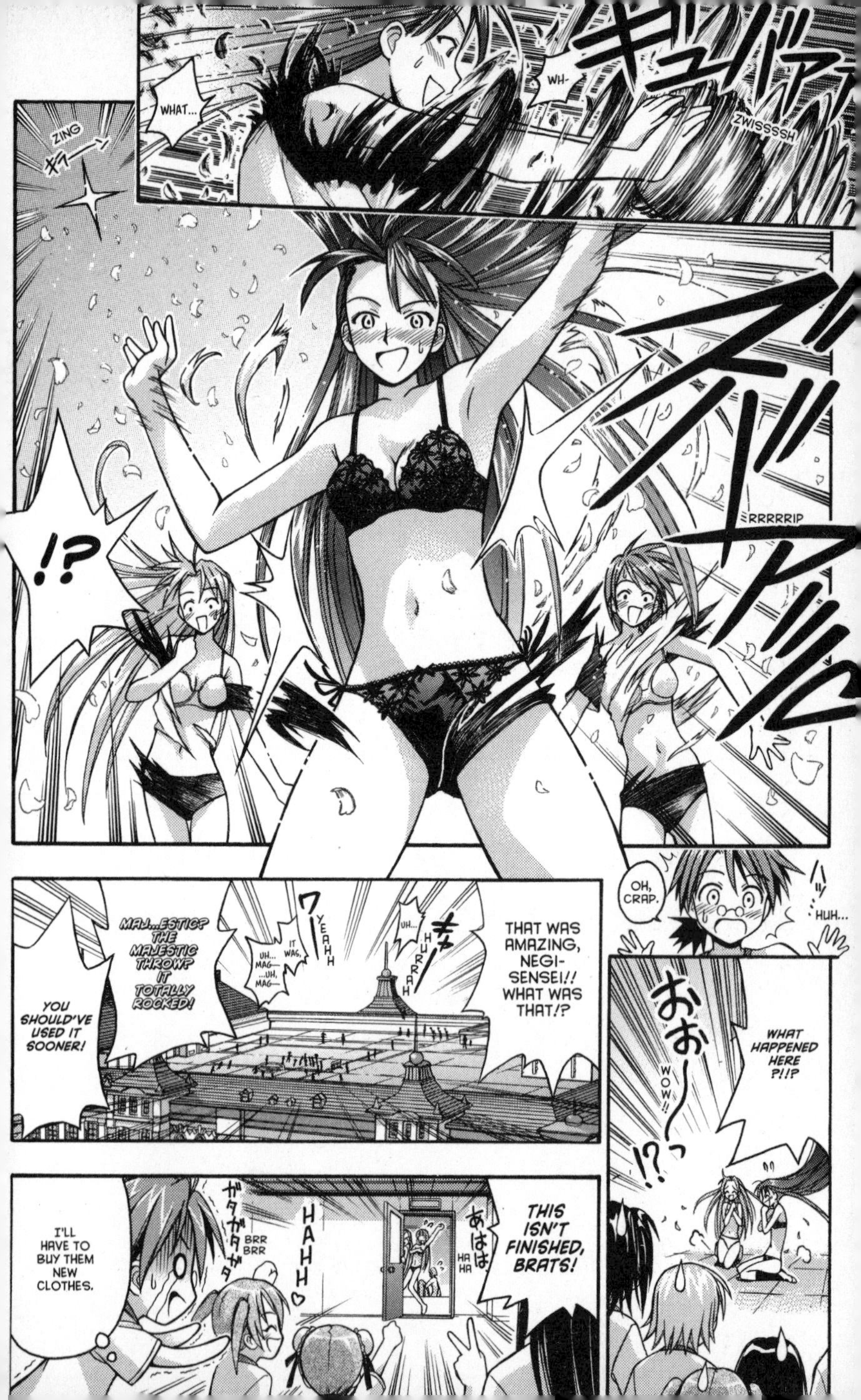
WH-
WHAT...
ZWISSSSSH
ZING
RRRRRIP
!?
OH, CRAP.
HUH...
THAT WAS AMAZING, NEGI-SENSEI!! WHAT WAS THAT!?
HURRAH
UH...
IT WAS,
UH... MAG— ...UH, MAG—
YEAHH
MAJ...ESTIC? THE MAJESTIC THROW? IT TOTALLY ROCKED!
YOU SHOULD'VE USED IT SOONER!
おお～
WOW!!
WHAT HAPPENED HERE?!!?
!?
THIS ISN'T FINISHED, BRATS!
あはは
HA HA
HAHH
ガタガタ
BRR BRR
I'LL HAVE TO BUY THEM NEW CLOTHES.

CONTINUED IN VOLUME 2

– STAFF –

Ken Akamatsu
Takashi Takemoto
Kenichi Nakamura
Masaki Ohyama
Keiichi Yamashita
Chigusa Amagasaki
Takaaki Miyahara
Kei Nishikawa

Thanks To

Ran Ayanaga
Toshiko Akamatsu

About the Creator

Negima! is only Ken Akamatsu's third manga, although he started working in the field in 1994 with *AI Ga Tomaranai*. Like all of Akamatsu's work to date, it was published in Kodansha's *Shonen Magazine*. *AI Ga Tomaranai* ran for five years before concluding in 1999. In 1998, however, Akamatsu began the work that would make him one of the most popular manga artists in Japan: *Love Hina*. *Love Hina* ran for four years, and before its conclusion in 2002, it would cause Akamatsu to be granted the prestigious Manga of the Year award from Kodansha, as well as going on to become one of the best-known and best-selling manga in the United Kingdom.

Volumes 1, 2 and 3 of *Negima!* are available now.

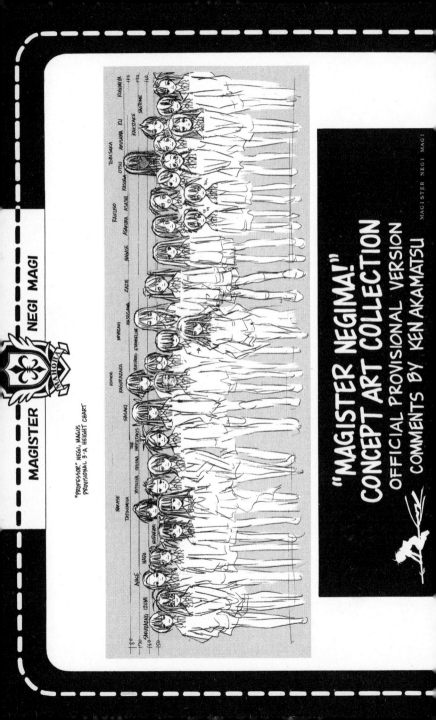

MAGISTER NEGI MAGI

"PROFESSOR" NEGI, MAGI'S
PROVISIONAL 3-A HEIGHT CHART

"MAGISTER NEGIMA!"
CONCEPT ART COLLECTION
OFFICIAL PROVISIONAL VERSION
COMMENTS BY KEN AKAMATSU

MAGISTER NEGI MAGI

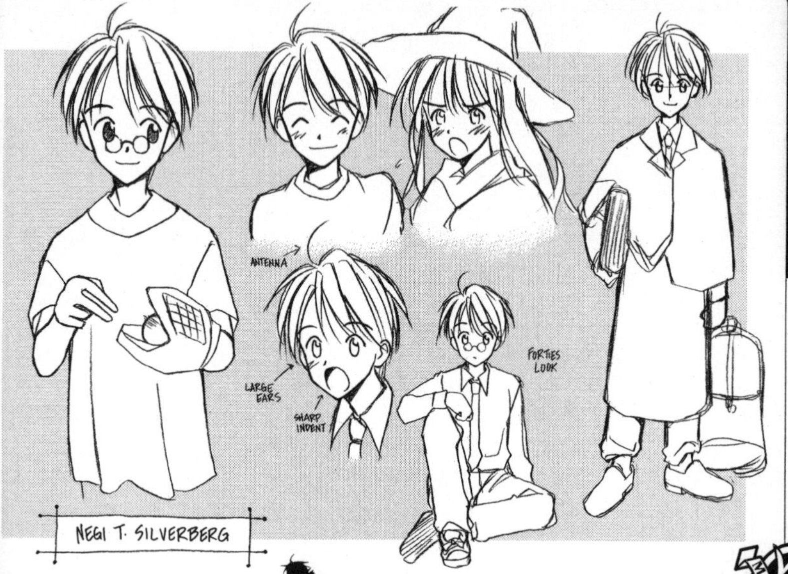
ANTENNA
LARGE EARS
SHARP INDENT
FORTIES LOOK
NEGI T. SILVERBERG

MAGISTER NEGI MAGI

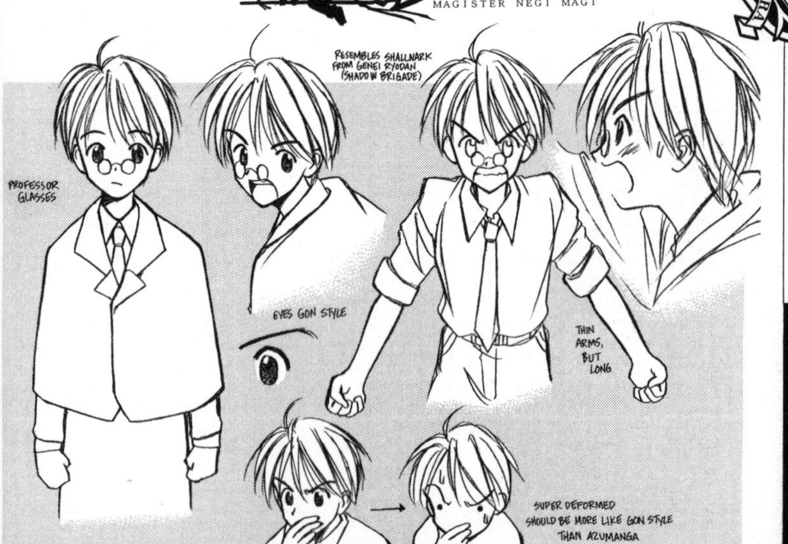
RESEMBLES SHALLNARK FROM GENEI RYODAN (SHADOW BRIGADE)
PROFESSOR GLASSES
EYES GON STYLE
THIN ARMS, BUT LONG
SUPER DEFORMED
SHOULD BE MORE LIKE GON STYLE
THAN AZUMANGA

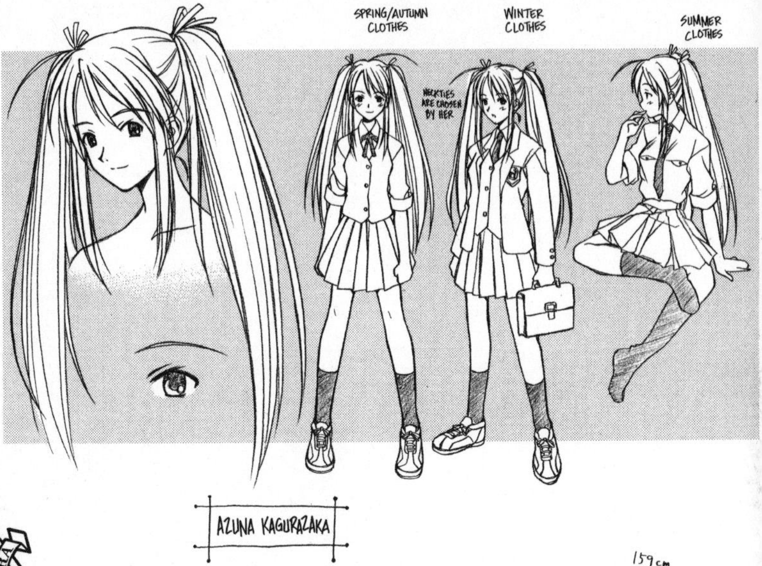
SPRING/AUTUMN CLOTHES
WINTER CLOTHES
SUMMER CLOTHES
NECKTIES ARE CHOSEN BY HER
AZUNA KAGURAZAKA

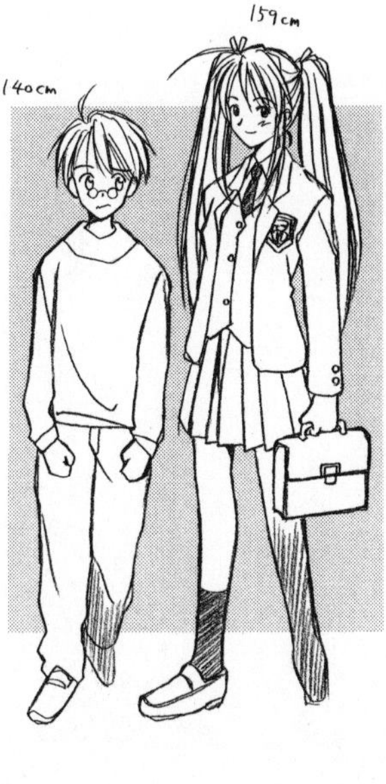
159cm
140cm

THE CONCEPT ART FOR THE MALE AND FEMALE PROTAGONIST. NEGI'S LIKE, "WHAT?" (^^;) WE ENDED UP REJECTING THIS VERSION, OPTING FOR A MORE CHILDISH, ROUND FACED CHARACTER.

HE IS CUTER THAT WAY AFTER ALL~ ♡

THE FEMALE PROTAGONIST IS BASICALLY TAKEN FROM A HEROINE CHARACTER FROM A CANCELLED PROJECT I WAS WORKING ON BEFORE "NEGIMA". THESE TWO ARE LIKE SIBLINGS, SO MAYBE IT'S A LITTLE ODD AS A LOVE COMEDY?

MAGISTER NEGI MAGI

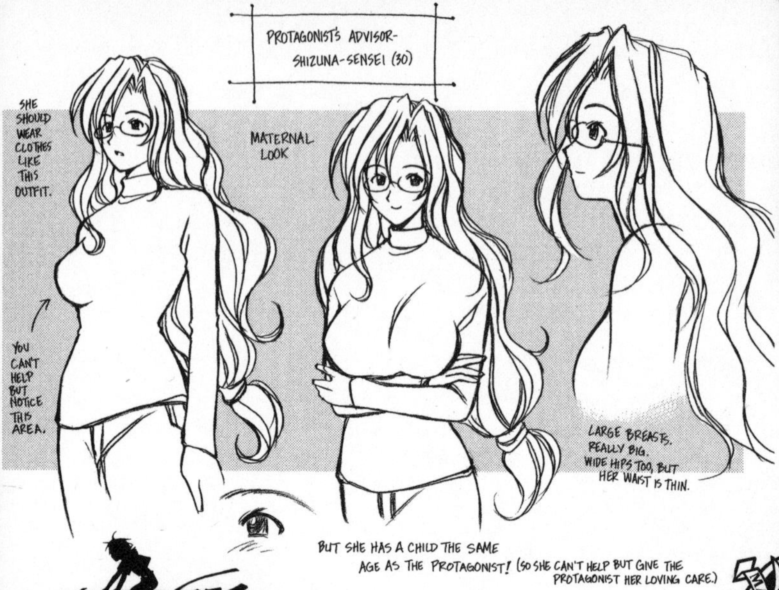
PROTAGONIST'S ADVISOR-
SHIZUNA-SENSEI (30)
SHE SHOULD WEAR CLOTHES LIKE THIS OUTFIT.
MATERNAL LOOK
YOU CAN'T HELP BUT NOTICE THIS AREA.
LARGE BREASTS. REALLY BIG. WIDE HIPS TOO, BUT HER WAIST IS THIN.
BUT SHE HAS A CHILD THE SAME AGE AS THE PROTAGONIST! (SO SHE CAN'T HELP BUT GIVE THE PROTAGONIST HER LOVING CARE.)

EVERY ONE OF THE 31 CLASSMATES HAVE THEIR OWN DETAILED CONCEPT DESIGNS, BUT RIGHT NOW I CAN'T PROVIDE A CHARACTER DESIGN CHART... SO I'LL START WITH SHIZUNA-SENSEI WHO DOESN'T HAVE MUCH OF A DETAILED CONCEPT DESIGN (HA HA)

I WONDER WHAT KIND OF RELATIONSHIP SHE HAS WITH TAKAHATA-SENSEI?

(* WE HAVE DECIDED THAT SHE DOESN'T HAVE CHILDREN AFTER ALL.)

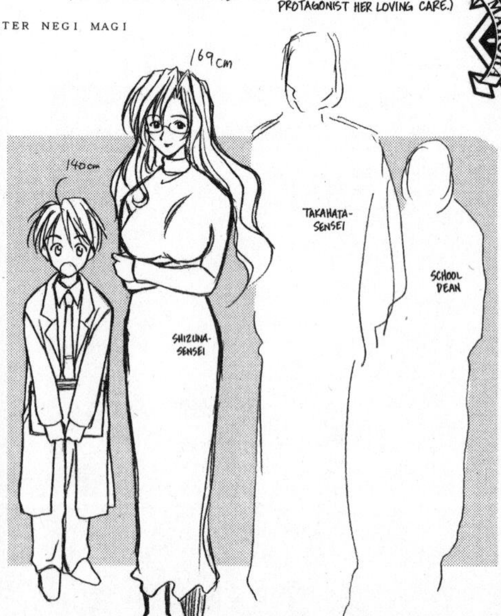
169cm
140cm
TAKAHATA-SENSEI
SCHOOL DEAN
SHIZUNA-SENSEI

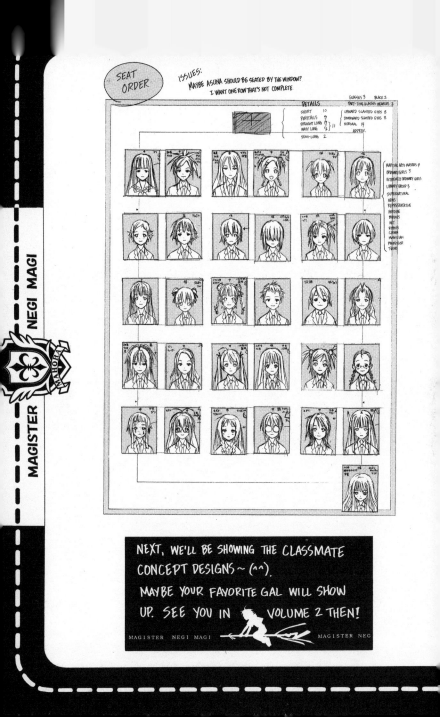

SEAT ORDER
ISSUES:
MAYBE ASUNA SHOULD BE SEATED BY THE WINDOW?
I WANT ONE ROW THAT'S NOT COMPLETE.
GLASSES 3
BLACK 2
DETAILS
PART-TIME GLASSES WEARERS 2
SHORT 10
PONYTAILS 7
STRAIGHT LONG 7
WAVY LONG 4
11
SEMI-LONG 2
UPWARD SLANTED EYES 8
DOWNWARD SLANTED EYES 8
NORMAL 14
APPROX.
MARTIAL ARTS MASTERS 4
ORDINARY GIRLS 3
EXTREMELY ORDINARY GIRLS
LIBRARY GROUP 3
SUPERNATURAL
NEWS
REPRESENTATIVE
HEROINE
BUDDIES
NET
ROBOTS
CLOWN
MAGICIAN
PROFESSOR
TWINS

NEXT, WE'LL BE SHOWING THE CLASSMATE CONCEPT DESIGNS~ (^^).
MAYBE YOUR FAVORITE GAL WILL SHOW UP. SEE YOU IN VOLUME 2 THEN!

MAGISTER NEGI MAGI MAGISTER NEG

Translation Notes

Japanese is a tricky language for most westerners, and translation is often more art than science. For your edification and reading pleasure, here are notes on some of the places where we could have gone in a different direction in our translation of the work, or where a Japanese cultural reference is used.

If you're reading all of the manga from the launch (and if you're not, go pick up *Guru Guru, Pon-Chan, Ghost Hunt, xxxHOLiC, Tsubasa* and *Basilisk* right now!), you'll have seen that we've gone to great effort to keep our translations as authentic as possible. Nowhere did that pose such a challenge, however, as with *Negima!*

Two decisions we made early on in planning the line were to maintain Japanese honorifics as appropriate (for example, if a manga were set in, say, England, there would be little point in keeping them), and to translate all sound effects. We've managed to do both of these things in all of our books, but *Negima!* has been the most—shall we say—troublesome.

To begin with, take a look through the book at all of the sound effects. Akamatsu-sensei sure does like to use them, doesn't he? Where in our other manga we were experiencing 0 to 5 sound effects per page, with several pages lacking effects entirely, *Negima!* has more like 2 to 10 effects and asides per page! As difficult as it was to translate them all (and I'm not certain, but it's possible we managed to miss some along the way), *Negima!* highlights why it is so necessary to do the extra translation work and provide the reader with a more complete, immersive reading experience.

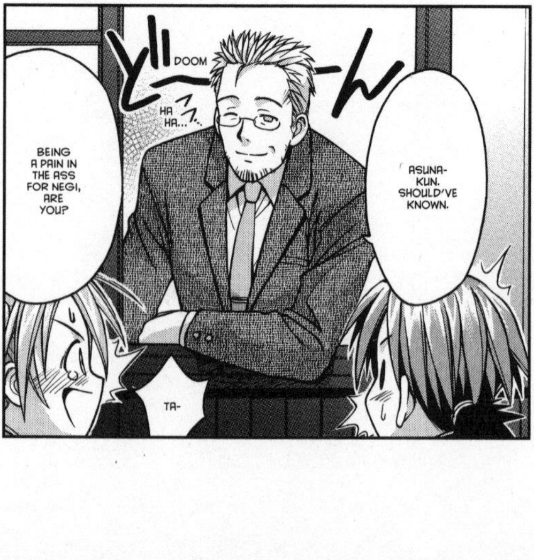
ASUNA-KUN. SHOULD'VE KNOWN.
DOOM
HA HA...
BEING A PAIN IN THE ASS FOR NEGI, ARE YOU?
TA-

While honorifics came up in our other manga, they were definitely a major necessity in *Negima!* because it takes place in a school—a very formal setting in Japan. An understanding of Japanese honorifics drives home the relationships between the characters. Look at when Negi first runs into Takahata—he calls him by his first name with no honorific at all, clearly indicating they are good friends.

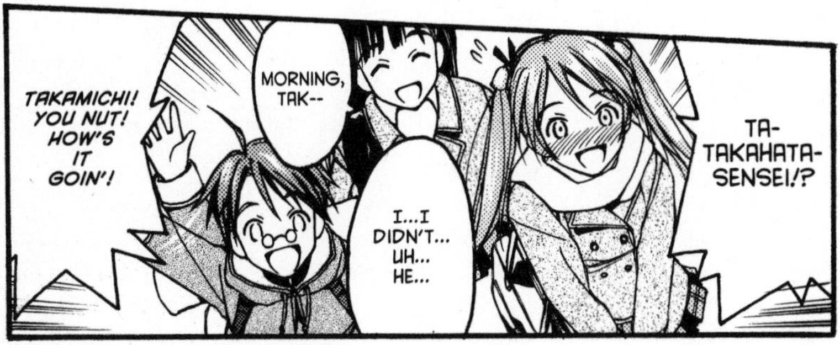
TA-
TAKAHATA-
SENSEI!?
MORNING, TAK--
I...I DIDN'T... UH... HE...
TAKAMICHI! YOU NUT! HOW'S IT GOIN'!

Likewise, when Takahata interrupts Asuna and Negi after school, he calls them both Asuna-kun and Negi-kun, which to Negi should indicate friendship, while to Asuna it's simply an acknowledgment that she is a student and Takahata is a teacher.

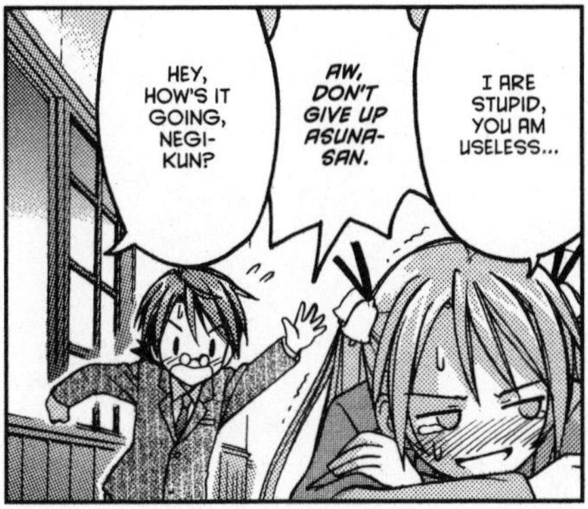
I ARE STUPID, YOU AM USELESS...
AW, DON'T GIVE UP ASUNA-SAN.
HEY, HOW'S IT GOING, NEGI-KUN?

Preview of Volume 2

We've pleased to present you a preview of volume 2. This volume is available in English, but we thought you might like to see a preview in the original Japanese.

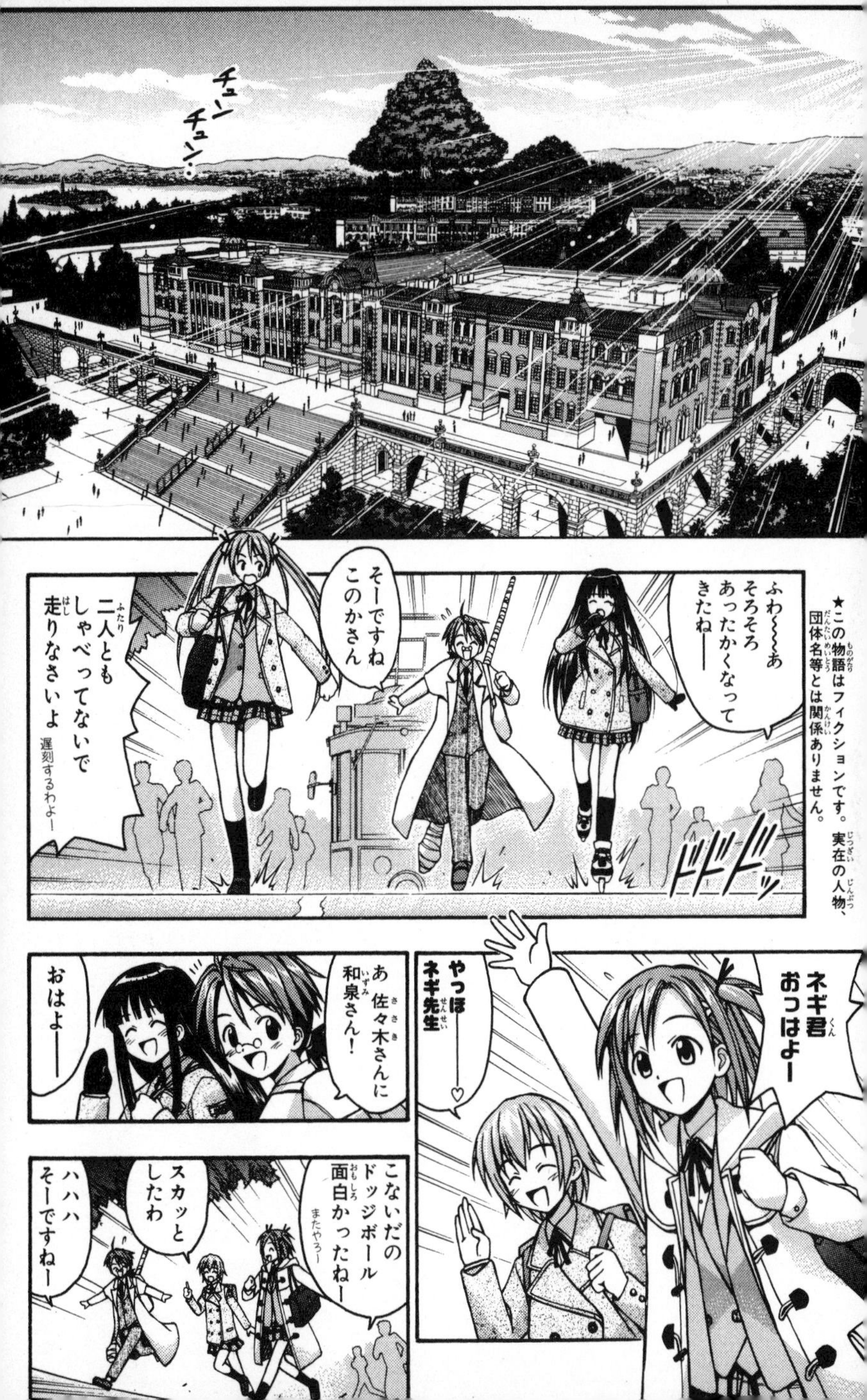
チュン
チュン…
ふわ〜〜あ そろそろ あったかくなって きたねー
そーですね このかさん
二人とも しゃべってないで 走りなさいよ
遅刻するわよ!
ドドドッ
ネギ君 おっはよー
やっほ ネギ先生ー♡
あ 佐々木さんに 和泉さん!
おはよー
こないだの ドッジボール 面白かったねー
またやろー
スカッと したわ
ハハハ そーですねー

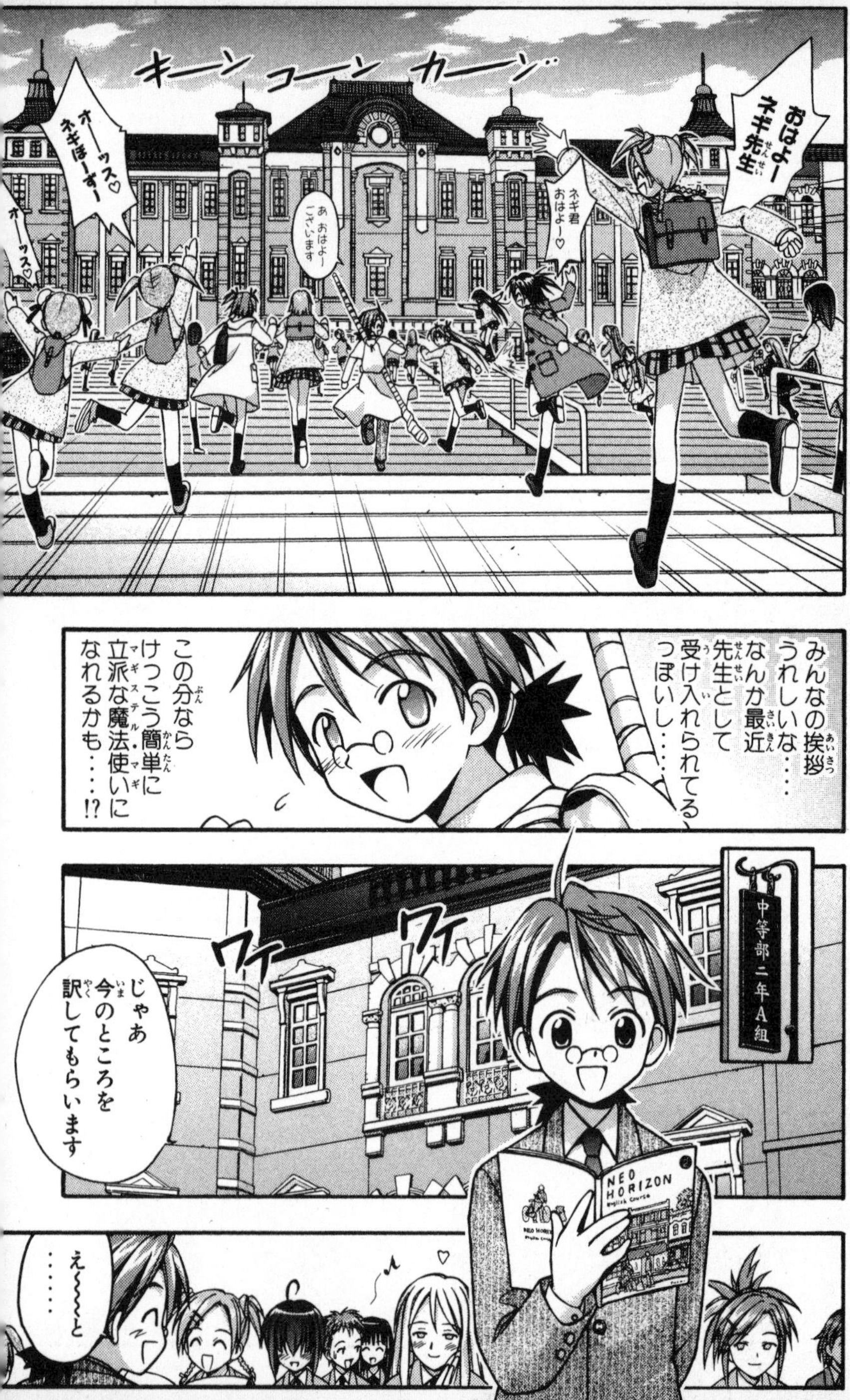
キーンコーンカーン
おはよーネギ先生
ネギ君おはよー♡
あ おはよーございます
オーッス♡ネギぼーずー
オーッス♡
みんなの挨拶うれしいな…… なんか最近先生として受け入れられてるっぽいし……
この分ならけっこう簡単に立派な魔法使いになれるかも……!?
中等部二年A組
ワイワイ
じゃあ今のところを訳してもらいます
NEO HORIZON English Course
え〜〜〜と……

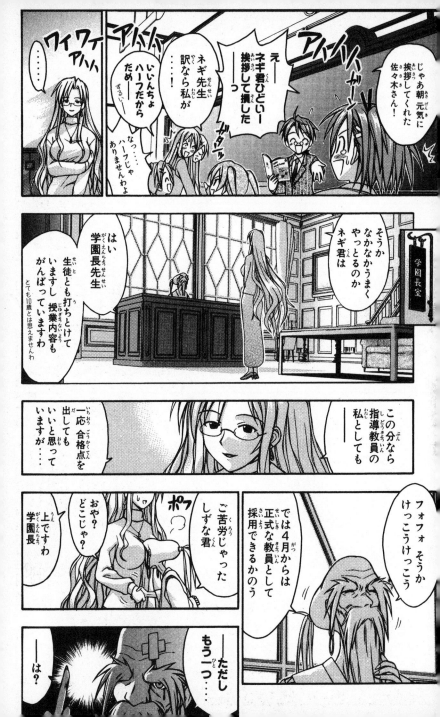

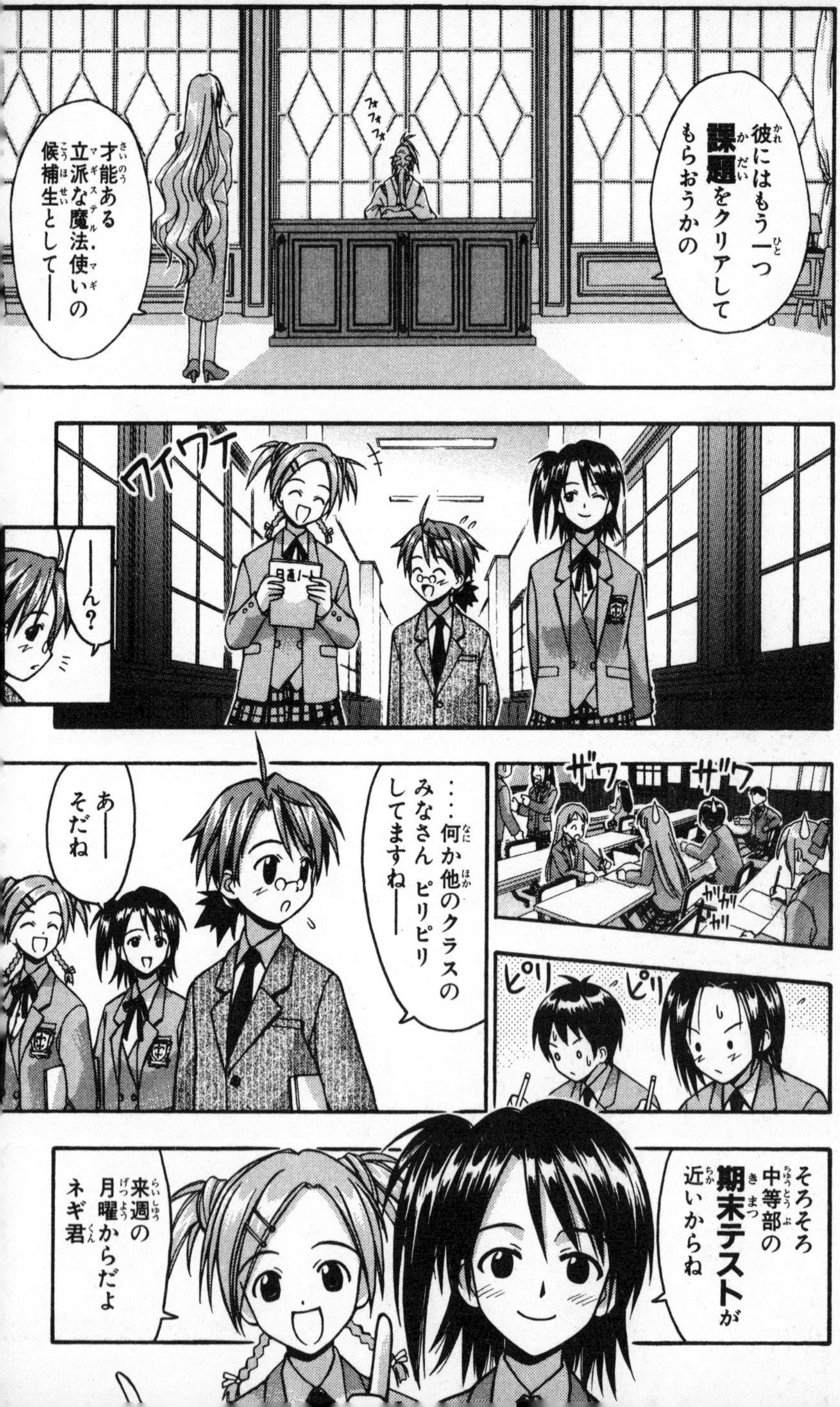
彼にはもう一つ課題をクリアしてもらおうかの
フォフォフォ
才能ある立派な魔法使いの候補生として──
ワイワイ
──ん？
ザワ
ザワ
ガリガリガリ
ピリ
ピリ
・・・何か他のクラスのみなさん ピリピリしてますね──
あ──そだね
そろそろ中等部の期末テストが近いからね
来週の月曜からだよネギ君

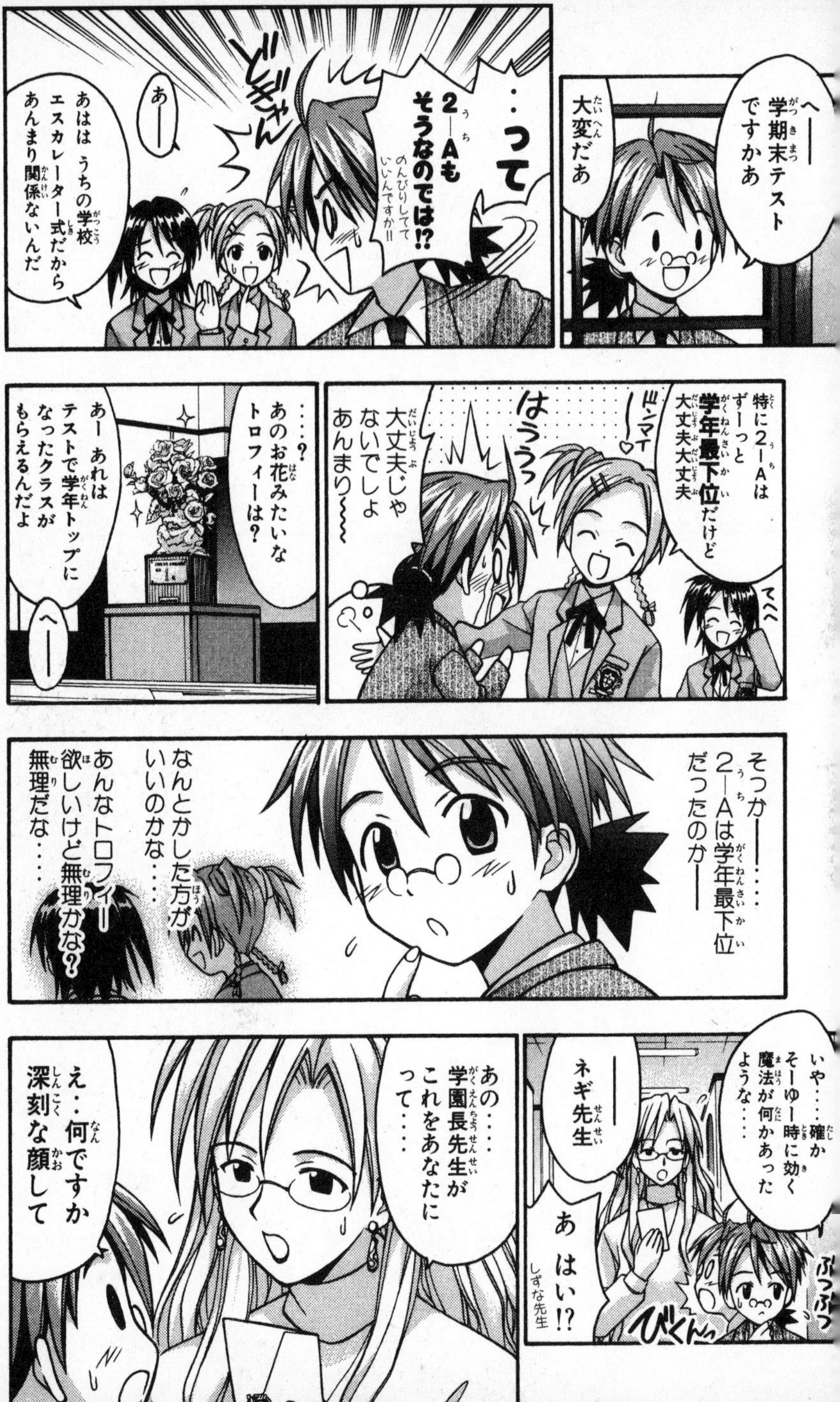

へーー 学期末テストですかあ
大変だあ
…って 2ーAもそうなのでは!?
のんびりしてていいんですか!!
どぎゃん
あーー
あはは うちの学校エスカレーター式だからあんまり関係ないんだ
特に2ーAはずーっと学年最下位だけど大丈夫大丈夫
ドンマイ～♡
はううっ
大丈夫じゃないでしょあんまり～～
てへへ
…? あのお花みたいなトロフィーは?
あー あれはテストで学年トップになったクラスがもらえるんだよ
へーー
そっかーー…2ーAは学年最下位だったのかーー
なんとかした方がいいのかな…
あんなトロフィー欲しいけど無理かな?
無理だな…
いや…確かそーゆー時に効く魔法が何かあったような…
ふっふっ
ーーネギ先生
びくんっ
あ はい!?
しずな先生
あの…学園長先生がこれをあなたにって…
え…何ですか深刻な顔して

xxxHOLiC

BY CLAMP

Watanuki Kimihiro is haunted by visions. When he finds himself irresistibly drawn into a shop owned by Yûko, a mysterious witch, he is offered the chance to rid himself of the spirits that plague him. He accepts, but soon realizes that he's just been tricked into working for the shop to pay off the cost of Yûko's services! But this isn't any ordinary kind of shop . . . In this shop, Yûko grants wishes to those in need. But they must have the strength of will not only to truly understand their need, but to give up something incredibly precious in return.

Ages: 13+

Special extras in each volume! Read them all!

TSUBASA

VOLUME 1
BY CLAMP

SAKURA AND SYAORAN RETURN!

But they're not the people you know. Sakura is the princess of Clow—and possessor of a mysterious, misunderstood power that promises to change the world. Syaoran is her childhood friend and leader of the archaeological dig that took his father's life. They reside in an alternate reality . . . where whatever you least expect can happen—and does. When Sakura ventures to the dig site to declare her love for Syaoran, a puzzling symbol is uncovered—which triggers a remarkable quest. Now Syaoran embarks upon a desperate journey through other worlds—all in the name of saving Sakura.

RESERVoir CHRoNiCLE
1
TSUBASA
by
CLAMP
NEW FROM THE CREATORS OF CHOBITS!

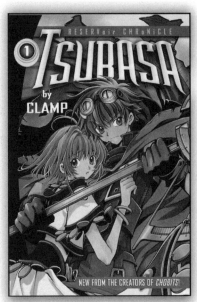

Ages: 13+

Includes special extras after the story!

tanoshimi

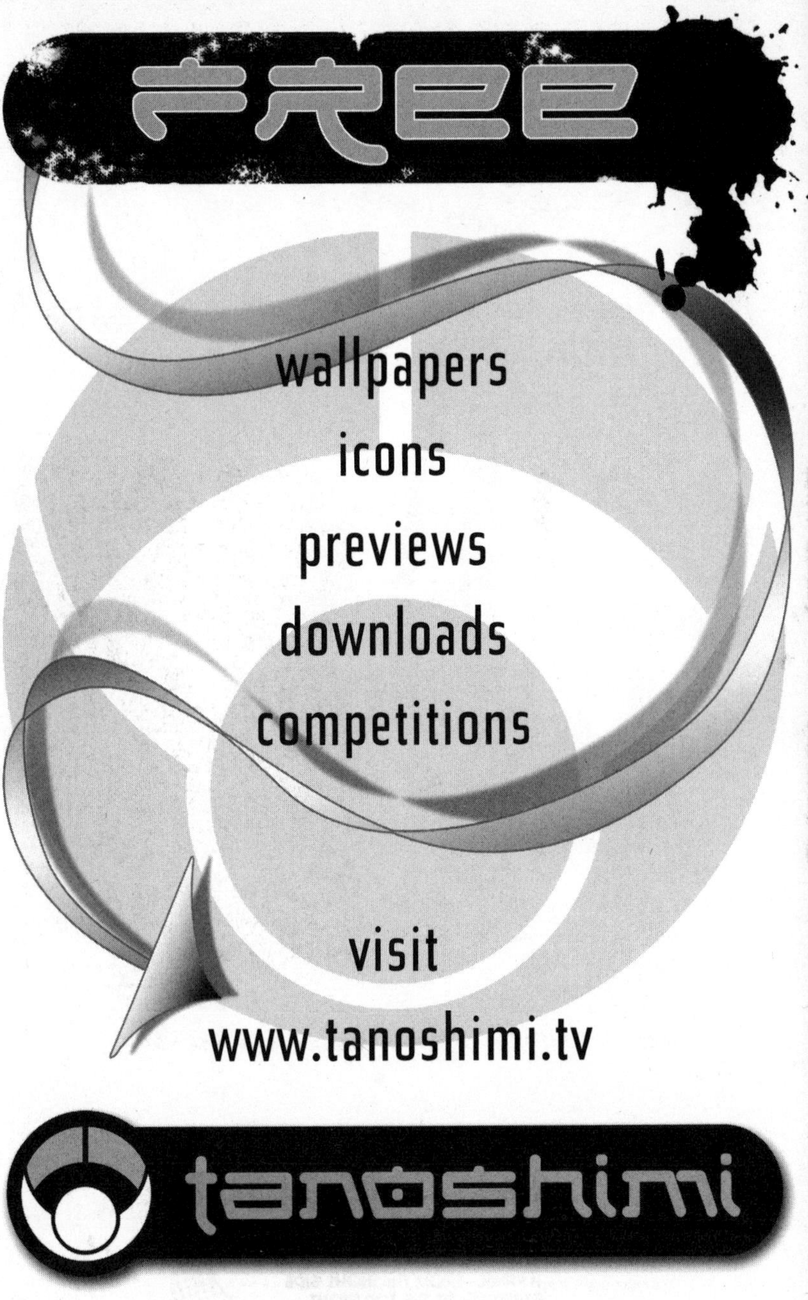
FREE
wallpapers
icons
previews
downloads
competitions
visit
www.tanoshimi.tv
tanoshimi